Real-World Newsletters
To Meet Your Unreal Demands

Linda B. Jorgensen

Publications from EEI Press

Guides to Editing, Writing, Proofreading, and Publishing

Error-Free Writing: A Lifetime Guide to Flawless Business Writing

The Great Grammar Challenge: Test Yourself on Punctuation, Usage, Grammar—and More

Letter Perfect: A Guide to Practical Proofreading

Mark My Words: Instruction & Practice in Proofreading

My Big Sourcebook: For People Who Work with Words or Pictures

New York Public Library Writer's Guide to Style and Usage

Real-World Newsletters to Meet Your Unreal Demands

Stet Again! More Tricks of the Trade for Publications People

Substance & Style: Instruction and Practice in Copyediting

Subscription Newsletter for Editors, Writers, Managers, Educators, and Journalists

The Editorial Eye: Focusing on Publications Standards and Practices

Real-World Newsletters

To Meet Your Unreal Demands

Linda B. Jorgensen

EEI PRESS®
A Division of EEI Communications

EEI Press publishes other books and *The Editorial Eye,* a subscription newsletter focusing on standards and practices for excellence in publications. For a free catalog, call 800-683-8380, send e-mail to press@eeicom.com, or use the Web form available at http://www.eeicom.com/press/.

EEI Press offers discounts for quantity orders from individuals, bookstores, corporations, nonprofit associations, and educational organizations. For more information, call, fax, or write to

EEI PRESS®
A Division of EEI Communications

66 Canal Center Plaza, Suite 200
Alexandria, VA 22314-5507
tel 703-683-0683; fax 703-683-4915

Library of Congress Cataloging-in-Publication Data
Jorgensen, Linda B.
    Real-world newsletters to meet your unreal demands / Linda B.
Jorgensen.
        p. cm.
    Includes bibliographical references (p.   ) and index.
    ISBN 0-935012-24-9
    1. Newsletters. 2. Journalism—Editing. I. Title.
PN4784.N5J67 1999
070.1'75--dc21
                                      98-31275
                                        CIP

Less isn't more. Less is less. More is more.
And enough is enough.

Dedication

This book is for Robin Cormier, one of the world's great listeners,
who acts like she believes you know what you're doing until
you believe it, too, and for Sally Smith, whose trust in real-world training
makes you wind up trusting yourself.

&

It's also honorarily for my father, Richard M. Bowles, who let me "read"
the newspaper to him when I was little. He taught me that words
have pictures in them, and medicine.

&

It's also (hey, it might be awhile before I write another book) for my son,
Benjamin. When he was little, by way of polite small talk he'd offer
news flashes about his three imaginary friends, the Freddies (Blue, Brown, Green).
Restless, curious guys, they took turns taking off: "Freddie (Blue, Brown, Green)
caught a plane for California (Ohio, Georgia) today." Aside from being invisible,
they were hard to tell apart. But Ben always knew who was who,
who was where, and what was what.

&

Long live the Freddies, wherever they may roam. Long live the tellers of
inside stories and long live their kindly listeners.

Contents

List of Sidebars

Preface

What you see here is the result of 10 years of working with newsletters—editing, writing, selling, critiquing, and helping to redesign them. I owe a lot to my colleagues here at EEI Communications. They've given me the kind of support that other editors can only dream of.

The students who have taken our basic news writing and newsletter editing workshops over the years have also helped me see what actually works (and what doesn't) in corporate, association, government, nonprofit, advocacy, marketing, public relations, and educational contexts.

What I'm getting at is that the advice in *Real-World Newsletters* isn't based on theory (although it acknowledges a few admirable theorists). It's based on practice, on the decisions that practitioners make (or should be making) every day. For years I've been stowing away anecdotes and collecting examples of newslettering so niched they're almost rockroses. This is my chance to show you a kind of newsletter family album—cute, squinty, squirmy kids; patient, pleased adults; stiff beauty queens and their hotshot dates; the token bibulous cousin; and the sweet old party with way too many cats.

The exchanges in our workshops are informal but thoughtful, occasionally blunt, full of humorous asides. In class, we think through frustrating, stubborn problems together and look for ways to get over there from stuck here. I hope this book feels a little like those conversations between editors. Not everybody loves troubleshooting the editing and writing and producing of newsletters, though, and it's potentially quite a messy job. One thing I've learned, and teach: Common sense and good will matter just as much as editorial skill. Why, that even rhymes. (It's true anyway.)

Most of all, a newsletter editor needs to develop a sense of confidence in the ability to meet several demands: Manage the details of the editorial and production processes. Please the busy and maybe skeptical people in the audience. Be responsive to the publisher orchestrating the performance. And somewhere in there, be a responsible practitioner of good reporting. Manage, please, be responsive, be responsible.

I want to reassure every editor that you don't have to go from 0 to 60 overnight. Becoming an intelligent observer, an analytical reporter, and a well-organized project manager happens gradually. If you're ready to get started, here's the deal:

- The core of the book is three main sections: an overview of the editing process, a survey of design and production considerations, and the essentials of reader-based news writing.

- Two "gallery" sections analyze actual, published examples of what's going on in contemporary newsletters. The design gallery covers some of the good and the bad as well as the better (a case study of a redesign). The writing gallery is like a hit list of the mistakes most commonly made by harried editors on deadline—the ones to guard against no matter what.

- Checklists throughout suggest ways to organize your time and target your efforts—adapt them for your own use. Sidebars summarize information it's nice to know sooner instead of later—and tell anecdotes to help you see that we're all in the same boat.

- An appendix offers perspective on the future with a discussion of computer-assisted journalism and samples of three online newsletters that serve as very different vehicles for their publishers.

- A selected bibliography lists great books for further study when you're ready to go beyond the overview this book provides. You may not be a newsletter editor forever, but everything you learn about this kind of journalism will translate to other publishing contexts. (Really.)

Happy newslettering. Yes, it's fairly serious business. But remember to have a little fun with it. And once you've learned how to deal with all those unreal demands, do me a favor. Promise me you'll never again say, "I'm just a newsletter editor."

—Linda B. Jorgensen

P.S. The only way they were able to finally pry the manuscript away from my death grip was to promise me I could put all the things I ran out of time to add in a future edition. So I've started source files already, and I'd love to hear from you if you have questions, ideas, solutions, or scary stories to tell. Please send them to me at EEI Press (see the copyright page for all the addresses).

Acknowledgments

Even simple books don't make themselves. I'm grateful to the EEI Communications people who braved the forest of early drafts and pitched their tents in the hellish suburbs of final revisions: Mary Stoughton, copyeditor; Merideth Menken, unflappable cheerleader and project manager, who asked all the right questions, as did Robin Cormier, vice president for publications; Jennifer Stewart, co-conspirator in doing and writing up the real-live redesign; Jayne Sutton, guru of the sane production process; Elizabeth McBurney, astute editorial proofreader, who silvered some badly tarnished spots; Pat Caudill, detective and arrester of idiocy; and Claire Kincaid, publisher, who against every instinct let it take as long as it took.

The layout had to work as both textbook and trade reference—and it was inseparable in my mind from the content. We began laying out the design and gallery sections first, figuring if we could nail them, the rest would be a snap. Hah! I'm a big fan of Lynn Whiteley, resilient, skilled designer; Davie Smith, former art director, creator of the apt little worried naked newsletter-guy concept and insightful design reviewer; and Gayle Dahlman, project manager for page design.

Finally, my morale and sections of the manuscript were improved by the generous critical review of Howard Penn Hudson, editor and publisher of *The Newsletter on Newsletters* and founder of the Newsletter Publishers Association (design); Susan Todd, managing editor for *Newsletter Resources* (editing); and Richard Weiner, public relations consultant and author of *Webster's New World Dictionary of Media and Communications* (writing). My thanks also to the astute Catharine Fishel, editor of *Dynamic Graphics* magazine and proprietor, Catharine & Sons, Inc., who reviewed the whole shebang. Susan Munsat of Lichtman, Trister, Singer, and Ross performed the legal review of design samples.

Whatever works here I gladly share the credit for. What's imperfect is all mine—but I'm working on it.

1 Editing Newsletters

Creating a Newsletter: Start to Finish

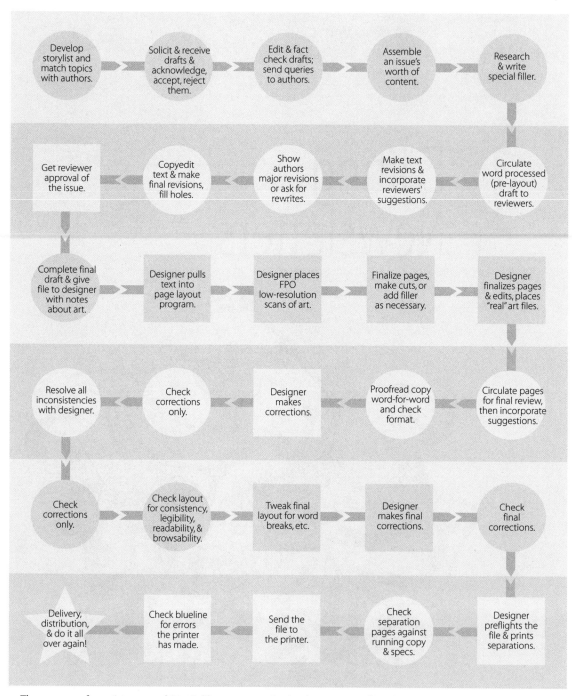

Develop storylist and match topics with authors. → Solicit & receive drafts & acknowledge, accept, reject them. → Edit & fact check drafts; send queries to authors. → Assemble an issue's worth of content. → Research & write special filler.

Get reviewer approval of the issue. ← Copyedit text & make final revisions, fill holes. ← Show authors major revisions or ask for rewrites. ← Make text revisions & incorporate reviewers' suggestions. ← Circulate word processed (pre-layout) draft to reviewers.

Complete final draft & give file to designer with notes about art. → Designer pulls text into page layout program. → Designer places FPO low-resolution scans of art. → Finalize pages, make cuts, or add filler as necessary. → Designer finalizes pages & edits, places "real" art files.

Resolve all inconsistencies with designer. ← Check corrections only. ← Designer makes corrections. ← Proofread copy word-for-word and check format. ← Circulate pages for final review, then incorporate suggestions.

Check corrections only. → Check layout for consistency, legibility, readability, & browsability. → Tweak final layout for word breaks, etc. → Designer makes final corrections. → Check final corrections.

Delivery, distribution, & do it all over again! ← Check blueline for errors the printer has made. ← Send the file to the printer. ← Check separation pages against running copy & specs. ← Designer preflights the file & prints separations.

The process of creating a newsletter is like a perpetual calendar: never-ending. On a given day, an editor is likely to be working on more than one issue—with each issue at a different stage of development.

1 Editing Newsletters

Managing the process without making a spectacle of yourself

Every year thousands of companies, associations, and other organizations hire editors to publish newsletters. There's a reason: Newsletters can be an effective and cost-efficient way to help a specialized message go public. That's one of a handful of generalizations worth making about "what newsletters are."

Here's another one: Newsletters are emphatic about aspiring to be a source of specific benefits for readers. That fact predisposes people to want to read them (as long as the medium doesn't get in the way of the message). The element of providing a service is utterly basic to being an effective editor, and it's at work in every successful newsletter no matter what the focus of the content is.

"Providing service" is interpreted in as many ways as there are dedicated editors—that means thousands and thousands. But for all editors it means creating snapshots of a milieu, a telescoped glimpse of news, advice, insider information, and a certain amount of cheerleading.

You can serve readers and still protect your publishing interests. The relationship between many newsletter editors and their readers is one of empathetic service; they edit "service newsletters." Even marketing, public affairs, and advocacy newsletter editors who have an agenda work hard to make sure they offer readers some solid information— "value added" content—as a courtesy for reading their pitches. Service journalism is a kind of bargain: Readers come to depend on and value what editors lead them to expect, but those expectations have to be met consistently.

Other newsletter editors pride themselves on a specialized focus that means the content isn't likely to be duplicated in any other publication. They edit subscription, association, alumni, affinity group, and business-to-business newsletters. Here, too, the service element is at work.

Whether widely distributed to an external public or restricted to a small, internal "public," newsletters have high visibility. A good newsletter gets talked about, passed around, and saved by readers—the ones you know about and other readers to whom it's passed along. By extension, being a newsletter editor means being in a position of public recognition, with the potential that implies for making a sweet spot for yourself or a spectacle of yourself. If you do things the hard way (like one of Rube Goldberg's elaborate machines), your goals will get caught up in the machinery. Being a newsletter editor is all about building relationships.

1.1   Working relationships: an overview

You may be doing the work of a newsletter editor even though that's not part of your title. Or you may be called a managing editor and report directly to the director of communications or human resources.

1.1.1   Who are you supposed to be?

The term *editor* and all its euphemisms cover a lot of ground. Although someone with many non-publication-related responsibilities may have a more stripped-down newsletter role, being editor means doing some or all of these things:

- Meeting regularly with the publisher (who may be your supervisor).
- Getting and line editing or rewriting contributions from peers or volunteers.
- Soliciting and developing articles from experts or professional writers.
- Doing original research and interviews.
- Writing filler, reviews, and articles on topics no one else will touch.
- Ghostwriting party-line columns and pieces by superiors.
- Attending events and meetings to report on them and analyze trends.
- Checking for grammar, style, factual, and formatting errors (copy-editing).

What's Substantive Editing? It's What You Do

To arrive at publishable copy, some articles need no more than the rearranging of a few paragraphs and a spell-checking pass for the whole thing to click. But in most cases, newsletter editors must substantively edit the drafts they receive (and write). What's that? Simply defined, substantive editing is the editing of meaning. It happens at the word, sentence, and paragraph levels, but at any level it's based primarily on analysis—separating the components of something to discover what's essential about it and looking for the logical relationships that make up the whole. As a result of a good substantive edit, important material won't have to fight for attention or require much mulling.

Substantive editing involves reorganizing sentences within paragraphs, moving paragraphs around till they feel at home, deleting irrelevant or redundant material, recommending changes in terminology or wording to authors, supplying missing words, and rewriting where necessary to clarify meaning and condense copy for the space where it must fit. Here are the basic substantive editing tasks newsletter editors perform:

Analyzing

Filling gaps in thought

Reducing

Reorganizing

Rewording

Rewriting

See section 4 for writing and revising advice and section 5 for substantive edits of real newsletter samples.

Don't be afraid to edit for clarity and conciseness.

- Interacting with an editorial board or peer reviewers.
- Taking photographs, suggesting illustrations, and conceptualizing images.
- Working with a designer on the layout or doing it all yourself.
- Working with a desktop publisher or printer, or both.
- Reading other publications and staying current in your field.
- Brainstorming ways to gain more readers and build their loyalty.
- Creating a forum for reader concerns.
- Putting the newsletter or a version of it on-line.

Until you've put a newsletter together, you might not believe that a full-time editor could work exclusively on, say, a 32-page quarterly association publication. Newsletter journalism is a deceptively simple genre. But because information must be condensed into relatively short articles that are—at the very least—useful *and* interesting *and* accurate, newsletter editing is hard work.

Some Advice for Newsletter Editors

A subscription newsletter, even one with a solid renewal rate of 50 percent or higher, loses readers and gains new ones every year. The rate of turnover may be even higher for a corporate newsletter. To ensure that almost all readers, almost all the time, find almost all of the content useful, editors check for signs of balance in each issue. The average newsletter audience has a shifting mixture of readers who look—consciously or not—for different things, and there should be something for everyone:

- The longtime loyal reader who asks, "Where's the page of photos from the party? Is my department's award mentioned? When is that course being offered again?"

- The newcomer who asks, "What does this acronym stand for? Who are the people in this photo? Is this column written by management? Is this supposed to be funny?"

- The busy browser who asks, "How can I follow articles that jump all over the place? What's the most important article on this page? What's this insert for?"

- The skeptic who asks, "Why are they printing another article about product secrecy leaks? Why should I care about another plaque being handed to another retiree?"

- The demanding colleague or superior who asks, "Why is national news given more coverage than regional? Any typos or omissions in the calendar this time?"

Perhaps the most telling question is the one every editor should ask when reviewing the storylist: "If I didn't have to, would I want to read this newsletter myself?"

It's important to learn where your efforts are best directed, especially if editing a newsletter is only a half-time responsibility. It helps even more if you're lucky enough to be able to put together a team to work with on each issue. People should have a clear description of duties and know just where and when they'll be called on in the course of production, for their own good as well as yours.

1.1.2   Where are you on the experience continuum?

As a newsletter editor, you may have to learn some things you've never paid much attention to about writing, graphics, and organizational politics. If you work alone or in a huge newsletter publishing business, you'll need to adapt the guidelines in this book for your needs because most of them are offered with the average organizational editor in mind.

Who is this stereotypical editor? He or she works alone or with a couple of associates, almost always answers to a team of reviewers, and may deal with volunteer or freelance writers. Sometimes there's a designer or a mysterious art director lurking in the background. Less often, editors do it all by themselves from start to finish within a corporate, association, or government context—many people standing around in the kitchen and waiting at the table, but there's only one cook.

Some new editors who have never written for publication before say the word *editing* makes them think of something vaguely literary that old and wise people do. Or else they think editing means copyediting the text that other people write for grammar errors and typos. The truth is so much more fun than that! And much less grand.

Most of the time, being a newsletter editor means knowing how to head off problems (then fix them when they happen anyway) and being nice to (busy) people who can help you out. You simply can't do it all yourself, yet you're responsible for making sure all the pieces come together. Even—no, especially—if you really are a one-person shop, you must develop a professional support system. The more resources you bring to developing content, the better it will be, and the more stamina you'll have for working simultaneously on future issues. Here are the extremes and the news:

You need professional resources and tools.

- If you're an inexperienced and overworked editor, you have finite reserves. The good news for you is that newsletters are bound by a finite set of conventions. This isn't an encyclopedia you're compiling; encyclopedic knowledge and talent aren't required. Keep things simple and consistent and you'll be doing better than most.

- If you've been doing newsletter editing for a while, morale can be a problem. You have to find enough energy and heart to care about the quality of the work issue after issue after issue. If you're tilting toward jaded, the good news for you is that newsletters offer an infinitely flexible set of possibilities, and the tools are better than ever.

Make things interesting for yourself as you go along. Learn enough to spearhead a retooling or even a redesign, if nothing has changed editorially or graphically in about five years. These aren't marble tablets for the ages you're pounding out; periodicals are ephemeral, after all. Invariability isn't required when creating them. Flexibility is.

1.1.3   Who are your colleagues?

As for titles, they're quite arbitrary since they're specific to how an organization is...organized. One newsletter's editor is another's managing editor with the same duties as another's assistant editor. Few publications have a massive listing; it's more common to give credit to a handful of people. Roughly, here are some newsletter staff positions that commonly show up on mastheads:

- **Publisher or executive editor.** Has final approval of content; acts as a consultant and reviewer; spearheads marketing efforts.

- **Editor.** Solicits, assigns, edits, and rewrites articles; works with authors; consults with the executive editor and publisher to steer content; approves layout; helps with promotion and marketing efforts.

- **Managing editor.** Shepherds manuscripts through the review cycle and oversees author contracts; makes copyfitting edits to articles; oversees or works with production staff; interacts with readers; helps with promotional efforts.

- **Assistant editor.** Performs administrative and reader support tasks; does research, fact checking, and proofreading; may correspond with authors and help with manuscript preparation.

- **Editorial assistant.** Has a largely clerical support position but may correspond with readers and proofread, research, and fact check copy.

- **Copy editor.** Checks the manuscript for grammatical and usage errors and typos; may smooth the writing and check facts. Count yourself blessed if you have one on staff, and find a freelance or contract editor to help you if you don't.

- **Contributing editor.** Regularly writes substantial material, usually but not always for a fee or some consideration, and usually comes from outside the organization; may be a largely honorary title for a volunteer, review board member, or former editor who helps brainstorm topics and authors for the storylist, passes along ideas, and acts generally as a booster.

- **Art director.** Conceptualizes and approves all graphics and text flow; checks layout for more and less reasonable loyalty to the template.

- **Designer or layout artist.** Creates the layout for the content; selects and places graphics; prepares files for the printer.

- **Production manager.** Polices the traffic patterns—rounds of layout revisions and preparation of final deliverable files and proofs—a manuscript must drive through while avoiding collisions, wrong turns, and unforseeable delays.

- **Photographer.** Takes, develops, and helps edit photos. But few newsletters have a person dedicated to taking photos.

- **Editorial board.** Members act as critical reviewers—list them to make the chain of command clear and to give them public recognition for helping.

On pages 14 and 15 are some actual examples of how differently organizations set up their rosters and list the lines of responsibility in the masthead. Really, anything goes—except giving *no* credit where it's due.

1.1.4 Editors have constituents, so they can't escape politics

In addition to being specialized in one way or another (by subject matter or readership), newsletters provide analysis and advice. These are the three hallmarks of newsletter content, although format varies from brochure to manuscript-page to newspaper size, length from one page to 52 pages, paper from photocopy-quality to slick coated stock, and frequency from weekly to quarterly or even annually.

According to an article by Anne Murphy in *Inc.* magazine, "Thanks to the age of the desktop press, newsletters are inheriting the earth." She explained:

> The weapon of choice for legions of frugal marketers, newsletters now bombard company mail rooms as heavily as catalogs once did. You can expect them from suppliers, bankers, lawyers, accountants, consultants, printers, and overnight couriers. Followed by others from insurers, distributors, and brokers.

Murphy also said, "Companies with successful newsletters attest that the process of producing the newsletter forces them to define their marketing goals and crystallize their message to customers. It also keeps them better informed about their own business."

But here's the rub: If readers are being bombarded by so many newsletters—suspect as a category in the first place by association with unsolicited "advertorial" propaganda—why would they want yet another shoved at them? What sets your message apart from the zillions of newsletters and newsletter-like pieces being cranked out on countless desktops for countless hapless readers?

Editors are, first and last, reader advocates.

The answer is the unique service you offer readers. The simplest four-page newsletter should make it clear even on a quick scanning what the practical benefits of reading it are—a handful of readily identifiable and clearly desirable ways readers get what they expect—defined and diagnosed symptoms, asked and answered questions, posed and solved problems, named and mapped roads, unlocked and opened doors. Newslettering is *service journalism*, and its chief task is to supply reader-based content. "News you can use," that clichéd tagline, is the truth about newsletters.

So newsletter editors are, first and last, advocates for the best interests of readers. And most of this book is intended to help editors do right by them.

But that's just for openers. An editor's second-most important reader is the publisher, the sponsoring organization that pays the salaries, the bills, and lots of attention to whether the newsletter serves its goals. It doesn't matter whether editors report to the CEO, human resources manager, or public relations v.p.: There's a specific reason for publishing. Doing the job for readers can't happen without knowing what

The Editor Who Wasn't

Editors have to pick their battles.

Problem: I was hired as a special projects coordinator for a 12-page quarterly newsletter. After several issues, it has become painfully clear to me that I'm not truly the editor. I fill out the purchase orders, stay in contact with the writers, and edit submissions. Then I funnel copy to my boss, who does more editing. Her boss does even more editing, usually a rewrite.

We decided to redesign the deadly dull format, so the artist and I worked on a mock-up. However, when it was revised and made final, I wasn't even notified of the meeting. In fact, my boss and her boss make all the decisions—topics, article assignments—without my input. But they want my name on this newsletter as editor. How can I get them to treat me like one?

Solution: Some perfectly acceptable newsletters are written and produced by an individual, but the truly successful ones represent the collective knowledge and opinions of a team of people. Collaboration isn't incompatible with editorial integrity. There's always a middle ground.

The key is determining which issues are important enough to debate and which aren't. I wouldn't suggest tendering your resignation over minor disputes about word choice or font size (if you do, you'll be changing jobs a lot). However, you must be able to come to an agreement about your level of involvement. Here are some steps you can take:

- Ask for a meeting with your boss and her boss to clarify the mission, goals, scope, and audience for the newsletter. If they do lots of editing, they must feel that the drafts are missing the mark. Possibly a fundamental source of disagreement has never been aired. If you don't figure out what the concerns are, you'll be spinning your wheels on every issue.

- Decide what you want. What ideal scenario would allow you to consider yourself the "true" newsletter editor? Sketch a detailed process for assembling and producing an issue and describe your desired involvement at each step. Explain how you will incorporate review comments. Ask your bosses if they feel you have the skills to carry out your plan.

- Boost your credibility by referencing outside sources—books you've read, seminars you've attended—so your bosses know you've done your homework.

- Meet with your boss and her boss to go over their edits for each issue so that you understand why they've requested changes. If you disagree, explain why. You'll earn their trust and respect if you can articulate the thinking behind your decisions.

Special project coordinator is a catch-all position for duties that don't fit elsewhere. It's up to you to help establish your role in a proactive, positive manner. With the proper mix of teamwork, trust, and respect, your newsletter can be a special project that you'll be proud to put your name on.

—Robin A. Cormier, from an article in *The Editorial Eye*

the publication is intended to accomplish from the organizational perspective.

That means you have to learn everything you can about your readers *and* your publishing context. Then, and only then, can you sell the publisher on your own ideas for bringing down to earth, onto the page, useful messages for real, live people.

To say it another way, filling newsletters full of good stuff requires not only a general understanding of what the format can do for readers but what *you* are specifically being asked to accomplish for *your* publisher.

Editors may play many roles on an average day: journalist, keyboarder, artist, accountant, manager, designer, psychologist, and marketer. But first of all, the newsletter editor is a politician charged with interpreting and communicating a point of view and establishing a coherent identity. If you and your publisher can agree on a vision of what your newsletter should do for readers, they'll be more likely to wade through the stuff on their desks looking for it—because it will look and sound and feel like something that can do them good.

The process of newsletter publishing begins with a set of related decisions about why and what and for whom to publish. All the rest is searching for ways to please and enlighten readers.

1.2   The publisher sets the agenda

Fortunately, few newsletter publishers overwhelm their editors with aggressive, surgical-strike objectives. After all, editors, who are hired for their ideas, discretion, and skill at putting puzzles together, are by nature idealistic. But they serve at the discretion of the folks with the agenda.

Unless publisher and editor independently select the same goals, their view of the enterprise may lead them to misunderstand each other and pull in different directions. Here are some generic publishing objectives, expressed as verbs, a number of combinations of which an editor might undertake to meet on behalf of readers. How can you tell which motives belong to whom? In a perfect shop, they'd dovetail. But that matters less than making sure there's no unnecessary antagonism.

teach	inform	market	sell	motivate
entertain	recruit	report	analyze	clarify
praise	persuade	impress	illustrate	interpret
inspire	define	justify	reassure	advocate
lobby	investigate	advise	empower	explain
network	help	answer	recommend	review

The most useful objectives set criteria for what will count as desirable reader response. Not to mention the fact that publishing objectives set boundaries for the amount of time and money and the number of people necessary to produce the newsletter, as well as, ultimately, the overall look, production values, and publishing frequency. Do you and your publisher want to

- inspire more donors to attend an upcoming alumni reunion?

- caution miners to pay more attention to safety rules so they have fewer on-the-job injuries?

- tempt clients to turn in a coupon for a free service so you can explain your new technology when you get there?

- add subscribers by reaching out to people slightly outside your core group?

- persuade your association members to sign up for low-cost workshops at the national conference?

- recruit new clients for your prepress services and get old clients to try them?

- motivate your employees to follow company "anti-espionage" policies?

- improve morale by telling home office readers what the field staff is up to?

- publicize the efforts of volunteers and encourage others to help?

Newsletters can accommodate all sorts of objectives. Not all of them at the same time, though; a standard 12-page title can support only about three distinct, complementary objectives. That's why many publishers use a print newsletter to spin off time-sensitive material from a less frequently published magazine, or use an online version to post miscellaneous "housekeeping" content that seems ill-at-ease in a more narrowly focused print newsletter.

In short, the more objectives you have in mind for a newsletter, the more different kinds of articles and additional pages you'll need—and the more it will cost to produce. Over time, it may make more sense to spin off a new title so that there's one for a closely related group of goals and another that's more general interest. Remember that the more ground a newsletter tries to cover, and the more kinds of readers it tries to reach, the less likely that it's covering enough territory, thoroughly enough, for most readers.

1.3 Always put your mission front and center (and stand behind it)

Publishers mandate the publishing mission, but editors have to buy into it or they'll find themselves working at cross-purposes with the folks whose help and approval they need. The first step toward creating a consensus is to write a working mission statement. That's where the editor's most significant communication goal and the publisher's most concrete objectives intersect. It's also a good place to remind readers and advertisers why you're asking them to pay attention to your message—so be sure to print it somewhere in the newsletter itself.

A mission statement is a succinct note about whom you're publishing your newsletter for, why it's being published, and who is publishing it—or some combination. Mission statements are "meant to be inspiring—editors create them both to stay true to their own focus and vision as well as to communicate it to others," writes Cheryl Woodard in *Starting & Running a Successful Newsletter or Magazine*. Also called *editorial statements* because they're based on editorial goals, they're anchored by the publisher's hoped-for tangible results. Such statements are traditionally printed as part of the name on the front page or in the masthead (also called a staff box). They can be a single statement or a longer paragraph—but they belong in each issue as a sign of editorial commitment and a reminder to readers. (Sometimes an entire column or a box or screened area may be necessary if the purpose of the newsletter isn't easy to summarize in a few choice words.)

Your publishing mission is the outreach engine.

The mission is really the engine for outreach. Especially if your organization publishes more than one newsletter or publishes regional versions of a parent newsletter, the mission statement helps readers to recognize each face in the crowd (there's bound to be some overlap in distribution).

If your newsletter is easily recognized by employees or association members as "their" publication, you may think printing a mission statement would be wasting space on the obvious. But remember that new readers need help getting a fix on why they should be reading—and newsletters have legs. You never know who may end up browsing your pages before they end up on the bottom of a birdcage.

Why not take advantage of every opportunity to state your case, both inside and outside your organization? Note the mission statements in the masthead samples on pages 14 and 15.

Fall 1995

*Publi*FORUM

MANAGING EDITOR	Theresa Best
EDITORS	Mark Coté
	Tonja Joyce
	Naomi Pauls
	Erin Prendergast
DESIGNERS	Vinita Phord
	David Schimpky
WEB DESIGN	John Maxwell
	Laila Straus
PRODUCTION	Mette Henrichsen
DISTRIBUTION	Luisa Canuto
	Marilyn Jones
PHOTOGRAPHY	Vinita Phord
	Laila Straus
ADVISORY BOARD	Jane Cowan
	Ralph Hancox
	Paul Heyer
	Rowland Lorimer
	Ron Woodward
EDITORIAL ASSISTANCE	Constance Brissenden
CREATIVE ASSISTANCE	Michael Lee
TECHNICAL ASSISTANCE	Michael Hayward

COLOUR SEPARATIONS
AND FILM BY
WYSIWYG PREPRESS
(604) 684-5466

©1995 Canadian Centre for Studies in Publishing

Publiforum is published by the Canadian Centre for Studies in Publishing. Portions of this newsletter may be reprinted or adapted for academic non-profit purposes without permission, provided that the source is clearly acknowledged.

For more information about the Canadian Centre for Studies in Publishing or the Master of Publishing program contact:

Canadian Centre for Studies in Publishing
Simon Fraser University at Harbour Centre
515 West Hastings Street
Vancouver, British Columbia
V6B 5K3
Canada

Telephone: (604) 291-5242
Fax: (604) 291-5239
E-mail: jray@sfu.ca

SIMON FRASER
UNIVERSITY
AT HARBOUR CENTRE

A

Key to Sample Mastheads

These toolboxes can contain as much or as little housekeeping information as you want your readers to have about the publisher, the newsletter staff, copyright, and contact information. They can take many shapes and come in all sizes—but they should run in the same place on the same page each time, just like the nameplate they're often confused with. These samples show a range of editorial and graphic treatments.

A. This column-width vertical masthead shows just how many people may need to be listed—even for an 8-page newsletter. Note that newsletter staffers come first, then a note about the mission of the newsletter, and finally the sponsoring organization's contact information. The university logo at the bottom anchors the column. Sometimes this order is exactly reversed.

B. Note that the vertical masthead is a column width set off by neatly centered lines within a block of white space. At the top, where the title is often repeated, a graphic invites reader interaction on the focus of the newsletter, which also happens to be its name. Type is small but legible.

C. This horizontal page-width masthead on the last page is as simple as they come—that's the style of the editor, and it's a one-person operation. Nice to add the reassuring information that the newsletter has served its target audience since 1983. Include an e-mail address if you have it so people can send you notes, and list a Web address if you have a site, whether or not you have an online version of the newsletter itself. (A new job title for editors who work with a corporate webmaster on their publication's part of the site is *docmaster*.)

D. Another horizontal masthead that takes the path of least layout resistance, but as complete as you'll see in a newsletter. Also on the last page, it's in a font so tiny as to defy reading—it doesn't compete with text, but if it's worth including, it needs to be legible. Since you can't really see it, here's what it contains: title, ISSN, mission, publication schedule, subscription rates, contact information, note to the postmaster, disclaimer advising readers to verify rates for travel arrangements, disclaimer stating that the mention of names and establishments doesn't indicate their sexual orientation, and then the staff is listed (Publisher, Editor, Art Director, "Circulation and lots more," Production, and individual columnists). Professional affiliation with the International Gay & Lesbian Travel Association is followed by—whew!—copyright notice.

E. This page-width horizontal masthead is placed early in the magazine-style newsletter. A screened box holds a notice that prohibits external distribution and the extraordinary (for an internal newsletter) legal disclaimer that all information and opinions belong to the authors and don't necessarily reflect the organization. Simple contact and staff information could also be printed alone in a smaller box if no disclaimer were necessary—it's just enough to do the trick.

Publisher
Loujean LaMalfa
•
Editor in Chief
Barry Prince
•
Mexico Senior Editor
G. Cunningham
•
Contributing Editors
Tod Jonson
Ed Bustamante
Curt Hyman
Darcie Beaumont
Barry Harte
Alex Cummings
Tom Webber
•
Copy Editor
John Hoopes
•
Editorial Manager
Donna Horne
•
Art Director
Sindy Poremba
•
Production Manager
Poremba Press & Communications

B

1.4   What makes a publication a *newsletter*?

Many of the contemporary-looking corporate and association publications that call themselves newsletters are virtually magazines. They have art on the cover, a main
article or two in a central feature well prefaced by news
bites and followed by columns and ads, and a table of contents spread replete with photos, graphics, oversized folios,
teasers for article titles, and pullquotes.

As desktop publishing has shamed most of the down-and-
dirty holdouts away from Courier typeface and bright
orange paper, the distinction is sometimes hard to make—
and frankly, it doesn't really matter unless using a "hybrid"
design means losing the advantages of both newsletter and
magazine format. But that's the problem. Most editors
don't know what they're missing when they default on
what newsletters do best.

1.4.1   If it's feathered like a newsletter....

Remember the earlier reference to Rube Goldberg? He was
a cartoonist who created fantastic machines; they made
something happen by means of an elaborate process when
a simpler process would have done as well. Good newslet-

Sid Cato's NEWSLETTER ON ANNUAL REPORTS has been published (on recycled paper) every month since September 1983. P.O.
Box 19850, Kalamazoo, MI 49019-0850 USA (616) 344-2286 (-4145 FAX) Copyright © Cato Communications, Inc. On the
Internet: *http://www.sidcato.com* *The Official Annual Report Website®* Send email to *sidcato@sidcato.com* ISSN 1083-6721.

C

OUT & ABOUT (ISSN 1066-7776) is a privately published newsletter providing travel information free from advertising bias for lesbian and gay travelers and their travel agents. It is
published ten times a year (monthly with combined issues January & February and July & August) for $49 per year in the United States ($59 in Canada/Mexico; $69 other addresses) by
Out & About Inc., 8 W 19th St., Ste. 401, New York, NY 10011 (telephone 212-645-6922; fax 645-6785; www.outandabout.com).Periodical class postage paid at New York, NY and at
additional mailing offices. POSTMASTER: Send address changes to Out & About Inc., P.O. Box 1792, New York, NY 10113-1792. Back issues $5 each. All rates and information in this
publication are subject to change without notice, and readers are encouraged to verify critical information with the travel supplier or a professional travel agent prior to making travel
arrangements. Publication of the name of any person or establishment is not an absolute indicator of the gay-friendliness or sexual orientation of such person or establishment, and all ratings
and descriptions reflect only the personal opinions of our editors and contributors. Publisher: David Alport; Editor: Billy Kolber-Stuart; Art Director: Fred Gates; Circulation and lots more:
Matthew Pealer; Production: Charlie Beavin, Barbara Kolber; Party Columnist: Alan Brown; Calendar Editor: Matt Farris. Travel Pack: Tom Loughlin. Out & About, Inc. is a member of
the International Gay & Lesbian Travel Association. © 1998 by Out & About, Inc. All rights reserved. No part of this publication may be reproduced or transmitted in any form or by any
means without permission in writing from the publisher.

D

Prudential Leader

Leader is for informational purposes and is intended for internal use
only. Further distribution is strictly prohibited. Any discussion about
Prudential products or services is not intended as an offer or solicitation
of such products or services. Comments about products and services are
based on information and data believed to be accurate at the time of publication. Any opinions that may be expressed are those of their authors
and do not necessarily reflect the views of Prudential or its employees.

Published by:
Prudential Communications Group
213 Washington St., Stop 061
Newark, NJ 07102-2992

Fax: (201) 802-9400

Office Vision nickname: "LEADER"

Copyright ©1996 The Prudential
Insurance Company of America
Litho in U.S.A.

Senior Editor
Debbie Meany
Editorial Staff
Dave Artuso, Ken Coles
Editorial Assistant
Suzanne Dzula Adams
Design
Nick Pazinko
Design Assistant
Rosemarie Rossi

E

ters follow the law of parsimony: They adopt the simplest means to reach an end.

Generally, newsletters are 8½ by 11 inches (11 by 17 inches folded) or tabloid-size (all pages are 8 by 14 or 11 by 17 inches). It's cheapest for most printers to output 8½-by-11 pages in signatures of 4 pages, which is why so many newsletters are 4, 8, 12, or 16 pages long.

Tabloids come in many shapes but are often kept to eight pages or so— they take a lot of copy to fill! But one 11-by-17 professional association tabloid has 52 pages, and a 10-by-14 university public relations tabloid has 24 pages.

Newsletters do down-to-earth work.

Less common are smaller sizes that fit neatly in the hand; they might seem like brochures except for their reliance on articles and other print journalism elements like headlines and photos. The smaller paper size doesn't necessarily cost more to use if your printer has a press that can handle it without special set-up fees and paper waste. The point is that newsletters come in all shapes and sizes, and the choices are largely designer-driven on the basis of how much content there will reliably be and how many and what kinds of graphics will figure into the mix.

1.4.2 If it honks like a newsletter....

Newsletters look and honk like...newsletters. What literally defines a periodical as a newsletter, as apart from a magazine, journal, or newspaper, is its observance of newsletter style conventions. (That fact makes it hard to define online newsletters, which lack most of the conventions of their printed cousins. See appendix on page 321.)

"Newsletter style" means short articles, an emphasis on reader-service, behind-the-scenes analysis of complex or technical topics, and a group of complementary articles that cover regular bases. In short, a balanced mix of how-to, help, highlights, and a bit of housekeeping. That means newsletters offer a lot of content in a carefully constructed package. No frills, nothing purely decorative or diversionary, nothing extraneous. Newsletters—even newsletters about exotic topics like sky diving or dowsing or raising ostriches—do down-to-earth work for a living. They take only scheduled leave of their mission; departures are few and deliberate. And may be accompanied by honking.

1.4.3 If it flies south every winter like a newsletter....

Okay. It looks and sounds like a newsletter. How time-sensitive is most of your content? How many subjects objectively exist and need to be reported on? How much money is available to subsidize editorial and printing costs (less subscription/membership/ad fees)? The answers will determine how frequently you can and should reasonably publish without going broke or crazy.

Printing half as often or half as many pages doesn't mean the newsletter will cost half as much; it's not a 1:1 ratio. There's no "average" amount of money it takes to produce a "model" newsletter; instead, there are countless financial variables and many, many editorial models. It may even make sense for some newsletters to keep publishing in the red for their value as identity pieces or as an integral part of other marketing collateral (brochures, catalogues, direct mail letters, and the like).

The best advice most seasoned publishers give newcomers is to write down all the pros and cons and do a break-even analysis. That means seeing what you can count on getting back, whether you measure your bottom line in sales, members, subscribers, fans, or having your stories picked up by wire services—and whether that value justifies the cost of

Breaking the Rule of Thumb: A Smaller Page Size Can Work, Too

More handsome tabloid-size (oversized) newsletters are being produced than ever. But the art director and designer chose a small format size for the *Focus on EEI Communications* client newsletter when they updated its design. Why?

- The editorial focus had shifted to shorter profiles of client successes instead of longer, overt marketing pieces about the company's way of doing business.

- One client "cameo" per page allowed the editor to highlight each success story, instead of ganging up several small competing pieces on each page.

- All art on each page was directly connected to one article instead of competing with other graphics for attention.

The designer summed up the tradeoffs involved: "The term 'bite-size' has a bad connotation for some editors, but these short pieces are easy to find, easy to read, and each page is more restful-looking. The 6- by 11-inch folded size isn't being used for many other corporate newsletters, and since we publish *Focus* only quarterly, we wanted each issue to be a standout."

The designer acknowledged, "Once the commitment to a small format was made, of course, the editor had to learn to write to fit the smaller page. It's certainly changed her life now that a 500-word article might take up three pages and has to shrink by two-thirds—but still say what it needs to say."

For the two-color *Focus,* a soft-edged effect is gained by using Mohawk Options paper, which has good ink absorption for the spot color and screens. Four colors from the corporate palette alternate each quarter. Photos of clients and their successful projects are the main graphics. Small can be beautiful, and in this case it doesn't cost more to print. (For a copy, write to the publisher at the address on the copyright page of this book.)

producing the newsletter (a) in the form and at the frequency you pre-fer, (b) some other way, or (c) not at all.

Venerable newsletter guru Howard Penn Hudson has the best answer to how long a newsletter should be and how often it should be pub-lished: "It depends."

Consumer-oriented titles are published less often than corporate or business newsletters. In *Success in Newsletter Publishing: A Practical Guide*, Hudson advises:

> While it is normally the depth and specificity of information published in a newsletter that leads to its success, rather than the timeliness—in the sense of rapid delivery of information—one school of thought does hold that frequency is important and that a publisher would be better off to promote a 4 page weekly than an 8 page biweekly.

Everything's a tradeoff in periodicals publishing. The (un)holy triad of time (enough), money (no more than necessary), and quality (the best) is the ideal. The shape of most operations is more like a three-legged chair propped up on a stack of books.

1.5   Nurturing a core readership

Some audiences are captive—they work at a company and they're a known quantity—but they should never be taken for granted. The American workforce is so diverse that the concept of "the reader" really needs to be expanded to include many different sub-audiences defined by variables such as age, education, professional experience, and so on.

Other newsletters need to find an audience that's actively involved in or interested in a field or topic. Realistically, only a fraction of the "universe" of all such people who might want to read a newsletter reg-ularly will actually do so. They become its *core audience*. Defining the likely candidates for a newsletter is directly correlated with how the newsletter will address their needs. At some point, the natural interests of readers and the editorial goals of a publisher have to coincide.

Enter the editor: an arbitrator for keeping those interests in balance. This book is aimed at editors who have walked into an existing pub-lishing venture or who have a good idea of who the intended audience is, but even then they can help publishers pinpoint answers to several basic questions about potential readers, as described by Cheryl Woodard. Here's a summary:

- **Participation.** How do people involve themselves in an activity? How long have they been involved? How often do they attend pro-fessional events? Determining how active or passive people are will influence things like the tone and scope of articles.

- **Information needs.** Are people looking for help advancing their careers? Buying or selling products? Finding out about new technologies? Traveling to pursue their activities? Meeting other people in their field? Are there influential people readers would like to hear from? The answers will determine the mix, scope, and difficulty level of articles.

- **Other sources of information.** What related magazines, books, or other newsletters about your subject are your readers familiar with? What can your publication give readers more of (if they like it) or less of (if they dislike it) than existing publications? What topics could be and should be discussed by other editors but aren't? The editorial focus will be driven by how your newsletter distinguishes itself from the competition (or from a void).

Newsletters serve an infinite variety of missions.

- **Demographics.** In addition to their level of engagement with a subject, most publishers and editors want to know in general what kinds of groups will be reading: young? old? men? women? working people? retired people? Writing with the reader in mind means all the readers—with something for everyone in each issue.

Newsletter format serves very different kinds of publishing missions equally well. It shows signs of having been put together by human beings—that's its chief virtue (or curse, depending on the skill and motivation an editor brings to the enterprise—without at least one of the two, it's shades of *PTA News and Views* badly typed by a tired school secretary). There's a sense of being part of a community, and readers are often work colleagues or belong to the same group as the editor.

In any case, your newsletter will give them information and guidance they can't get anywhere else, on topics that hit home—where they work, live, or play. That's the *least* you can do.

1.6   Basic types of newsletters

An *internal* newsletter is a great way to let employees know what's going on and where things are headed. (That's why associations and nonprofit organizations publish newsletters, too.)

External newsletters (professional, marketing, public relations) and specialty *subscription* newsletters (free or paid) are a good way to educate, motivate, and inform a diverse readership while adding to the visibility and reputation for responsiveness of the sponsoring organization.

Newsletters provide a platform, a stage, for a publisher. They come in countless flavors and sizes, but they're all aimed at "clients." All target a qualified readership. And all are in the publicity business.

But wait, isn't publicity what direct mail brochures, ads, press releases, and media spot promos are for? Yes, but unless people are in the market for something *right now* or in the mood to shop for it, they tend to resist direct sales messages. Newsletters look like journalism.

Besides, many newsletters aren't in the business of selling anything except information itself. These newsletters publish for a *niche*—that is, they diligently digest statistics, spot trends, offer guidelines, provide analysis, and collect bits of insider gossip, anecdotes, and wisdom for a certain kind of reader interested in a highly defined topic.

Niche newsletters keep that "target audience" in mind and make readers feel they're part of an in-group. Service newsletters can build a wide and loyal readership by serving up practical benefits and advice that's the mental equivalent of holding something in the hand: in short, news that feels concrete because it makes a difference.

1.6.1   You need to define your editorial goals

An editor should be given—or better, participate in devising—clear guidelines for the range of content and production values that will be appropriate to serve the publisher's objectives—within the allotted time and budget for production.

But it's the editor's job to make sure that for each publishing objective there's valuable content in each issue for readers—a corresponding reader-based benefit. You're also going to try to produce a newsletter that's distinctive but recognizable over time. You're the guiding force in achieving these two main editorial goals.

Decide what's

in it for you.

These are the goals you use to explain to yourself what you're doing and why you're putting *this* article but not *that* one in the newsletter. Some editors say they have personal goals that they derive private, professional pride from meeting: say, creating a column for running reader comments and answering their questions, or adding a second color so some short pieces can be attractively formatted in boxes, or even completely redesigning the newsletter.

Sometimes an ambitious editor casts a wider net to include goals like "motivating employees to read each issue before throwing it away" or "showcasing employees who care about the community in which they work." Meeting those kinds of goals isn't easily measurable, but they're part of the canon for creating a quality publication apart from the bottom-line objectives. (If you self-publish, asking a few selected readers for feedback can help pinpoint whether what you say your mission is matches what people see.)

Of course, the universal editorial goal is to provide interesting, beneficial copy. No editor sets out to take advantage of readers, bore or misinform them, or beat them senseless with trivia. But the editor's

Computer-Assisted Editing and Human Error

Editing newsletters with the help of database software that compiles and analyzes statistical information isn't foolproof. Editors have to make good choices about which online sources to trust, verify the accuracy of percentages and correlations, and make sure that numerical data have relevance for their readers.

The appendix presents some online resources for learning about the new discipline of *computer-assisted journalism*. But there's nothing magic about online data; they are researched, assembled, keyed, and verified (or not) by human beings, who make mistakes. And all data are only as good as their interpretation and analysis. Dazzled by university and government databases, we may be tempted to overload articles with half-baked information just because it's so readily available—and free.

Andrew Schneider, in an article for the *Columbia Journalism Review* (now the *American Journalism Review*), examined "The Downside of Wonderland"—the ease with which uncritical computer searches can seed errors and bad (or unnecessary) statistics into copy. He reported the results of a survey of seasoned newsroom editors:

> When asked whether computers improved the overall quality and readability of stories, 28 percent of the editors said they saw improvement, and 16 percent noted no change, but 56 percent said the impact, the relevance of the topic, and the overall quality had diminished. …Inaccurate information is another concern. Most of us who have done many stories based on databases have learned that it's only too easy for bad data to get into stories.

"A well-structured computer database can generate enough statistics to kill the best-written story," said a metro projects editor for *The Washington Post*. "Reporters must fight to keep the human factor in their copy. Editors must keep all but the most relevant statistics in a box or out of the story. Numbers, even those never before reported, should be used only when examples of real people can't be gotten."

personal investment in good journalism is the only way any newsletter has a prayer of rising above mediocrity.

1.6.2 What if your publisher's goals are different?

Editorial goals aren't necessarily at odds with meeting the publisher's stated objectives, but sometimes there's a conflict. You may be successful by your own measure, but in real life corporate newslettering, "desired reader responses"—desired by the publisher, that is—largely map the boundaries of a particular newsletter's content. You have to find the realistic places where everyone's good intentions intersect and compromises can be made. Those sweet spots will be easier to find if editors remember which loyal reader is, to borrow from Orwell, a bit "more equal" than the rest (sort of like the loyal opposition?). That would be your publisher.

Even an editor who believes in a consensus process has to negotiate some decisions—and "no" is always a possible answer. Wise publishers know that the best work comes from editors who feel they have the autonomy to act on their vision of "a good newsletter." If they have nothing more than the responsibility and the headaches of editing a newsletter to everyone's standards except their own, editors have little incentive to get the best quote, seek out the best photo, run that statistic down to be sure it's right, and constantly find interesting people and things to write about.

One obvious way to make editorial goals clear is to make them a part of normal daily conversation. Mention them when speaking to people—supervisors, members of the editorial board, and other newsletter participants. Others you work with are more likely to understand and support your ideas, as well as temper them with healthy perspective, if you ask them to help you think things through. For example: "I'm thinking that if we run short updates about field projects, regional staff might feel more connected to our central office. Do you think we could ask for a couple of volunteers to send monthly e-mail reports?" The answers you get will be a reality check.

Who's really in control? Mark Beach, author of the seminal *Editing Your Newsletter*, says that the most frequent problem newsletter editors face is "control over content. The editor feels responsible for content, loyal to readers, and pressured by the deadline. The publisher wants to approve every word." Newsletter editing, then, thrives on a healthy tension between the editor's vision and the reality of the publishing mission. A little friendly contention can be productive; service journalism doesn't mean lip service.

1.6.3   Newsletters are famous for what they *don't* do

One of the reasons there are so many newsletters being published each year—about 5,000 subscription newsletters alone, give or take a few that fold and others that start up—is what they *don't* do: They don't make heavy demands on the people who read them. They don't come across as didactic, although they may be relaying quite definite views and asking readers for serious commitments of time, energy, and money in activities or products.

Successful newsletters *offer* information, *invite* attention, *encourage* participation, *reward* loyalty, *ask for* feedback, and *express* a sense of mission. The whole idea is to be a source of periodical news that people recognize and look forward to. As Rene J. Cappon, author of the *Associated Press Guide to News Writing* said, "To gather information is not enough; we must also get people to read it."

In short, what you leave out of your newsletter is as important as what you pack into it. Successful newsletter editors try to give readers the sense that they're part of a select in-group, or the kind of content they can't find anywhere else, or preferably both. Just as *The Shelby Daily Star* is the newspaper of record for a circumscribed part of Cleveland County, NC, a newsletter is the "paper of record" for its editorially defined constituency. Newsletter content has to interest a range of readers with both common bonds and special interests. And then there's the final challenge: Most readers aren't readers at all but browsers—not in the market for clichés, generalizations, and propaganda.

So although editors aren't supposed to make reading seem like a lot of extra work, readers themselves expect quite a lot from newsletters. And if you're like most editors, the newsletter is just *one* of the projects you're expected to crank out. You've got your work cut out for you, all right. That's what an editorial process is for: containing the mayhem and increasing the odds of getting a good product.

1.7 Meeting multiple unreal demands

Being an editor means that the responsibility for the quality of the content falls to you. That means overseeing everything that affects it from the amount of leading between the lines of type and the amount of time it takes to get an issue through production and to the printer—and everything in between.

If you've been picked to take over a newsletter or start one, you're not alone if you feel a sort of frantic discouragement. A lot of people think editing a newsletter is no big deal, but editors themselves know better. Here's what three articulate new editors have said they're up against:

*It's **all** in your job description.*

- *I have to do everything by myself.* I've been asked to take over our employee newsletter and start including news about all our field offices. It's only four pages now so we want to redesign it. I have to learn PageMaker so I can do the layout, too, while assisting the marketing director, handling correspondence, and answering phones. The first issue has to come out in three months.

- *I can't make a single independent decision.* The chapter president of an association that I do a newsletter for has to approve every word of my copy. He comes from the old school—for example, I can't ever use first person or any contractions—and I have to run a long, rambling letter from him on the front page of every issue. I know people think it's boring, but I have no freedom to make changes.

- *I have no say in how things end up looking.* I've just been promoted to newsletter editor. I can write, but I'm having problems with our designer, who's been here a long time. Sometimes typos turn up that weren't there when I gave the copy to him. He adds clip art wherever he likes, and it can be pretty strange. I don't see the news-letter until it's printed—it's embarrassing to have my name on it.

The demands are many, but literally anyone who's willing to do the homework can learn what makes successful newsletters tick. If you're in a hurry, you can go right to the very detailed index of this book, follow the leads to what you want to know more about right now, then come back for more help in managing the editorial process. But remember to come back: There's a reason all the steps of creating a newsletter—planning, talking, writing, editing, fitting copy into the layout, taking photos, getting approvals, checking for errors—may seem to be happening at the same time, in a blur. They are, in fact. While working on any issue, you should be planning at least one more and scouring your landscape for future ideas—all the time. So managing the steps matters.

1.7.1   A note about optimism vs. pessimism

Nobody, but nobody, ever produces a perfect newsletter. Not editors in publications, marketing, public affairs, or human resources offices. Not editors in associations, corporations, universities, the government, or nonprofit organizations. Not freelance editors who in theory have all the time in the world and call their own shots—except that time is money.

If you're optimistic, your newsletter will be interactive.

Perfection just isn't in the cards for evolving, responsive, deadline-driven news-based periodicals like the ones most of us produce. Perfec-tion's not a realistic goal for newsletters for another reason, as we'll see in the writing section. Something that's without fault may not seem as if it's been created for real people by real people. Real-world newslet-ters have a few signs of humanity somewhere, including rough edges.

Newslettering is a labor of love as well as a necessity for those who enjoy this kind of publishing. The enthusiasm you bring to the cycle of doing a newsletter all over again and again is crucial. The best real-world newsletters are created by people who've learned how to keep their own natural curiosity alive while appealing to the "enlightened self-interest" of their publisher and readers.

These editors give their publishing mission a human face and a voice that readers trust. And they know that, more so than other kinds of editors, they're participating in a process. Each issue is a fresh chance to tell the story they're trying to tell.

Another thing newsletter editors who are "naturals" have in common is a tendency to create forums for reader concerns and ideas. In that sense, any newsletter can be "interactive," whether it's published on paper or the Internet. The bottom line is that readers, like skittish horses, dogs, children, and strangers, will sense your attitude and your energy. *That* can't be taught. Personal goodwill shows up in countless small matters that show care has been taken.

1.7.2   The heart of the matter is that you're a journalist

Editors are responsible for selecting, enhancing, and arranging newsworthy messages, and they have a lot of leeway. Although content must be accurate and deliver practical benefits to your readers, the way it's written and presented can be conversational and informal, even personal. You have a vision and a voice all your own, and the publication's tone will reflect them.

As a journalist, you can't escape learning how to write persuasively, revise and organize information logically, and edit graphics intelligently. You're in the business of making strong psychological connections with your readers so they'll be receptive to your publishing mission. You have a voice.

You have a position of genuine power as a communicator and it can be a professional steppingstone, if you keep your balance. The project management skills you acquire will transfer to many other publishing contexts. In short—you have a future.

1.8   Editors manage a process, not a thing

Editors have to learn to be competent project managers—more than just "word people." You need to know how to approach the overlapping details and steps involved in getting a useful newsletter into print. You have to learn what the format can and can't achieve and understand the working relationships, planning decisions, and quality control processes involved in editing each issue.

All editors need to develop a system—a set of regular processes—for getting things done within their organization. The flowchart at the beginning of this section is a graphic overview of these processes. Of course, the steps to getting a newsletter into print are different from place to place but at minimum include

- assembling a balanced issue,

- negotiating changes with authors,

- incorporating changes from reviewers,

- producing a layout, and

- checking for editorial and design problems.

But as Arthur Plotnik says in *The Elements of Editing*, "The editorial 'process' exists only to assure that a particular result will come about consistently and economically. The process, however, should never become so overwhelming as to create unalterable patterns and smother editorial initiative. Each editor brings unique enhancements to the meaning of 'editing.' These individualized approaches distinguish and enliven a medium."

If deadlines are routinely getting missed, errors are going to print uncaught, readers are complaining or unsubscribing, and your reviewers are in a perpetual snit, something's broken down somewhere in the process. Editors, like ostriches, have to keep their ears close to the ground to discern the drumming of danger while it's still far enough away to head off.

In the background, you'll be building a future storylist so that you don't face a tabula rasa when it's time—already!—for a new issue. You'll also want to know that, in case an article has to be pulled for any reason, you've got a backup ready to go.

1.8.1   Editorial committees don't have to mean trouble

Informal communication links that you may already have with others in your organization can be formalized to your advantage by asking energetic, creative people to serve a term as members of the editorial board. Their names imply support from many departments and thus lend your newsletter credibility and authority. But does everyone really need an editorial board of advisors?

You don't need a cast of thousands.

Not necessarily, but the addition of even a pro forma editorial board to the masthead can be an effective way to let readers know whom to contact if they have news in a particular area, a bone to pick, or questions. Colleagues who have agreed to be on an editorial board may like seeing their names in the masthead; from your point of view, they're your own official "stringers" and should be encouraged to suggest material or perhaps even write articles.

Reader morale and rapport—hard to measure but an important intangible—can be boosted by the cooperation and support for the organizational newsletter that a management- or expert-stocked board implies. A cast of thousands, however, can look pretty intimidating and serve to remind people what a huge bureaucracy they work for. So it's not advisable to print the name of everyone who holds any position whatsoever in the organization—a space-waster that does nothing at all for readers.

Having too many editorial advisors also makes a newsletter operation look sort of silly or top-heavy and suggests that the editor is either a master politician or a hapless flunky. Being forced to roll each issue uphill past a committee of people who don't know what the right or the left hand is doing, preferring instead to help the editorial foot into the editorial mouth, is a common frustration.

Working with a Review Board

Editorial boards have wide-ranging responsibilities, from giving a scholarly journal the right intellectual cachet to steering a true editorial course. A well-chosen board can both strengthen a publication and support its editor. Working with an editorial board is not the same as editing by committee—an unsatisfying and potentially disastrous situation. Rather, the editorial board provides the editor a forum in which to debate ideas, structure content, and refine language.

In some instances the editorial board consists of subject specialists who determine the acceptability of submissions. In their roles as peer reviewers, board members serve as resources for the editor and protect the periodical from publishing inferior research. The editor, who is usually a publications expert rather than a subject expert, then has full authority over the number and kinds of editorial changes necessary to make accepted manuscripts presentable to the journal's audience.

In other cases, the editor controls content and the editorial board acts as a kind of Greek chorus, commenting on the substance and the expression of the various articles. The editor then gathers all the written comments, incorporating the best and most relevant and ignoring the rest. This exercise can be particularly interesting: Each member of the board will tend to focus on a different aspect of an article or an entire issue, often forcing the editor to see it from a new and perhaps clearer point of view. It can also be time-consuming, requiring one or more additional cycles in the review process.

There is, of course, a delicate balance between the value of a variety of perspectives and the potential for a truly sour broth. The members of the editorial board should therefore be chosen with extreme care. All should bring to the content not only their diverse educational and editorial backgrounds, but a unique personal perspective as well. Obviously, in any such bouillabaisse, one person must clearly be the final authority on all matters of content and style. Ideally, this person is the editor, although, for political or other reasons, someone else may be the arbiter.

One of the most valuable functions of any good editorial board is to protect the editor from acute tunnel vision. The interaction between the editor and the board is, at its best, a lively intellectual exchange that benefits both the participants and the periodical.

—adapted from an article in *The Editorial Eye*

An enthusiastic "working" editorial board can, however, work out well. Choose people who are part of your organization or outside it, depending on the nature of the relationship you're asking for; boards can provide either active or relatively inconspicuous support, and some members won't always pull their weight. Start with a half dozen people; if someone who has agreed to be on the board doesn't perform, explain that it's only fair to rotate the honor and the burden and find someone else.

As an editorial board member once admitted, "The image of the editorial board as a body that bogs down in trivia and never reaches a clear consensus is, unfortunately, often accurate." But the relationship between an editor and an editorial board doesn't have to be adversarial. Brainstorming meetings not only help the editor shape the periodical but also give the board a stake in the product that makes cooperation the default.

1.8.2   Editorial balance or hotfoot?

The newsletter editor acts as a moderator for a forum that many voices will contribute to—inhouse authors, third-party experts, readers, outside news sources. The attributes of good newslettering can seem at first glance to be contradictory. That's only because they are. A newsletter is both more and little less than strictly a news vehicle. A modest 12-page newsletter can be/contain/have/offer/be characterized by…

Newsletters are both more and less than strictly news vehicles.

this…	but also this.
Niche, vested interest	Analytical, forecasting
Sharp straight-news focus	Service focus on reader benefits
Distinctive flavor	Recognizable voice
Limited in scope	Provides context and overview
Closed universe	Open doors
Tight prose	Descriptive, persuasive prose
Informal tone	Authoritative tone
Personal, even slangy	Pragmatic
Brief articles	Comprehensive treatment
Quickly browsable	Worth keeping
Informative, educational	Fun to read
Unpretentious diction	Goal-oriented messages
Aimed at the median reader	Written by experts
Reader-centered	Publisher-driven agenda
Appealing to an in-group	Jargon-free
Periodic	Builds long-term loyalty
Familiar format	Interesting
Consistent editorial	Offers new twists on old stories
Soft news and features	Knowledgeable sources
Attributed—fact checked, quoted	First-person reports and essays

1.9   Message strategies and natural selection

As we've seen, a newsletter's reason for being is determined by the messenger, the message, the recipient, and the desired reaction. Taken together, all these factors define the publishing mission. Each newsletter editor has to decide what message strategies will support it.

- Who the publisher is and what the publisher has to say (its expertise) define the publishing specialty, or niche—education, nonprofit, public interest, consumer, entertainment, advocacy, affinity, public relations, marketing, sales, association, corporate internal and external, professional subscription, and on and on. What works for one niche will backfire in another.

- The people who are intended to benefit from the message or expertise determine the focus and scope of the content—and research teaches us that we need to be careful to take into account the diversity of subgroups in an audience rather than thinking monolithically in terms of "the reader." What some readers enjoy may offend other readers.

Newsletter editors have a message strategy—if only by default.

- What the audience is supposed to do with the message or expertise—what the benefits are—determines a lot about how a newsletter is organized and presented. What some readers will tolerate is unacceptable to others.

Choosing message strategies is really just putting the principles of natural selection to work for you: If you choose wrong, you'll extinguish the feckless interest of your readers and lose their attention.

Caution: You can be sure that if you're not setting about a message strategy by intention, you're doing it by default. There's no way around it: A newsletter editor is in the business of making choices. Every single issue is a little feat of empathy and manipulation. The ability to decide what readers will find interesting or helpful depends on balancing what *they* want to know about with what *you* want them to know about. That's hard to do if you aren't making conscious decisions like these for each issue:

- What must go in; what's optional; what's gravy.

- What deserves a lot of space; what can be cut or crunched.

- What should be highlighted; what's subordinate.

- What the ratio of news or sell is to features or benefits.

If you're not aware that you're making such choices, that's the wrong kind of strategy.

1.9.1   Analyze your content formula

Try this: List the titles of all the articles in the last three issues of your newsletter or all the topics you plan for the first issue of the newsletter you're starting. Group similar titles into categories to see how many overlap, and give them names: regional news, national news, employee award, annual conference, training opportunities, messages from management.

Do the simple math necessary to create a table or pie chart with slices representing the amount of "real estate" each category takes up (and therefore the explicit message strategy).

Newsletter content comprises strategically selected messages that serve readers' short-term goals and a publisher's long-term objectives. Here are some of the kinds of strategies and content an editor has to choose from:

Content	Strategy
News reports	Interest, educate
News analysis	Give perspective
News roundups	Inform, give an overview
Special topics (features)	Motivate, interest, educate
Recurring topics (departments)	Reassure, build loyalty
Personality profiles	Persuade, provide human interest
Question-and-answer interviews	Inform, offer insight
Editorials (columns)	Persuade, motivate
Reader letters	Appeal to an in-group, amuse
Thought pieces	Persuade, interest, analyze
Photo essays	Inspire, amuse, provide human interest
Case histories	Analyze, educate, offer insight
Surveys	Give perspective, indicate trends
Reviews of resources	Inform, educate, persuade
Stand-alone fact boxes	Inform, persuade, interest

1.9.2   Develop a formula just for *your* readers

Editing a newsletter is *not* merely the act of filling up a certain number of pages (or computer screens, for an online publication) with paragraphs and clip art. The understandable but counterproductive tendency toward a "brain-dump" school of editing results in stuff nobody wants to read. Here are a few axioms about editing reader-based service newsletters:

- You don't have to write about everything there is to know and say everything there is to say about it.

- Readers don't want to read everything there is to know—just the stuff they care about, and they want it to be palatable.

- You have to know what matters most to readers and present it to them in a way that makes sense without demanding a high level of engagement.

Offer a spectrum of viewpoints for all readers.

Learning how to select and emphasize information that's germane to both readers and the publishing mission is a balancing act. Here's Cheryl Woodard's advice:

> Even if you have found the best, most enthusiastic and loyal audience possible, you won't be able to build a profitable [literally or figuratively] relationship with them unless you produce a quality product that appeals to their interests. To do this, always keep the reader's viewpoint uppermost in mind.

Any newsletter worth its salt offers a spectrum of points of enlightenment. That's because unless you're publishing *The Stepford Quarterly,* your newsletter has to include several kinds of content to appeal to all the categories of readers who will read it. Even in a company where everyone's doing the same kind of work, *demographic variables* have to be taken into account. "Know your audience," every book ever published for writers and editors says.

This time, think of it this way: You need to know a lot about your *average* reader—most of the core audience—and also about your *median* reader—taking into account the people at the far ends of, for example, the old-young spectrum.

An editor has to keep in mind three pushme-pullyou imperatives for a balanced issue:

- Most articles ought to offer editorial benefits to most readers—the core audience.

- Each subset of readers should find content that applies directly only to them.

- Publishing objectives should correspond to the content formula.

That's why it's important to distinguish between *publishing objectives* and *editorial objectives.* They're two halves of the publishing mission. The tie that binds is the hope-in-common of providing something for everyone—more often than not and sooner rather than later.

Deciding on a content formula means making a commitment to covering a regular list of topics (perhaps in regular departments) in a predictable ratio, weighted according to where the majority of your readers fall along the Bell curve. Here's a possible content formula for a generic 12-page newsletter whose editor has decided how much space should be allocated to eight kinds of boilerplate articles aimed at segments of the audience. Numbers are approximate and rounded off—they'll vary from issue to issue—but the ballpark estimates will help steer editorial planning:

Content	% of the issue	Pages	Articles/ blurbs needed
Departments/ Columns	33	4	2 to 4
News	17	2	4 to 8
Features	17	2	2 or 3
Resources	17	2	2 or 3
Kudos/Self-promo	4	0.5	1
Humor/Fillers	4	0.5	1
Calendar	4	0.5	As needed
Viewpoint/Opinion	4	0.5	1

Trying to adhere to a formula like this one too strictly won't work out very well because the content will vary from issue to issue. It's more sensible to decide how much of one category of information your newsletter should contain over time. That translates into the number of articles that should be in development at any given time.

But the formula doesn't tell the whole story, especially if you're developing content for, say, a 32-page newsletter and planning alternating features by different authors that cover similar territory. To see why a simple set of departments doesn't give enough of an overview, let's take a closer look at that formula. At first glance it looks as if news, features, and resources—the bread and butter of service journalism—aren't very prominent, when in fact they predominate once you identify similar kinds of content. To illustrate that point, look at how the percentages shift if similar categories of content are combined:

News/Features/Resources/Calendar	55%
Departments/Columns/Viewpoint/Opinion	37%
Kudos/Self-promo/Humor/Fillers	8%

Plan content for an issue by listing all the articles in the *storylist* and then double-checking to make sure they represent appropriate slices of the overall goals for categories of content. You may have too much of a good thing.

1.9.3   How much is too much information?

What do editors owe readers? News that's short, sweet, and cut and dried. But individual editors and individual readers define those criteria differently. Deciding how much detail readers need to get the point is one of the hardest things to learn. How much can you assume they already know? Will they remember the first part of this two-part article or do you need to summarize it? Has everyone seen the movie *Titanic* by now and will they get that witty aside? Editors have to make educated guesses all the time about what the telling details are and how many are enough.

A word about "refrigerator journalism." It's used widely as a synonym for "service journalism," and though the concept behind the terms is similar, there's a big difference in what's owed to readers.

Much that's worth knowing can't be cut to a sound bite.

Refrigerator journalists replace words with graphics, bulleted lists, and small text boxes whenever possible. Sometimes even when

- simple sentences would be clearer,

- bulleted items are cryptic phrases, and

- context is sorely lacking.

Taken to an illogical extreme, this kind of telegraphic journalism means that readers are spared the need to do their own extrapolation and analysis. They're also spared real writing. If you believe what some refrigerator entrepreneurs say about readers, there aren't really very many of them (readers, that is; there are plenty of doomsayers) around anymore. Sound-bite journalists believe that people who will read—really read, not just browse—a 12-page newsletter of their own free will on the subway or while they eat lunch at their desk are the exception. A promotional flyer for one newsletter editing seminar sounded the death knell for bona fide readers:

> "Only" 70 percent of the public has graduated from high school—and most of them read at a junior high level. People are afraid of print.

> People are so busy they want to be told what to think and do. Give them news that's the mental equivalent of a grocery list parked under a magnet on a refrigerator door.

> Advertising language gets attention in news stories. Make claims and use words like handy, quick, easy, revolutionary, innovative, improved.

But much that's worth knowing isn't reducible to formula journalism. Many things worth learning won't make your life easier, just richer. Much that newsletter editors have to tell their readers isn't revolutionary, just bread-and-butter basic. Important matters aren't *always* quick and easy to understand. And if everything is improved, nothing is just plain good, is it?

Genuine service journalists (that includes editors of newsletters, magazines, and their hybrid forms) make a contract with their readers to produce practical information and guidance. Content is useful not merely because it's presented in short articles but because it has been carefully researched, fact-checked, compiled, surveyed, organized, and written with the reader in mind.

Publications that provide real service resist condescending, manipulative copy aimed at a profile of the least motivated reader. Editors who respect readers know they have the good sense to recognize what's important and are willing to extend to good writers the courtesy of paying attention. People want the facts so they can make up their own minds—or at least let them cherish the delusion that they're independent thinkers, even as you create persuasive copy that serves your own interests.

1.9.4   Relevance means 'need to know'

Let's say that you respect your readers and you have no plans to write least-common-denominator copy for them. Still you have a problem: How on earth can you know that they'll perceive what you select as relevant, useful, or entertaining? "Nice to know" information can take many forms; you have to use your imagination and weigh it against what you know about your readers' tolerance for what they think of as fluff. But all "need to know" articles show signs of having several of these qualities:

- Significance (timely, timeless, rare, universal)
- Human interest (anecdotal, amusing, applicable, astonishing)
- Accuracy (details, quotes, definitions, statistics)
- Perspective (context, history, implications, consequences)
- Evaluation (insight, interpretation, demonstration, prediction)

The acronym just formed vertically by the list (SHAPE) might help you remember these qualities, but what all reporters must give their readers, foremost and always, is accuracy.

In a pinch, you may have to print articles that don't go into as much detail as you'd like, don't reach out and grab the reader, and offer only a glimpse of the big picture. But if you develop a reputation for accurate reporting, people will indeed listen to what you have to say.

1.10 Getting the editorial process under control

A service, consumer, or business-to-business newsletter publisher with the goal of gaining paid subscriptions has very different start-up and ongoing production issues than a printing and prepress shop trying to gain clients or an advocacy group publicizing issues and looking for sponsorship.

Literally anyone can print what they call a newsletter and distribute it to as narrow a group as embroiderers or as wide a group as the employees of a global security company—but in *Starting & Running a Successful Newsletter or Magazine*, Cheryl Woodard identifies three main kinds of periodicals: solo operators, lean-team staffs, and full-house publishers.

- **Solo operators**—mostly newsletter publishers who outsource all or some of the writing, production, and distribution. The publisher concentrates on an underlying publishing mission, such as offering clients "value added" or bonus information (free just because I value your business). Breaking even financially is good enough.

- **Lean teams**—3 to 10 people who may work with freelancers and farm out some or all of the production and distribution tasks. Woodard says this model is mostly used by nonprofits or other organizations that value high-level communication but have to keep expenses small—she cites the Menninger Clinic's *Letter*, put out by a full-time staff of only 7 people for 80,000 subscribers. The lean-and-mean model is also used for niche periodicals created for small but highly knowledgeable readerships such as association and professional journals; affinity groups (hobbyists, political lobbyists, special-issue advocates); and investment, computing, management, and religious newsletters.

Big niche, little niche: we all need an editorial plan.

- **Full-scale publishers**—for special interest or consumer publications with a broad audience. The *Kiplinger Washington Letter* is produced by 50-plus employees for 350,000 subscribers. Phillips Business Information, Inc., publishes hundreds of specialized business-to-business subscription newsletters but uses small editorial teams for each title; so does United Communications Group, which makes individual "publishers" responsible for a newsletter's successful marketing. The stakes are higher, so financial reporting and forecasting are important, and the pressure for winning and keeping high-ticket subscriptions is fierce. If ads don't underwrite the development of the editorial side, annual rates may be as high as $1,000, and copyright tends to be closely guarded.

1.10.1   Core editorial and design concepts

An editor can't work well without knowing the fundamental concepts of news writing, page design, and editorial accountability—to a publisher, to an audience, and to professional journalistic standards. But these are concepts that can be learned on the job.

Valuable content and attractive design are so closely related in newsletter format that it's almost impossible to practice one without learning about the other. In fact, a newsletter editor who "designs" content for an issue can learn from the graphic principles below, which are adapted from Robin Williams' advice to page designers in *The Non-Designer's Design Book*:

- Start with a focal point for each article—graphically and journalistically. Decide what you want readers to pay attention to first and what you want them to remember longest. "Nothing should be placed on the page arbitrarily," Williams tells designers. The same with content.

- Place closely related pieces of copy and graphics like main articles and complementary sidebars, photos, and charts near each other and separate contrasting information so it's clear to readers what's what. (Make need-to-know and nice-to-know articles look different, too.)

- Work toward unity in your package of facts, quotes, ideas, opinions, instructions, and advice. Avoid scattering your forces. "Every element should have some visual connection with another element on the page," Williams advised. Articles need to be written within the framework of a consistent vision and show some clear connection to the mission.

With these principles in mind (they're discussed further in the design chapter) and any luck at all, you'll provide a more or less useful product to a more or less enthusiastic audience. What's the difference between more and less? It lies in whether you choose to do (or can get away with doing) more...or less than the bare minimum.

1.10.2   What does 'editorial oversight' mean?

What you don't want *oversight* to mean is "something the editor overlooked." The newsletter editor is the point person for seeing that all aspects of the work are moving forward in three basic, sequential stages:

- Copy preparation and review
- Layout and production of pages
- Quality control and file preparation for printing

Newsletters, like other periodicals, get assembled piece by piece. It's easy to lose track of details, even key details, but it's your job to know what needs to happen and noodge it into reality. And it's preferable that everyone still be speaking to one another when the dust settles—you're going to need these people for the next issue.

In essence, a newsletter editor is 50 percent project manager, 25 percent developer of ideas, and 25 percent editor of words. And 100 percent cheerleader.

Editing is 50 percent project management.

That's why having a schedule is important. All the players deserve to know what's expected of them, and the editor deserves to know what he or she can depend on getting from contributors and other staff. In between the ideal and what really happens, editors perform as small-scale crisis managers 25 percent of the time. (That makes 125 percent of effort from you so far. And that's not counting your own writing. Aren't you glad you bought this book?)

1.10.3 One newsletter's planning and scheduling routines

The sample on this page gives you an idea of what a simple review schedule looks like. The box on page 38 shows what an informal running editorial calendar (list of assigned articles and story ideas in all stages of development) looks like. Both are used by the editors of *The Editorial Eye* newsletter, along with regular person-to-person brainstorming sessions, story conferences, and back-and-forth by e-mail and phone with individual authors. (Not to mention drive-by audits and status reports in the hallway and bathroom.)

Eye reviewers get a copy of the editorial schedule so they know when their comments are needed; the production schedule officially begins when a draft of the lead is given to the designer for planning cover art.

The first review step for *The Eye* is a chance for senior management and an outside reviewer to evaluate the overall usefulness and readability of the articles. These reviewers also evaluate content to see whether the advice and information offered reflect the best publications standards and practices—that's the mission of this particular newsletter. Either the editor or the assistant editor keys revisions.

After first review comments have been weighed and changes made to the file, a hard copy is copyedited thoroughly for tone, wording, and logical fallacies, and suggestions may be made for alternative wording and reorganization. (The editor is the final arbiter.)

November *Eye* Review Schedule	
October 5	To 1st review (due back October 7)
October 9	Copyediting
October 13	For coding, am
October 16	To 2d review (due back October 19)
October 20	Proofreading
October 21	QC
October 22	QC seps
October 23	To press
October 27	Bluelines
November 2	Delivery

The *Editorial Eye* Storylist 9/98-12/98

Authors	Month/Topic	Rec'd	Paid	Contract
Lead authors				
Gary Smith	Dec./Scholarly Authorship			
Cathy Fishel	Nov./Case Study: Magazine			
Chris Callahan	Oct./Internet mailing lists			
Staff	Sep./Edward Tufte's Info. Design			
Regular columnists and guest contributors				
Gabe Goldberg Sites Worth Seeing	Aug., Oct., December			
Reid Goldsborough Computerdom	Start new col. 11/98			
Art Plotnik Americanspeak	Small, Grander/Blander Aug., Oct., Dec.			
Richard Weiner Decoding Insider Jargon	British English Nov., start new cols. 1/99			
Elizabeth Whalen Second Thoughts/ Eye on Education Stereotypes	Nov./Editors and the Scientific Method Dec. Editorial			
Keith Ivey Untangling the Web	Nov./Validation, Integrity, Accessibility of Site			
Evan Morris Infernal English	Curious Case of Hopefully			
Kathryn Hall Production Techniques & Technology	Oct./Word Bugs & Fixes			
Priscilla Taylor The Watchful Eye	Nov./Elements of Style— Copyeditor who revised it			

By now the editors and the designer have agreed on a cover concept. An image is purchased from an online vendor or a photo shoot is arranged. Work in Photoshop begins at the layout stage.

A cleaned-up and fact-checked draft is brought to a desktop specialist for coding and the issue is laid out in QuarkXPress. *Eye* editors work directly with the designer to plug holes, cut articles to fit, and tweak editable graphic elements like subheads and block indented quotes so that awkward text blocks and wraps are avoided and the alignment at the bottom of the page looks pleasing. The cover image is critiqued for placement and sizing, etc.

Make sure a proofreader reads every syllable of your copy.

The Eye then goes to senior reviewers for a second look at the logic and appeal of the layout and a second chance to ask questions or suggest revisions to new filler and the by-now twice revised original articles.

Next *The Eye* goes to a proofreader, who reads it syllable by syllable and writes queries on anything that seems false or idiotic. Corrections at this point are keyed by the desktop designer—because the manuscript is now a Quark file and access to it is restricted to the designer.

Final checking steps behind each round of corrections end at a word-for-word quality control review that includes a critique of the layout.

After all this, the designer prepares files for the printer, and color separation pages are checked for the correct graphic specs and copy that may have moved around or been inadvertently dropped.

When the blueline arrives from the printer about three days later, it's checked for printer's errors and any final problems that *Eye* editors or the designer simply can't live with—even though making changes at this point means paying the printer an extra fee because your "reservation" on press is being held for you while you fiddle with changing the file. Also, the printer has to carefully make the change to the film that's already on press. Delivery within 7 working days for distribution means *The Eye* is being mailed out just as the next issue is moving into first review.

1.11 Tailor production to your editorial process

The basic steps of the process that's shown on the flow chart at the beginning of this chapter are pretty similar for all editors. Use the simplest forms and tracking systems that work for you; they're a tool to promote efficiency, not a tool of the devil intended to make editors play beat the clock. In fact, if there are problems that will delay production, only a schedule will bring them to light so that Plan B or even Plan C can be put into place for catching up on lost time.

A simple photocopied form may be enough; if you work with many authors and reviewers, you may want to use project management software or an online calendar to keep track of things. Where you fit on the sophistication spectrum was determined when you made fundamental decisions about your publication's mission, budget, and format, which in turn govern production values, publishing frequency, and staffing. But even if you publish "just" eight pages every other month, you need a written schedule—and it should be distributed to all the players.

Everybody needs a written schedule.

Here are some scenarios to help you see the range of production schedules possible:

- **My team is me.** If you're working solo to write and produce all of it, it's still important to stick to a simple schedule so that issues are printed on time. Most printers prefer to receive a newsletter within the same regular timeframe (and put it in the contract), so they can reserve press time and get the job to you as quickly as you need it for distribution. All production schedules are set up by reckoning backward a step at a time from the preferred date of delivery or distribution.

- **I'm a team leader.** If you're an editor whose job means that you negotiate with authors, supervise assistants, interact with reviewers, work directly with designers (or do the layout yourself), market subscriptions, attend events, and perform other work for your organization—while also staying in touch with your readers and keeping up with developments in your part of the world—a schedule is your only hope of success. With luck, you have a managing editor to act as the "enforcer" for deadlines.

- **We're a frequent publisher.** If you've chosen to publish weekly or monthly, you'll need to devise a schedule that allows you to work with your staff on several issues at once. One issue will always be in layout, one in editorial review, and one in the drafting stage—with some articles always in development for use at a moment's notice.

- **We're an infrequent publisher.** If your newsletter is published quarterly (like many alumni, corporate external, marketing, and nonprofit newsletters) or only occasionally (like some entrepreneurial, public relations, and—it's a mistake, you need to be out there regularly—some corporate external newsletters), the temptation will be to wait until the last minute. You'll have to hold space for fresher articles that really can't be written months ahead, but map out what needs to happen as soon as possible so you don't end up with a newsletter that seems either canned or half-baked.

A Sane and Civil Production Checklist

____ Plan schedule, working back from distribution date

____ Verify availability of key staff members; write contracts as needed

____ Write text

____ Plan all elements of design with costs and standards in mind (paper, ink, etc.)

____ Create artwork and shoot photos

____ Edit text for layout

____ Obtain bids for page layout and printing

____ Obtain all needed approvals

____ Scan artwork or other camera-ready materials

____ Lay out pages

____ Proofread pages carefully; return for second proofs

____ Check corrections

____ Complete proofreader's final checklist

____ Perform final check of electronic files for specifications such as
- ❑ colors and color overprinting applied correctly
- ❑ rules properly defined

____ Perform final check of disk for
- ❑ printer and screen fonts (including those used in graphics) included
- ❑ all imported and linked graphics included

____ Make ready for the printer
- ❑ instructions (establish responsibility to set traps if necessary)
- ❑ print order with specifications and price
- ❑ composite laser proof at 100% (tile and/or fold into a dummy if necessary)
- ❑ file names of all imported and linked graphics written on the composite proof
- ❑ color-separated laser proof (if necessary)
- ❑ list of all electronic files supplied
- ❑ any camera-ready materials identified and marked for return

____ Check bluelines carefully for broken type, smudges, placement of graphics, etc.

____ Check delivered job before accepting it: evenness of inking, quantity, correct order of pages, binding, etc.

1.11.1   Frontload the planning process as much as you can

The most frequent piece of advice given to new editors is "stick to a schedule," as if there were some magic linear train you could board and ride straight through to the station. We wish.

Instead, the way real newsletters get put together is a little messier. Several activities have to be going on in the background at all times so that you never run out of articles (or steam). The best way to see an issue to completion, and to keep material coming your way for future issues, is to frontload your editorial planning process and bring the cleanest, most complete manuscript you can muster to the production phase. Frontloading is an investment in future sanity. It means *not* saying, "I'll take care of it later, this is good enough for now." It means making the drafts closer to good with each and every round of revisions.

Work back from your target publication date.

What does frontloading translate to in practical terms? Working backwards from the target date for publication and distribution, compose a realistic schedule that takes into account how long every step of the process from initial review to printing will take.

Most newsletters can be printed in about seven business days. Start by subtracting that time from the target date and back up to the date the newsletter will be ready for layout. *The Editorial Eye* spends two weeks in this stage and a week in final review and QC; some newsletters spend two months in production alone.

Keep in mind the date by which the issue must be assembled for first review in order to leave enough time for layout. Estimate how much time you'll need for making each round of revisions between each step of the process outlined earlier. Leave time for meeting with authors, fact checking, pinning down loose data, and writing filler—for everything that will take "just half an hour or so" but has to happen before moving forward. (A word to the wise: Nothing ever takes just half an

Trolling the Internet for Material

Editing newsletters is essentially a human undertaking—and that means making good choices about which sources to trust. Editors have to verify the accuracy and currency of all the information they find. That goes double for databases and online publications.

But without firsthand knowledge about the provenance of an online publication, how can you be sure it's a credible source? Repeating the content of discussion lists or of proprietary Web sites may be violating copyright; repeating undigested material even with permission and attribution is a shortcut you can't afford to take if it turns out later to have been a myth, political propaganda, or the half-baked pipe dream of a graduate student or loner with too much time to spare. Anyone can publish on the Web. Bring a skeptical eye to what you find there.

hour. Even if you're correcting very few things, it takes that long to locate a file, open it, work in it, save it, and print out the new version for checking.)

Here are some ways editors can help their project stay on schedule starting with the first draft of an issue:

- Give reviewers an entire issue at a time rather than routing separate articles.

- Do as much as you humanly can ahead of time to edit material tightly and roughly organize articles in the order in which you want them to appear and with any special treatments—headlines, boxes, pullquotes, tables, photos—you envision for them.

- Even though it's "just a draft" as it goes through stages of editorial revisions, try to anticipate and head off what could be trouble spots in the layout. That means you'll have to learn the basics of putting a workable layout together, and that's why there's a design primer in this book. You'll also have to learn about copyfitting, which is why techniques for cutting copy (no, you can't just take out every third word—I heard that) are suggested in the writing section (see "Editing to fit," page 237).

- Prepare more material than you actually need for the upcoming issue and archive what you don't use right away for future issues. You may have heard that editors should run every piece as soon as it's written or writers will be offended. Don't you believe it. Yes, writers (even volunteers) are eager to be seen in print, but they'll respect an editor who plans ahead—as long as they know where they fall in the scheme of things. Never promise exactly when you'll run a piece unless you know you absolutely will.

1.11.2   Create a back-up file of articles for your publication

How does a newsletter (or any other) editor set about creating a backlog of interesting articles?

- **Keep up with the literature**—and other newsletters—in your field. Track trends to identify creative voices who have something to say, and to get the jump on the competition by publishing new ideas as they develop. You must be willing to take some risks, but the reward is to be identified as a trendsetter.

- **Cultivate relationships** with the movers and shakers in the industry. They can give you a sense of the big picture that others, like you, who seldom have the luxury of becoming generalists, can't. By talking to the people who know what the big picture looks like, then faithfully reporting what you learn, you can help readers make reasoned decisions.

- **Scan the competition** for interesting tidbits. This is an overworked editor's default tactic, but it has its useful aspects. Not all readers have the time or the inclination to read every periodical in their field, and newsletter editors can do a real service by offering digested bits of new information.

- **Make it a practice to assign more material** than you need for each issue. If all goes according to plan, the surfeit will soon have your files bulging with articles competing for space on the printed page. If not, at least there should be enough to fill that last half-page.

- **Keep a commonplace book or file of article ideas** that can be turned into an article on short notice if a chief contributor scheduled to write a major piece has a midlife crisis and begs off.

- **Look around** and make use of the resources at hand—even unlikely ones. Seeing the potential in a staff person previously unthought-of as a contributor sets the visionary editor apart from the pedestrian one. The clerical staff in a publishing house may have a fresh perspective on what it takes to prepare a manuscript for publication.

Building and maintaining a file of back-up articles for a periodical requires constant thought, research, and vigilance. Most editors simply don't have the time or are too preoccupied with deadlines to become ruminants. Failing all else, though, you yourself can contribute that luminosity of thought, clarity of vision, and literacy of expression that will satisfy both the reader's thirst for information and your own need for a moment of creativity. Go ahead and write it yourself! And if it's a major piece, take a byline; tell the ego cops I said you could.

To Potential *Editorial Eye* Authors

We're delighted that you'd like to write for *The Editorial Eye*. We'd say that 98 percent of all our dealings with authors are a pleasure; the better the writer, the likelier that we all walk away happy. One big piece of advice: Please don't send us an article if you haven't (a) inquired first and (b) asked for a recent sample. We'll be glad to discuss article ideas by e-mail. We prefer seeing an outline before giving the nod to a lead article (1,500 words). We send a standard contract once an assignment is mutually agreed on. When we have a draft we're both happy with, we'll decide where in the storylist the article will be placed. We have a careful editorial process; we look forward to working with *Eye* authors throughout the revision cycle to resolve queries, but we must reserve the right to edit as required for the needs of our readers. Articles are subject to further copyfit and QC edits; authors receive a checking copy before publication. Here's a guide to the process. If it doesn't scare you off, we encourage you to talk to us—and in any event we appreciate your interest. [See Fact Sheet on page 47.]

—The Editors

1.11.3 Develop story ideas with writers

Editors who rely heavily on freelance or outside writers to generate the content of their publications sometimes become frustrated with disappointing drafts that require extensive revisions or plain can't be salvaged. This situation often arises when an editor must deal with people who are subject matter experts instead of trained writers. If you don't always get what you want from freelancers, these suggestions should help.

Head off disappointment by telling writers what you expect.

Solicit articles from proven authors. Read other publications in your field looking for good authors whose talents you can also use. Seek out well-respected, well-spoken authorities in your field and speakers at your industry's conferences. Send writers' guidelines and sample copies of your publication to prospective writers to help them grasp your editorial style. In return, ask for writing samples before you give an assignment to a new writer.

Communicate your vision. When assigning an article, most editors envision the story clearly but sometimes have trouble communicating the idea to the writer. The ways you discuss a story will differ depending on the type of writer you use. Editors with limited budgets can't always afford experienced professionals whose skills—and alas, fees—weigh in more heavily than those of less experienced freelancers or volunteer subject matter experts who aren't great writers. Those editors will need to give their writers more direction.

Look for signs of reluctance. Professional writers have developed the ability to research and write on almost any topic. Subject experts and volunteers may be more hesitant. Ask questions like, "Do you have time to write an in-depth article? Would you like me to help you outline it? Would you prefer to pass on this topic and do an interview or a survey piece later on?" Reply neutrally if the relieved author takes the out you offer. If the topic and the writer aren't a good match, don't force the issue even if this person is your last resort. Writers produce their best work when they're interested in the assignment. Assure the writer that future assignments will be forthcoming.

Provide a paradigm. In addition to providing writers' guidelines, include sample copies of your publication (specifically, issues dealing with a similar subject), background material on the topic, and samples of outside articles treating the topic or written in the style you wish to follow for this assignment. Explain what you like about the samples so that the writer will know how to shape the article. This discussion should be specific; if you use a formula for writing certain types of articles (book reviews for example), give the writer a checklist.

Make sure you both have the same focus. Your vision of the article is clear and so is the author's—but is it the same? From your point of view, what's the story's overall purpose, what tone and level of detail are needed to support it, and why is the topic important? What needs to be said? What needs to be left out? What do you hope readers will learn? Should the style be reportorial or human interest? Serious or casual? Do you envision an interview, a profile, a survey, or an analytical forecast? Will extensive research be necessary? How long should the piece be? As you bring up and nail down the parameters, the story will take shape in the writer's mind.

Consider providing a rough outline of what you have in mind. Sometimes untrained writers are reluctant to ask questions or to admit that they don't follow your train of thought. An outline will help steer the first draft closer toward the finished piece you expect with less editing and rewriting. Even experienced writers usually appreciate an outline with pertinent questions and issues made explicit.

Writing isn't a science, and neither is revising.

Follow up and send encouragement. Send e-mail or call periodically to see how the writer is doing and to answer any questions. Stories can take a different turn once the writer delves into the topic, and your guidance will be appreciated. To ensure that you've communicated your needs, ask to see a revised outline before the writing begins. You may also ask for a rough preliminary draft to make sure the writer is on track and to avoid mutual frustration later on.

Review articles promptly. When the manuscript arrives, let the writer know you've received it, even if you aren't yet prepared to discuss it. Review it as soon as you can and relay your preliminary evaluation while the article is still fresh in the writer's mind. Go over the positive points first, then discuss areas that need to be strengthened, and follow up with detailed notes.

Write down editorial suggestions. Mail, e-mail, or fax them in a separate memo, in the margins of the draft, or embedded in a word processing file attached to an e-mail. When a manuscript requires substantive reorganization, some editors number the manuscript's paragraphs to make their suggestions easier to follow: "Move para. 3 to p. 4, and insert new material after para. 12." Some editors prefer to note all questions and comments on a separate sheet; others insert comments manually on a printout or online in text. Still other editors and writers prefer to work through an edit on the phone while both have the document on their computer screens. Use the techniques that work best for you both, but be sure to put your comments and suggestions in writing.

Remember that writing isn't a science and neither is revising. Sometimes writers just don't think their work needs the edits you propose. But most writers aim to please, once they understand what's wanted.

Finally, say thank you. And pay them promptly, sending a couple of copies of the issue in which their article appears. There's no substitute

Fact Sheet for Potential *Editorial Eye* Authors

- Drafts of all articles, unsolicited or solicited, are considered to be submitted on speculation. That is, any article is subject to acceptance by the editor. The conditions and terms of acceptance as defined by the editor are not negotiable. However, once the article has been accepted, the author is a partner in the revision process and all substantive edits are negotiable with the editor up to the point at which the deadline and the needs of our readers will dictate an end to quibbling.

- An author who engages in this process must be prepared to field criticism. Authors who feel they shouldn't have to negotiate with us over changes will not be published here. The author whose work requires substantive edits but who doesn't want to make timely, responsive revisions and answer questions will not succeed here. We treat authors with respect, but articles must meet our standards.

- Our standard contract will be offered on acceptance of an article. We retain first North American serial rights only but request the right to reprint articles as part of EEI Communications training materials and for a limited time to include them as part of the *Editorial Eye* Web marketing sampler. All other uses are negotiable with the author, including the right to include articles in textbooks and anthologies. These terms do not apply to material that has already been published elsewhere.

- Payment will be processed on acceptance. Please allow a month from the date of acceptance for payment to arrive. We try to print an article within 2 to 4 months of acceptance, but we work several months ahead and conflicts may arise. We reserve the right *not* to publish an article for which full payment has been made.

- *The Editorial Eye* offers a "kill fee" for any article that has been solicited and submitted in good faith but that does not, for whatever reason, meet the editor's terms for acceptance. The kill fee will be 40 percent of the original fee agreed upon.

- We ask that an article under serious consideration or that has been accepted by the *Eye* editor not be submitted for publication elsewhere simultaneously or before publication in *The Eye*.

- An author byline and brief biographical information will usually be offered, as well as 6 copies of the issue in which the article is printed. We can create a direct link to your Web site from your article if we include it in our EEI Press Web sampler. We're happy to mention an author's published works and print ordering information.

- All drafts accepted for publication are edited substantively, formatted for *Editorial Eye* style, and subject to copyfitting edits; the author will receive a checking copy before publication. The editor retains the right to make final decisions after collaborating with the author. What's good for readers governs, and my definition of that will rarely do an author a disservice.

- Each issue is reviewed by an editorial board and copyedited and proofread by senior-level staff; the author may be asked to quickly resolve queries or rewrite such items as introduction, transitions, conclusions, or to supply additional information. All additional work to achieve a final draft publishable in the *Editorial Eye* is considered to be part of the original fee.

- In light of the fact that an article published in *The Eye* has received the equivalent of an intensive peer review, if the author grants reprint permission to another publication, we request the courtesy of a notice to the effect that the article first appeared in *The Editorial Eye*.

- After publication, we'll forward directly to the author requests from our readers for reprint permission. On request, we'll print extra copies of the issue in which an article appears for a special workshop or presentation by an author.

for a respectful rapport with the writers who help you create eye-opening content for your readers.

1.11.4   Style suggestions for more appealing articles

One of the simplest ways to make your newsletter seem down-to-earth is to use direct address when you can. Using the rhetorical *you* in stories builds reader rapport. Remember we're editing news*letters*, not news*papers*, so strict formality and objectivity aren't always necessary. Take the following lead, for example:

> Are you still trying to figure out how to program your VCR? Well, get ready for new challenges. The Winter Consumer Electronics Show is exhibiting thousands of new toys and gadgets—and some of them are likely to be in your future.

Here are some additional ways to make articles more appealing to readers:

- Avoid hypothetical case studies. Nothing grips readers as much as real life. Name names, use dollar signs, use ratios and numbers, and quote people directly. Don't depend on the reader to translate abstract information into practical application.

- Be evenhanded, even if you're writing an advocacy piece. Discuss both the success and the failure of pet projects and highly touted ventures. "Lessons learned" pieces are always welcome.

- Don't be wishy-washy and subjunctive when you're educating people. Readers appreciate clear recommendations. You can include pros and cons to satisfy standards of objective reporting, but at the same time make your point of view clear and give the reader a compass.

- Don't give headlines short shrift but don't use them to hype the article. They help you sell the story, but be sure you're not guilty of bait and switch.

- Favor dramatic attributive verbs over prosaic ones. Write the way your readers talk, most of the time. Don't write the way lawyers talk, ever, unless they're your readers. No matter who your readers are, they all speak plain English and prefer to read it.

- Think like your readers and ask the questions they're likely to ask. Don't just report. Challenge the information the way your most skeptical reader will. Consider bouncing story ideas off a few readers before you publish.

- Don't play it too safe. Make it a habit to debunk myths, uncover secrets, demystify confusing subjects, and tackle controversy. Readers appreciate the newsletter that shoots down hot air balloons and saves them from making mistakes or being taken advantage of.

1.12 Editing a credible in-house publication is an art

The goal in editing any newsletter—even though there's always an agenda—is to provide truthful communication, not what's perceived as propaganda. In the minds of most writers, the corporate in-house publication ranks among the least challenging of all nonfiction forms. It's widely believed to lack the glamour of consumer publications and the substance of technical and trade journals. What's more, an in-house magazine or newsletter is often perceived as an extension of the management memo pad.

Readers can sniff out propaganda.

Despite these perceptions, producing an in-house publication can be rewarding and challenging. Although the primary aim of such a publication is to communicate company news to employees, it can also recognize employee achievements and motivate and educate staff members. Here are six steps toward starting or improving a corporate publication, adapted from an *Editorial Eye* article.

1.12.1 Know your readers

Before you can plan the first issue, you must know who your readers are and what they want and need to know about the organization. Obtain demographics from the personnel department, discuss employee makeup with division managers, conduct formal and informal employee polls, and use your own instincts to develop an accurate reader profile.

Do You Need a Contract with Your Authors?

Yes, you do, if you're paying money to professional writers who have mortgages and car payments and have to meet your expectations to make it into print. These are litigious times. One editor who had responded to a query from a writer-lawyer assigned an article—on speculation—about copyright. A few months later, after several phone calls discussing what the article should cover to be most useful to the intended audience, a draft arrived. It was written as the barn swallow flies, in great dips and tailspins of logic. Key terms went undefined. No practical examples were provided to illustrate concepts. There was no lead paragraph, no conclusion, really no message—just a series of disjointed thoughts. When the editor mentioned several serious problems with the draft and concluded that not only wasn't it publishable but it might not be editable, the author immediately threatened to sue unless she received full payment. Her rationale? She had turned in a draft on time, and it was the required number of words. Bad luck if it wasn't any good. Exit good faith. Enter the contract.

Keys to Producing a High-Quality Newsletter

- Use a style manual and designate a dictionary.
- Spell check every draft.
- Proofread in layout and after copyfitting edits.
- Check corrections after every round of revisions.
- Check facts and numbers.
- Follow a production schedule.
- Take a reader survey.
- Get a professional critique.
- Cooperate with an editorial committee.
- Subscribe to publications in your field.
- Keep "evergreen" back-up articles on hand.
- Work several issues ahead on the storylist.

1.12.2   Find the stories

Once you understand your audience, you can develop appropriate story ideas. Content also depends on management's objectives for publishing the newsletter or magazine and on your own instincts. As editor, you should strive for a balance between news stories and features, and between stories that address corporate activities and those that cover employee issues.

Before you plan stories, make a list of your most important sources for each section of the publication. This list should include contacts at headquarters and field offices and in the advertising, public relations, and human resources divisions.

District managers often are good sources of employee information because they work closely with field staff. You can also appoint "regional correspondents" to write articles or provide information that you work into stories.

Gather article ideas and leads by listening to what's going on around you. Spend a few extra minutes chatting with co-workers at the coffee machine—it could save you embarrassment when a worker whom you plan to feature as employee of the month in the Chicago office is transferred to Seattle—and besides, these conversations often lead to good stories.

You can also generate story leads by inserting a postage-paid reply card in your publication. Ask readers to write a one-sentence description of a story they would like to see published and include a contact name, phone number, and address. This tactic works best when you offer the readers an incentive (a T-shirt or company gift item) to return the postcard.

Periodic reviews of past issues may also alert you to aspects of corporate life that haven't been featured recently.

1.12.3   Write the stories

In all of your writing, strive to *express*, not *impress*. Your goal is communicating with your audience, not creating a new art form.

News stories are the easiest ones to write because information is usually available from headquarters and the facts are usually unambiguous. When writing news stories, follow the basic rules of journalism: Cover the who, what, where, when, why, and how of the story. Use quotes and avoid flowery language.

Features—"human interest" articles about particular workers—are often the most challenging and enjoyable stories to write. To locate good prospects for features, express interest in your co-workers, ask

---

'Quality' Differs, Like Personality

The equation for a balancing act could be sketched as *corporate goals + editorial integrity = quality*. Balancing corporate goals with editorial integrity is the hardest part of a newsletter editor's job. The definition of what represents "quality" to your readers is at stake, yet you must also honor the corporate definition of your newsletter's mission. Mark Beach, veteran newsletter guru, advises editors to keep these points in mind when editorial vision starts blurring:

How your newsletter looks and reads affects how well it accomplishes its objectives.

Readers notice tangible traits such as paper and printing and intangible features such as design and writing. The intangible aspects matter more than the tangible ones. Fancy paper or color printing cannot make up for dull writing, careless editing, or poor design.

Money helps buy quality, but budget isn't the only factor. Time and skill make a big difference. Design of the nameplate alone heavily influences perception of quality.

Quality reflects personality. Your publication may seem neighborly, concerned, or authoritative. You may want readers to view you as an objective observer or as an enthusiastic insider. Your writing can be intimate or detached.

The way you want readers to perceive your organization [your style] should affect quality. Filling each issue with professional photos may suit the marketing department of a bank, but would seem excessive from a neighborhood volunteer agency.... Each newsletter has its own appropriate quality level.

—from *Editing Your Newsletter*

Skirting the Generic *He*

Newsletter content may be proprietary, but it mustn't seem biased—and that means editors have to watch out for sexist language. That doesn't mean *never* using what's called the "generic *he*" (*To each his own*); however, always defaulting to *he* as a generic pronoun is a problem because not everyone understands it to include both men and women. The English language doesn't offer an all-purpose, gender-free third-person singular pronoun, so editing is the answer.

Obviously, *To each his own* could be recast as *To all their own* or *To each his or her own*, but straining self-consciously for gender neutrality can do serious damage to readable prose. Always saying *he or she*, *him or her*, and *his or hers*, or alternating *he* and *she* as generics in the same article or publication, is clumsy. The "singular *they*" (*Every editor should make sure that their office is soundproof before screaming*) has been used for almost two centuries, but writers can't rely on it in more scholarly newsletters.

Make sure prose avoids *both* the potentially offensive and distracting use of *man…he…his…him* to refer to both genders and the cumbersome, wordy *he or she* edits. A bonus: Rewrites can sharpen copy as you steer around stereotypes. Try these edits on the next suspect sentence that tries to slip past your scanner:

Rewrite the sentence with plural nouns—often the easiest solution. *A careful editor will couch his queries in neutral terms* suffers no loss from a rewrite to *Careful editors will couch their queries in neutral terms*.

Recast the sentence using *we/us/our*. *Each must do his best* can become *We must all do our best*.

Rewrite the sentence in the second person. *No man knows what he's got until it's gone* can become *You don't know what you've got until it's gone*.

Replace *he* with inclusive words such as *someone, anyone, one, the one, no one,* etc., and replace *his* with an article (*the, a, an*). Clayton Rawson's *Can't a critic give his opinion of an omelet without being asked to lay an egg*? could be changed to *Can't a critic give an opinion…?* Or leave out the pronoun entirely: *The average American travels abroad with a few stilted phrases he has memorized from a guidebook* could be changed to *…with a few stilted phrases memorized from a guidebook.*

Replace the pronoun with a noun. *He who betrays a friend loses him* could be changed to *To betray a friend is to lose one*.

Finally, remember that famous quotes should either be used as is or not used at all. They're not editable after the fact. Even ardent feminist editors resist revisionist history.

questions, and listen carefully. A factory supervisor, asked if any of his employees had unusual hobbies or backgrounds, said disparagingly, "You won't find anything interesting in this lot."

But in a casual tour around the factory, talking with workers along the way, a reporter unearthed a former professional soccer player, a scuba diver, a man who hadn't missed a day of work in 20 years, and someone who restored antique furniture in his spare time. (See "Getting printworthy quotes from interviews," page 62.)

Listen to people, respond, then listen some more.

Part of your job involves breaking down artificial barriers between management and workers and demonstrating that we each achieve in a unique way, no matter what our occupation or position in the company. Listening and talking also work with management. When you interview someone in his or her office, look around you. Does he have a photograph of himself leading a Scout troop? Does she have an unusual paperweight or achievement award on her desk? These talking points may provide a lead to move the conversation beyond well-worn paths.

Keep features short and write leads that pique readers' interest. Use anecdotes and quotes, and while it's permissible to tidy up someone's grammar, don't put words in your subject's mouth. Always mention the person's position in the company, work location, and job responsibilities.

1.12.4   Make your publication look interesting

Visual appeal is extremely important. An attention-grabbing layout is far more likely to attract readers than long columns of uninterrupted type. Experiment with bold designs and if possible use at least one additional color. Don't cram too much information into the nameplate or onto the front page. The name (*The Editorial Eye*, for example), a subtitle that clarifies the topic or audience (*Focusing on Publications Standards and Practices*), the company logo, and volume number are sufficient. Put the publication's mailing address and other details either in the masthead or on the back page.

Use bold headlines for the lead article. Use the daily newspaper as a layout guide to make the publication's pages look "newsy." Add photographs whenever possible. Balance shots of large groups with smaller head-and-shoulders shots, and vary the subject matter. Write interesting captions that pull readers into the story. If photos aren't available, use illustrations or clip art to add interest to the pages. (For three steps to better photos, see page 119.)

Whether your publication is a four-page newsletter output from a word processor or a 64-page, four-color magazine, keep the design clean, inviting, and easy to read.

Should You Use a 'Filler' Service?

Q. "I do a monthly newsletter for a small hometown bank. I am constantly looking for information to write about because I never have enough content for each issue. Do you know of any services or people who offer a service that deals with the banking industry? "

A. Filler services exist to provide editors with general-interest blurbs. This is the way most of them work: You pay for a subscription to a newsletter-like booklet that arrives at intervals and contains a variety of copyright-free articles or cartoons. You can use or reprint any article you choose in your own newsletter, sometimes even without attributing the filler service. The problem is that the topics are necessarily generic (much like stock photos) and therefore not likely to be terribly relevant to your publishing mission. The writing also sounds "canned" rather than fresh.

You'll still have to decide what kinds of articles serve your mission, so why not create your own copy? Of course, you have to know why you're doing the newsletter. Who are your readers? What kinds of things do they want to know about? What do you want them to be able to do with the information?

Nobody can decide for you what should be in the newsletter, and you know more than you think you do. But resources and ideas won't fall into your lap. Dig them up! Internet searches can lead you to a wealth of helpful people, books, and periodicals. You can read FAQs about your industry or even ask someone a question and get e-mail back, if you find an author who invites feedback. Without trying very hard, we found the Web site for the *The American Banker* (www.americanbanker.com), which says it offers "all the banking and finance news you need to keep ahead." We also found an online *Primer on the Banking Industry*, which offers "an introduction to commercial banking" that includes definitions for terms commonly used in the industry. As you learn the lingo, you might even want to run a short glossary of banking jargon in your newsletter.

If you're not set up to do Web research, newsstand magazines and newspapers report on financial and socioeconomic trends that affect your industry: *Newsweek*, the *Economist*, and the *New York Times* are a few. You can paraphrase the information or news angles you find (citing the original source and writer) or use them to give you ideas for further research or interviews of the people in your local financial community.

You'll feel less isolated if you join an association for editors and get access to its publications and workshops. Subscribe to or do a trade for a newsletter in your industry. Take a workshop to learn about all the pieces of newsletter editing. Each time you come up with a good idea and develop it into an article, the easier it is to do the next time—really. Soon topics and resources will be popping up everywhere, and you'll have more than you need for one issue.

The truth is that building a "futures file" is a better long-term solution for your blank pages than a filler service.

Dividing your publication into departments creates a sense of continuity and ensures that the publication regularly covers topics of importance within the organization. By devoting a column in each issue to a specific region or division, the department format also guarantees equal coverage to various groups within the company. When cleverly designed, departments also add to a publication's visual appeal.

1.12.5   Check your sources

Making sure that facts are correct is critical. However, checking with your sources doesn't mean you should change a story to reflect the way the subject believes he or she should be portrayed. Always verify the correct spelling of subject's full name and his or her correct title, address, and phone number.

When management is involved or when a story includes many facts, obtain written confirmation of the story's accuracy. I learned this lesson the hard way when I had to take the blame for an error in an explanation of the corporate structure—an error that originated in the chairman's office. As the Russian proverb says, "Trust—but verify."

To produce a professional, credible publication, proofread each article. It's difficult to spot errors in your own copy, so ask another staff member to help you. Add that person's name to the masthead in appreciation.

1.12.6   Always tell the truth

Your in-house publication should not be management propaganda; if it is, you will lose respect, and the magazine or newsletter will lose credibility. And credibility and communication are what an in-house publication should be about. You may never write the Great American Novel or crack a Watergate-style story, but there's great satisfaction in producing a balanced, informative, well-written, and innovative corporate publication.

1.12.7   Avoid the A.S.A.P. trap

If you're having trouble getting people to turn in articles and sign off on copy for your corporate newsletter, give them the benefit of the doubt: Maybe they don't realize they're holding things up. They may care, but the newsletter isn't their priority; managers and colleagues have daily fires to put out and long-range planning to do. Maybe you're stuck in the A.S.A.P. trap: A deadline of "as soon as possible" is usually translated by busy people as "when I get around to it."

Scheduling creative output takes continual effort to make people aware that the newsletter won't go out on time if it stalls at any point.

The RWD Technology Report Newsletter
Editorial Calendar
1998–1999

Issue	**Article Titles Author Names Assigned Mgr Names Due	Client Permission Letter Required? Yes? No?	**First Draft Copy and Graphics Due	**Final Text and Graphics Due	Layout	**Internal Review	Final Production	Print and Distribute
Fall '98 Vol. 9 No. 3	7/6/98– 7/10/98		7/13/98– 7/17/98	8/17/98– 8/21/98	8/24/98– 8/28/98	9/1/98– 9/11/98	9/14/98– 9/18/98	9/28/98– 10/2/98
Winter '98–'99 Vol. 9 No. 4	10/05/98– 10/09/98		10/12/98– 10/16/98	11/16/98– 11/20/98	11/23/98– 11/30/98	12/2/98– 12/11/98	12/14/98– 12/21/98	12/28/98– 1/4/99
Spring '99 Vol. 10 No. 1	1/4/99– 1/8/99		1/11/99– 1/15/99	2/15/99– 2/19/99	2/22/99– 3/1/99	3/3/99– 3/12/99	3/17/99– 3/24/99	3/29/99– 4/2/99
Summer '99 Vol. 10 No. 2	4/5/99– 4/9/99		4/12/99– 4/16/99	5/17/99– 5/21/99	5/24/99– 6/1/99	6/2/99– 6/11/99	6/14/99– 6/21/99	6/28/99– 7/2/99
Fall '99 Vol. 10 No. 3	7/6/99– 7/12/99		7/13/99– 7/19/99	8/16/99– 8/20/99	8/23/99– 8/30/99	9/1/99– 9/10/99	9/13/99– 9/20/99	9/27/99– 10/1/99

**Time frames for author, editor, manager interactions

That's true for newsletters published less frequently as well as for week-lies and monthlies. The long lead time that quarterlies seem to have is deceptive—unless you've nailed down due dates, they'll sneak up and find you empty-handed.

One editor of a quarterly corporate marketing newsletter gives a five-issue editorial/production calendar to all his reviewers and writers. Editing the newsletter is something he does in his spare time, so he doesn't want to be rushing around in production. Week-long time frames dedicated to each stage of compiling and producing the quarter-ly allow varying author, editor, and manager interactions to occur flex-ibly. The editor allocates a time block for assigning future stories; drafting copy and graphics; finalizing copy and graphics; and layout, internal review, and printing. Behind the scenes, the editor is working ahead—developing articles, working with authors on revisions, and getting permission from clients to mention them in upcoming issues. (See the calendar on page 56.)

He sets drop-dead dates for deliverables and feedback, even though, he said, "I know I won't get material on time. There's always a mad dash at the end." Block scheduling takes into account what he knows about his overbooked colleagues: They don't know exactly when they'll have time to write an article, create graphics, or review an issue, but at least people know when the editor will be knocking on their door.

This isn't a traditional editorial calendar listing authors and assign-ments. It's a hybrid pegged to all the contributions from everyone who could hold the schedule hostage. "Have you had a chance to look at the newsletter yet?" and other personal reminders supplement the more formal nag of a cover sheet stapled to the calendar, spelling out what's needed from whom and calling attention to when. The editor isn't directly involved in layout, production, or printing/distribution, but he has to schedule them.

1.13 A hit list of make-or-break editorial elements

Plot your progress with an ongoing self-critique by doing a postmortem after each issue is printed. Use the questions in sections 1.13.1 and 1.13.2 to create your own checklist—really a "hit list" of key make-or-break elements—by putting a check mark by any area you feel might need improvement. Or pass a checklist out to co-workers to get their responses (anonymously); be sure to ask for examples of what bothers them. These checklist elements cover editorial quality and overall readability; be picky. That's how you get good.

1.13.1   Editorial Quality

Keep in mind the need for an appropriate tone, an approachable but correct level of language and standard usage, logical organization within articles and throughout the publication, clarity of publishing mission, and a reader-centered approach.

____ Is the writing as free of jargon as possible? Plain English is always welcomed, even by professionals.

____ Is the writing at the simplest appropriate level for the audience? Long strings of phrases and passive constructions detract from discussions—direct quotes from interviews are fine, though.

____ Is the writing free of gender, age, race, ethnic, and other biases?

____ Is paragraph length about right?

____ Does each paragraph move the article forward?

____ Is sentence length kept to an average of about 20 words, with most shorter than that?

____ Is there a good variety of sentence types? If they're all declarative sentences with linking verbs or cast in the passive, the overall tone will be monotonous—even boring.

____ Is the writing clear and concise? Do you trip over phrasing as you read?

____ Does the newsletter offer a variety of perspectives?

____ Is the tone of stories appropriate to content?

____ Is humor used sparingly and appropriately?

____ Are direct quotations edited tightly? If they go on for too long the effect of lively speech is dulled.

____ Are quotes embedded in narrative as part of discussion or analysis?

____ Are punctuation and capitalization correct and consistent with your style?

____ Are lines free of bad breaks, widows, and orphans?

____ If copy is justified, have holes and rivers been avoided?

____ Are single quotes used within double quotes and in headlines?

____ Are all bullets aligned and elements parallel in construction?

____ Is punctuation with lead-ins and within bulleted material correct?

____ Has typeset, not typewritten, punctuation been used? Avoid underlining of heads and titles, inchmarks instead of curly quotes, and two hyphens instead of em dashes.

____ Are all continuations where promised? Jumping long articles helps to break up copy blocks and to make sure something new is happening on each page.

____ Are jumps (continuation lines or heads) in consistent style?

____ Do articles seem to be complete, with a beginning and an end and a clear payoff?

____ Is copy free of typos or basic grammatical errors?

____ Is it clear where each article stops and others begin?

____ Is art clearly placed so that it's connected to the copy it goes with?

____ Do graphics compete with copy for the reader's attention?

___ Have pullquotes been limited to one key thought? They should be edited tightly to be short and crystal clear.

___ Are most pullquotes limited to four lines or less?

___ Is direct address ("you") used in stories where appropriate? You may not be able to do much of this, but it can personalize newsletter copy.

___ Are vague qualifiers like *much, many, often,* and *some* kept to a minimum?

___ Are strong, active verbs used in headlines and as often as possible in text?

___ Does the present tense predominate over past tense for narrative development?

___ Does the writing resemble the way the audience talks or writes normally? Even if your audience has a technical or scholarly bent, most jargon and passive language needs to be translated into plain English.

___ Are errors of fact acknowledged and corrected in print in subsequent issues?

___ Are readers encouraged to contribute ideas and ask questions? Consider asking them to submit case scenarios/what-ifs/problems; run the answers in a Q&A format.

___ Is a complete masthead included?

___ Is a clear mission statement included? Without one, only by inference can readers get a clear sense of the intended publishing mission and where the newsletter fits into their lives.

___ Is a journalistic reporting style used?

___ Are adjectives and adverbs used sparingly? They take up space but contribute little. Show, don't tell.

___ Is the passive voice used sparingly? Watch out for expletive constructions (*there is, there are*).

___ Is parallel construction observed? If sentences are long, this will be lost as a logical device. Subheads need to be made parallel.

___ Is the percentage of "hard words" kept to 10 to 12 percent?

___ Is the newsletter educational? Offer "value added" information even if your primary mission is marketing.

___ Does the newsletter seem to serve as a forum offering the chance for give and take between readers and between readers and editors?

___ Does the newsletter have readily apparent practical value—that is, information you can use?

___ Are regular departments clearly and consistently flagged as such? This is one of the hallmarks of a newsletter.

___ Is each story built around one important point, even if it's a longer or complex narrative article?

___ Is there a clear distinction between news and features?

___ Do you make space for squibs or roundups of short news bites?

1.13.2   Overall Readability

Newsletter content should be accessible and attractive to readers. Keep in mind the need for interesting and varied content, a balance of different topics, a good mix of article types, easy-to-follow layout jumps and page makeup, an appealing reporting/narrative style, and evidence of a reader-based perspective.

____ Are titles or headlines imaginatively written to capture the readers' interest?

____ Are subheads easy to find and of appropriate size and weight?

____ Are italics or boldface used correctly and consistently to format special material?

____ Are the leads strong attention-getters?

____ Are all articles equally weighted so that, unfortunately, none stand out?

____ Are stories informative?

____ Do you offer readers a variety of story presentations?

____ Is there an appropriate variety in paragraph lengths? Very gray, uniform pages result if every paragraph is the same size.

____ Do the stories make readers feel like an integral part of the association, organization, or affinity group?

____ Is content too confined to strict reportage with little room for reader involvement?

____ Is the news reinforced by showing the readers how they are affected by the event, or subject, written about? Anecdotal sidebars and related stories are welcomed for giving the bare facts a more human context.

____ Are some stories made more interesting by being presented in a more conversational, or lighthearted, manner?

____ Are some articles quickly browsable or do they all require a great deal of commitment from readers?

____ Is there a good mix of story lengths?

____ Are the stories written in such a way that they avoid talking down to readers?

____ Do stories read as deadpan presentation of facts with little human interest?

____ Is the publication designed so that the first thing you see creates interest regardless of how you pick it up?

____ Are all pages laid out with a unified theme (instead of being laid out separately with no thought to the other pages)?

____ Is there a regular column for reader letters or comments?

____ Are interviews with experts in the field included?

____ Are interviews with rank-and-file staff or readers included as counterpoint to expert talking heads?

____ Does the newsletter avoid overt marketing or at least set it off from editorial?

____ Are serious articles well-backed with analytical discussion of regulations and policies?

Newsletter Proofreading Checklist

____ Are all quotation marks and parentheses both opened and closed?

____ Are single quotation marks used within double?

____ Do all italic and boldface treatments start and stop on the right word?

____ Are there no repetitions (same letters at end of line and start of next) in word division?

____ Are there no doublets (same word at end of line and start of next)?

____ Are all word divisions correct?

____ Do the page numbers and titles in the table of contents match the articles?

____ Is there need for further fact checking? Have all addresses, phone numbers, and spellings of proper names been verified?

____ Does the date of any event on a calendar fall before newsletter publication date?

____ Is the sequence of items in each list appropriate?

____ Do captions match photos?

____ Have all corrections been made from the previous draft or proofs?

____ Have corrected pages been checked for new errors?

____ Are all titles and headings formatted consistently?

____ Are the headers and footers formatted consistently?

____ Do the page numbers mirror each other in a spread?

____ Are page numbers in order?

____ Do facing pages balance?

____ Do columns balance on multiple-column pages?

____ Are right margins consistent? They may vary between body copy and sidebars.

____ Do all characters at the left margins align?

____ Are all bullets aligned?

____ Are paragraphs indented consistently? Indentation may be different for the first paragraph after a heading and subsequent paragraphs in the copy.

____ Are all transitions (from column to column, from page to page) correct?

____ Are all continuations where promised?

____ Are jump lines in consistent style?

____ For tables, charts, and figures:
 ❏ Are they in the correct sequence?
 ❏ Are legends or titles appropriate?
 ❏ Are they formatted consistently?
 ❏ Are the columns in tables aligned?
 ❏ Are they placed in the text appropriately?

____ Is the type quality acceptable (consistent density, not obscured, no stray marks)?

____ Is there unnecessary crowding anywhere?

____ Is there unnecessary white space anywhere?

____ Do you see anything that could be improved? Is there anything that "jumps out" at you?

1.14 Getting print-worthy quotes from interviews

As writer-editors who specialize in publications for and about companies and organizations, the team of Susan Bury and David Stauffer conducts some 200 telephone interviews annually from their office in Washington, DC. These are not journalistic *60 Minutes*-type interviews, but interviews to get quotes for annual reports, testimonials, speeches, and newsletters.

Sometimes the people they interview work for the client; they cooperate because they have no choice! Most often, however, the interview subjects are busy executives and professionals with expertise who stand to gain little more than some decidedly limited exposure by patiently answering a lot of questions.

At one time or another most of us have secretly wished we could just make quotes up, but that would be missing the point of an interview: authenticity. People can say thoughtful, surprising things—the words just need a little help getting out. Bury and Stauffer have developed some interviewing techniques that are quite effective in getting the last drop of information from the know-it-all who has no interest in being a tell-it-all. Here's their advice:

1.14.1   Schedule an appointment for the interview

Then call to do the interview. We began this practice for our own convenience, realizing that there's no reason to spend time formulating questions for someone we may not be able to reach. But we found that setting appointments also boosted our success rate in getting interviews by about 30 percent, maybe because people will agree to anything to postpone being put on the spot just then. But there's always someone who says, "I'm leaving on vacation tomorrow, so let's talk now." For these opportunities, we keep at hand a list of all-purpose questions that are appropriate for many contexts.

Don't you wish we could make quotes up?

You can also fax a "request for interview" memo before calling to set up an appointment. In this fax introduce yourself, state your purpose, estimate the time involved, and provide sample questions. The fax gives you the chance to say more about what's in it for the person to be interviewed. In the management newsletter we write, for example, each article quotes only one expert. We mention this in our fax so our subjects know they don't have to share the spotlight with others or risk unfavorable comparison.

1.14.2   Start the interview with low-key, open-ended questions

You may be tempted to get right to the heart of the matter immediately by challenging an expert's most controversial opinions or prompting a consultant for hot tips right away. But even people who are experienced at being interviewed need a chance to warm up and become focused. A possible opener: "How did you first become interested in [this topic]?" People get to talk about themselves for a moment and, even if you don't actually use what they give you, the interchange smoothes the way for the first real content question.

Readability and the Fog Index

Newsletter content needs to be clearly expressed—and that means editors have to watch out for foggy writing that obscures the point. The Fog Index (a service mark of the Gunning-Mueller Clear Writing Institute) measures the readability of a discrete piece of copy. It can be a helpful tool for editors trying to encourage an author to find simpler ways of saying things. Grammar checkers will compute the Fog Index (or an equivalent) and judge the difficulty of a piece of copy, but you'll have to decide what edits will make copy clearer. It's instructive to see the factors that affect overall readability—they'll help you learn what to watch out for when you're editing. Here's the formula, with criteria revealed:

1. Pick a sample paragraph about 100 words long (you can get a quick word count from your spell checker).

2. Write down the number of words in each sentence. Count the number of sentences—count all independent clauses as separate sentences. Then divide the total number of words by the number of sentences to get the average sentence length.

3. Count the number of words that have three or more syllables and divide the total by the number of words in the sample passage. When counting, omit proper (capitalized) words, common compounds (*bookkeeper*), and simple verbs that have been made into three syllables by adding *-es* or *-ed* (*surmises, promoted*).

4. Add the numbers from step 2 (average sentence length) and step 3 (percentage of long words) and multiply this total by 0.4. (Ignore the digits after the decimal point.)

5. The result of these calculations will give you the Fog Index—which means the approximate years of schooling your readers would need to have in order to understand the sample paragraph with ease. A score of 17 or more represents the college graduate level and should be considered heavy going for the purposes of most newsletters.

Douglas Mueller, one of the developers of the Fog Index, says that the typical popular news magazine article has an average sentence length of 15 to 20 words, with relatively few "hard words" (between only 10 and 12 percent), and a Fog Index of 10 to 12. That score translates to someone with a high school education being able to understand the point of the article on the first reading. Such prescriptions are somewhat arbitrary, but the point is obvious. Needless complexity has got to go.

1.14.3   Don't rush in with words to fill dead air

It's a trait endemic in middle-class American society: the fear of a pause in the conversation. Mystery novelist Tony Hillerman's fictional Navajo detective, Joe Leaphorn, knows about the "white abhorrence for conversational silences. Sometimes the resulting uneasiness caused [white] witnesses to blurt out more than they intended to say." People do feel responsible for saying something—and often what pops into the air, unguarded, is the truth. We've never gotten a confession by out-pausing someone, but we've often gotten our lead quote.

Always get more than 'enough' quotes, just in case.

1.14.4   Always ask "What one thing…?"

Make this question a standard part of every interview. For example, "You're known across the country for your expertise in human resources management. What one thing do you most often see applicants doing wrong?" The opening flattery, coupled with the open-ended opportunity to expound, can produce some intriguing answers.

1.14.5   Don't cut off the interview process too early

You may have "enough" quotes from someone to fill the space they're intended for, but often the real gold comes 15 to 30 minutes into an individual conversation. And even if you have lots of bright quotes from one person, keep going until you have more than enough material from more than one person. A surplus of quotes gives you more flexibility in where and how you'll use them and extras in case any subjects withdraw. For an annual report, we asked each customer for comments on the same items: cleanliness, pricing, display, and so forth. Overkill? No. Insurance.

One thing that works for us when we reach the question third or fourth from the bottom of our list is to say, "One last thing: What do think about…." You get double duty from this tactic. People, all-too-likely to be restive by now, stop worrying about the time because it's almost up. And people may noticeably relax and become more open because a stressful situation has been weathered. Not once have we ever been subsequently challenged with "You said that was the last question."

1.14.6   Challenge interviewees—but stay on their side

Sometimes you'll want to ask for an opinion about a controversial viewpoint or challenge a possible flaw in the thinking behind the answers you're getting. But you don't want to make anyone feel defensive or irritated. A ploy that works for us is to ascribe the contrary ideas to others: "Some say that's not possible" or "I've read claims that your study was flawed. How do you respond to such critics?"

Editing Spoken Comments for a Print Article

Should editors clean up spoken comments for print? The answer depends on your editorial policy, but the rules differ from those for published material. Speech is "thinking out loud" and almost always needs editing; how much is a matter of editorial judgment. People don't call or send e-mail to editors saying, "I'm not going to take this—you made me sound too good!" But the speaker's meaning must always be preserved, and it's best to print 99 percent of the original phrasing verbatim. Here are some rules of thumb:

- Get approval in advance to print attributed comments. Sooner is better than later, when quoted material is a substantial part of final copy, so you can clear up any misunderstanding and substitute another quote or paraphrase instead, if necessary.

- Double-check all direct quotes if you've taped the interview. Transcribing from tape is tricky.

- Edit a quote if necessary to save your interviewee from being embarrassed in print by the awkward or colloquial English most of us use in conversation.

- Preserve individual style that reveals character and spices up the content, but avoid quotes that border on caricature or stereotype.

- Use common sense when deciding how much idiomatic expression to keep. A little colorful vocabulary or quirky syntax can humanize copy. But too much patois may make the speaker look foolish, and dialect and substandard English can be hard to read and annoy readers. Take care not to put uncharacteristic words in someone else's mouth—never make someone sorry for having spoken to you.

- Help an interviewee who skips around, backtracks, or repeats statements in the course of an interview by imposing a logical sequence on the quotes you select for print. Paraphrase as necessary for transition, but be sure to use ellipses when you leave out a substantial part of an answer. If you impose logical order, don't create misleading transitions or gaps that misrepresent the original answers.

- Remember that extensive paraphrasing in an article defeats the purpose of doing an interview: to get lively voices, warmth, an approachable tone, and different perspectives into print. Keep your scene-setting observations to a minimum.

- Finally, the Q & A print format seems simple but really works well only for short profiles or for a group interview limited to a clear core of ideas.

—from *The Editorial Eye*

1.14.7   Make it clear what the payback is

As you're winding things down, be careful to get the interviewee's name, title, address, and the like exactly right. Mention that the person will be identified in your publication as a reminder that his or her remarks are understood to be for attribution—make it sound like a good thing: "I want to make sure I give you credit." Ask for the preferred business bio line, for example, "a management consultant who specializes in identifying challenging and satisfying new positions for dissatisfied star performers." Countless interviewees have thanked us for allowing such free-advertising tags to be used, so if you have the option, it's appreciated.

1.14.8   Send complimentary copies of the finished piece

Many interview subjects have told us that this follow-up is often promised but seldom delivered. Make sure you offer this tangible form of thanks. Some day, someone you interviewed may be perfect for another project. We interviewed one consultant for a management newsletter article. Later, he turned out to be the perfect expert to interview for the feature section of another client's annual report. And he was willing to cooperate with us again because we had shared the results of the previous interview with him.

1.14.9   The more specific and defined your purpose for interviewing, the more names you need

In our experience, out of every 10 names you're given as possible interview subjects, 2 or 3 will seem to have vanished from the planet, another 2 or 3 won't return your phone calls, and 1 or 2 won't say anything worth using. That usually leaves about 40 percent of the original list (not all quotes will be germane or print-worthy). When one company asked us to approach community leaders for favorable quotes for its annual report, only one-third of those identified as sources made it into the printed piece.

1.14.10   Hazards to getting the quotes you need lie everywhere along the production path

Once we interviewed retirees to be featured in an organization's annual report. We got wonderful quotes from one gentleman; later in the process, our client learned that he had brought numerous lawsuits against the organization during his employment. Sadly, one retiree died before the report was finished; the client accepted our suggestion to keep the interview in, prefaced with a brief memorial statement.

An executive we interviewed for a corporate newsletter defected to the company's chief competitor right about press time. For another client's annual report, we got a quote with glowing praise from the chairman of a major retail chain. He approved for printing not only the version of his remarks but also a full two-page layout, only to withdraw permission to quote him in any way at the last minute. The client was left with an embarrassing hole in the copy and an expensive production problem.

The moral is, of course, to line up three or more names for every one quotable interviewee you need. Once you have a live prospect (and we do mean live), follow the steps we've outlined for a successful telephone interview. At least the odds will be in your favor.

1.15 Everyone's an interview

Newsletters can do the work of a forum only if they're filled with the sound of human voices—and that means editors have to talk to people and listen to them talk back. As Nancy Brigham said in *How to Do Leaflets, Newsletters & Newspapers* (Writers Digest Books), "It's impossible to exaggerate the value of personal experiences. More than anything else, they make readers feel that your paper or newsletter is theirs, too."

The best way to give your readers the sense that you value their ideas and experiences is to interview them. Make listening interactively a regular part of your dealings with your colleagues. You don't need a formal appointment to ask people what they think or what they've been doing. Informally interview anyone interesting you meet: That means asking a few questions and taking sharp mental note of the answers. If your interest is genuine, people won't feel you're putting them on the spot. Your curiosity needn't be intrusive: Most people are flattered to be asked to talk about themselves. Editorially, it's good business: Readers are always curious to see what their peers have to say for themselves, as long as what's quoted doesn't sound forced or canned.

Asking good questions can help an editor acquire information that gives boilerplate articles the zing of recognizable reality instead of the musty taste of recycled set-pieces. Articles like these get read:

- A kudos piece that highlights a group's special contribution or an individual's one-of-a-kind achievement.

- A "top/down" piece from Mount Management to the befuddled masses about why a policy change is being made.

- A think piece that offers a fresh perspective on a persistent problem or gives voice to "what everybody knows" but nobody's saying.

- A 5-Ws report on a conference, speech, or trade show that makes readers feel they were there for all of the high spots and none of the tedium.

People who would never dream of sitting down to write a letter to the editor or volunteering to write about the efficient new procedure they dreamed up will talk to you one-on-one. This is the single easiest way for an editor to avoid the impression that content is homogenized and predictable. Keep these points in mind when you're thinking of staging a drive-by interview with a colleague:

- Prepare a list of questions for the interview.

- Think about the article you want to end up with.

- Show your genuine interest in the person's responses.

- Keep the interview on track to avoid ending up empty-handed.

- Listen carefully and paraphrase responses for verification if you're not sure you understand.

- Ask open-ended questions—and ask them one at a time.

- Ask brief questions—the point is not to offer a disquisition on what you know.

- Try asking a slightly negative question to get an animated answer.

1.16 Copyright should be a concern

Sooner or later, every newsletter editor has to learn the basics about intellectual property rights. Why? To avoid legal difficulties that could arise from using someone else's published work—words and images, printed and electronic—without permission. And you wouldn't want to see your own hard work turn up reprinted and credited to some other publisher or editor, would you? So you have to come up with a clear policy about letting others use the content you've created or paid others to create for you. There you have it, the two sides of the rights issue: You want to protect your right to profit from, package, and control the distribution of your own work, and you must observe the rules for using someone else's protected work. Copyright balances the rights of creators and users.

1.16.1   Protecting your own work

If you don't want people to reprint your articles, edit and reuse your photos, or photocopy your entire newsletter, be sure to run a note in the masthead saying just that. If you want to be sure that your claim is protected, you can print the copyright notice as a footer on each page.

(Some notices have gone so far as to warn that the publisher is willing to prosecute copyright violators, and court cases have been decided in favor of such publishers.)

If you want to charge for reprints, the Copyright Clearance Center will, for a fee, collect and periodically remit to you set fees that others pay for photocopying your articles. Companies and educational institutions honest enough to report their reproduction of copyrighted content get a good deal at pennies per copy. Many large companies and universities pay for a one site license that lets them make as many copies as they like.

But maybe you don't mind if others reprint your material or distribute photocopies of your entire newsletter; maybe you welcome the publicity. If you do, be sure to say that, too. If you want people to print a credit line giving your publication as the original source, state exactly how it should be worded.

If you've bought only first serial rights to a bylined article written under contract, remember that future rights revert to the author after publication. Requests for reprint should be forwarded to the author as a professional courtesy—for freelancers, each article has the potential for secondary income.

Some editors mistakenly think that getting an ISSN (International Standard Serial Number) is the same as copyrighting the content. It isn't. Even if you haven't registered for copyright, claiming copyright in print with a notice or using the © symbol has legal force. If you've gone to the trouble to register for an ISSN, you simply make it clear to the world that you're a serious publisher. If you're publishing regularly to a wide, external audience, it's a good idea to get an ISSN; librarians who catalog periodicals and others who compile directories require it. Print it in your masthead along with your notice of copyright. The copyright office of the Library of Congress maintains a useful, informative Web site from which forms can be downloaded. Visit http://lcweb. loc.gov/copyright.)

1.16.2 Determining 'fair use' of someone else's work

People can own rights only to original work that's actually been executed in a fixed form—written down, photographed, drawn, recorded, or stored electronically. Great ideas and good intentions can't be owned. But the law is quite clear that regardless of claims of originality, certain circumstances override copyright in favor of the public's need for information and education. Reproduction and reuse of copyrighted work go on all the time under legally approved circumstances known as "fair use." (It's still a courtesy to request permission, however.)

All editors—even those who are sure that their content doesn't need legal review and seldom reprint material—need to know the four factors that underlie the concept of fair use. Briefly, fair use means it's okay to reprint previously published material without getting explicit

Trademarks and Service Marks

Editors should just assume that writing and graphics are protected and request permission to use more than brief fair use excerpts. Names, logos, and other distinctive marketing devices that show up in newsletters may also be protected (though not titles of articles, short phrases, or slogans that don't constitute a unique service mark or trademark.) It can get tricky: One newsletter's mission statement, printed as a tagline, doubles as a protected service mark—*We bring people and technology together.* Here are the basic definitions:

Copyright. Reserves to the owner the exclusive legal right to reproduce, publish, and sell the creative content and fixed form of an original literary, musical, or artistic work. Copyright is held automatically regardless of whether it's been registered with the Library of Congress, and it may be used without registration to announce the intention to protect distribution rights.

Trademark. Reserves to the owner the exclusive legal right to make and sell proprietary material or merchandise. Rights are enforced by affixing a mark of claim (the ® symbol of registered claim or the words "a registered trademark of"). A trademarked name points to the origin or ownership of the item to which it's attached.

Trade name. A name adopted by a producer for an article or service that distinguishes it from the competition and identifies its origins; may be used and protected as a trademark. The International Trademark Association (call 212-768-9887) sells a list of protected names with guidelines for the usage preferred by the manufacturer. When rendering someone's trade name in print, however, an editor needs to be literally faithful to only correct spelling, capitalization, and special graphic treatments as far as possible. If it's your trade name, use the trademark symbol to protect it. If it's not your name, you have no duty to use the trademark symbol at every iteration, which is good news since copy pockmarked with little symbols is pretty annoying to try to read and can make end punctuation look silly.

Service mark. Reserves the exclusive legal right to use a statement that identifies a service offered to customers and makes a claim to uniqueness. The ^{SM} symbol is used to show a link back to the origins of such claims and the owner of the rights to the statement. A corporate service mark makes a nice tagline for a marketing newsletter.

permission from the original author or publisher. Transforming or incorporating properly attributed work into something newly useful, rather than just copying the original, is something newsletter editors take as their right, but that's not the whole story.

Think of the following factors as four test questions that all have to be answered correctly—that is, your publishing intentions have to meet a set of criteria. Decisions about whether a reprint is within legally acceptable limits have to be made on a case-by-case, but these test questions apply every time.

- What's the copyrighted material being used for? Is your intention to use it for commercial gain? Though nonprofit, educational uses are favored over commercial ones, if you plan to make money from your "educational" consumer or subscription newsletter, the stakes are little different. Using copyrighted work for the purposes of criticism, comment, news reporting, teaching (including multiple copies for classroom use), scholarship, or research is not infringement. But your intentions are just one factor; even if you're teaching or reporting, you're not exempt from the other three.

Fair use isn't the same as 'fair game.'

- What's the nature of the copyrighted work? The more creative a publication, the more likely that reprinting from it without permission is iffy. In fact, the degree of innovation is one of the two criteria (along with being in a fixed form) that qualify a work for copyright in the first place. A newsletter that's a pure digest of information from other newsletters probably can't claim copyright for the act of assembling a collection and certainly can't give others permission to reprint work original to others. When in doubt, always ask the original source.

- How much copyrighted material are you using and how substantial is it? What proportion of the original does the material you want to use represent? In the eyes of the law, the amount reused is measured qualitatively as well as quantitatively. So shorter excerpts are more likely to be fair use, but if you take the heart of the work and use it as your own, that's not.

- How does your use of the copyrighted material affect its value or potential market? This can be a hard test to pass, and some judges consider it the most important factor. If you use either a lot of material or what could be considered substantial (essential, unique) material for free, or distribute it to your readers for free or for the price of a subscription, you're making a dent in someone else's profits. Increasingly, reprinting newsletter articles as part of coursepacks for educational purposes isn't considered fair to publishers who would otherwise have sold subscriptions.

Ah, the ring of authority in someone else's voice! The lure of someone else's finished work! You may be planning to quote "only" a few borrowed paragraphs in your subscription newsletter and closely paraphrase only a few more, but if the original copyrighted document is just 1,000 words long, and it's specialized information researched from scratch, and your readers would have had to subscribe to the publication in which the article first appeared to get their hands on that material—you're on the edge of infringement.

Forget about the apocryphal "300 words" that some editors still think is the magic cutoff point. Even appropriating one or two words, if they constitute a service mark, can get you into trouble. A case in point: *The Editorial Eye* had to discontinue its widely loved "Ms. Grammar" column when a litigious association publisher told us to "cease and desist" its use, citing its ownership of the "Miss Grammar" mark for its language column for a few years longer than ours had existed.

Assume all graphics are copyrighted.

As for graphic rights, your best bet is to assume that behind every image is a fiercely possessive freelance photographer or graphic artist or cartoonist and that behind every piece of stock art is a publisher that keeps its house counsel busy tracking down people who aren't paying for using copyrighted images. Digitizing and manipulating images in Photoshop doesn't make them yours. If key elements of the original can be detected, you might be in for a lawsuit. Don't take shortcuts when it comes to paying for art in your newsletter.

1.16.3   Asking for permission

If you're sure that your intended reuse of someone's original content in your newsletter is either unrestricted or fair, you're home free. But if what you want to use fails any of the four fair use tests, you'll need to get permission from the copyright owner. Remember that

- A possible answer is "No, you may not reprint or adapt my material." Reasons may be offered but they're not required.

- A fee may be involved, and it can be minimal or deliberately prohibitive. Some editors split the fee with the author and use permissions income to help subsidize their publishing operation.

- Editors are being increasingly asked to give away their rights for material in whole or in part, in all media, forever and ever, as part of a new collection or a database, but few are eager to do so. Be prepared to scale back your plans to appropriate content for more than a one-time use. And be sure you're not signing a form that gives away more rights to your own content than the simple, one-time, in-print, limited distribution deal you intended.

- Most editors prefer such requests in writing. Send a polite letter or e-mail that explains thoroughly what you have in mind and describe the material precisely—in fact, send a photocopy if you're using postal mail or fax. Indicate a place for the copyright owner to sign granting permission—you need it in writing. "Silence is not permission," as Kenneth D. Crews said in his on-line copyright tutorial hosted by Indiana University. Offer to print a credit line acknowledging the author and publication in which material was first published.

Twelve Ways to Gain Feedback and Encourage Reader Participation

Try some of these ideas for building reader loyalty.

1. Conduct a reader survey.
2. Insert reader response postcards.
3. Run a regular column of letters to the editor.
4. Call readers at random.
5. Hold a contest and offer a prize.
6. Organize a focus group or hold a brainstorming brunch.
7. Challenge readers to react to a controversial topic.
8. Set up a hotline to answer questions.
9. Give credit in print to readers who have suggested articles.
10. Answer all letters and return all calls.
11. Turn routine inquiries and requests into ideas for editorial.
12. "Reward" readers with bonus editorial.

Some of these require more funding and energy than others, but the editor of even a high-readership publication needs to pick up the telephone each week and speak briefly with a few readers about their interests and concerns.

As the managing editor of a trade publication once advised in a *Folio:* seminar on keeping readers involved: "We have to make each reader feel like a member of the 'in-group' by doggedly appealing to a sense that we're all in this together. Every issue should remind readers that they belong to this exclusive 'club' and can't afford to miss a single issue."

Cultivating a lively exchange with readers requires careful planning, creative execution, and resolute follow-up, but the result—readers who read and respond to your newsletter—is worth the extra administrative effort.

1.17 How to encourage subscriber loyalty

The rule of thumb in subscription publishing is that a renewal rate of at least 50 percent is a sign of health, and renewal rates of 65 percent or higher are best for the profit margin. Small publications, especially, live and die by their renewal rates because it costs far more to capture new subscribers than to keep old ones.

Even if you edit a controlled subscription newsletter, all that hard work toward your editorial goals will be wasted if people stop reading.

How can an editor cultivate and sustain a high renewal rate? Your readers must *enjoy* and *need* your publication so much that they wouldn't consider letting the subscription lapse. That kind of loyalty is anchored in content that rewards people for sticking around.

- Make sure you run plenty of small nuggets of information that readers can actually use. That includes information on resources, books, software, products, associations, conferences, contests, and the like. Make it easy for readers to follow up on this information by printing contact addresses and phone numbers.

Reward readers for sticking around.

- Mention your readers often. A newsletter's community of readers is usually rather specialized and cohesive. Help your readers feel as if they are part of this community by setting up one or more columns that give them a chance to see their names in print. Invite comments and if they're not calling or writing, why not call a few subscribers yourself? Ask a question and get permission to print their answers. In short, readers who feel involved with the content also feel bonded to a publication.

- Always emphasize the *breaking news* element of your articles. After a while, readers may feel they've heard it all before. Taking a fresh approach to headlines for familiar topics can put a new slant on things, even if you have to run yet another President's Message. If you as an editor can't think of anything new to say in a headline, that article needs rewriting.

- Always return every phone call and answer every letter you get from a reader—sometimes a postcard with a short note will do just as well. Always accept a chance to speak at a small gathering or brown bag lunch. It's good for you to get out among your colleagues, and a bit of editorial visibility will keep you from being taken for granted. This is the simplest way to build a reputation for being responsive.

1.18 How to conduct a reader survey: a case study

Problem: I recently took over as the editor of a bimonthly employee newsletter for a federal agency. As a first step toward improving the publication's effectiveness, I attempted to survey our 700 readers. To my dismay, I received only a 2 percent response rate. How should I interpret that? I'd like to give it another try, but obviously I need some new survey strategies. Do you have any suggestions?

Solution: You're right to be concerned that so few people responded to your survey. Either your readers have little interest in the newsletter, or your survey methods were seriously flawed. A 100 percent response

Basic Dos and Don'ts for Reader Surveys

Do

- Use a prepared list of questions, no matter which survey method you choose.
- Select the survey method likely to yield the highest number of responses.
- Test your questionnaire with a sample group before sending it out.
- Elicit responses not only from those who read your publication but also from those who don't.
- Use the group-administered survey when you are able to poll a significant number of your audience in one place while you wait.
- Follow up the group-administered survey with another method to collect data from those not present.
- Publicize the mailed survey in advance.
- Set a deadline for mailed survey replies.
- Include an addressed, stamped envelope with mailed surveys.
- Publish reminders for people to return mailed surveys.
- Survey a representative random sample if you can't poll your entire readership.
- Follow up all surveys by reporting to the respondents what changes, if any, will be made as a result of the responses.

Don't

- Ask questions that are judgmental or emotionally loaded.
- Expect only positive responses.
- Make major changes based on survey responses of less than 50 percent.
- Include a mailed survey in your publication if you can avoid it; mail the survey separately.
- Mail surveys in the summer when readership is normally smaller.
- Hand-select names for a sample; to generate a truly random sample, choose names at a regular interval (for example, every third name).

Sample Survey Form
Flight Times Feedback
McDonnell Douglas

In the interest of improving *Flight Times*, we want to know what you like and don't like about the publication. Please take a few minutes to complete this survey, then return it to: *Flight Times* Survey, McDonnell Douglas Helicopter Systems, 5000 E. McDowell Road, Bldg. 510, MS A387, Mesa, AZ 85215-9797. We'll compile all responses received by Sept. 15, and publish the results in an upcoming issue.

Naturally, we would be delighted if everyone read every single issue of *Flight Times*. But, realistically, we know better. If you feel you don't read *Flight Times* often enough to give meaningful answers to the questions in this survey, please skip to the section labeled "Some Information About Yourself." You can still give us very useful information by circling the appropriate responses on those items.

Here's how one editor of a corporate newsletter surveys its employee-readers.

1. Does the layout and design of *Flight Times* make it inviting and easy to read?

No				Yes
1	2	3	4	5

2. How much of *Flight Times* do you read?

Almost all				25 percent or less
1	2	3	4	5

3. Rate your interest in each of the following topics with 5 being the most interesting, and 1 being the least interesting:

___Financial news and business outlook

___Stories about teammates on or off the job

___MDC's plans for the future

___Milestones (deaths and retirements)

___Legislation/regulations affecting the company/industry

___Company-sponsored clubs, teams and other recreational activities

___News about our competitors

___Development of new products, services, technologies

___Benefits and other Human Resources issues

___Quality improvement initiatives (ISO 9000, etc.)

___Contract announcements

___Employee recognition and rewards

___Actions and perspectives of MDHS leadership

___News from MDA and other components of MDC

___Letters to the editor

4. Rate the clarity of writing in *Flight Times*:

Difficult to understand				Easy to understand
1	2	3	4	5

5. *Flight Times* seems to be written:

For management		For everyone		For non management
1	2	3	4	5

6. Rate the accuracy of the information contained in *Flight Times*:

Inaccurate				Very accurate
1	2	3	4	5

7. Rate the credibility of *Flight Times*:

Not credible				Very credible
1	2	3	4	5

8. How much of *Flight Times* is "new" news?

Mostly old news		A mixture		Mostly "new" news
1	2	3	4	5

9. *Flight Times* is published every other week. That is:

Not frequent enough		Great		Too frequent
1	2	3	4	5

10. Are copies of *Flight Times* easily available?

No				Yes
1	2	3	4	5

11. Overall, how would you rate *Flight Times*?

Poor				Excellent
1	2	3	4	5

It's a good idea to ask at least one open-ended question (13).

12. If you were in charge of *Flight Times*, what changes would you make?

13. What specific topics would you like to see covered in future issues of *Flight Times*?

Some Information About Yourself:

14. I am a:
❑ Regular employee   ❑ Contract employee   ❑ Retiree   ❑ Other

15. Years of service in the organization:
❑ Less than 1 year   ❑ 1 to 5 years   ❑ 6 to 10 years   ❑ 11 to 20 years
❑ More than 20 years

16. Age:
❑ Under 25   ❑ 25 to 35   ❑ 36 to 45   ❑ 46 to 55   ❑ Over 55

17. Sex:
❑ Male   ❑ Female

18. Job Type: (if you are retired, your last position held.)
❑ Managerial   ❑ Non-managerial, salaried   ❑ Non-managerial, hourly

19. Highest level of education attained:
❑ Some high school   ❑ High school graduate   ❑ Some college
❑ College graduate   ❑ Post-graduate degree

Thank you for responding to this survey.

rate is almost never achieved; most polling experts consider anything over a 50 percent response as significant ("adequate") and consider 60 percent "good" and 70 percent or more "very good."

In general, a 100 percent return from a small sample is better than a 50 percent return from a large one. Think of it this way: If 70 percent of your readers respond, and if 80 percent of those who respond say that they enjoy reading "The Hobby Corner," the math tells you that only about half of your readers enjoy this feature. But that's a flawed conclusion because it's based on the assumption that those who did not respond don't like the feature—and that's probably not true. The people you don't hear from are often the ones who are satisfied.

Be willing to make changes based on the survey responses.

The process of surveying need not be complicated or costly, but if you have any say in the matter, don't undertake a survey unless you're sure management will take the results seriously and support your efforts to make the content more appealing. Careful planning and willingness to make changes based on the survey responses are the only requisites for dealing with the reader apathy you seem to be facing. Ask yourself some fundamental questions before you try again.

What do I want to know? In his book, *How to Conduct a Readership Survey,* Charles Redding suggests that editors spell out in detail exactly the kinds of information they need. Wording is very important: Simply asking readers if they "enjoy" your newsletter is not enough—readers may enjoy the same newsletter for different reasons. Breaking questions down into several parts or constructing follow-up questions from a different slant is essential to getting the full picture.

Once you have an outline of the types of information you need, structure the survey so that the answers—multiple choice, rankings, categories—will be revealing, easy to tabulate, and unintimidating. One axiom applies: Keep it simple. Don't leave any room for ambiguity or vagueness. For example, if readers are supposed to rank the importance to them of certain kinds of information (staff accomplishments and awards, personnel policies, fiscal performance), make it clear that *1* means "I care a lot" and *10* means "I couldn't care less."

How will I collect the data? The three basic data-collection methods are

- *Mailed questionnaires.* These are better for relatively small target groups because you can survey all members and follow up with phone calls. (As a survey method, however, mailed questionnaires are far from perfect, so make sure you have a follow-up plan for soliciting responses from those who don't send back the questionnaire.) To survey a large readership (more than 1,000) by mail, select what you think is a representative number. Redding and other experts frown on the "shotgun survey" sent to all readers because a balanced response is unlikely. Readers who feel strongly negative or

Survey Your Readers Before You Redesign

See if you fit any of the profiles—all showing signs of a publication in need of retooling.

Fill in the blank: "You need to do a reader survey because..."

- **Your publication is moving toward a different editorial mission or audience.** For example, if the sales force you're trying to motivate has become international, you'll need a slightly different look. Also, you'll probably need to create some new departments to interest your new readers—and to educate your old ones. A survey can tell you about cultural concerns to consider if you go global.

- **You're ready to upgrade the quality and design of the publication.** A complete redesign or partial retooling every four years is a good idea. If management wants to completely overhaul your publication, do you do a survey before or after? Or both? Most publishers have limited resources, and readers have limited patience with being asked to play critic—they just want information. As one *Eye* survey respondent commented: "It's fine! I like it! Quit worrying!" If those involved know what the new look is intended to say about your organization or mission and if you have a lot of design talent available, be brave and redesign before doing a survey. Be sure to acknowledge the new look in print and briefly explain the rationale in a note. A survey before redesigning can help you decide what still works and what to change; a survey afterward can tell you how people reacted to the changes.

- **Your profession or industry is changing rapidly.** This applies to a lot of us. But does it mean that your newsletter needs to change? Every three years or so, we send a survey to everyone who subscribes to *The Editorial Eye*, not because we plan to change our mission, but because we know we have to keep up with what's going on if we want to be a key resource for editors and writers. A survey can help editors stay on track and help publishers decide whether a spinoff title is needed for a sizable segment of the audience.

- **You haven't heard from your readers for a couple of years and it's just plain time.** In fact, a lot of marketing managers would say that's much too long to wait. With an average turnover rate of 30 to 40 percent (that's equivalent to a 60 to 70 percent renewal or retention rate), you have a lot of new readers every year. How will you know whether your content and design are appropriate for the audience you're trying to reach if you're operating under old assumptions about who they are? The nature of the workforce is changing so fast that alumni and association newsletters and magazines, in particular, can't count on a uniform reader profile. A survey can tell you how the demographics have changed and whether your publication has a mandate for changing or for staying just the way it is.

positive will be the ones most likely to respond, and that can skew your results. Instead, select a sampling of people from each department or geographical area. The difficulty in simply getting your readers to send their responses back to you by mail is another reason experts think sampling is a good idea for larger mailings.

- *Focus group interviews.* Here's how a national sports magazine uses a "subscribers board." Twelve readers of the magazine work directly with the editors on each issue, giving feedback on stories and artwork. Board members also participate in long-range editorial planning sessions. Editors credit the subscribers board with improving the quality of the magazine and increasing overall reader satisfaction. A more reasonable approach for editors with more limited means might be to sponsor an occasional working breakfast or brownbag lunch with local readers.

Weigh criticism, but don't let it bowl you over.

- *Telephone interviews.* Make random telephone calls to readers. Set a certain number of calls as your weekly goal, and each month should bring a wide range of comments. The advantage of this method is that you collect responses immediately. Readers may hesitate to give negative criticism one-to-one, so ask for rankings or positive comments: "If you could change one thing about the newsletter, what would it be?" If your readers are government workers, be sure that you have permission to make these calls; perhaps you could precede them with a memo to alert supervisors that the calls are authorized.

How will I compile the responses? This aspect of surveying is perhaps the most daunting to editorial types because they assume that it involves number crunching. In fact, a variety of computer programs can help you tabulate and analyze your data. To save you from the tedium of pencil-and-paper tabulations, you might want to consult a computer expert from your organization.

What will I do with the information? There are two musts in surveying: Always disclose the final results—publish an overall analysis as soon as possible—and take action based on what you've found out. From the outset, keep readers informed about the progress of the tabulations, and let them know how you're proceeding to analyze the responses.

Tell readers what changes you plan to make and invite them to let you know how they feel about them. If you've decided to set up a network of in-house reporters, for example, tell readers how to reach them with story ideas or criticism. Above all, thank readers for responding to your survey and assure them that their answers have helped you shape your newsletter's content and format. But don't natter on too long; after all, this is housekeeping, not news.

The reasons for doing a survey are to stay current with the needs of your readers and serve your organization's goals. A good reader survey can help you keep the lines of communication open, but be prepared for some harsh criticism and a few off-the-wall suggestions. Weigh them in the light of your own vision for the newsletter. In trying to be responsive, don't lose sight of your responsibility to exercise editorial judgment. You can use survey results to educate both readers and management about what you see as the newsletter's mission, as well as to confirm that your efforts are on track.

1.19 When and why you should redesign

The human tendency is toward inertia: "If it ain't broke, don't fix it." If most of your readers seem to like your newsletter—or at least, they don't complain about it to you—why should you fiddle with the formula? An editor in one of our newsletter editing classes was thinking that maybe it was time for a little refurbishment since the newsletter hadn't been redesigned—ever. *It had looked exactly the same for 20 years.* We applauded her, literally: We gave her a round of applause for the wrenching, unentrenching effort ahead of her and her gameness in tackling it.

At some point, every periodical definitely needs to break away from the thoroughly comfortable, in terms of content as well as design, and make a move toward the slightly surprising. Newsletters aren't static, if they're doing their work well. They should acknowledge and reflect their world and lead their readers a bit beyond the status quo. Even the sturdiest design has a limited life and eventually will need to be retired in favor of one that's even better for *this* time, *this* new editorial slant, *this* new type of reader we know we've gained. How do we know? We've surveyed our readership.

Most newsletter publishers seek out a fresh format every four years or so, but there's no golden layout waiting to be discovered. Trendy styles in design pop up and then start looking dated just like popular preferences in clothing, food, and music do. Nobody in the new millennium is going to want a newsletter that looks like the equivalent of an avocado-green shag carpet from the 1970s (unless it's a newsletter for aficionados of retro home decoration, of course).

But publication design isn't just about being trendy. It's part of the continuing work of editors and designers to communicate content and create an image of the content provider—without making readers work too hard. As graphic designer Alex White wrote in an article for *The Editorial Eye*, "Messages that requite minimal exertion by the reader require design decisions that lead to a balanced, orderly page." What those decisions look like and feel like will be very different for different newsletters and for the same newsletter over time.

People may be reading less than ever before, but they're picking what they choose to read with more care. Lots of exposure to sophisticated graphics from other media has given readers a more demanding palate—that is, ugly-looking stuff isn't palatable. For editors and writers who care about communicative design, and for designers who respect editorial goals, boring is not an option. Enterprising editors work with their designers to stay a step ahead of ordinary, too-safe, too-prevalent graphic and editorial clichés—and a step ahead of readers' expectations. The only way to do that is by trying out new visual relationships as a publication evolves.

The package matters. People *do* judge content by the shape, color, size, and heft of the container. They don't want to hear that contents may have settled in shipping, either. That's why you need to take a look at the design section that follows.

2 Designing and Producing Newsletters

Creating a Newsletter: Start to Finish

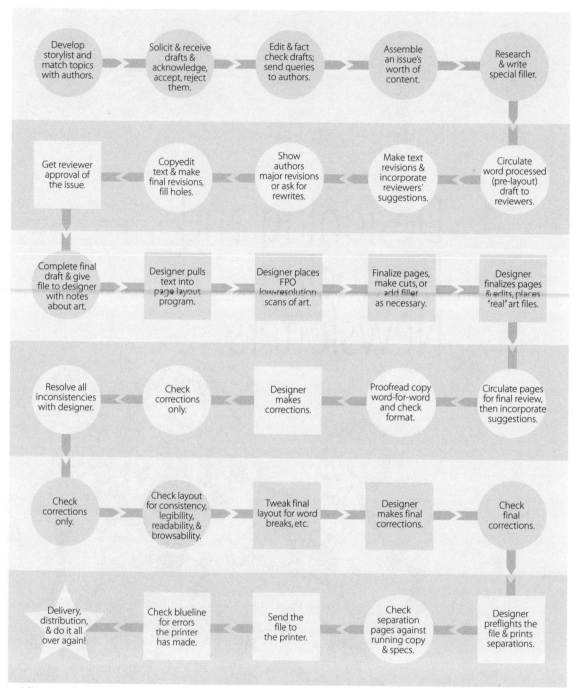

Develop storylist and match topics with authors. → Solicit & receive drafts & acknowledge, accept, reject them. → Edit & fact check drafts; send queries to authors. → Assemble an issue's worth of content. → Research & write special filler.

Get reviewer approval of the issue. ← Copyedit text & make final revisions, fill holes. ← Show authors major revisions or ask for rewrites. ← Make text revisions & incorporate reviewers' suggestions. ← Circulate word processed (pre-layout) draft to reviewers.

Complete final draft & give file to designer with notes about art. → Designer pulls text into page layout program. → Designer places FPO low-resolution scans of art. → Finalize pages, make cuts, or add filler as necessary. → Designer finalizes pages & edits, places "real" art files.

Resolve all inconsistencies with designer. ← Check corrections only. ← Designer makes corrections. ← Proofread copy word-for-word and check format. ← Circulate pages for final review, then incorporate suggestions.

Check corrections only. → Check layout for consistency, legibility, readability, & browsability. → Tweak final layout for word breaks, etc. → Designer makes final corrections. → Check final corrections.

Delivery, distribution, & do it all over again! ← Check blueline for errors the printer has made. ← Send the file to the printer. ← Check separation pages against running copy & specs. ← Designer preflights the file & prints separations.

Editors can help simplify the production phase of the process—the creation of a layout that "packages" content effectively—by learning some basic concepts, rules of thumb, and vocabulary. Then QC the final product ruthlessly.

2 Designing and Producing Newsletters

The bare essentials for editors

I t's simple enough to parse newslettering into its working parts, start-ing with decisions about how often to publish, for whom, and in what format. You can justify almost any combination of editorial ele-ments—as long as they work, which means *work together* to interest readers. The same can be said of design elements.

It's more difficult to talk about the process of making decisions about where things will go in the newsletter and what they'll look like. Think of newsletter production as a series of fresh chances, randomly presented over time, to get it right. If the content is interesting, read-ers will forgive errors and omissions more than editors (for whom each issue is risky performance art) will ever forgive themselves. Not perfec-tion but thoughtful piecing together of elements into a complete pack-age is what sets apart the newsletters people want to read.

The same can be said of the bundle of graphic pieces that constitute a newsletter's image. Research by the American Society of Newspaper Editors and the Poynter Institute for Media Studies shows that people will read plain vanilla text if they're interested in the topic; they won't read what they're not interested in, no matter how beautifully it's laid out.

2.1   Good design is a set of good choices

Design is a just a tool for presenting a message. No great claims can be made for any one surefire formula for hypnotizing readers into paying attention. We have a lot less control over how people read any publication than we like to think—and newsletters, with their built-in browsability, are even less subject to control.

Nevertheless, there are design conventions that work most of the time for most newsletters. And there are mistakes that we all must learn to avoid—errors in judgment or execution that get in the way instead of smoothing it.

2.1.1   Solve the layout puzzle

Newsletter layout is a puzzle, but it must arrive already solved for readers. Identifying a group of good choices for a particular audience from among many theoretical options is just as important when it comes to design as it is for the content being presented. Like service-based editorial formulas, content-based newsletter design templates rely on an appeal to familiar categories (or conventions) each time out of the gate.

There's a lot of information about periodicals design out there; the only problem is that most of it is intended to help designers "enhance the message." There are entire books on typography, layout, and clip art; specific page layout and illustration software guides; and magazines that focus solely on production and file preparation—new ones every year. (The bibliography on page 345 lists some of the best for editors.)

Editors need to know what contributes to legibility.

For editors—who, like designers, need to think about how to create selective emphasis and to recognize what contributes to legibility—the resources have tended to be fewer. Newsletter textbooks used to say sternly, "Leave design to designers." No more.

Good editors try to balance a variety of content (so things don't seem monotonous) within a unified whole (so they seem under control). This same sense of balance is required for presenting a variety of story sizes and shapes on the page, as well as using graphic elements to best advantage.

Experienced editors who know a little about how to get the best from layout software may not be designers, but they've developed an eye for the best ways both to fit copy to layout and to use layout to highlight copy. Whether or not they're responsible for using a layout program to produce a newsletter from a template, new editors should become familiar with the vocabulary used by professional newsletter designers—that's the first step toward becoming familiar with the concepts.

A glossary of essential terms at the end of this chapter (page 125) is followed by "Anatomy of design conventions for newsletters," which identifies the essential graphic elements that can help organize newsletter content (page 131). Simply knowing they exist is a start.

But memorizing the definitions for design elements won't help you much unless you're actively wondering what they should be doing for your readers—and how you can edit them. The most significant places in any layout for gaining reader interest are shown in the sidebar.

Relative Importance of Various Newsletter Elements to Readers Who Are Browsing			
Element	Readers notice in this order	Percentage of readers who read element	Potential for impact on readers of element
Headlines	1	70%–90%	Negligible
Subheads	2	60%–90%	Negligible
Captions	2	60%–90%	Low
Lead-ins	3	40%–70%	Negligible
Body copy	4	5%–10%	95%

—The Newsletter Factory

2.1.2 Heads up

Headlines are the chief tool for ordering copy.

The chief way that editors create a sense of order and copy flow is by creating—and consistently using—a system of headlines. Heads give readers a way to pick and choose what they want to read first by signposting categories. Heads also demonstrate the range of content and thus reinforce the publishing mission. In section 1, we saw that editors have to remember to cover all the bases, all the time—monotony and lack of perspective are the biggest traps waiting for editorial. Writing these heads is important to emphasizing the focus of an article. On pages 134–139 are illustrations of these elements as used in a real newsletter.

For now, the point is that they function as primary graphic cues. Sections 2.1.3–2.1.6 are a guide to the basics of placing headlines, including kickers, deckheads, and crossheads, as well as captions, pull-quotes, and sidebars. These are the essential display elements that editors should build into copy early, not as an afterthought.

2.1.3   Main and subordinate headlines

Headlines that grab attention are especially important for newsletters, which are more likely to be skimmed through quickly than pondered. See the "Anatomy of design conventions for newsletters," on pages 131–139, for graphic examples of each. Newsletter headlines can lead the reader further into the story if you follow these rules:

■ Keep them short—they don't have to be complete sentences.

■ Use short words—so you don't have to hyphenate (never break a proper noun).

Use special typographic headline treatments consistently

■ Use strong verbs in the active voice.

■ Highlight the most important point of the story.

■ Avoid "empty heads"—get rid of vague, abstract wording.

■ Distinguish between clever and cute.

■ Avoid editorializing.

■ Avoid biased language—offended readers stop reading.

■ Vary headlines—ask a question, include a brief quote.

■ Proofread carefully—errors often hide in plain sight.

2.1.4   Sidebars add interest to a main story

A sidebar is any short story accompanying a longer one, and it's usually formatted as a fact box or a screened text box. But a good sidebar is more than that—it's an entertaining alternative, a fresh perspective, a reader-friendly hook. Sidebars provide an opportunity to add extra reader appeal to any story, whether news or feature.

There are three things to remember about sidebars:

■ They should be tightly written. They're condiments, not the main course.

■ They shouldn't be too long—certainly they shouldn't be as long as the main story. A sidebar that long should be formatted as a related story.

■ They'll be read first before the main article they accompany, so they're influential. Don't just dump a list of facts into a box without making a connection to the main article.

Sidebars offer an alternative to narrative text. If done properly, they carve up complicated material into bite-sized chunks—while providing graphic relief at the same time.

A Checklist of Style Conventions for Heads, Captions, and Pullquotes

___ Avoid all-uppercase headlines. Headline style varies according to the preferences of a publication:

- *up style*—All Significant Words Are Capitalized (like that). This is traditional newspaper style.

- *down style*—In "down" or "sentence style," only the first word and proper nouns are capitalized. Heads are easier to read and take up less room; this style is currently in favor. But style also depends on your hierarchy of heads—you can use down style for subheads (Head B) if main heads (Head A) are up, for example.

___ Headlines don't have to be sentences and don't need end punctuation if they are sentences. (The period stops the reader.)

___ It's standard to use single quotes instead of double quotes in all display type.

___ Write headlines to fit no more than three-fourths the width of the column(s) over which they will run. Don't be afraid not to fill the whole line—create "found" white space. Pick a style:

- *Centered.* Often just looks a little "off" when a long head extends over an entire column. Best over a full page.

- *Flush left.* Works best in conjunction with kickers and deckheads. Also works best over narrow columns.

___ *Kickers* (above the headline), usually a descriptive or explanatory phrase, are set off from headlines with italics, underlining, or type reversed out of a screened bar. The type is normally smaller than headline type. Sometimes department heads are formatted as kickers.

___ *Deckheads* (below the headline) can be as long as a complete sentence to explain a cryptic headline. Also usually set off with italics and sometimes set in type larger than body copy. Most effective when they span more than a column width. Use only for clarity.

___ *Crossheads (subheads)* are short transitional heads within an article. They show a shift in narrative direction and make a longer article seem more approachable by providing browsing points. As for subpoints in an outline, you need at least two crossheads in an article.

___ *Captions* for photos, tables, and graphs are usually set in type smaller than body text. Keep them brief and informative; longer captions should be carefully constructed and clear. The exception is the photo feature.

___ *Pullquotes* are a graphic way to highlight a point in a story. They provide visual relief on the page—but only if set off from body text with enough space and a distinctive treatment, however simple. Place close to but not right beside the copy they echo. They don't have to be a direct quote and may be—should be—edited for punch. Placement varies; use to balance another graphic or to copyfit a short page.

___ Use special typographic headline treatments consistently throughout your publication and limit them to no more than you really need to set off levels of information—three are enough for most newsletters that are still trying to be newsletters and not magazines, which can and do mix dozens of styles.

2.1.5 Pullquotes enhance and humanize layout

Newsletters are often text-heavy and in need of graphic leavening. Pullquotes are a graphic element traditionally found in magazines, but they're a wonderful way to help newsletters look less gray—if used carefully. Too often they're shoehorned into text without enough white space around them.

- A pullquote can be a sentence or direct quote lifted verbatim from a story, or it can be a paraphrased or slightly edited version of a significant or interesting statement.

- Pullquotes serve three editorial purposes. They

  1. draw attention to a point within an article or to the thesis,

  2. invite readers to dip into an article, and

  3. make the layout more appealing.

  That is, they can be an invitation if they're not placed at the very top or bottom of a page or in the middle of a short paragraph of text.

Newsletters are often text-heavy.

- Pullquotes can be quite simple or play a large graphic role complete with oversize quotation marks; there are many acceptable formats. The point is to pick a consistent style that stands out from body copy (usually a different size or type style) yet is consonant with other layout components. Use pullquotes sparingly or your readers may find them irritating interruptions.

- A pullquote should be placed somewhere near the original version but not right beside it—that would defeat the purpose of "leading into" the article. Slight edits are often necessary to keep a quote from seeming pedantic or odd, but don't trick readers so that they look in vain for more about the statement that interested them. Keep punctuation and shifts in tense to a minimum and avoid using ellipses or adding bracketed comments that break the impact of the quote. Below is an example of a cryptic pullquote published in a national newspaper. It's been edited (the brackets tell us that) but it still is filled with confusing pronouns we have no antecedents for— we haven't read the story yet, remember—so although it's punchy enough, it has no direct appeal:

  > "[Investigators] repeatedly told me that
  > 'people like you' make them sick."

- An effective pullquote crystallizes some high point or is a summary of the article's message, so pick a crisp, articulate, or even controversial statement. A bland one does harm because it invites a "So what?" reaction. Running no pullquote at all is better than running a boring one—even if your designer has placed a nice big hole on the page labeled "pull-quote here." However, if as an editor you can't supply a pullquote, maybe your copy could use a second look.

Samples of Pullquotes

These published samples are all great sound bites that surely drew readers' attention. The quotes, all well placed to offer visual interest without crowding or competing with copy, used plenty of white space and a type treatment distinctive from body text. Note that rules are optional and white space alone can be just as effective—even preferable.

A. A little long, but this single-column, centered pullquote says right away that the rather text-heavy article is going to pay off in practical advice. A slightly larger size of the body font and hairline rules set it off. Well placed to avoid bumping up against subheads in adjacent columns.

B. There's no question that this single-column screened pullquote grabbed attention. It's so compelling that it's almost curt—and that's a plus in a quote. Rules and italic in a larger size of the headline font ensure there's no confusion with body text.

C. The short, punchy pullquote hanging in the scholar's margin works almost like setting out a shingle that says, "You need to know what this article says." The smallish but heavy, down-to-earth sans serif echoes the rest of display copy and complements body copy without hectoring it.

D. The large, heavy sans serif pullquote centered across two columns hints at something else we like to be consistent—but what? We want to find out. Carefully placed to avoid competing with the subhead beneath it.

A

attitude questions: How do you feel about this? They don't always lead you

---

One tip to keep in mind: Always include a place on the survey where respondents can write comments.

---

to action," Sinickas says. Generally, her preferred method of response is

---

B

Common critical performance elements are a set of critical elements

There will be no more automatic performance awards.

that consist of duties and responsibilities that contribute towards ac-

---

C

How fast do your images download?
The answer might determine the success of your intranet

"You don't want users to ever be hanging around waiting for graphics."

Everyone wants to create attractive pages for their intranet, with beautiful images that help create an interesting experience for users. Unfortunately, large, rich images take longer to download—and the speed at which

"JPEGs are good for photographic images; GIFs are good for large blocks of solid color," according to Neal Bayless, president of Brooklyn-based Web developer SMLXL Design (www.smlxl.com). "If an image contains color gradients or a

---

D

grandparent who still refers to their refrigerator as a *Frigidaire*?

Purity is another parameter by which product quality is judged. We

We like the box of *Cheerios* we buy one week to be identical to the one purchased last week. No variations, changes or surprises.

Quality parameters
What is it about those products that qualify them for the "quality" label in

don't want our gasoline to have water or other contaminants in it, nor do we want our pails of bentgrass

Surely something is worth highlighting? The pullquotes in this book will give you an idea of how they can serve to draw interest and summarize key points.

2.1.6 Captions require special care

These informative blurbs appear below or next to photos or illustrations or central to a group of them. Captions must be

Captions shouldn't be too tiny.

- brief (unless they're expanded for a photo essay),
- clearly descriptive of the image,
- accurate (names, places, events, dates),
- ordered the way the people or things appear, and
- linked to the story in some way.

Captions are usually smaller than body copy and may be set in italic or sans serif to further set them apart from body copy. But have a heart: Captions, like headlines, are there to add information. In fact, captions can be used to contribute information that you don't have room for in the accompanying article itself. Don't make captions tiny candidates for a magnifying glass.

2.1.7 Rules of thumb about using graphics

What we're after is to balance a sense of variety within a consistent framework—a neat trick. The risk is that we'll fail and end up with the extremes of chaos or monotony. Editorial judgment must overrule excessive graphic high jinks, but editors need to listen to designers when it comes to trying out new ways to highlight material.

In a typical issue of either *The New York Times* or *USA Today*, 70 percent of the stories run without any art, 25 percent use just one piece of art (a photo, chart, or map), and only 5 percent use two or more pieces of art. Likewise, most of the stories that most newsletter editors prepare will consist of just headlines and text.

Because there are only a few ways to design stories without art, it's fairly hard to foul text up. But we manage to do it—by using inappropriate type and margins, by jamming text into boxes or ignoring the grid so that copy seems to float on the page, and by jumping articles that would be better trimmed. Perhaps the single most important page design guideline is this one: Whether they're vertical, horizontal or square, stories should always be shaped like a rectangle. (You'll find an example of copy with a *dogleg* in the Gallery of Don'ts on page 177.)

Horizontal legs of text create the illusion that stories are shorter than they really are, and flow left to right the way readers naturally read.

Ten Types of Sidebars That Add Reader-Friendly Content

1. **Lists.** The Top 10 anything, a sequence of events, helpful phone numbers.

2. **Quizzes.** Factual questions and answers, brief person-to-person interviews and quotes.

3. **Checklists, guides, and fast-fact boxes.** Capsules of who-what-when-where-why information, entertaining trivia, statistics, signs to watch for, changes to implement, step-by-step how to, books to read.

4. **Calendar.** Upcoming events and activities, training opportunities.

5. **Glossaries.** Definitions of technical terms, jargon, abbreviations.

6. **Excerpts.** Brief, representative sample of someone's work to accompany a profile or a book review.

7. **Extended quotes and anecdotes.** First-person embellishment of a profile or personalizing of a straight news story.

8. **Reader challenges and contests.** A prize for responses to a question or a request for an opinion.

9. **Tables.** For readers to make comparisons and see patterns.

10. **Maps.** Add mileage scales when possible, use screens cautiously (10 percent is best), match the map to the story, center maps within the box, assume the reader is lost.

Keep legs of text between 2 and 10 inches deep. Headlines should cover the story and begin above the first line of the text.

In a perfect periodical, every long story would have some sort of art: a photo, a chart, a map, or—at the very least—a pullquote. In reality, though, producing that much art would take a colossal amount of work and might actually be too distracting for readers.

A better rule of thumb is: Make every page at least one-third art. This is counting photos, graphics, teasers, white space, and display type. But when there is simply no time and no artist to help you prevent your pages from being gray, instead of stacking stories in rows, try

- boxing stories that are important or different (but not just to box them),

- using bastard measures (breaking columns out of the basic grid, like the layout on this very page), or

- using text wraps and alternative headline treatments.

Editors will have to write headlines to accommodate these formats and work with the person doing the layout to fatten up or shrink headlines to work with stories most effectively.

Finally, remember that most readers prefer to find the same material in the same spot in each issue: the table of contents, photo or calendar features, editorials, reader forums—regular columns and features, in short.

2.1.8 Twenty mistakes newsletter desktop publishers often make

Run-of-the-mill newsletters are full of these mistakes. Avoiding them boosts your credibility. Pick a handful to check and watch yourself get better.

1. Not getting at least the newsletter's nameplate professionally designed.

2. Not providing enough contrast between heads (and subheads) and text.

3. Not emphasizing some kinds of content more than others. If everything has equal weight, the overall dull gray look doesn't encourage browsing.

4. Not using enough visual elements—stock art, photos, and charts.

5. Using stock photos and clip art unimaginatively. Two or three pieces of harmonious stock art can be combined; one piece can be used very large and then screened down with the type overprinting it.

6. Letting the (often limited) capability of a computer program or its operator dictate the design. Get design training or hire a designer.

Editors have to distill pullquotes.

7. Changing the grid so many times that each page looks unrelated to the ones before and after.

8. Using initial drop caps in a newsletter with many short news items. It takes extra care and time to insert them. They can also become too spotty on the page, especially if they're too large. (They can also spell dirty words all over the page, something to watch out for.)

9. Using pullquotes (breakouts, lift quotes) unattractively and undistilled. The rule of thumb is: One thought only; four lines maximum. In other words, don't pack multiple thoughts or sentences into pullquotes. And don't let them run too deep on the page: Like a billboard, they need to be absorbed at a glance.

10. Using too many different kinds of typefaces in one newsletter. Three are enough—one for body type (and possibly the captions), one for headlines (preferably in bold), and one for the nameplate and standing heads (preferably a different font from your headline typeface).

11. Using too many different art styles or clip art sources.

12. Using too many different styles of boxes.

Type That Makes Things Easy for Readers

- Only about 7 percent of readers said they find body copy easy to read when it's set in capitals, according to a survey conducted by Colin Wheildon, an Australian journalist and typographer.

- Most respondents found black body type most attractive to the eye when seen against a 10 percent cyan background (blue-green hue). Legibility dropped sharply when the tint darkened to 20 percent.

- As for reverse text, 88 percent of readers found comprehension poor for white-on-black copy. (However, reverses can provide visual impact for department heads, and screened reverses can work well as headers or footers.)

- As for column width, 38 percent of respondents found copy hard to read when set in a measure wider than 60 characters per line; 8 percent found text hard to read when set at a measure narrower than 20 characters.

13. Using coarse laser printer screens instead of imagesetter output.

14. Using vertical rules that are too heavy. Vertical rules between columns should be hairline, ½ pt. or 1 pt. The reader can handle much fatter horizontal rules—they can be 2, 4, or 6 pt. in black, heavier if in a second color. But use the thinnest rule that does the job.

15. Using typewriter punctuation marks instead of typeset punctuation—that is, up-and-down quotes instead of curly quotes, two hyphens instead of an em dash, and underlined instead of italicized type.

Stay away from
too-heavy rules.

16. Setting captions for three-column photographs in a small, italicized type—often justified, too! Shorter captions, set flush-left/ragged-right, are often far more readable.

17. Lack of kerning. Few newsletter desktop publishers appear to take the time to reduce letter spacing in headlines, with the result that the headlines occupy more horizontal space than they need to.

18. Using centered headlines and subheads that may unnecessarily complicate browsing and trap white space.

19. Relying on unedited photographic images instead of cropping and sizing. Many photographs contain distracting foreground or background information that competes with the primary subject. Artwork placed between columns, causing lines to wrap on both the left and right sides, is also visually annoying.

20. Setting up background screens and drop shadows in the electronic file to be reproduced on a 300-dpi laser printer. If drop shadows or screens are needed, indicate their placement and let your commercial printer add them.

2.1.9   Twelve dos and don'ts for better newsletter design

1.   Research shows that most Americans scan a page diagonally from the upper-left-hand corner to the lower-right-hand corner. Position important elements where they're most likely to be seen.

2.   The prime area on any page is the center. An item in this location will rarely be missed.

3.   The poorest viewing area is the lower-left-hand corner. Never place an important article there.

Don't put
important
news in the
lower left
corner.

4.   Use the "dollar bill" rule to check your layout. A dollar bill should touch or cover at least one graphic element (headline, illustration, box, etc.) no matter where it's placed horizontally on a page.

5.   Try not to box more than one item per page. For maximum effect, limit boxes to two or three different kinds of content.

You Be the Judge

Look at three consecutive issues of your newsletter and use this checklist to rate its design as if you were a contest judge. This is the form actually used by one association's panel of judges. Each item is worth 4 points.

_____Stories of highest importance are on page 1.

_____Front page space is not given to routine coverage of past events (routine chapter meetings).

_____Each page has a focal point that dominates the page, gives it order, and characterizes the subject matter. It may be a major story, a photo, or a piece of art.

_____A consistent typeface has been used throughout the newsletter.

_____Headlines do not bump (run into each other at the tops of columns).

_____Each page includes a page number, the name of the publication, and the date of issue (running feet or running heads).

_____Stories are displayed in patterns that separate and spotlight each piece of content.

_____Story layout is simple and recognizes that readers read from left to right.

_____Columns are used.

_____White space is used effectively. It is floated to the outside margins of the publication and not trapped.

_____Graphics and illustrations enhance the meaning of the printed work they accompany.

_____The body type is set in a point size no smaller than 9 points, except in lists, which may use a smaller type size.

_____Material related to an article is packaged close to it (for example, a small, boxed story or graph).

_____Headlines generally fit their space, neither falling too short nor extending beyond column edges.

_____Headline type becomes smaller as readers move down the page.

_____Headlines mostly appear above or to the left of stories.

_____Headlines are easy to read. (They are in a readable type—generally sans serif—and are not all uppercase.)

_____The newsletter has a masthead (where the editor's name, phone number, and address are clearly apparent).

_____The nameplate is simple and easily readable.

_____The nameplate includes the date of issue and the name of the organization.

_____The newsletter uses subheads and bullets or boxes to break up long stretches of type.

_____Reproduction is clear and sharp, neither too light nor too dark.

_____Photos are used to preview and follow up events, picture people in the news, and identify writers.

_____Photos have captions that clearly define their contents.

_____Graphic statements are made using special typefaces, special headline arrangements, rules, screens, boxes and other devices.

Score:_____ (100 possible pts.)

40 (Weak)   60 (Fair)   80 (Good)   100 (Excellent)

Use this checklist to do a postmortem on your next issue

6. When using "rules" (horizontal and vertical lines), apply the Rule of Half. That is, select the line you want to use, then use one only half as thick. Subtler is better.

7. Frame each page with a consistent border of white space on the top, bottom, and sides of the page.

8. The ideal width of a column is 40 to 45 characters of type. This is the optimum distance the human eye can travel without strain.

9. For headlines, use type that's three times larger than the type used for body copy.

10. Never use type smaller than 9 points for text. If you have a large number of older readers, you may want to use 11- or 12-point type.

11. Each issue needs to be long enough to cover the subject, but short enough for a quick read. The same goes for the length of the articles in each issue.

12. If your readers save back issues, consider using three-hole-punched paper so they can put them in a binder.

2.1.10   The graphic ante has been upped for all publications

The odds of arriving at a successful layout are even better when a talented professional designer is on the case, detecting the likeliest graphic relationships and points of emphasis. But even when production reverts to lesser mortals, there's no excuse for a haphazard layout that has laziness or carelessness written all over it.

Good copy-fitting requires a relish for graphic details.

The plain truth is that readers won't tolerate confusing layout and unfriendly-looking type. They can tell the difference between generic clip art and a hand-drawn illustration style—and they resist overly slick or canned-looking art, period. Nobody enjoys peering into dark photos at groups of pinheaded strangers, and nobody reads captions set three columns wide in 7-point italic to find out who they are. Newsletters may be an informal vehicle, but they're inevitably compared on some level with all the sophisticated electronic graphics that show up even in magazine ads. The graphics ante has been permanently upped for news periodicals, too.

If a design is right for its content, it offers editors a flexible repertoire of contrasting and complementary layout possibilities within a consistent, recognizable design framework. Even if it's "only" four pages produced in WordPerfect for Windows and photocopied in black, a newsletter can be well designed within the production values chosen for it.

Thus this primer for well-intentioned newsletter editors who want to make sure the layout is as intentional as the content. If you're one of

About the Team of Word-People and Picture-People

Editors and designers must work together as a team. To function optimally they should keep two very important factors in mind:

Readers won't tolerate a confusing layout.

1. There's nothing new under the sun. Someone somewhere thought up the same idea or used the same trick. There is no point in trying to reinvent the wheel. All that is needed is to use common sense and intelligence in order to turn the same old tried-and-true materials into a fresh and unexpected mix. Such a new mix may well turn out to be clever and innovative, even original. Wonderful! But that's just gravy. Originality per se is not the purpose of the exercise. The true purpose is to make dull material interesting, thus to catch the reader's attention, hold it and transmit a message. To do this successfully means that we must make the most of those special qualities that are inherent in the material, be they thoughts, facts, words, images, charts, tables, diagrams or whatnot. We must bring those qualities out and give them unmistakable visibility, so they can do their attention-attracting and story-telling.

2. The vast majority of raw material we are faced with using in our publications is just plain dull. Most of it is repetition of, or (if we're lucky) variation on the same old themes whose importance lies in the information they contain. There's nothing wrong with that prosaic dullness. On the contrary: it provides an opportunity for editors and designers to become alchemists who transmute the dross into editorial gold.

Needed are imagination; ingenuity; courage; time; effort; and some investment of treasure of course. But above all, what is needed is clear editing: a lucid understanding of what the point of all the material is—the reason for publishing. Once that is articulated, it can be given visibility and emphasis by graphics. In fact, GRAPHICS = EDITORIAL TOOL. That is the secret formula. Like all such "secrets" it is both obvious and deceptively simple.

—Jan V. White, from *Graphic Idea Notebook*, 1980.

those normal people who plans to be newsletter editor for only a few years, you still need to do a creditable job during your stint.

But be warned: A little taste of the power of design may prove addictive. Many editors secretly think that designers have more fun than word people, who have to overcome readers' built-in resistance to… well, words. Editors who learn the concepts and some of the vocabulary can lend a hand in the "fun part," which is actually the pretty serious business of creating nonverbal cues.

2.2   Everybody understands what 'good' is...right?

As they perform quality control checks, all newsletter editors need to keep in their mind's eye the conventions that apply to newsletters from early in the process and on throughout. The goal is to present professional-looking content to readers, which means tailoring copy from the beginning to some extent to fit within the framework. Anyone can learn how to use these conventions and how to tighten copy when fitting it with edits to the layout. These are, at a minimum, the design-related tasks of editors. They can't be delegated to designers.

Beyond that, getting good at fitting copy requires a certain relish for noticing graphic details over time, looking critically at every direct mail letter, news-based magazine, daily newspaper, newsletter, and frozen pizza box that comes your way. Watch how other publications handle copy flow and place art. Listen to your designer.

But what does "professional-looking" mean, exactly? That's what all editors want, but it's not the same thing for every publication. (Not even the same thing for different editors of the same publication.)

In fact, everyone except trained editors and designers acknowledges good design mostly by ignoring it. That is, they pay attention to the content and read with interest. What they don't do is stop and remark admiringly, "What a crisp, contemporary display typeface this book uses! Optima combines the best of a subtle serif and a slightly condensed sans, while remaining within the ballpark of a typeface perfectly appropriate for the relatively conservative field of newsletter design itself."

The simplest layout should telegraph, 'Read me.'

We like what we like about design by letting it do its work as an unconscious persuader—and we come to recognize the quality of its performance with reflexive ease, the way we'd greet a friend.

We also recognize good design by what we don't do when we don't stop, stare, and marvel—out loud or in a quick, unconscious recoil from the cheesiness before us: "What the heck is going on here? I can't deal with this. What were they thinking? Did anybody actually think about any of this or just tape it together? My kid could design better than this." Editors, whose job it is to look at layout through the eyes of their readers, have to learn to see signs of under-design or over-design. Design is a tool, just like words are.

2.2.1   An infinite number of ways to succeed

Less than sterling newsletter design is bad in the same handful of ways. Good-looking design comes in many packages. (It's the opposite of Tolstoy's maxim about all happy families being alike, and all unhappy families being unhappy differently.)

What I mean is that there's a finite set of design conventions that should be observed (or broken deliberately—not by default from not knowing about them). There's a finite set of careless or mistaken design notions that can be avoided. And editors can learn these things. And must.

At a minimum, an editor of even the most conservative newsletter squelched by an unimaginative review board can advocate for presenting content to readers efficiently, unobtrusively, carefully. A simple layout doesn't have to be grim. The package should telegraph, "This is worth bothering to read."

2.2.2   Editors have to care about design

Page design—including type—is the face of the newsletter; words are the voice; art and photos are the expressive hands. Each newsletter has a distinctive message that isn't a fluid simply to be poured into an arbitrary container. If you've taken care with the layout, readers will trust at first glance that you've taken care with the content.

Good design is the absence of complexity.

Okay. We may not be able to specify how it got that way, but most of us can agree that in a well-designed newsletter several optimal situations will exist for readers. They will be able to tell, without guessing or straining, how to weigh the dozens of possible relationships between bits and pieces of graphics and text that exist in even the most straightforward four-page newsletter.

Designer Alex White says, "Good design is not the abundance of simplicity. It is the absence of complexity." Good newsletter design may not be easy to execute, but it makes information easy to track. Whether alone at the screen or working with a designer's preliminary proofs, editors must learn to ask the following questions and find answers for them as part of the layout process:

- Where does each new piece of information start and where does it stop—in each article, page, and spread, and across pages, too?

- Do closely related pieces of information on a page or a spread look like parts of a whole?

- Are unrelated pieces of information on a page or a spread set off clearly from each other?

- Do headlines provide clues to each piece of copy, no matter how small?

- Do articles that everybody needs to read look more important than "housekeeping" or lighter articles?

- Are all graphics and photos placed sensibly so they relate at first glance to the context of an article?

- Is any of the text hard to read for any reason? If so, why?

- Does every page have a few elements to break up gray body copy? But only one large, dominant graphic (if any)?

2.3 Design vs. production

It's helpful to make a distinction between design and production, though those if us who work with newsletters sometimes use these terms as if they're interchangeable.

- Design of any periodical is something that you do once every few years and essentially stick with until you do a redesign (though design decisions are made with every issue and, over time, alter the "purity" of the original template).

- Production is what you do every time you put an issue together— the making of countless specific decisions that vary with content.

Design is the artistic enterprise of creating images and impressions that result in a publication with a recognizable identity. It governs such basic decisions as the kind of grid, type, paper, illustration style, and colors you'll use each month.

Readers acknowledge good design mostly by ignoring it.

Production is the practical enterprise of creating pages within the framework of a design. Page design involves making decisions specific to each issue's little challenges—what to do about how dark the photos came out, how to fill the hole caused by the writer who didn't turn in the assigned article, and how much of the issue you can lay out and proofread before the holiday. Ultimately, production is all about deciding what gets put in, what gets left out, and what gets put where. Software is a means to those ends. This chapter won't tell you how to use your particular software, but it *will* give you an overview of all the design considerations that newsletter editors have to take into account.

It's worth the expense to have a professional designer create a one-of-a-kind design—or, at the very least, design a unique nameplate, pick a typeface, and set up a variety of complementary text formats within a template. It's lovely to have a staff designer to hand off the editorial to and to work with on fine-tuning the layout. And you'll require the services of a designer if you ever decide to redesign.

Even if you're not the person in your organization responsible for laying out each issue with desktop publishing software or if you use the services of a freelance or contract designer, as an editor you're part of the production process—issue after issue after issue.

Alex White's Advice for Communicative Design

It's tempting to change text size, mix several display typefaces, or alter the line spacing to stretch or compress type to fit the column, simply because the software makes it so easy to do. But the work of design is to compose elements so that they are maximally interesting and comprehensible to the reader. Maximally interesting does not mean Hey! Wow! Pow! Zoom! It means revealing the content of the story instantly and efficiently.

As a visual communicator, your job is to make sure the message is read and absorbed, not just to fill in all the space. Editors, writers, and designers, regardless of title, can contribute to the effectiveness of the visual material presented to the reader.

What will make someone want to read?

Design has evolved to reveal the relative importance of text elements and can affect a reader's first impression of whether the content is valuable, which is why bad design matters: People do judge a book by its cover (and a newsletter by its typeface).

To produce communicative design, you must put yourself in the reader's place. What will make someone want to read? Use well-written, informative headlines and subheads and select pictures that invite attention—not necessarily the prettiest ones. Don't go overboard with variety in an attempt to make the page look more interesting (in this regard, self-discipline is vital). Consider these four conventions:

- Good design requires sharply defined visual relationships. It requires the self-discipline to make similar elements consistently similar; after all, you can't make something pop out with importance if the surroundings are all busy being special.

- Good design requires breaking long blocks of copy into smaller, nonthreatening, undemanding segments. It requires different ways for the eye to enter copy easily, not just a linear path that begins with a title or a headline and abandons the reader to gray pages.

- Good design requires a clear page structure. Readers expect to glean information quickly, so scanning the page to find entrances must be effortless. Because the hierarchy of information must be neon bright, the designer must understand the material. Too much design is done without the designer's having read the material.

- Good design uses an external format, or grid, to organize material. A grid is simply a plan that gives starting points for the placement of elements. Unfortunately, a relentless grid may be substituted for thinking, and the result is a suffocating sameness throughout a publication. Knowing when to break the grid is an essential aspect of having one in the first place.

—adapted from an article by Alex White in *The Editorial Eye*

2.3.1 The role of editors in production

During production, the page designer's responsibilities are to

- format display and body copy according to the layout stylesheet,

- arrange articles starting with the cover page's primary or lead article or articles, then place features, departments, and columns working around the givens—standing material such as the table of contents, masthead, a self-mailer, and regular departments may need to appear on the same pages in each issue,

- choose appropriate variations within the grid for sizing blocks of copy and grouping related boxes, photos, and art (while separating them from other articles),

- incorporate revisions from proofreading and editorial review, and

- prepare files for printing.

The editor's chief contribution at the production stage is to help make sure the design uses all available space wisely. "Wisely" means (a) articles are arranged for maximum readability and proper emphasis and (b) the issue seems to contain an optimal amount and balance of useful content (not too much, not too little). It can be tempting to say "It all fits" and call it good, but an editor has to be sure that the value of the content isn't eclipsed by layout expediencies. That means keeping out graphic treatments that get in the way and encouraging or requesting graphics that make the layout easy to browse.

Here are the cardinal rules of the production process:

- **Cardinal Rule 1:** There's never "just enough" text. There's always too much or too little.

Text never, ever, ever fits just perfectly.

- **Cardinal Rule 2:** There's no prescribed way to go about completing a layout.

These "rules" require the editor to sit there and fill up space or cut copy out, either directly onscreen or by marking changes on a printout—onscreen can be faster, but marking on paper leaves a paper trail for proofreading changes carefully to make sure they haven't introduced errors.

Depending on your editorial mix, you may end up trimming several articles, leaving out some articles or photos entirely, writing copy to fit holes, cutting longer articles into two parts, with one to be held over, or all of these. (See "Putting the design into practice," pages 203–206, on putting an issue together from scratch by using a template.) The point is that editors are part of the production team, and the more they know about the production process, the better the communication back and forth will be.

2.3.2 Some core design concepts

There are a lot of ways to talk about the same core concepts, so it's a good idea to become familiar with the vocabulary of design.

Robin Williams, in *The Non-Designer's Design Book*, uses four organizing concepts when discussing a balanced layout: proximity, contrast, alignment, and repetition. They are techniques for highlighting content and shifts in content.

Alex White, in *Type in Use*, speaks of hierarchies that clearly align like elements and differentiate components, offering relationships and contrasts to the human eye. He speaks of the need to choose images based on the clues they offer to genuine expository content rather than on their prettiness or trendiness.

These designers are both really talking about using design to achieve unity—a harmonious cumulative effect, an overall image of things belonging where they are. Regardless of the vocabulary, editors need to look out for five main favors design can do for readers:

- Make things that aren't the same look different.
- Make things that are related look related.
- Make key editorial and images look dominant.
- Make secondary editorial and images look subordinate.
- Make editorial elements look familiar by signposting the same thing the same way each time with recurring graphic elements.

Newsletters are either text-dominant or image-dominant, depending on what the message is. The rule of consistent formatting applies in both cases, so as not to wear readers out with trying to interpret erratic variations. Jan V. White, in his book *Graphic Idea Notebook*, speaks of organizing information in "logical, accessible units" but also applying "verbo-visual spice"—novel graphic treatments that echo the meaning of the content. "Page layout," he writes, "is merely the last step of the editing process."

2.4 What editors need to know about the production phase

Production is the part of the editorial process when an issue is put together for readers within the framework of a comprehensive design (or template) that governs specific choices such as the number of columns (grid), typefaces, and so forth.

In the indexes of most books about desktop publishing and editing newsletters, there are only a few spotty, single-page references to pro-

Roasting Layout Chestnuts: These 'Rules of Thumb' Aren't True

Don't believe it when a well-meaning "helper" tells you to follow these "rules" that are really popular misconceptions.

- Two spaces are needed after periods and colons.
- All-caps heads grab attention.
- Extra space is needed between paragraphs as well as indents for every paragraph.
- It's a good idea to make some words bigger than others in heads and copy.
- Sans serif type for all body copy is modern looking and "clean."
- A lot of boldface will make copy stand out and readers pay attention.
- Italic type makes a long section or article look special and makes people want to read it.
- Red, brown, green, and yellow are happy colors to use for display type and body type, too. Yellow ink on gray paper is really special.
- Lots of exclamation points in heads and copy make readers enthusiastic!
- Horizontal and vertical rules should be placed between every article and photo on every page to contain content—kind of like a wire fence.
- Headlines have to fill the whole space over the article.
- Headlines have to summarize the content of an article.
- Pullquotes should be long and unedited.
- The bottoms of columns of an article have to align exactly.
- Justified type is more correct and professional and easier to read.
- A subhead should be placed every three paragraphs just to break up copy.
- If an article is about only one thing or one person, captions for photos in it are unnecessary.
- It's clever to jump an article three times to keep readers actively moving through the issue.

duction. There are two reasons for that: Production isn't a surgical shift from word processed text to finished layout—it's a painstaking sequence of draft layouts that incorporate rounds of editorial revision and become increasingly polished. And desktop publishers are often not responsible for moving the layout through rounds of review and revisions—but editors are.

During the production phase (misleadingly called the design phase as shorthand for designing pages), all the conventional elements of newsletter design at our disposal are considered as we search for solutions to the problems that arise. Choices don't happen all at once;

they can't, because they have concurrent consequences—making one little change here affects the way things work there.

That's why you need a schedule. You'll never be able to guess how quickly or how slowly the layout will evolve if left to its own rhythms—every issue is different. Every step in the process has to be allowed for, with a little wiggle room thrown in, and the process must move forward toward a printing and distribution deadline. Every snag along the way puts pressure on the rest of the steps down the line.

Every issue evolves a bit differently.

Editors who oversee production for even the simplest newsletter must know that it encompasses these basic steps (more or less, depending on how you combine them):

- Cleaning up files for importing into a desktop publishing program

- Creating a layout that places articles logically and attractively

- Choosing, creating, and placing heads, captions, and pullquotes and text boxes, photos, and art

- Copyfitting articles by cutting or reparagraphing, adding new copy, enlarging or shrinking photos and illustrations

- Proofreading the text and layout for typos, style inconsistencies, formatting errors, and garbled, incomplete, or missing copy

- Preparing files to go to the printer

- Checking the blueline (last chance before printing the run) for errors of imposition and registration, pagination, folding, trimming, and perhaps checking a color proof for color and trapping.

2.4.1   Keep production in mind from the start

For editors, production really starts the day the first draft is assembled for review, and it continues down the line with each improved version. It's probably best to keep making revisions in word processed copy for as long as possible—it's more efficient for editors to finalize text and get the necessary signoff for the draft manuscript before trying to lay it out. Editors who are trying to do it all, typing directly into a layout program and fitting as they go, may find it less stressful to make edits first and then import word processed text so they can concentrate on layout issues separately.

You have to be awfully skilled (or an old newspaper person) to type directly into layout. Work in your word processing software as long as you can so ideas can take the shape they need to take instead of the shape of the space that happens to be on a certain page at a certain time. Copy needs to be written first (so you know that all the key points are there) and only then tailored to fit the space.

Each round of revisions must be carefully made so that as far as possible the draft coming in for layout is clean (free from typos and extraneous formatting, complete, and organized roughly the way final copy should look. At each step, editorial revisions must be checked—it's a mistake to wait until the very end, when it may be impossible to find any errors that have been introduced.

And because each time a change is made—a text wrap adjusted, a new paragraph indented, three hyphens in a row corrected by rebreaking words at the end of the lines, a subhead added—text shrinks or flows forward, so new layout tweakings are inevitable. A lot of patience is required to stick with the increasingly small but telling details of layout editing.

At least three classic newsletter references advise editors to "let things go" when they get close to acceptable. With desktop publishing in every office, the standards are higher for us all and we're tempted to tweak the tweaks.

Check every round of revisions and the changes they cause.

As long as there's anything important out of whack, keep looking for solutions. "Good enough" for newsletters means something different now—in the early 1990s, we couldn't have imagined sending film directly to print for "just a newsletter."

Simple, uncluttered pages are fine, but pages that are dingy, crowded, or pockmarked with trapped white space won't do—whether from a homeowners' association, a district legislator, or a local PTA group. We don't want to force our readers to bob and weave defensively to dodge aggressive graphics, but we do want to lighten a page that would lack all relief from serious black type. Editors are the guardians of the compromise between the two extremes.

That's also what a production schedule is for—to assign an expiration date to the inclination of editors (or at least the ones like you and me—you know, the good ones) to press toward perfection when good enough really has been reached.

Without deadlines, no newsletter would ever emerge. Nor would any newsletter editors and designers maintain their sanity. The following section lists possible layout errors worth detecting and fixing before sending files to the printer.

2.4.2 The cornerstones of every good layout

Use the questions in the checklist on pages 108–110 as a diagnostic check-up to help you home in on both the structural fine points and the overall "face" your newsletter presents to the world. With your almost-final layout in front of you, look at each page and then each spread and appraise, as honestly as you can, what you see—while there's still time to change it.

Keep in mind that, although production values and budgets vary, all editors need a layout characterized by its *legibility*, *readability*, and *browsability*. This entire checklist boils down to two cornerstones:

- Consistent, legible type—large enough, dark enough, with enough leading—and generous white space are required for readability and logical organization of a variety of content for serious readers.

- Consistent, unintrusive graphics—art and photos that reinforce copy points without detracting from them—steer readers as they browse, help editorial priorities emerge, and make the act of reading feel less yeomanlike.

Remember the ultimate question to ask yourself: If you weren't being paid to do this, if you had to read it on your own time, and if you didn't know all the work it took to get it into being, would *you* want to read it?

____ Is the logotype or nameplate memorable?

____ Is the publication designed so the first thing you see creates interest regardless of whether you start with the front or back page first?

____ Do table of contents page numbers match the actual locations of articles?

____ Is standing or recurring material easy to find from issue to issue?

____ Is it clear where articles end and new ones begin?

____ Is there a good mix of article lengths—some short, some longer, perhaps a roundup of news items?

____ Is the text typeface of appropriate size and weight (9 to 11 points)?

____ Is typographic unity achieved in headlines, department heads, and pullquotes by using bold, extra bold, italic, etc., in one or at most two display typefaces?

____ Are captions, bylines, and pullquotes treated consistently?

____ Have pullquotes been limited to one clear thought set off sufficiently from body copy?

____ Is the same type treatment used throughout for equivalent kinds of content?

____ Is a typographic hierarchy achieved by using consistent typeface treatments throughout for each head level (kicker, main headline, deck, subheads, run-in subheads)?

____ Are the layouts clean rather than cluttered or gimmicky?

____ Do too many rules and boxes clutter the page?

____ Are the pages laid out so that important stories have headlines at the top of the page and related stories or boxes are clearly subordinate?

____ Are heads vertically stacked too deeply or tombstoned (placed side by side horizontally)?

____ Do run-in heads offer a break from the relentless march of either subheads or unadorned paragraphs?

___ Does display type for heads create appropriate contrast with body copy?

___ Are all headlines free of typos?

___ Have subheads been used in longer articles as both transitional devices and entry points for browsers?

___ Are italics or boldface used correctly, consistently, and effectively to format special material?

___ Do elements such as drop caps, sidebars, and text variation within the grid enhance layout and break up copy?

___ Are subheads bold enough to contrast with body type without competing with main heads?

___ Are cutlines (captions) smaller so that they don't compete with body copy or other heads?

___ Does one—and only one—element (story, head, photo, etc.) dominate each page?

___ Are dominant page elements balanced on each page and relative to elements across each spread?

___ Do facing pages balance without being boringly symmetrical?

___ Do pages seem too plain or stripped down?

___ Does the layout reward browsers with many "gold coins" of visual interest?

___ Does each page offer readers several different points of entry into copy?

___ Do screened boxes add variety and contrast to the layouts?

___ Is spot color used effectively (not overdone)?

___ Can readers follow a story without guessing when it jumps from column to column or page to page?

___ Are all graphics and clip art well executed, colorful, and related to content?

___ Do charts and graphs have clear captions and stubs, and is the information easy to extract?

___ Do line lengths (columns) seem too wide or too narrow for comfortable reading?

___ Does word spacing in body copy avoid being "holey" or too crowded? Are the layouts "clean" and uncluttered looking?

___ Do margins offer enough white space?

___ Is enough white space used to set off pullquotes and other editorial elements?

___ Is unnecessary white space "trapped" anywhere?

___ Do all characters at the left margin align?

___ Does copy avoid word division repetitions (the same letters at the end of one line and the beginning of the next) and doublets (the same word at the end of one line and the beginning of the next)?

___ Are page lengths consistently within the ballpark even if they don't align perfectly across the bottom? (The exception is an intentionally scalloped alignment.)

continued on page 110

continued from page 109

___ Is paragraph length about right but not monotonously the same?

___ Are lines free of bad breaks, widows, and orphans?

___ Has the right margin been adjusted (ragged) to avoid excessive hyphenation and holes?

___ Are complex or lengthy lists of items formatted as bulleted lists?

___ Is bulleted material punctuated correctly and formatted consistently?

___ Has typeset, not typewritten, punctuation been used throughout?

___ Are all continuations where promised?

___ Does the layout avoid jumping from—or to—a little bit of copy that could be copyfitted to avoid the jump?

___ Are photos of generally high quality?

___ Is distracting background cropped out of photos?

___ Do photo captions give the reader a reason to turn to body copy for more information?

___ Do photos related to an article make sense where they're placed?

___ Do standalone photos carry enough of a caption to work as a photo essay?

___ Will readers see evidence that a coherent editorial vision underpins each issue?

___ Does the overall look set the right tone: professional, friendly, cutting-edge, reassuringly conservative?

___ Overall, does the layout accommodate the somewhat indefinable "human element"? How reader-based is it? Check for some or all of these:

- ❑ Plenty of high-quality photos and direct quotations
- ❑ Short Q & A features or reader-friendly surveys
- ❑ Fact boxes: important who-what-when-where-why
- ❑ Helpful nuggets: hotlines, how-to, dos-and-don'ts
- ❑ Reviews of resources and analysis of news events
- ❑ Bulleted lists that outline complex or numerous items
- ❑ Advice and news about professional advancement

___ Overall, does this newsletter seem tired or does it seem filled with signs of life, energy, and commitment to reporting time-worn issues with a fresh spin?

2.5   How editors can help simplify production

For every newsletter, there's always a layout revision stage—really a series of giant steps followed by the baby steps of final quality control review. Editors can help this process go more smoothly by cleaning up text before it's imported into layout software and formatting copy right from the beginning as close to the way it needs to appear as possible. Here are some specific examples:

- Print the storylist and the entire word processed draft. Group articles in the order that you'd like to see repeated in the layout; note sidebar material, possible pullquotes, and filler that can go anywhere. Write captions and note where they will go. The designer will create separate files for placing articles, but the printout with notes is a helpful master plan that shows how pieces of copy are intended to work together.

- Apply italic, boldface, real fractions, typeset dashes, and ellipses where you want them. Use your master printout to check whether they've been coded and applied properly in the layout. There's nothing quite so sad as good writing that shows up in print without professional-looking typesetting.

- Break out any long direct quotes (longer than five lines) into block indented paragraphs. That will help avoid long paragraphs.

- Make sure sentences aren't much longer than 35 words and paragraphs are only three to five sentences long. But all sentences and paragraphs shouldn't be exactly the same length: One long sentence may be an entire paragraph, especially in a three-column layout. The idea is to not blot out the sun with too much dark type—"gray" pages look like too much work to read.

Build in room for subheads and captions from the start

- Write subheads and captions early. Build them in, don't "wait and see if there's room," because these elements aren't luxuries. It's easier to cut copy now than to make room for subheads later in the layout.

- Break out any long series (of names, items, steps, requirements, and such) in text to be a bulleted list (wherever it makes sense editorially—see page 262). This builds white space into body copy and highlights the material in the list.

- Ask for a runover page (also called *overset copy*—the concluding text of articles that are too long for their slot in the layout) to be printed out so you can look at overflow copy while deciding how you want to revise articles. It's easy when cutting copy to lose key transitions and important information if you trap yourself into just sticking words into the rectangles of a layout. If the writing seems disconnected, the layout's no good no matter how good it looks.

2.5.1 Keep things predictable from issue to issue

Be aware of your limitations—of time and energy. Recognize that you need more rather than less structure, and try to reduce unnecessary editorial variables. That means good planning before layout begins. Try to work with your designer (or the designer part of your own brain) to set the layout up so that your need for content and graphics becomes fairly predictable for each issue. You'll know about how many articles your storylist needs to include and about how long they can be.

You're going to have to compromise.

The more copyfitting and copy expanding edits you do, the more accurate you get at providing content that works in the first few passes for your design. And if you have a short list of preferences for article placement, speak up, but understand that the designer may not be able to honor them all...unless you trade off something else that's become a sticking point.

At the production stage, everything's a trade-off. You can have it fast or you can have it good or you can have it cheap. But you can't have all three. You can claustrophobically preserve every last word of your draft, or you can have orderly pages that give text breathing room. But you can't have both.

2.5.2 Proofread so nothing gets lost in the shuffle

Newsletters are, by their discontinuous nature, vulnerable to errors that nobody sees until it's too late. Layout requires both mechanical and aesthetic decisions about shape, size, and proportion, such as how to crop and place photos. Proofreading is where you find mistakes you've made in layout and incongruities that crept in as copy and art were moved around and tweaked.

At every checking step, read through for copy that's been left out and for garbled copy. At layout, neither editor nor designer is reading words anymore: Both are moving chunks of information around. Besides, by now the editor has seen too many versions of the text to be aware of discrepancies.

If you cut a paragraph, did you paste it somewhere? If you cut a paragraph, did you paste it twice? If you've cropped someone out of a photo, did you edit that person out of the caption—and vice versa? Remember:

- *Never* make a change without checking it, especially if it's a single, "simple" change.

- *Always* get somebody else to read the newsletter all the way through at one sitting.

It's the no-brainers that nobody's paying close attention to that wind up in print as mistakes that make editors look like...no-brainers. (See the Newsletter Proofreading Checklist on page 61.)

2.6 Production and printing decisions

One of the things that novice editors get themselves into trouble over is not knowing the implications of their decisions for printing quality and costs. For example, if you're sending off camera-ready laser pages directly for printing, you don't want to have screens or photos— because they'll reproduce badly. Going to the trouble of setting things up in your software and putting pretty scanned images on a page is a waste of time if it doesn't mean those pages will print well.

Become best friends with a good printer.

If your goal is to hand over an electronic file to the printer (and your newsletter will look better if you do), you have to know something about setting files up properly. That means working directly with your printer. Some editors rely on their printer to create a layout from their copy and photos, but most printers don't want you to hand them a finished newsletter in a word processing software. They prefer the relative predictability and reliability of a PageMaker or QuarkXPress file. If you're going to use something else, you (or your designer) will have to learn to create PostScript files. Make sure you research ahead of time what your printer's capabilities and requirements are, and ask questions about compatibility with the layout software and platform you plan to use.

In fact, one of the best things an editor can do is learn just enough about printing to be able to hand off properly prepared files. Knowing your limitations and making best friends with a conscientious, responsive printer are the two best ways to avoid expensive on-press corrections and disappointing print quality.

2.7 What editors need to know about typography

As Alex White says, "the music is not in the violin" when it comes to computer-assisted page layout; it still takes human orchestration. Although software makes templates and lots of options available, the newsletter editor sitting at the computer is not often trained to be a page designer—that is, not trained to know what will appeal to readers.

What editors have to learn, White says, is that "the human eye looks for relationships and contrasts (similarities and differences); they're flip sides of the same coin. Two or more typographic, photographic, or illustrative elements that share qualities—same size, shape, color, or position—create a relationship." The reverse is also true.

Three Basic Printing Concepts

Like computers, printing presses are stupid. They're either on or off, yes or no, ink or no ink. Three concepts control everything about putting ink on paper:

1. For every color, a plate is used on press (one plate equals one color). In the electronic file, you have to arrange for color breaks and color separations. More plates mean more costs.

2. Line art, tone art, shades of gray, scans—all break down into dots, the linchpin of printing. The resolution at which the dots are printed (the linescreen) determines the quality of the image.

3. Process colors and spot colors are used differently.

Editors who don't have a lot of experience and lack design help should rely on the printer to output halftones. Place a scan FPO (for position only) to help the printer place photos and other art, and let him or her deal with appropriate linescreens and color separations.

A big problem for printers is graphics files produced in, say, a presentation software that isn't meant to go out for printing—colors are defined differently when the image is meant to be produced as a negative for slides. If your printer has to bring files into an illustration program first and manipulate and edit them for you, you'll pay extra.

Another problem is inconsistent definition of colors in software. There are three shades of black—which do you want? The available color palette has to be used selectively or you may inadvertently be telling the printer to use more color plates than you meant to and end up with a color you didn't want—and pay more for the privilege, too.

Establishing relationships and contrasts means making sure that readers aren't distracted or confused by what they see. The countless small decisions that an editor makes about what goes where on a page add up. White says: "If two or three out of ten decisions made for a single page are bad—for example, too many characters per line, misalignment of headline and subhead, and too narrow an outside margin—the page will be sufficiently disturbed to slightly repel readers."

2.7.1 Learning to look at type

Noted typographer and author Daniel Will-Harris made a strong case in an article in *The Editorial Eye* that type is the newsletter editor's closest ally. He believes that type "sets the style and tone of a document, colors readers' interpretation of the words, and defines the feeling of the page. While most readers don't consciously notice typefaces, they work as powerful if unconscious persuaders." People will notice that a newsletter seems serious, or silly, or modern, without realizing that type is at work.

Overall, the basics of good type are a matter of personal preference and common sense. Here are Will-Harris's simple rules for using type. You don't even have to memorize them if you don't want to; just tape them up on the wall and check them once in a while:

■ Body text should be between 10 and 12 point, with 11 point best for printing to 300 dots-per-inch (dpi) printers. Use the same typeface, type size, and leading (or line spacing) for all body copy within a document.

Replace underlining with real italic.

■ To be sure you're using enough leading, always add at least 1 or 2 points to the type size: If you're using 10-point type, use 12-point leading. (Automatic line height in most layout software will do this for you.) Never use less leading than this or your text will be too dense.

■ Don't make your lines too short or too long. The optimum length is more than 30 characters but fewer than 70.

■ Use only one space after a period, not two.

■ Don't justify text unless you have to because if you do, you must use hyphenation.

■ Make paragraph beginnings clear. Choose either indent or block style. Don't use both.

■ Use italics instead of underlines throughout copy.

■ Don't set blocks of more than a few words in italics, bold, or all caps because they're hard to read.

■ Don't put rules under heads or subheads. Instead of adding emphasis, rules isolate heads from the body text to which they belong.

■ Leave more space above headlines and subheads than below them, and avoid setting them in all caps. Use subheads liberally to help readers find what they're looking for.

2.7.2 "What font should I use?"

Typefaces are neither good nor bad, but instead more or less appropriate. The key to choosing the best typeface for the job is finding the most appropriate one. Here's Will-Harris's advice for choosing type.

> If your copy has to be easy for anyone of any age with any kind of eyesight to read under any kind of lighting, then the typeface must fit those criteria. You'll probably end up with something that has a large x-height such as Cheltenham, Melior, or Serifa.

> If the piece needs to look traditional, then you should choose a typeface such as Centaur, Bembo, Bodoni, Galliard, Palatino, or Weiss. If

Typography Is the Thread That Binds

Type holds a publication together. It's the constant, the thread leading from spread to spread. It's crucial to the life of your publication that type be presented consistently and in a way that makes sense to the reader. Steady use of a single typeface family unifies the pages of a publication. You'll tire of your typography long before your readers do. Develop a system that works for your particular needs and stick to it.

Type choices are crucial to your publication's image.

- **Restrict your use of typefaces.** Use the least possible number of typefaces, sizes, and weights to create clear differentiation and hierarchy, while still allowing for flexibility as unusual circumstances warrant. When in doubt, do not make a special change. Your readers are well served if you err on the side of typographic consistency. If your system is thoughtfully devised, the variations in your regular typographic arsenal will cover any situation. Making special changes or experimenting from page to page or issue to issue confuses and severely weakens the unity of your product. Minor typographic variations distract the reader from the content. And creating style exceptions takes a lot of time and invites formatting errors, as well.

- **Standardize columns and type specifications.** Column structure and text type together create a publication's personality. Taking a standard three-column format and shoving interesting display type at the tops of the columns results in uninformed design. Using a unique column structure so that all type looks distinctive to this publication is informed design. Flush-left/ragged-right type is an all-purpose setting in which word spacing is always consistent, regardless of the column width. Justified type, in contrast, achieves two smooth edges at the expense of even word spacing: Each line of type is sucked out to or shoved into the full measure, and word spacing is automatically inserted or deleted as needed. This is a minor distraction in lines that have at least 40 characters, but shorter justified lines can create horrible word spaces. You can avoid the problem by setting all type flush left/ragged right and allowing hyphenation. The idea that justified type looks more dignified is nonsense.

- **Catalog all essential typographic treatments** for the past year's worth of issues of your publication, and develop a system of text settings and column placements that can accommodate all those circumstances. It is extremely likely that future stories can be made to behave like one of those past articles.

- **Standardize type placement.** After you have decided on type specifications, determine exactly where every element will be placed, how far from the trim, how far from other type elements. Also decide how much space there will be between picture and caption, between headline and subhead, between subhead and text. This space management makes your publication look clear and well organized. It will make readers trust and value the content.

—Alex White, from an article in *The Editorial Eye*

you want something casual and friendly, choose something like Souvenir or Bitstream Cooper.

Check out Esperfonto on my Web site at **http://www.willharris.com/ esp**. Esperfonto is an interactive (hypertext) system that helps you choose the most appropriate typeface for your particular job. Tell it whether your piece is formal or casual, and then choose from a number of impressions. Esperfonto will provide you with a list of typefaces that fit your needs. If you don't know what they look like, Esperfonto even provides on-screen samples. Or look at type samples in books and decide for yourself.

2.8   Choosing, placing, and editing images

Collections of illustrations can be bought from clip art and stock photo publishers; digital cameras may be a solution for some editors who need a lot of relatively simple original photos. Printers can size, crop, and place such graphics for you if you (or your designer) can scan images and photos into position. You'll want to choose a page layout program that's compatible with the graphics programs you have access to and expertise with so that all art can be part of the electronic file. Colors can be set in the program or specified for the printer.

Not all newsletter editors have the luxury of a designer who can use paint and image editing programs or the budget to buy stock art and color reproduction. Their newsletters will need to take advantage of intelligent grayscale design and scanning. Most scanner software saves files as halftones or grayscale images, and there are books dedicated to the art of making do with only black as a "color." Remember that nothing is as legible as black type on white paper, so if you use grayscale images, use only high-quality originals. A black and white and gray newsletter on bright white paper can be as striking—or boring— as one with a second color. But it'll cost less no matter what.

Nobody loves content like the editor.

Who's responsible for choosing, placing, and editing images—editors or designers? Yes. Together. Not every editor will be able to put a request in to an art director for a photo shoot and contact sheets or ask a designer to pick a batch of PhotoCD images for approval. Not every editor can even count on someone's off-kilter candid photos of the annual picnic. And being a designer doesn't mean knowing the best angle for a photo or knowing what the chief copy points are—even if he or she has read the whole thing. Remember, nobody loves your content as much as you do and nobody is a better judge of whether the proposed graphics serve them. Here are the main things to remember:

- Hold out for the best image you can find or create to illustrate a copy point or topic. Refuse to accept second best until you have to.

- If you have to use a mediocre photo or a less-than-artistic illustration, make up for it with a killer caption or tasteful screening and subordinate placement that doesn't call undue attention to the image.

- Never use even a high-quality image if it doesn't contribute something strong to the editorial. Art for art's sake doesn't apply in newslettering.

- Trust your designer to choose images and edit them to fit the layout, but reserve the right to ask for them to be placed more or less prominently in light of your editorial intentions.

- When things go right and graphics add life to your copy, and photos of real, live people make your pages pop with energy, remember to thank your designer or your printer, or, if you did it, treat yourself to something chocolate. It's no mean feat when graphics and copy work together.

2.8.1 Photos are the graphic most often used in newsletters

Photos are associated with breaking news, reality as opposed to fiction, and being worth a thousand words. The good ones, that is.

Light, shadow, and strong forms are the three basic building blocks of photographic composition. Most newsletter editors have to use photos that aren't of very high quality: The ideal photo has one dominant focal point and is cleanly framed, crisply focused, well lit, creatively posed, and identifiable at a glance as something interesting. (See the gallery of Don'ts for examples and discussions of photos.)

The best photos are full of life.

Amateur photographers are often uncertain about what to focus on and settle for capturing the obvious. The main offenders to avoid if you can (and you won't always be able to) are really problems of perspective—as in lack of life, which is the very thing photos can add to a layout:

- "grip and grin" award and greeting shots of people facing the camera head-on

- group shots with too many people arranged in institutional rows

- extraneous background or foreground "stuff" distracting from the central person

- small people too far away under a huge sky or ceiling

- static shots of buildings and landscapes that look like either postcards or advertising brochures

2.8.2   Three steps to better photos

A fat envelope arrives from the photographer. With a sense of hope tinged with worry, you slide a finger under the flap and peek inside. The quality of what lies on the contact sheets you pull out depends on several factors.

Access to a talented photographer helps, and so does having a photogenic subject or event. But that's the ideal. Usually you have only one or neither. As a result, many corporate newsletter and magazine layouts are filled with gray, lifeless shots called "grip-and-grins": Ernest Salesguy Accepts a Quota Completion Certificate from Joe Superior. Yawn.

The best photos tell a story.

If you don't have an art director on staff, you can still work toward a more professional appearance for the images you want to publish. Try these three steps:

- Define what a good photo is for your publication.

- Take control of the assignment process and photo specs.

- Think of dynamic photo placement when it comes to layout.

2.8.3   Define 'a good photo'

A good photo—of even an ordinary scene—manages to convey human emotion and pulls the viewer in. It may also define an extraordinary moment. For instance, a shot of Ernest Salesguy getting a high-five from his peers as he returns to his seat at the awards dinner shows a lot more about the excitement behind his award than the stock grip-and-grin.

A good photo is, of course, in focus and lighted correctly. Even one fuzzy, dark, or flashed-out photo can degrade the reader's perception of an entire layout, and it ruins the effect of an otherwise engaging image.

But the best photos don't just show something: They *say* something. They tell a story. Let's say that you have two photos from a speaking engagement, one of the speaker and one of the crowd giving him a standing ovation. And let's say that the technical quality of both images is excellent. But everybody already knows what a person standing behind a podium looks like. The other shot, the more interesting one, actually says something about what happened; it would be the better choice (at the least, it should be run larger than the speaker shot).

2.8.4   Take control of the specs

Maybe the photographer is just as sick of boring photos as you are and is itching to display more creativity. The trouble is, you've both been operating under the HWADI (How We've Always Done It) Plan. Be sensitive, but introduce the idea that you need to rethink the kinds of photos you've been using. If you work with a number of outside photographers, draft a set of specifications for all of them that spell out exactly what you want. Include samples of photos you like as well as ones you don't. Specify whether you want black-and-white or color shots and what form they should be delivered in (slides, prints, contact sheets, or undeveloped film).

You're not publishing scrapbook pages.

Next, create an assignment sheet that can be filled out for each new job; an electronic template you can fill out on screen is convenient. Note whether you need a vertical or horizontal shot (or both, for the most options at layout time); what the photo should show; specific emotions you'd like to see; how many frames you need; what the deadline and fee are; and other particulars. Include some blank lines for handwritten notes, as well as your name, phone number, and e-mail address in the event questions should arise.

If you're not in charge of the quality—that is, photos are plopped onto your desk and you're expected to use them—make it known that you will no longer be running crummy images. When you begin to accept only high-quality shots, contributors will hesitate before sending you anything less.

2.8.5 Think 'dynamic placement'

Page design may or may not be your domain, but it pays to remember that the goal in laying out photos is to create attention-grabbing spreads, not scrapbook pages. Even before layout begins, you must call into action the same editing skills you use on text: Select only the best photos (in terms of quality and content) and crop them tightly to eliminate clutter and excess information.

Contrast of scale is your best tool when laying out photos. Here's why: A page full of same-size photos is as dull and lifeless as a lunar landscape. There's no focal point to attract the eye. If you use one or two photos that are larger than all the other elements on the page, you create a doorway the viewer can use to enter the page and get involved. Or pick one great shot, enlarge it, and use it by itself. (But don't enlarge poor-quality photos: You'll only emphasize the grain in the film, the lack of focus, or both.)

Other ideas:

- Run a photo or two at a slight angle.

- Apply a filter in a photo-manipulation program that fuzzes out everything but the main subject of the photo (ideal for picking the main subject out of a crowd shot).

Graphic Resources

There are more resources for newsletters than you can ever investigate. Here are a few, just to give you an idea of the scope of what's out there:

Aridi Computer Graphics Library. Five volumes of borders, initial caps, and ornaments on a "hybrid" CD-ROM (for both PC and Mac). Call 800-755-6441 or 214-404-9171.

Arrowglyphs Clip Art Collection. About 600 hand-drawn color and black-and-white illustrations on nature, wildlife, energy, pollution, recycling, and general environmental themes. Call Arisen Corporation at 800-243-1515 or 717-296-5490.

Art on the Net Project. Works like a public gallery; images can be viewed, copied, and distributed electronically. Users must verify copyright status, request permission from creators to re-use images, and meet their stipulations. Most images may not be edited but may be resized. Visit http://www.art.net.

Arts and Letters Graphics Software. Downloadable free fonts, clip art, and graphics software demos. Also bargains on PC-based software and accessories. Visit www.art-letters.com or call 800-752-9057.

Designer's Club. A monthly subscription art and idea service. Includes *Ideas and Images* magazine. View images at www.dgusa.com. Call Dynamic Graphics, Inc. at 800-255-8800 for a free brochure.

Fontek DesignFonts. Fully editable spot illustrations in a range of styles "from medieval drawings to funky high-tech objects" at a cost of about a dollar an image. Call Letraset, 800-343-TYPE.

FontHaus Picture Fonts. An offbeat collection of startling and humorous clip art illustrations. Call MVB, 800-942-9110 or 203-367-1993.

The Graphic Designer's Sourcebook. Poppy Evans has collected more than 1,000 listings that tell you how to find studio supplies, illustrations, clip art, photographic stock and resources, computer fonts, printing and finishing services, papers, packaging, and more. Call North Light Books, 800-289-0963.

Megatoons. More than 1,000 original Phil Frank illustrations intended to enliven stale layouts and defuse potentially sensitive editorial with gentle humor. Call CMS, 800-358-2278 or 510-843-3408.

Past-Tints Antique Illustrations. Detailed clip art images, all 100 years old, for a wide range of traditional topics. Call Periwinkle Software at 800-730-3556 or 909-593-5062.

PhotoDisc Starter Kit. Over 9,000 royalty-free photographic images plus 300-page reference book. Call 800-528-3472.

Publisher's Toolbox: A Catalog for Digital Artists and Designers. Discounted software, accessories, EPS images of corporate and association logos and trademarks, computer medical illustrations, and high resolution, royalty-free (photographic) images on CD-ROM. Call 800-390-0461.

United Media's Comic Search Electronic Library. For a fee that can be applied against the reprint cost, this service checks archives for a selection of comics on your topic. Fees somewhat negotiable. Call 800-211-4816, ext. 603.

Resources for clip art and other graphics are more abundant and affordable than they've ever been.

- Use three or four photos showing different stages of the same action to indicate process.

- Try a round crop (head shots only).

- Crop to create another unusual shape, say, extremely thin and vertical.

- If you're dealing with mug shots, don't run them in a checkerboard-like block. Instead, place them in a horizontal or vertical line, or use them as insets to the text.

For inspiration in layout, the coffee-table-size annuals published by the Society of Publication Designers (212-983-8585) can be found in most larger libraries. North Light Books (800-239-0963) also publishes how-to books on publication design, many of which are in bookstores.

(The material on better photography was adapted from an article by Catharine Fishel in *The Editorial Eye*.)

2.8.6   Using clip art well is an art

Newsletter editors have a wonderful resource in the many CD-ROMs of images organized by editorial topic and kind of image. As Chuck Green says in *Clip Art Crazy* (which comes with a disk of 500 royalty-free images),

> The beauty of electronic clip art is that virtually every desktop publishing, word processing, and presentation software package has the tools to import, size, and crop it. Graphics software gives you the power to edit it, and both laser and graphics printers will print it. All you need is a CD-ROM drive attached to your computer and you're ready for liftoff.

Don't get carried away with witches.

The two main kinds of electronic files for clip art are what's known as object-oriented or "draw" graphics (they use lines, ovals, rectangles, curves) and bitmapped or "paint" graphics (they divide artwork into tiny dots and give a more nearly photographic likeness).

The problem is that new editors and designers can get carried away with all the options: little witches and people on bicycles and generic shadow people in the grip of silhouetted handshakes. (See the Design Gallery for examples of clip art that works and clip art that doesn't work.)

2.8.7   Clip art basics

A few editors may still be using cut-and-paste clip art books like the ones Dover Press (still) publishes, but most editors and designers try to make the best use they can of editable electronic clip art. Clip art for newsletters usually encompasses "spot" pictures, illustrations, or images

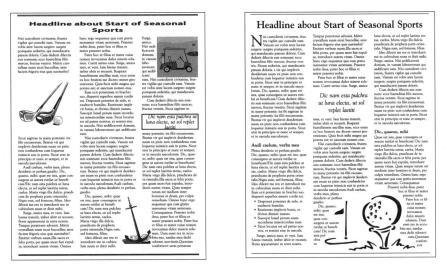

On the left, too many dated, miscellaneous images add little to content; awkward, intrusive, space-trapping placement in grid and bad text wraps make graphics a liability rather than an asset. On the right, the display cap is a better graphic entry point than huge golf clubs floating in space. Using subheads and a bulleted list breaks copy into digestible pieces. A single contemporary "tee off" graphic underlines the seasonal topic without intruding, and it's balanced by a restful pullquote that's not squeezed into a tight box.

originally drawn by somebody else, though it also covers icons, symbols, logos, borders, and display type that can be added with a keystroke from font software.

There's nothing inherently amateurish about clip art despite frequent sneers that it's by definition inferior to "original" spot illustrations. Chosen and incorporated with care, clip art can be a good way to spice up pages, not clutter them. Even collections of images that come bundled with other products can be used effectively—if they're used with restraint and imagination. (Once again the need for newsletter editors and designers to use a fairly conservative hand in the service of a discerning, twinkling eye.)

Clip art doesn't kill a layout— careless artists do.

Not only is the graphic quality of contemporary images better, the sheer variety now available on CD-ROM and downloadable from the Internet gives editors-who-do-it-all a better shot at creating handsome layouts. Newsletters on a tight budget no longer have to look as if a musty grab bag of illustrations was brought down from the attic and plundered at the last minute. (A range of clip art publishers can be found on page 121.)

Here are some guidelines for editors:

- Most CD-ROM collections of images come with a license agreement that spells out what you can do with them. Some images are sold for one-time use; others may be used an unlimited number of times.

- Remember that editing an image in Photoshop doesn't make it yours. The test for infringement is whether someone looking at the original alongside your adaptation can tell that you've made a copy, albeit edited. Assume that all images are protected by copyright.

- Avoid buying dated-looking, overly familiar bulk clip art images— "50,000 generic images of 1950s-style silhouettes for $19.95." Most of them aren't worth your consideration aesthetically to begin with, and few will be relevant to your content. You can choose from countless distinctive styles, a couple of which will surely be appropriate for your content and compatible with your design.

Don't ask for image edits that will take forever.

- Pick a style of clip art from one publisher and stick with it, perhaps with a compatible back-up source for hard-to-find images. One of the biggest temptations new and volunteer editors face is the Sin of Excess Clip Art—too many bits and pieces of it on each page and too many different styles scattered throughout.

- Every desktop publishing program lets you import, size, and crop clip art; you'll have to learn which file format takes best advantage of your page layout program and, conversely, which tools you'll need to add to handle the images you want to use. Graphics software lets you edit images—add light or shadow, add or subtract details, highlight curves or lines—and graphics conversion tools help you import images (both in software and from the Web) that you want to use when your page layout program balks at an incompatible file format.

- Editing clip art is something designers do, but editors need to understand that it *can* be edited and *you are allowed to ask for changes.* However, ask your designer how long it will take to make the changes you'd like to see—you may be asking for eight hours worth of work for what you think is a minor tweaking.

2.8.8   The three biggest liabilities of clip art

There are lots of little ways to go wrong with clip art, but editing these three big liabilities out of your layout will immediately make it look more professional:

1. **Bad art.** If a particular clip art image is being used "because we need some art and this is what we have," it's mere decoration— and thoughtful readers will see it as useless filler. Effective images (a) highlight and (b) support some aspect of the content. First, they draw attention and then they subtly enhance copy points. But only after the editor and designer do some brainstorming about the copy together. That requires that the designer read and the editor listen to ideas and be willing to rewrite headlines and perhaps even a lead to work with art.

2. **Bad placement.** Images should be (a) integrated with the text block so they don't compete with it and (b) placed pleasingly within (or break pleasingly out of) the grid so they don't crowd copy or trap white space. There's an art to designing a page that's pleasing alone and compatible as part of a spread, but editors can stand back from the technicalities of layout and make sure no art will force readers to wonder where copy starts or stops—or read around it to get from the first half of a paragraph to the last half.

3. **Bad text wrap.** One of the surest ways to wear readers out is wrapping lines of text that are too short or too long around a piece of clip art. Physically, it's tiring because the eye has more work to do, and, since ease of comprehension is reduced, there's less chance that readers will retain information. It also looks crummy.

2.9 Essential type and design terms for newsletter editors

Learning some of the jargon of graphics and design techniques is a way to become aware of the concepts underlying successful execution. See the bibliography, page 345, for several comprehensive dictionaries and guidebooks that go into more technical detail, if you need it.

alignment—the relationship of type and graphics to margins and the underlying grid of the layout. The four types are

- flush-left alignment: Body or display text lines up with the left margin (the right margin is ragged).
- flush-right alignment: Body or display text lines up with the right margin (the left margin is ragged).
- center alignment: Text is centered on the line; lines of type are centered over each other, or display type is centered over columns.
- justification: Body or display text is set with variable interline spacing and end-of-line hyphenation so that all lines are the same length.

anchoring—in software, linking a graphic to specific text or to a fixed place in the layout. Used loosely to mean "aligned" or placed in a clear relationship to text or within the grid rather than floating in trapped white space.

bars—thick rules. They look sort of silly running across the top of every page of a newsletter when only occasional or short lines of information are printed across them or reversed out of them. The use of bars as a header is a convention that requires rethinking—it's like overhearing an editor muttering to a designer, "We need something here, but what?"

baselines—the invisible horizontal lines on which type is set.

bleeds—a graphic element—color, a rule, a photo, an illustration—that's printed to the edge of the page (actually "bleeds" or runs off it to the eye). A bleed can give the sense of expanse and variety to a page, but it adds to printing costs.

boldface—a heavy (darker) weight of a typeface or font.

caption—copy that identifies the people, places, things, activities, and significance of photos. In newsletters, most photos require captions; they're read first and can be a hot link back to a main article.

color separations—physically breaking apart the different colors used in a publication. Used to create plates for printing (one color per plate).

continued (jumped, linking) articles—this technique of jumping the last part of an article to another page speeds up layout although it can slow readers down. Some editors jump articles deliberately as a technique for getting readers to move around and sample something on each page.

continued (jump) lines—a note set the same way each time that says "Continued on page x" before jumping and "Continued from page x" above the concluding copy. A few key words from the main headline can be repeated in the continuation line. This editorial courtesy isn't necessary across a spread unless continued copy is likely to be lost among several short blocks of similar-looking copy.

contrast—strictly speaking, the range of black and white tones in a photo. More generally, the principle of highlighting type or graphics by making them look different from body text.

cropping—eliminating distracting details from photos or illustrations along the top or sides or in the background. As distinct from a silhouette, the shape of the photo remains rectangular (or oval).

dingbats—small, decorative graphics, usually limited for newsletters to filled (black or a screen of a color) round bullets, square boxes, and diamonds; also simple stylized ornaments used to identify recurring elements—the end of an article, a pullquote. Dingbats can also set off items in a list; use a pointing finger, checkmarks, and smiley or sad faces gingerly. Fresher choices are small, screened triangles, diamonds, round bullets, and squares.

display type—a typeface for titles, distinguishable from body type by size, weight, and serif/sans serif contrast. Usually larger and heavier than the predominant body typeface for headings; larger and set off with space and/or rules for pullquotes; smaller and often sans serif for captions, even if a serif face is used for heads.

downloadable fonts—software that can be loaded from disks or the Internet into a printer. Add typefaces, weights, sizes, styles, and dingbats beyond the default fonts that the manufacturer installed.

drop shadow—a black or shaded edging lightly offset behind or around a photo or box. Creates a three-dimensional effect; drastically overused in thick 100 percent black in many newsletters—should highlight, not overwhelm a text box. Easy does it around photos; fresher looking than rules when gently shaded.

ellipsis—a special character set of three dots that indicates text has been omitted.

folios—page numbers. Can be minimized or used as an ornament with a distinctive graphic treatment (e.g., a white number reversed out of a color circle). The optimal placement for folios in a newsletter is the outer corner of the bottom of a page—important if articles are jumped.

font—one member of a type family: italic, boldface, bold italic, small capitals, body and display faces, and often ornaments.

formatting—a consistent set of choices for each category of type in a word processed file. Type, margins, spacing, styles, and so forth must be selected and specified as part of a desktop publishing software style-sheet to support an editorial hierarchy of information.

grayscale values—the levels of gray in a photo or art that are reproducible by using a scanner or laser printer—something many newsletter editors must resort to. A grayscale range of 256 levels (256 different shifts between shades of gray) approaches almost photo-quality images.

grid—the underlying (invisible) pattern of lines that defines how and where copy and art can be placed in a layout. Creates a consistent columned format and, by extension, mathematical variations within it. Allows harmonious placement of different sizes and shapes of content across spreads and on a page. Sets up a system of orderly relationships among text blocks, column and page margins, boxes, photos, and art—and, within that order, a set of complementary variations. The opposite of chaotic layout; essential to a professional look.

halftone photo—printed as a pattern of dots. The more dots, the higher the resolution, or clarity, of an image's details and light and shading.

hierarchy of information—the sum of all stylesheet decisions that specify what kinds and sizes of type are to be consistently used for each display element in the newsletter. The integrity of this hierarchy is directly tied to an image of competence and credibility. Covers kickers, main headlines, feature headlines, deckheads, crossheads (subheads), captions, pullquotes, sidebar heads, authors' bylines and bios, editor's notes, and other content-based clues. Arises out of the nature of the content and then becomes the standard for both editor and designer when formatting copy for efficient access by readers. This is the governing basis for creating a software template. Creates and rewards reader expectations on both editorial and graphic levels.

high-resolution output—for the best quality in printing, electronic files (particularly graphic files) must support 1200 dpi ("high res") output in addition to the 300-dpi laser printer output commonly used.

image scanner—hardware that converts a photo to an electronic file that can then be manipulated, edited, and imported into a layout program.

initial (display) capital letters—oversized display (contrasting with body type) type used as a graphic invitation by drawing the reader's eye to the first letter of the first word in an article. Can also be judiciously used as a transitional graphic device in a long article with the first word of a new paragraph that marks a shift in the narrative.

- drop cap—set below the baseline, embedded within the first three or so lines, with white space and text wrapped around it, aligning with the top of the first line of text.
- side cap—set in a scholar's margin adjacent to copy but not intruding into the paragraph. Drawback: Far away from the rest of the letters of the word, so possibly forcing readers to go back and try to read it again.
- raised cap—set on the baseline and rising above the rest of the type on the line. Drawback: Requires extra vertical space.

italic—a slanted version of a typeface, used to set off titles of books and the like, as well as limited blocks of other special material (editor's notes, author bio notes) from roman body type.

justified copy—all lines are the same length. Some publishers consider this a more "formal" look for copy blocks.

kerning—fitting certain pairs of letters more closely together to close up the extra space that occurs naturally between them because of their shapes. Used especially with capital letters in display type where spacing is magnified.

knockout—the technique of overprinting text or a graphic as an outline against a photo or colored background. Should be used sparingly in text-dominant newsletters.

landscape orientation—type printed vertically across a sheet of paper (so it has to be turned 90° to be read). Some newsletter editors like to print a center spread landscape in order to showcase special material like a long chart, calendar, or photo essay. Normal orientation is called "portrait."

layout—the formal arrangement of type and graphics on a page or a screen. Layout varies from issue to issue within the style specifications of a governing design.

leading—the spacing between vertically set lines of type, from baseline to baseline. Add 2 points of leading to the point size to get an average setting for leading in newsletters: 10 points of type set over 12 points of leading, for example.

logotype—a nameplate that uses a stylized type treatment for the name of a publication rather than either simple display type or a graphic as a logo.

masthead—a standing block of information that appears in the same place each time. Lists newsletter staff, publisher's address, subscription information, ISSN, copyright notice, and reprint policy. May contain the organizational logo, a mission statement, and a note inviting and directing reader comments and questions to the editor.

nameplate (or banner or flag or headline, but never masthead!)—the title of a newsletter designed with special type and graphics with information such as (in descending order of importance) publishing mission and/or the name of the publisher, the date of publication, volume and number, logo. Proprietary logos don't usually work very well with other designed elements and art but a nameplate can be built around an attractive logo (better to use it in the masthead).

Pantone colors vs. process colors—Pantone Matching System (PMS) colors are obtained by mixing inks to match the specifications of this widely used reference system. Process colors are approximated by over-printing the four process colors (cyan, magenta, yellow, and black).

picas and points—a pica is the unit of measurement for specifying line lengths when setting type. Six picas equal an inch. A pica is subdivided into 12 points. A point equals 1/72 of an inch, the size of a pixel on most computer screens, which is why this measuring system has transferred to digital typesetting.

preprinting—stock that's prepared in advance of copy with standing material involving spot color and original artwork such as a nameplate, masthead, self-mailer panel, or recurring departments. A second pass through, usually with black for text, completes the printing of the issue. This process is still used by some editors who rely on printers (they store the preprinted stock) to lay out their newsletters.

proof (blueline)—a penultimate printout of the newsletter—last chance for catching errors and making changes, and they'll cost you.

pullquote—a short, snappy sentence from an article or a person quoted in an article. Set near the original context to attract reader interest.

ragged (scalloped) margins—every line is a different length. Considered preferable by many designers for columned publications like newsletters because ragged copy is easier to produce and easier to read.

reverse—type or graphics printed as white (with color "knocked out") against a dark background of at least a 60 percent screen. The most difficult reverse to read is small white sans serif letters against a 100 percent black background, no matter how good designers think that looks because of its utter contrast.

rules—solid horizontal and vertical lines that separate articles, form boxes, or provide decorative borders. Rules are used in various thicknesses of black or a color from hairline (very thin) to a bar. Dotted rules, less intrusive and less formal, are sometimes used instead.

sans serif—a typeface that lacks finishing strokes (serifs). The nearly monotonous shapes have a clean appearance, but in small sizes and for large blocks of text, they are more work to read than serif type.

scholar's margin—white space built into the outside margins of each spread in a layout. Usually no larger or smaller than about half of the regular column width. Body copy is set immediately adjacent, with or without a dividing rule, so material in the scholar's margin can complement it but mustn't compete with it.

screen—a percentage of a color less than 100 percent used as background for text or in graphics. Sometimes mixed with a tint of black to achieve the effect of an additional color. Also, the process of breaking a photo into dots for printing.

serif—a typeface with serifs, or finishing strokes, that give letter stems an edge. Serifs range in width and shape from a recognizable cross-stroke that looks like a line to a curved or wedge-shaped stroke. Serif type offers the reading eye quick clues to letter shapes.

sidebar—a short article that relates to a longer one. Also called a box because that's what it is: "boxed-off" copy set on a screened background or within rules.

silhouette—eliminating all or some of the background from a photo to highlight the actors or other prominent image. The photo assumes the interesting shape of its primary image, and even boring portraits take on more visual interest.

spread—facing pages, left and right. Should be designed as complements with regard to shape, size, and placement of articles and graphics. Only one dominant image on a page; significant articles or graphics should run on the right page or the right side of the left page.

standing head (eyebrow)—word or phrase that serves as a headline for a recurring feature or department. Remains the same every time. Often centered over the main headline. Offers browsers a clue to content.

template—layout file containing formatting instructions for a newsletter. Can contain standing material such as the nameplate.

tint—a shade of gray used as background for text or in graphics. Often used interchangeably with *screen* to mean a shade of gray or of a color.

tombstoned headlines—run parallel across the top of adjacent columns so that readers are tricked into reading across headlines instead of vertically down the columns.

tracking—desktop publishing software option that permits adapting (tightening or loosening) normal wordspacing to fit copy to layout or make it more legible.

trim size—final printed size.

type family—a collection of complementary fonts (think "family members") in different weights and treatments (italic, small caps) that are designed to be used together.

typeface—a set of designed characters that includes all or some of these: lowercase and uppercase alphabet, numbers, symbols, punctuation, and special characters.

white space—paper blessedly free of text or graphics. Needed for contrast, relief, physical separation of elements, and organizing margins.

- "trapped white space" is the leftover bits of space that results from badly laid-out copy and creates awkwardness rather than relief.
- leading is the white space between lines.
- the gutter is the vertical white space between two columns or the combined margins between facing pages.
- letterspacing is the space between letters that can be adjusted by kerning.
- word spacing is the space between words that is affected by justification and that can be adjusted by tracking.
- margins are the spaces around columns of type (also the framing space around the live area of a page in which headers and footers are placed).
- the "sink" is the amount of white space between the top of the page and the start of columns of text—should be the same for each page in the layout.

x-height—the size of a lowercase x in a typeface (not including ascenders—the upper part of a letter like h, or descenders—the lower part of a letter like y). The smaller the x-height, the more compensatory leading is necessary for legibility.

2.10 Anatomy of design conventions for newsletters

Not all newsletters need all the optional elements that exist to mark different kinds of editorial information, but a newsletter's look and feel derive from using basic elements that serve a clear editorial purpose. Putting big page numbers and a table of contents in a four-page newsletter is clutter, for example, because it's editorially unnecessary. But readers need both if you publish eight pages.

The diagram of *The Editorial Eye* that begins on page 134 demonstrates standard design elements at work in a real newsletter that doesn't use all possible elements in every issue. Neither will yours, probably. When they strengthen the layout, though, these elements are not just niceties but conventions. It's conventional to use a hammer to drive a nail, though the back of a pipe wrench will work too. It's conventional to use page numbers in a table of contents so people can find the articles listed—if page numbers are in fact used throughout. Graphic conventions can make information recognizable and accessible, and they make a newsletter look like the work of professionals. They make an editor's job easier in the long run.

Graphic conventions make a newsletter editor's job easier.

The level of editorial complexity will determine how much definition of content is required on the page—and the nature of the content in turn determines in many ways its corresponding graphic. For example, if you don't ever print articles by outside authors because you write them all yourself, you don't need to use a byline (and in fact really shouldn't, lest you seem egotistical). But if you need a byline style, you have your choice of several. And if you use bylines, you may want to print short author biographical notes at the beginning or end of the article. These elements are connected.

If you print long articles that must be continued across pages, you'll need continued-to and continued-from lines to help readers follow the story or backtrack to the beginning in case they start reading in the middle. But if all your articles are 150-word news briefs and most paragraphs are only one or two sentences long, you don't need to use continued lines—or, most likely, subheads, pullquotes, sidebars, bulleted lists, or end dingbats. Doing some serious work with your grid to allocate white space and writing crisp headlines in a sturdy display face will be your chief graphic challenges.

This is a list of elements identified in the examples of newsletter layout that follow. How many do you need? How many are you using now?

____ Author bio

____ Author byline

____ Back page (location of content popular with readers)

____ Bleeds

____ Block indented quote

____ Blurbs

____ Breaking the grid

____ Bulk mail indicia

____ Bullet points

____ Bullets, round

____ Bullets, square

____ Captions

____ Cataloging data

____ Chart

____ Collage

____ Consistent spacing between columns

____ "Continued from" dingbat

____ "Continued from" line

____ "Continued on" line

____ "Continued on" dingbat

___ Copyright

___ Correction notice

___ Date

___ Department head

___ Display letter

___ Dotted line separating articles horizontally

___ Drop shadow

___ Editorial invitation

___ Editorial note

___ End dingbat

___ Even spacing around photo

___ Folio

___ Graphics

___ Grid

___ Gutter

___ Halftone

___ Indented list

___ Initial capital letter

___ Initials as byline

___ Insert

___ ISSN (International Standard Serial Number)

___ Lead article

___ Lead headline

___ Lead paragraph

___ Level 1 head

___ Level 2 head

___ Level 3 head (run-in)

___ Logotype

___ Masthead

___ Mission statement

___ Mission statement, amplified

___ Nameplate

___ Numbered list

___ Ordering information

___ Production specs

___ Publisher information and address

___ Pullquote

___ Question set off by screened box

___ Reader forum

___ Reprint policy

___ Return address

___ Reviewers

___ Runover

___ Running header (date and title)

___ Scholar's margin

___ Screened box

___ Screened box separating articles vertically

___ Screened bullets

___ Screened sidebar

___ Screened-back art

___ Self-mailer

___ Sidebar

___ Single quotes

___ Squibs

___ Staff listing

___ Stylized display treatment with color

___ Subhead (two lines maximum length)

___ Table of contents

___ Tables

___ Tag

___ Teaser

___ Templates

___ Text wraps

___ Two colors

___ Vertical rule separating runover

You don't have to use all these elements. But you need to know they exist as options.

133

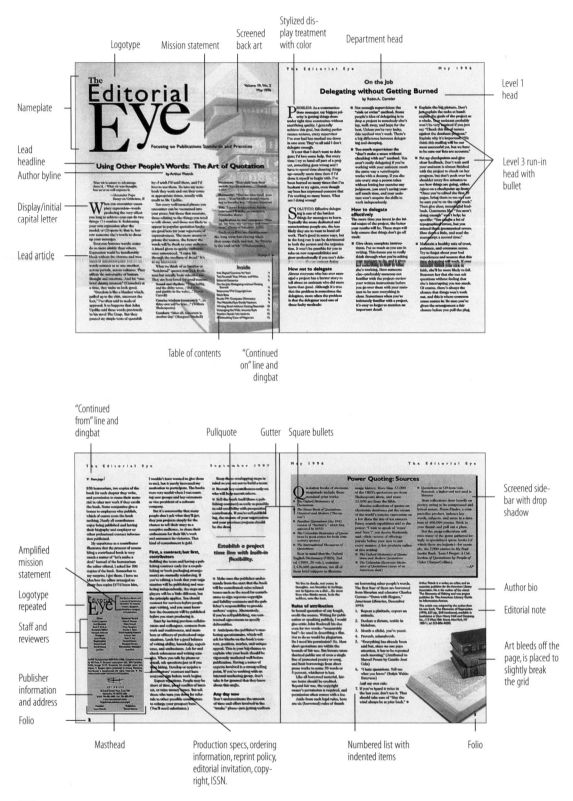

Logotype

Mission statement

Screened back art

Stylized display treatment with color

Department head

Level 1 head

Nameplate

Lead headline

Author byline

Display/initial capital letter

Lead article

Level 3 run-in head with bullet

Table of contents

"Continued on" line and dingbat

"Continued from" line and dingbat

Pullquote

Gutter

Square bullets

Screened sidebar with drop shadow

Amplified mission statement

Logotype repeated

Staff and reviewers

Publisher information and address

Folio

Author bio

Editorial note

Art bleeds off the page, is placed to slightly break the grid

Masthead

Production specs, ordering information, reprint policy, editorial invitation, copyright, ISSN.

Numbered list with indented items

Folio

Running header, date and title

Screened box separates 3rd article from other 2 vertically

Dotted line separates articles horizontally

Halftone photo screened in percentage of blue and shadowed

Even spacing around photo

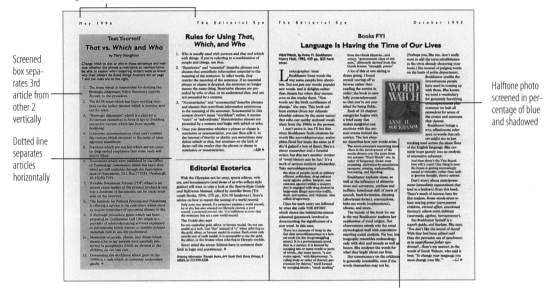

Vertical rule separating a runover from a new article

Continued dingbat

Level 2 subhead

Sidebar used as a fact box of bulleted items

Initials as byline when same person identified elsewhere in issue

Reader forum department

Departments separated by a screened box

Initial caps in color show transition within article

March 1997 The Editorial Eye

Readers Speak

Freelancing in Canada and 'See the Above'

The Editorial Eye March 1997

Getting There from Here

Editor Creates Her Own Niche

by Sally Smith

Resource FYI

INTECOM

Correction

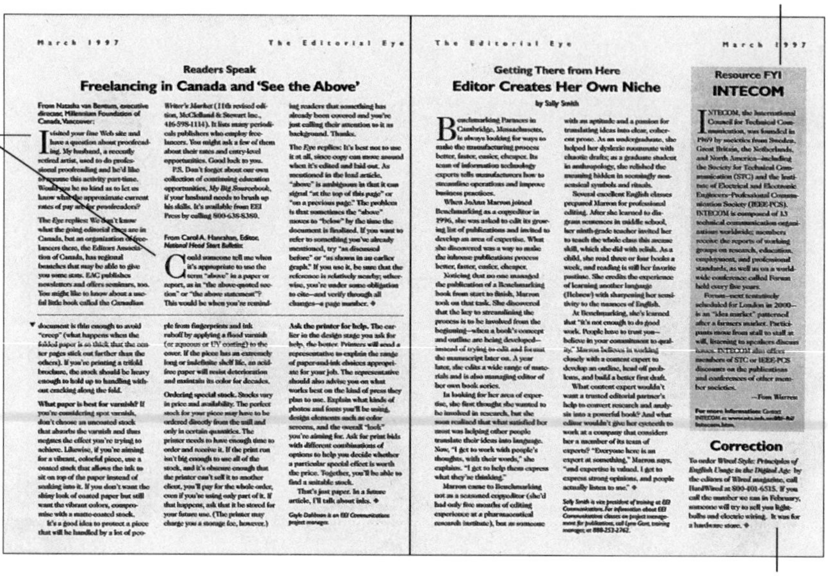

Correction notice

Chart placed in the grid across two columns

Question set off by a screened box immediately above the answer

The Editorial Eye July 1996

Part of an actual storyboard script (DELOS Inc.)

The storyboard script is a diagram

Project storyboarding precedes the script

July 1996 The Editorial Eye

Untangling the Web

Unicode: Making the Web Safe for Furriners

by Keith C. Ivey

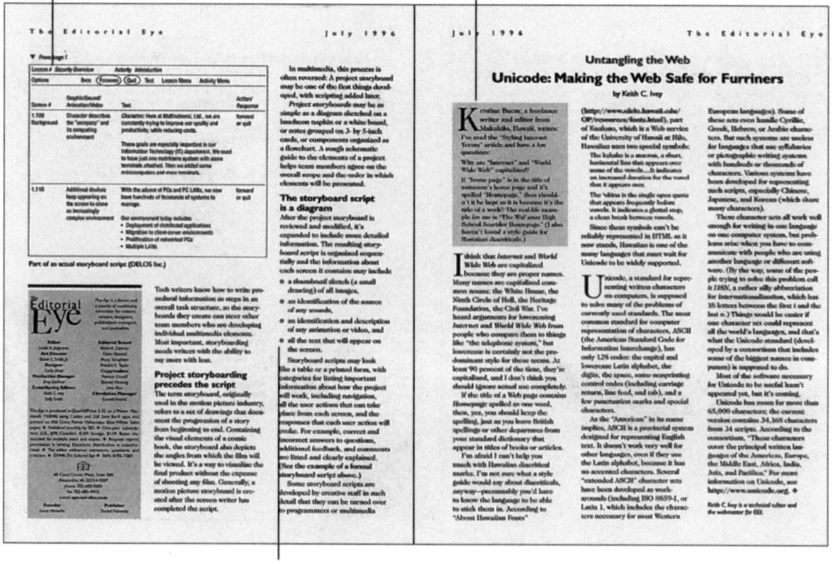

Round bullets used to list a series

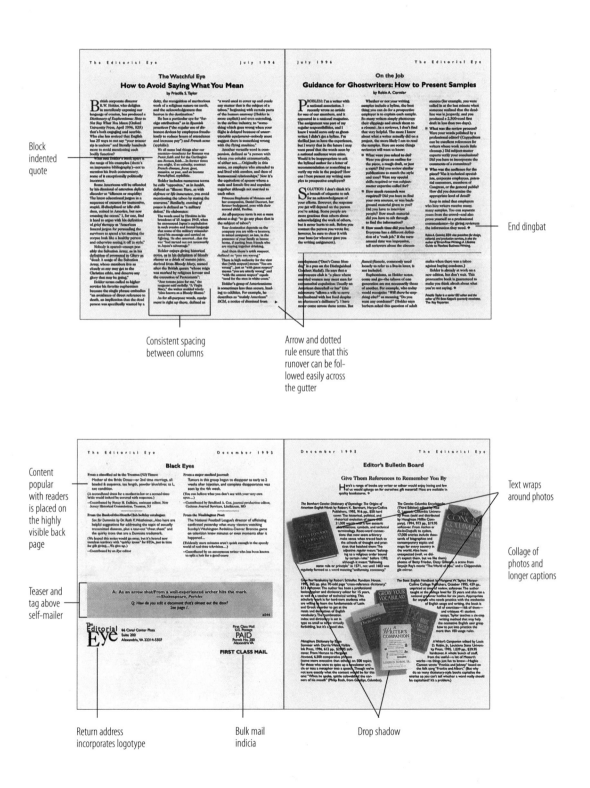

Block indented quote

End dingbat

Consistent spacing between columns

Arrow and dotted rule ensure that this runover can be followed easily across the gutter

Content popular with readers is placed on the highly visible back page

Text wraps around photos

Teaser and tag above self-mailer

Collage of photos and longer captions

Return address incorporates logotype

Bulk mail indicia

Drop shadow

Date and cata-
loging data

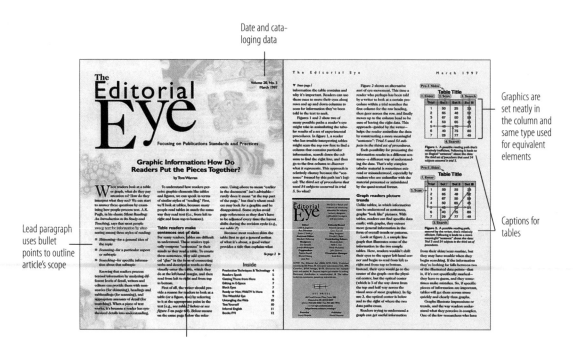

Graphics are
set neatly in
the column and
same type used
for equivalent
elements

Lead paragraph
uses bullet
points to outline
article's scope

Captions for
tables

Two-line subhead (level 2
head) is maximum length

Single quotes
in headline

Line of three
screened bul-
lets between
squibs

Insert about a
special topic

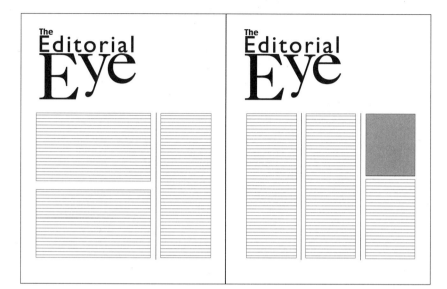

These templates show how easily and attractively the sizes and shapes of articles and graphics can be varied within the framework of a consistent grid. The goal is always to balance visual interest with editorial coherence.

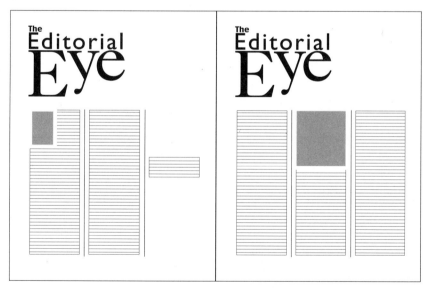

Immediately above left, the righthand column (scholar's margin) can be used for a table of contents, pullquotes, coming attractions, factlets, or author bios—or left blank.

3 Real-World Newsletter Design Gallery

3 Real-World Newsletter Design Gallery

The good, the bad, and the better

Newsletters look deceptively simple to produce, but the format is a challenge. It imposes a condensed, stylized format, limits content to fairly short articles, and yet is protean—flexible enough to hold a range of information for different kinds of readers but liable for that very reason to seeming disorganized. Newsletters are usually produced, designed, and printed on a tight schedule so time-sensitive news will still be fresh. Newsletterers never have enough time or enough helping hands. Ever. In fact, many editors operate entirely solo, relying on the advice of a printer but otherwise self-sufficient.

Some editors must snake their newsletter through a chain of supervisory review to be sure it advances the publisher's mission. *And yet* these editors want to put a recognizable human face on the organizational message so people will want to get it. *And yet* it must retain credibility as a reliable source of news-based reporting so people will believe it. It's not surprising that editors have trouble holding onto a sense of vision and mission while juggling these seemingly contradictory day-to-day demands. But that's what you're there for. The voice you hear may be your own! (Try not to talk to yourself in public, though. Editors already have a rap to beat about being mere "word people.")

Sometimes it seems that everybody's a critic. It's hard not to get defensive when nitpickers who have no idea how a newsletter is put together gleefully point out errors. After all, "Criticism comes easier than craftsmanship" (Pliny). But a case can be made—in fact, let's make it right now—that getting almost any kind of feedback is better than working in a vacuum. (That's on the condition that you allow yourself to think of mistakes as profitable learning opportunities—yeah, I know, it's corny but I mean it—and allow yourself to become confident that you're getting better all the time—no fair feeling defeated by every little misstep.)

Many editors do, however, feel a little uneasy about the quality of their work because, as a newsletter workshop participant once put it, "I have pretty good instincts, but I don't ever get any validation, just criticism. I always feel like I'm making it up as I go." When you work in isolation, it's easy to take readers for granted and focus on drumming content into the issue. Maybe you never have time to look at things through the eyes of your readers. Or maybe you're so invested in writing articles that you never look up long enough to realize that there's a better way to present them graphically.

In any case, when you're busy trying to cover all the bases, it's easy to lose track of how well the total package holds together. Even if you're trying to look at your newsletter critically immediately after reading the previous design section word for word.

3.1   Problems and solutions

Practice using your critical eye on the gallery of problems and successful and interesting solutions that begins on page 147. This isn't solely a design gallery; the fact is that editorial and design elements have to be closely calibrated in order to produce the desired effect. These snapshots reflect choices made quickly, maybe instantly, using shortcuts and a collegial shorthand we can only guess at. Good editor-designer relationships are grounded in shared assumptions about who the readers are, what they'll stomach, and what the publisher requires.

The choices behind the samples shown here aren't likely to have been made nearly so deliberately as the accompanying discussions might suggest. But when one is learning the anatomy behind the talent to walk upright, it's necessary to learn the names of the bones.

Our critical take on the samples might not match your own—we'd all do things differently if they were ours to do. The editors and designers who thought up the elements we showcase in this gallery have found ways to integrate change and predictability in their publications—and what they have chosen to do works for their readers. If you disagree with our comments or with a solution, the exercise of figuring out how you would prefer to have solved the problem is even more valuable than understanding the little lectures.

That's what all editors are trying to do, really: figure out new ways to adapt new content to an efficient (but limiting) template and spice overly familiar content with surprising (not jarring) graphics. All the time, a juggling act. But please note: We all make mistakes in judging the arcs from eye to hand and brain to mouth. In periodicals publishing, we always get another chance to do it better. "Next time, let's remember to…." "Next time, let's try…."

Newsletter publishers are up to a lot of tricks. Of the thousands of newsletters being published (and that doesn't count news briefings or intranet titles), countless editorial styles and kinds of subject matter are being poured into a wild variety of designs. All call themselves "newsletters," and their editors have personalized the content for their readership within the basic conventions of newsletter style. But there's a thread running throughout the samples here: It's the thread of care taken, homework done, and challenge accepted. The newsletters included here show editorial energy, a clear purpose for publishing, and openness to reader concerns.

Every issue brings its knotty little sticking places.

At one end of the spectrum are editors with a lot of freedom to gather and present material—they may actually produce the newsletter as well, using page layout software, clip art, and a scanner for photos.

Other editors hand over their copy to outside designers or their own production department, feeling as if they have to defer to whatever the designer "gives" them. Many of these editors feel it's beyond their power to control the quality of the package, given a multilayered review process, a roster of reluctant nonwriters who are volunteers (or worse, uneditable technical experts), an entirely too hands-on and voluble editorial board, and design "experts" who resist all attempts at editing their graphics to support the content.

The best way to master the many small details that can make or break a publication is to absorb the graphic evidence of how other editors (who have time, money, and energy constraints just like you do) have served their audience well.

The cumulative decisions that define a newsletter's look and "voice" can be learned. They're arbitrary, though, so rules about newsletter design are in dire need of breaking at times. Some rules are just conventions. Sometimes bad design is bad design no matter what.

Every issue brings its little knotty sticking places. Regardless of your niche—advocacy, alumni/affinity group, association, corporate internal or external, marketing, public interest, sales, or service journalism—what works for other editors may well work for your newsletter. But it may not. You'll have to be a good judge of what to borrow.

Sometimes "closer to good" is good enough in the world of newsletters. The samples shown here are snapshots of a given solution for a given problem on a given day by the editors and designers who had to make them. Please don't consider this a gallery of art. It's a gallery of down-to-earth craftiness.

Excerpts from 43 newsletters have been selected to show a range of the ways an editor-driven (by a driven editor?) layout can personalize and spice up copy, organize it for pleasant browsing, and use graphic elements to enhance some aspects of the publishing mission. Credits for the newsletters represented here are on page 353.

Not every solution here is elegant; all are, however, ingenious and demonstrate the truth of a simple theorem: Editing the newsletter package depends on equal parts common sense, expedience, perfectionism, and fatalism. There's always something to learn from the work of others—maybe even (surprise!) that you can be pretty proud of what you're doing.

A MONTHLY BREEDER'S REPORT

July 1994 Vol. 1, No. 3   CIRCULATION 10,000

The Adjustment of the Ostrich Market

The beginning of the *real* industry   *by Teresa Barbanell*

*L*ast week I received a telephone call from a newcomer to the ostrich industry asking if I were concerned about the downward trend of ostrich prices. Concerned? Absolutely not.

and add $200 million into the Texas economy by the year 2000. Imagine, if you will, these statistics on a nationwide scale by taking into

tinue over a long-term period. With bird population expanding, we are reaching the point at which the cumulative yearly chick hatch is

Ask the Edito

Q:

Editor:

I am writing to you as a concerned citizen and compassionate founding member of an animal rights group here in Atlanta, Georgia, urging you to stop breeding ostriches for their wholesale

First, contrary to your u ostriches are rare, they ar most prolific animals on e many as 100 eggs per yea sexually at 2 - 3 years of a 40 - 50 years, and living f 80 years, the ostrich has t overrun the planet were it tors and the commercial w products.

Second, we do not agree that "all living creatures a nected and each animal (b

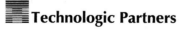 **Technologic Partners**

Marketing

Problem: Selling a subscription newsletter to a highly specialized group.

Solution: Evocative Nameplate. One of the best things about *Blue Ridge Ostrich Review* is the way the nameplate blends shameless self-promotion with professional pride. The exotic name rolls off the tongue and the simple expanse of rolling blue hills echoes the name of the publisher, Blue Ridge Ostrich Ranch, Inc. The fancy initial script capitals contrast with the plainer type. The nameplate as a whole gives off a whiff of the "what's over the next hill?" entrepreneurship the pages are full of. The tagline "A Monthly Breeder's Report" is just right. It says I'm a breeder, you're a breeder, and we're in this great business together. (Compare that wording with "Your Monthly Breeder's Report" or "A Monthly Report for Ostrich Breeders and Friends.") Posting the circulation in the nameplate is a little unusual but appropriate given the upbeat, even upstart, tone of this chatty, blunt vehicle. In the photo above her column, the editor's wearing a wonderful cowperson hat.

Corporate Proprietary Subscription

Problem: Retaining copyright for exclusive information.

Solution: Restrictive notice in the masthead. *ComputerLetter* doesn't fool around. The publisher, Technologic Partners, can get people to pay $595 for information about the Internet and "business issues in technology" only if the content is exclusively available to subscribers. Note the caveat against legal liability and the full-disclosure admission that the folks who bring you the content may have business relationships with the companies mentioned in articles.

Scholarly

Problem: Launch—win a national audience outside the community for a research quarterly that showcases a university's accomplishments.

Solution: Simultaneous launch in print and on the Web designed by a nationally prestigious design firm; distinctive logo. Both versions of Columbia University's *21stC* were designed by Roger Black, Incorporated (of *Esquire*, *Newsweek*, *Premiere*), to be a vehicle for more than the typical research-based quarterly report. Its director of publications said of the inaugural issue that "it strives to show how particular subjects of research may be dealt with very differently in various disciplines, with different implications for the university itself and society at large. Huge display type, a bright second color, and a "Metnews" feature running at the bottom of the page across spreads are examples of arresting elements in a tabloid format. Pages are printed both horizontally and vertically as necessary to accommodate long articles. The real surprise is that the design is relatively conservative. It's more that Black's design is one of very few high-end newsletters to make effective use of tabloid size, nice thick paper instead of common cheesy newsprint. The Web version can be found at **http://www.21st.org**.

Scholarly Public Relations

Problem: PR newsletter published once a year.

Solution: *Publishing Forum* isn't fancy; it's a demo of the education offered to the students of Simon Fraser University's Master of Publishing program: They produce it. The front-page mission statement keeps the goals of the program in front of readers. With only one annual shot at credibility, every element matters. Keeping the publisher, the Canadian Centre for Studies in Publishing, in the background (on the back page masthead) puts the focus on the professional goals of the program instead of on recruiting. Also in the masthead is generous permission to reprint articles—of course!

Corporate Internal

Problem: Selling readers—employees—on a four-color redesign from a "newspaper" to magazine format in a climate of downsizing.

Solution: Editorial honesty, lots of columns for reader feedback and exchanges with the editor, and the tone and feel of a newsletter! In the second edition of *The Prudential Leader's* new design, the editor fields criticism by explaining that the redesign costs no more than a small cup of coffee *per reader* from the cafeteria and is a sign of management concern—external advertising was cut to divert funds to the magazine. An additional note about the issue acknowledges the controversy and steers readers to both a "Letters" column and a page of pro-and-con feedback called "How Are We Doing?" A feedback form is stitched in opposite the negative comments—a subtly confident message to readers that they can speak up because (a) the *Leader* can take it and (b) readers are the whole point: They're actively courted. This magazine is a newsletter in its heart, serving as a forum for blunt, even cynical comments and countering them smartly. Articles are employee-focused: a "Prudential People" profile, a report of company-sponsored community activities, an invitation to readers to send cartoons, photos, and artwork—and an "Employee Perspective" subhead in an article about losing a long-standing contract.

Marketing Newsletter for Business-to-Business Marketers

Problem: Preserving the rights to distribute and profit from a newsletter that publishes proprietary industry information and the results of original research.

Solution: A copyright declaration and stated reprint policy that permits not even the faint stirrings of any ifs, ands, or buts. One of the more stringent we've seen, offering readers a bounty for reporting directly to the editor's legal counsel anyone who reproduces or stores articles without permission.

Association

Problem: Where to put housekeeping details?

Solution: Effective use of the back page. The Georgia Psychiatric Physicians Association *Update* doesn't give space to a masthead in its eight pages—though there's an editor's column and credit is given to several contributors. The newsletter is full of articles. But on the back page there's a calendar of professional events (accompanied by an adjacent notice of a featured speaker at one of the events listed) and contact information for anyone who wants to submit an article, ask a question, or a correct an address (adjacent to the mailing label itself). Rarely is this kind of information so neatly and visibly presented by association newsletters; it's too tempting to scatter bits of it through pages as a bit of space presents itself. The choice here keeps editorial content uncluttered and ups the odds that someone will actually notice the mundane but important "housekeeping" details of both association events and running a member-responsive newsletter.

Corporate Internal

Problem: Fostering a climate of employee optimism.

Solution: Give them a newsletter bursting with energy. Published for the employees and retirees of a Canadian company, this tabloid serves up a mixture of graphics, illustrations, and photos. The intended effect—highly creative staff are just part of a company-wide "shared leadership" initiative—is exemplified by having co-editors whose photos run along with their joint letter. It's side by side with a reader letter and editorial answer. For companies committed to cultural change in the form of "quality teams" and "employee empowerment," an internal newsletter like this is a way for management to put its money (instead of its foot) where its mouth is. The editors swear this redesign cost no more than its less sophisticated predecessor because of production trade-offs such as using two colors instead of four.

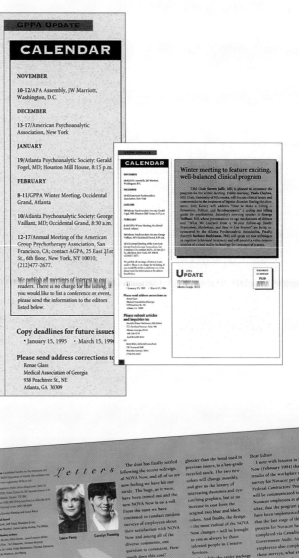

Our hard work produced impressive policy yields

Grassroots efforts helped achieve successes

By Dean Kleckner

₂₄ith the close of the 104th Congress, Farm agricultu

• The self-employed health insurance tax deduction is now permanent, rising from 25 percent to 80 percent eventually.
• The archaic, zero-risk Delaney clause that regulated pesticide residues was eliminated and replaced with a reasonable standard.
• The Safe Drinking Water Act that passed contained reasonable and workable standards for

ing retaliatory tariffs and boycotts of U.S. farm products.
• A balanced budget amendment failed by just one vote, the closest we've ever come to forcing Washington to live within its means.
• The president has been empowered with the line-item veto to control pork barrel spending.
If this list fails to impress you, then vow to get

THE VANCE INTERNATIONAL REPORT

A Security Newsletter for Clients and Employees   November 1995

Vance On Vance INTERNATIONAL

Press reports about the Detroit newspaper strike often mention "security guards"—but did you know that those anonymous guards are part of our own Asset Protection Team?

Starting in January of this year, APT sent a handful of security team leaders superbly led by George Beach to assist with strike contingency plans and prevent equipment sabotage; when a strike actually began on July 13, we substantially increased our security force in Detroit. They have played a critical role in enabling our client, the Detroit News Agency, to continue publishing for both Gannett and Knight-Ridder.

It hasn't been easy. This is a very emotional, divisive situation. I've made 3 trips to Detroit, and have observed more violence there than in any strike since the 1989 strike year in West Virginia's coal fields. Two of our men had to be hospitalized (both are recovering well), and more than a dozen others have been injured. Day and night our team contends with verbal provocation, spitting, rock-throwing and worse. Through it all, I'm

very proud to report that morale is high, and every single man has maintained his professional demeanor.

This assignment has contributed to APT's successful year, and of course that's gratifying. But I really am most proud of the performance of our personnel—some of whom are relatively new employees. We've also broken the 1,000 mark for total APT staff in the field. These records don't just "happen."

Vance headquarters staff—recruitment, training, equipment managers, payroll, and accounting, all pulled together to achieve this. Many people who thought they had 9-to-5 jobs with Vance discovered a new sense of solidarity with their APT brothers who always work 12 hour shifts!

I can't finish this salute to the APT team without mentioning another record-breaking performance—this one for longevity—with Caterpillar, who we've served at 5 sites for 427 days at this writing. We're proud to have earned Caterpillar's trust by helping maintain operations.

Chuck Vance

Association (Federation)

Problem: Highlighting lobbying gains made for members.

Solution: A special section with a distinctive nameplate. This four-color banner crowing "A Bountiful Harvest" sets the tone for a four-page special insert: a staunch farmer, surrounded by glowing produce, looks over his shoulder toward Congress. Parts of this illustration appear as spot art inside. This section, a report on state and national legislation favoring small farms is set off from the rest of the issue by a three-column grid. Special display script, bullets, subheads, and longer articles stand out. The writing makes the message stand out, too: "There have been few legislative sessions in our recent history in which more of our policy goals were accomplished.... This is a tribute to your grassroots lobbying, your State Farm Bureau's efforts and your American Farm Bureau Federation governmental relations program." No guessing about who to thank for this harvest. The encouraging message and graphics were surely welcomed by members.

Corporate Client and Employee

Problem: Using the letter from the president on the front page—usually suspect as fluff or propaganda.

Solution: A tightly written letter that goes beyond the usual congratulations-to-the-team-for-a-job-well-done to create a vivid scenario of the company's security services performing on the job—on the firing line during the Detroit newspaper strike. This letter never pulls punches— "This is a very emotional, divisive situation.... [but] every single [person] maintained a professional demeanor." The president demonstrates his detailed knowledge of the hardships employees are weathering by reporting on their heroic efforts, rather than emphasizing the trips he himself made to observe events. This "see yourself as I see you and be proud" technique is clever and sounds genuine.

Corporate Subscription

Problem: Reporting statistical survey information on several topics, each with several questions and respondent categories.

Solution: Wide two-column format, consistent typographical treatment, soothing second color. The two-column format lets *The Polling Report* pack a lot of information on each page without looking crowded because of the spacey "response" columns. The format also handles large pullquotes by opinion mavens. Brown ink, a low-key bit of visual relief from tiny black type, is used for headers, subheads, pullquotes, and occasional graphics. Each survey question is printed in the same size of italic and between quotation marks. Readers get reliable clues to each new topic and new respondent categories: All, Whites, Blacks. When polling is regional rather than national, results are set off by reversed-out heads. All in all, this ungimmicky report organizes data clearly for subscribers looking for popular preferences and voting patterns.

Subscription (Vanity)

Problem: Aggressive, self-indulgent posturing by a self-styled loudmouthed entrepreneur editor who loves shocking his readers.

Solution: The editor allows a reader to skewer him and says "Touché!" *The Affable Curmudgeon* is apparently published for the editor's friends and family (one issue was dedicated to "David and Joanne, my first and second grandchildren—twins") but he writes it for himself. Tirades against politicians, lawyers, and hotels that charge for local phone calls, mixed in with wandering "Suggested Auto Trip" travel pieces, are redolent (rank?) with random opinions. But at least once a reader got even: See the letter demanding a "readership fee" for tolerating the "unnatural wisdom" of the Curmudgeon. All editors should be willing to accept a barb and parry it gracefully—if they want readers to feel free to talk back to them, that is.

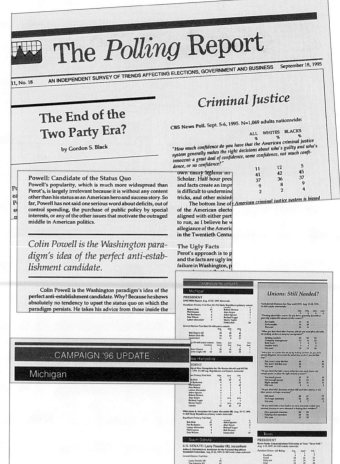

Seniorlines
Information for our senior customers

Potomac Electric Power Company

1900 Pennsylvania Avenue, N.W., Room 502
Washington, D.C. 20068

Mall Walks Grow in Popularity

In recent years, early morning walking programs sponsored by area malls and hospitals have drawn more and more people into a healthy fitness routine. Walking is one of the best exercises for overall fitness and one of the easiest to do. All you need are good walking shoes, comfortable clothing and a good alarm clock.

Participating malls generally open specified doors to walkers every day about 7:30 a.m. Some programs are more structured than others—the "I Love To Walk" program at White Flint in North Bethesda, Maryland is sponsored by Washington Hospital Center and awards T-shirts after 25 and 100 miles. But no matter how simple or sophisticated the program, all have two common benefits: they provide a flat, smooth surface and they're free.

Regular walkers will be quick to add that it's a great opportunity to meet new friends and perhaps to linger for coffee or breakfast after your walk. And you can get in some great window shopping as you add up the miles.

Give your nearest indoor mall a call to ask about their walking program. If they don't have one, maybe you and your friends can start one in partnership with your senior center or a local hospital.

Speaking of Fitness:
Energy Exercises For Your Home

You can strive for year-round energy fitness for your home just as you strive for physical fitness for yourself. It's easy with Pepco's Powerwatchers options, which offer many ways to save money and energy without sacrificing your comfort or convenience. To request a free copy of Powerwatching with Pepco, call (202) 833-7500 anytime, and enjoy the benefits of being a Powerwatcher!—an energy-efficient home and big savings in your pocket.

Seniors Race to Victory in United Way 10K

The 15th Annual United Way 10K, sponsored by Pepco and IBEW Local Union 1900, was another winner for all concerned, with more than 3,000 participants raising more than $40,000 for the United Way of the National Capital Area. Pictured here are three of the senior winners, whose exemplary racing times prove that exercise is ageless. From left to right are Paul Lackey, first place male age 65-69; Hedy Harper, first place female age 70 and over; and William Burnes, first place male age 70 and over. (Photos by Rick Greenwood.)

Corporate External (Customer Service)

Problem: Community public relations (senior citizens).

Solution: Service articles in large type with lots of photos and soft-edged corporate flacking. Potomac Electric Power Company's *Seniorlines* is tagged "Information for our senior customers," and they probably read it from cover to cover. "Information" is a bit vague in this issue; two brief mentions of energy-saving programs appear. Pieces about senior fitness programs and ways to prevent crime predominate, and larger type makes reading easy—clip art, boxes, and photos range from large to huge. Seniors are pictured engaged in community outreach programs, and company's staff are pictured doing good things like sponsoring charity races. A telling difference between marketing and public relations: the size of the power company's full name in the nameplate and in the return address is tiny—not suggestive at all of a huge utility. The friendlier "PEPCO" is used exclusively in the copy...which is all about pep, getup and go, and doing good.

WATER ENVIRONMENT Regulation Watch

Vol

Water Environment Regulation Watch is published monthly by the Water Environment Federation. Comments or questions should be directed to the Government Affairs Group at (703) 684-2400, ext. 6501. Subscriptions are available to WEF members for $35/year and to non-members for $79/year. For more information or to subscribe, call the Federation's Member Services Center at (800) 666-0206.

Association (Federation)

Problem: In a newsletter that doesn't go exclusively to members and prefers not to give bylines or run a staff box, how can you spell out housekeeping details for readers who want more information about the content or want to subscribe?

Solution: Run an abbreviated masthead anyway. The notice makes it clear who the publisher is, what the subscription rates are, which internal group will answer questions, and where to call to join the federation or subscribe to the newsletter—without involving the reader extensively in bureaucracy. The conscious decision to de-emphasize personalities—to the extent of giving no reporting credit—is a trade-off: Informality and the potential for reader involvement are forgone to avoid any appearance of politicizing the issues.

Association

Problem: Soliciting submissions.

Solution: Tell readers what topics you need articles written about. *Family Therapy News*, one of several newsletters and a journal intended for the same audience of marriage and family therapists, wants to get readers to submit articles. Traditionally, editors who welcome letters and articles say so in the masthead. But unlike other publications that hedge their bets by asking people to come up with ideas and get in touch with the editor—all initiative resting with the would be-contributor—the editor is very clear about what kinds of articles are welcome and why. In this issue, a boxed item below a "Speak Out" column encourages readers to write about a topic "from the heart"—about "dilemmas you face in research, practice and/or teaching" or as a lobbyist or a trainer. A standalone invitation for articles on alternatives to traditional family relationships explains that they're often overlooked in the literature—and lists them. A small box below the column welcomes letters to the editor and gives guidelines. Offering writers guidelines for substantive articles—or inviting authors to request them—would be a good idea, too.

Corporate/Internal

Problem: Getting the widely dispersed readers of Sara Lee Hosiery's *NEWSlink*, which the nameplate reminds them is published for all employees and their families, to suggest ideas for content that will interest and benefit them.

Solution: Include a box in the newsletter with an encouraging note and a reply form with room for brief comments—and clear instructions for where to mail it or send it via interoffice mail. (Surprisingly often editors "welcome comments" and leave it a mystery where to send them.) The brief form sends the message that responding won't take long and leaves the door open for freeform comments—no boxes to check off that can seem like taking a test.

Submissions Wanted to *Family Therapy News*

Family relationships lie at the core of marriage and family therapists' practices. But these relationships include many that are often given short shrift in the literature and in therapy. *Family Therapy News* seeks articles on the following subjects:

- adult children and their parents
- grandparents and grandchildren
- infant mental health
- aunts and uncles, nephews and nieces
- cousins
- chosen families

Letters to the editor are welcomed. They should not exceed 250 words. All letters selected for publication are subject to editing for clarity and condensation. We regret that we are not able to respond to or publish all submitted letters.

What Do You Think?

Share your thoughts with the readers of *Family Therapy News*! Write from the heart. Tell us about the dilemmas you face in research, practice and/or teaching. Add your voice to the issues discussed in this column. Or describe your experiences as a marriage and family therapist lobbying for change, training the next generation or researching families in crisis. Send to: Joan Rachel Goldberg, *Family Therapy News*, 1100 17th St., NW, 10th Fl., Washington, DC 20036.

Don't Be the Missing Link . . .

NEWSlink lives up to its name only when it represents all Sara Lee Hosiery divisions and employees. You are our direct link to the news.

Use this space to send information or story ideas so that the *NEWSlink* staff can investigate and write the articles that are both interesting and beneficial to you.

You may also use this space to respond to the information you read in *NEWSlink*. Thanks for your help.

_____

_____

_____

_____

For extra copies of NEWSlink, please call 919-519-3414.

Send your suggestions or comments to:

NEWSlink
Sara Lee Hosiery
P.O. Box 2495
Winston-Salem,
NC 27102-2495
Attn: Judy Bourne

or

(Interoffice)
5660 Madison Park,
3rd Floor

PROBABLE CAUSE

Vol. 2, No. 1 • Winter 1995 • No bad poetry or your money back   a literary revue™

Subscription/'Newszine'

Problem: Make a tabloid format "literary revue" that's not quite a newsletter, newspaper, magazine, or journal seem like fun to read and yet not a joke. It's an alternative vehicle with a liberal bias that specializes in darkly humorous profiles and critical articles and book reviews.

Solution: A conservative red rectangle of a nameplate with the title reversed out in slightly funky type—the name itself is evocative and...arresting. An unusually direct but cheerful mission statement sets the tone for the content: "No bad poetry or your money back." The can-can reader-dancers clip art is corny—a cue that the content will be a bit spicy yet safely within the urbane sphere of arts, letters, and the humanities. Plus, we just liked it and wanted to put it in this book to cheer you up.

Church Membership

Problem: Encourage church members to start attending a weekly fund-raising after-service lunch—and help run it.

Sunday Lunches Resume!

Lunch each Sunday after church in Davenport Center features delicious specialties by Arlene LaPenta (*pictured above left*)! Volunteers help Arlene serve her fabulous food. Recently Randall LeCocq and Sheri Sprigg (*above*) served and helped clear the lunch. If you would like to help serve one Sunday, call Gwen Galloway at (202) 363-4698.

Try out the lunch soon for fun and fellowship with other Foundry folks! Or come get your takeout before going to your meeting! The price is right — $5, $4 for seniors and children under 12, and $15 maximum for families.

Solution: Use the highly visible back page for short photo-essay, with the headline and blurb immediately underneath a charming photo of the woman who does all the cooking and a couple of people who have recently helped serve and clean up. The ceiling should have been cropped and the lighting in the kitchen could have been better, but hey, this is amateur photography. The semicircular pose is successful, with the cook properly in the foreground stirring something. They all look so genuinely happy.

Marketing

Problem: In a four-page self-mailing promotional newsletter, Prince Michel Vineyards must find room for a calendar of events associated with a newly opened restaurant.

PRINCE MICHEL VINEYARDS
HCR 4, BOX 77 / LEON VIRGINIA 22725
PHONE (703) 547-3707 FAX (703)547-3088

Mark Your Calendars

NOVEMBER 6, 1993
Don't miss this opportunity for a very special dinner and evening of entertainment to celebrate the release of Le Ducq Lot 88 and the premier release of our 1991 Brut Sparkling Wine at the Prince Michel Restaurant. Seating is limited so call 1-800-869-8242 to reserve.

NOVEMBER 25, 1993
THANKSGIVING DINNER
Put your pans away and let Chef Alain Lecomte do the rest. Last year's feast was unforgettable. Call 1-800-800 WINE for details.

DECEMBER 11, 1993
Make us a part of your Holiday Season with a special evening out. An elegant dinner highlighted by readings from Dickens, a barrel tasting and the sounds of classical music. Evening starts at 7pm. Call the winery 1-800-869-8242 for information.

Solution: Use the back page to list events in neat bullets just above the return address—reminding people where they're being invited to come—that ingeniously incorporates a small, clear map.

Subscription (Consumer/ Educational)

Problem: Helping a general audience learn about rights and permissions without resorting to complex concepts or intimidating legalese.

Solution: Journalistic rather than academic language. The tone of *copyRights* is neutral, but it's adamant on one point: The law is the authority of last resort, and "good faith efforts will not protect you from the consequences of copyright infringement." There are legitimate reasons for "borrowing" original work, but educators and others must ask for and meet the copyright holder's conditions. The editor-publisher also owns a copyright consulting company, but that's the expertise behind this newsletter rather than a marketing agenda. Specific instances of fair and not-so-fair use and short, bulleted checklist-style articles break rights issues into digestible installments.

University/Alumni

Problem: It's tempting to fill tabloid-size pages with splashy graphics; all that white space makes some editors and designers nervous. But a scholarly institution has much to say to its alumni and only eight pages to say it in, so each page must present a lot of text. How can pages be brightened and balanced for comfortable browsing?

Solution: A conservative three-column layout embellished with a few attractive typographical elements is the right approach. Instead of scattering many related small pieces throughout, an umbrella head organizes them onto one copy-dense spread. The second color is welcome in a few spots: subheads, rules between articles, triangular dingbats, rules around pullquotes (but legible black type for the quote), and a header/bar. At first glance, the spread looks like one long article with two sidebars but is really five distinct pieces. Readers can skip around or read straight through, but at no point will they feel at the mercy of text, graphics, random white space, or whimsical organization.

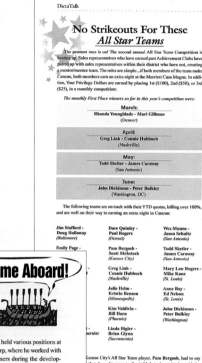

DictaTalk

No Strikeouts For These All Star Teams

The pennant race is on! The second annual All Star Team Competition is heating up. Sales representatives who have earned past Achievement Clubs have paired up with sales representatives within their district who have not, creating a mentor/mentee team. The rules are simple...if both members of the team make Cancun, both members earn an extra night at the Marriott Casa Magna. In addition, Your Privilege Dollars are earned by placing 1st ($100), 2nd ($50), or 3rd ($25), in a monthly competition:

The monthly First Place winners so far in this year's competition were:

March:
Rhonda Youngblade - Mari Gillman
(Denver)

April:
Greg Link - Connie Hubbuch
(Nashville)

May:
Todd Shelter - James Caraway
(San Antonio)

June:
John Dickinson - Peter Bulkley
(Washington, DC)

The following teams are on track with their YTD quotas, billing over 100%, and are well on their way to earning an extra night in Cancun:

Jim Stafford - Doug Holloway (Baltimore)	Dave Quinley - Paul Rogers (Detroit)	Wes Munns - Jason Schultz (San Antonio)
Emily Page -	Pam Bergosh - Scott McIntosh (Kansas City)	Todd Shelter - James Caraway (San Antonio)
	Greg Link - Connie Hubbuch (Nashville)	Mary Lou Rogers - Mike Kane (St. Louis)
	Julie Helm - Kristin Benson (Minneapolis)	Anne Ray - Ed Nelson (St. Louis)
	Kim Valdivia - Bill Horn (Phoenix)	John Dickinson - Peter Bulkley (Washington)
...urnier	Linda Bigler - Brian Glynn (Sacramento)	

...Kansas City's All Star Team player, Pam Bergosh, had to say ...that she and teammate, Scott McIntosh, are having with the

...Star Competition, Scott and I are motivated to bill quota every ...en us an opportunity to find ways to be creative, and it makes ...ility for each other's success. I really am looking forward to Achievement Club."

...kout for monthly results in the All Star '95 Competition. Good ...eams in earning that extra night in Cancun – *Turn Up The Heat!*

Welcome Aboard!

NED O'DONOVAN is the new Healthcare Marketing Manager (Stratford) reporting to Larry Bergeron, Vice President, Systems Marketing. Ned is responsible for the Digital Express® product line. Prior to joining Dictaphone, O'Donovan held various positions at Pratt & Whitney/United Technologies Corp, where he worked with the Boeing Company and airline customers during the development stage of a new high-tech turbine engine for the 777 airplane, also, Ned was involved in hardware design, controlling schedules, budget procurement, and testing. In addition, he acted as liaison with the FAA and foreign regulatory agencies in which he directed certification programs to comply with the agency's air-worthiness requirements. Ned is a graduate of Pratt Institute, Brooklyn, as a Bachelor of Mechanical Engineering, and earned his MBA in Marketing and Finance at the University of Connecticut. We're sure that with Ned's knowledge and experience, the Digital Express product line will soar to new heights! •

Corporate Internal/ International Sales and Service Force

Problem: Motivate employees in a demanding, quota-driven work environment to persevere in their efforts to sell digital equipment worldwide.

Solution: A content formula of 90 percent praise for—and lists and photos of—people who have met competitive sales goals. The colorful tabloid-size format is attractive, but it's the editor's insider humor and upbeat assumption that everybody's a potential winner that shine through. About 10 percent of the content reports on employee benefits and international division news. A lead article may highlight one record-breaking sales rep's success, and the rest of the issue might be a couple of features sprinkled with bits of upbeat news and kudos followed by readable lists of names. (Too many editors bury those presumably being honored in dense paragraphs of indistinguishable name after name complicated by parenthetical affiliation, job title, team, region, etc.) Generous graphic embellishment and the editor's cheery, straightforward energy pull off what could otherwise be cloying. Note the amusing "slave galleon" clip art welcoming a new manager.

University/Staff, Alumni, 'Friends'

Problem: Photograph a stock situation—a groundbreaking ceremony—without posing people stiffly holding shovels.

Solution: Get the "host of dignitaries" (a phrase from the caption we like) to lean into it and really shovel dirt! The semicircle of people in nice suits with mortarboard tassels swinging as the shovels are lifted offers a nice set of contrasts. The unexpected bonus of what seem to be sheepish grins is welcome. The expanded caption identifies the players and the significance of the scene, tells us who else showed up but didn't make it into the picture, and—after the news—names everybody there.

Bricks and Mortarboards Governor Parris N. Glendening joined Chancellor Langenberg and a host of other dignitaries to break ground for a new education facility at the UMS Shady Grove Center. The officials pictured above were joined by members of the Montgomery County business community, legislators, state and UMS officials, and other friends of the University System. (*See article, p. 2*). *Left to right: Maryland State Treasurer Lucille Maurer; Montgomery County Council Chairman Derick Berlage, State Sen. Ida Ruben, Comptroller Louis Goldstein, Sen. Paul Sarbanes, Chancellor Langenberg, Governor Glendening, Montgomery County Executive Douglas Duncan, Shady Grove student Peter Yared, Montgomery County High Technology Council Executive Director Dyan Brasington, University of Maryland University College President T. Benjamin Massey.*

Service/Internal

Problem: Dealing with a seemingly small but potentially divisive problem at a senior assisted living community. The problem? Food pilfering from the early breakfast buffet.

Solution: This little anecdote is a sly, well-turned version of the time-honored technique of reporting troublesome events through the persona of a disinterested bystander—here, a cat. (We presume it's clear to all that the cat is fictional, since most such communities, though not all, discourage cats in residence.) The interesting thing is that the persona is doubly masked. The complaint about a lack of doughnuts comes not from someone who showed up for the later breakfast shift and was cheated, but from someone who got theirs at the 8 a.m. breakfast. So the "cat," speaking for someone who saw the earlybirds pocket extra treats for private consumption, is merely meowing—not really an aggrieved party: in fact, a nobody. This is a graphic way to point out bad citizenship without pointing an angry finger. For a publication amateurs produce in their spare time for peers, a sermon would backfire. But in this case, point made and I'll bet someone's ears burned.

Scholarly Society/ Membership

Problem: Printing many contributions to a "Letters to the Editor" department in an already text-dense newsletter.

Solution: *The Key Reporter*, although legible, is packed with text. Its readers aren't afraid of words, though; in fact, they're full of words themselves, and they appreciate the "Letter to the Editors" forum. Because the newsletter appears only four times a year, the editor prints as many as a dozen letters in a 16-page issue, some 500 words long. Using display caps, rules, or extra white space to set notes off would be considered a waste of good air time by this group. The simple device of using topical subheads in blue makes it easy to browse through batches of notes on a variety of subjects. The blue also brightens pages.

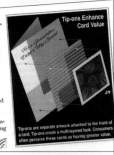

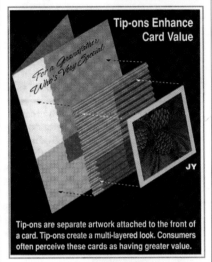

New "Environmental" Art Look for Father's Day

The evolving children's line is not the only change. **Rick Davis**, Creative Developer, Product Group IV, and his team were asked to create an upscale Father's Day feature to build retail sales.

"Creating innovative masculine cards has its own set of design challenges," says Rick. "Classic subject matter, such as sailboats and decoys, can quickly become overused.

We wanted the final product to feel natural, yet rich," continues Rick. "Because we know that consumers today are concerned about nature and the environment we gave the new cards a simple, honest, handmade look."

They did that by using recycled materials to make the cards. "With recycled brown paper, corrugated cardboard and natural jute, as well as colors inspired by nature — rust, forest green and ocean blue — the cards take on an environmental look," says Rick.

The final result is new card art that has the look of etchings or engravings. Artwork includes nature scenes, fish and other wildlife. Cost is $4 per card, a price consumers don't mind paying when they have the added value of heavier paper stocks, verse inserts, foil stamping and full-color tip-ons.

Tip-ons Enhance Card Value

Tip-ons are separate artwork attached to the front of a card. Tip-ons create a multi-layered look. Consumers often perceive these cards as having greater value.

Corporate/Internal

Problem: "Raising awareness, understanding, and activity of associates in support of business goals" is the stated mission of American Greetings Corporation's internal newsletter—and the unstated goal of all other internal newsletters. But most people resist any sign of top-down propaganda.

Solution: When describing the success of a new product line—a primary topic—the editors use direct quotes from the employees involved and avoid overly gung-ho editorial asides. Here, just in time for Father's Day, a creative team member explains the challenge of creating an upscale "masculine card" without resorting to duck decoy or sailboat motifs. The new card art used recycled paper, cardboard, and natural colors for "a simple, honest, handmade look" and "tip-ons," which turn out to be separate layers of artwork attached to the front of a card. A graphic shows the technique, and the caption reminds employees that "consumers often perceive these cards as having greater value." Corporate values are matter-of-factly shown—creative teamwork translates to sales—without inspiring cynicism.

Advocacy

Problem: How can the Office Workers Division of the Service Employees International Union use the cover to showcase 16 pages packed with 22 articles and reports and make people want to read them?

Solution: Highlight key topics, magazine-style. Here, the editors pitch four main categories of information—cover story, survey, strategies, job safety—and advertise four meaty articles. A photo collage of the people the newsletter is trying to reach with one important piece, part-time office workers, would be suspect in any but an advocacy context. They're posed believably at recognizable tasks, so these "generic" types escape seeming canned.

Consumer/Public Relations

Problem: Many people resist reading unsolicited material that's "for their own good." How, then, can health-related information be presented palatably to a general readership of more than 300,000 members of a health plan? Consider the widely varying levels of education, along with low human tolerance for warnings and unsolicited advice. Articles about taking personal responsibility for preventing accidents or losing weight and lists of wellness and support seminars just aren't intrinsically compelling to the casual reader.

Solution: Kaiser-Permanente uses a spacious tabloid format with clip art that seems hand-drawn to humanize its practical newsletter for mid-Atlantic members. The pastel spot illustrations are literal cues to the copy they accompany—it ain't cutting edge, but that's not the goal. It's meant to be accessible and nonthreatening, just like the writing; the mild-mannered clip art helps. The ultimate message is that the health plan you've chosen knows how to talk with people—like you. Skimming squibs about clinical cholesterol and when to go to the emergency room rewards readers with little effort.

Marketing/'Flyletter'

Problem: A travel agency wants to make traveling sound like a good idea and advertise trip packages. This free one-pager is distributed like a flyer but formatted like a mini-newsletter.

Solution: Production values are low, but care is taken to write catchier headlines than you tend to find in such flyletters. Each "issue" features a couple of themes, here, winter travel: trips to warm climates and good European tour deals. Headlines let readers know what country a blurb's about and reward those who enjoy—and get—corny puns like "Peso Little for Spain." This is bottom-line service journalism and it's not to be sneezed at.

Budget Cuts Threaten Societal Safety Net For The Mentally Ill

Gregory B. Collins, M.D., President

These are indeed perilous times for the mentally ill. In addition to harsh cutbacks in private insurance, government plans may be facing similar austerity measures.

This week, the House and Senate will be debating the merits of balancing the Federal budget, with sharp focus on current entitlement programs like Medicaid and Medicare. Pending proposals would chop Medicare by $280 million and Medicaid by $170 million over the next seven years. These programs have evolved into the underpinnings of our societal safety net for medical and psychiatric care for the elderly, the poor, and the chronically ill. Most state, public, and private programs now depend on a large infusion of these federal funds to maintain program integrity and support

valuable services. There is no way that budget reductions of this magnitude can be made up by private insurance or charitable philanthropy.

If these cuts are enacted, programs will have to be downsized or dismantled and important services will be eliminated. Social, medical, and psychiatric services depend on available funding. If no funding is available, these safety nets for our citizens will simply not be there. Please take the time to get involved in this political debate. Encourage our senators and congressmen to preserve these programs. Write to our President, Bill Clinton, urging his veto on any sizeable cutbacks. If we, and our patients, don't get involved, we may have to live with a drastically curtailed network of services for the mentally ill, the aged, and the poor. Please let Washington know where you stand.

Workman Receives APA Award

Philip A. Workman, Executive Director of OPA, was the recipient of the 1995 Area 4 Warren Williams Award at the APA Assembly Meeting in November, held in Washington, D.C. Each Area Council of the Assembly bestows the award on a person or program for outstanding contributions to the field of psychiatry and mental health. The other recipient of the award is Robert Irisay, owner of the Indianapolis Colts.

Mr. Workman has been Executive Director of the Ohio Psychiatric Association since 1983. His loyalty to the organization and his success in this position have been exceptional. During his tenure the membership of the association has more than doubled and he is noted for his helpful and supportive attitude toward all members.

Joining Dr. Michael Pierce in the presentation to Mr. Workman are (L to R) Drs. Norman Clemens, Bernard Foster, Dale Svendsen, Melvin Chavinson, Robert McDevitt, and Mary Kay Smith.

Mr. Workman has been very effective in supporting the work of individual members as

Continued on page 13

Volume 20, Number 3
November, 1995

Association/District Branch of a National Group

Problem: If you start two articles on the front page and one or both are accompanied by a small photo, where should you put the nameplate so there's room for everything? In this case, the nameplate has to include the names of the newsletter, the district branch (and logo), the national organization, and the date, volume, and number.

Solution: The president's letter is always short and ends on the cover, but a news lead usually continues inside. A professional designer set up the nameplate to run vertically on the far left with the district and national association names reversed and printed over the newsletter's name—an ingenious graphic statement for an audience of psychiatrists. There's room for two healthy horizontal story shapes plus photos—and the layout doesn't seem crowded. (Ideally, only prominent news stories should be on the cover page. But editors break this rule all the time and the world keeps turning.)

Corporate/Internal

Problem: Support staff for an international ad campaign both in the United States and abroad.

Solution: Research findings connect the corporate agenda to reality, and Avon's goal "to be the company that best understands and satisfies the product, service, and self-fulfillment needs of women" globally meant that management's vision had to be translated for the front-line sales associates abroad for whom the *Outlook* newsletter is also published. Special articles about the "Women Are Beautiful" campaign quote brand managers saying that Avon knows beauty means "who you are, not how you look." Of course, Avon does want its sales force to actually sell things for the outermost woman, and *Outlook* presented them with an outside research firm's survey results—objective evidence "relevant to Avon's vision." Motivational writing like this works because it doesn't feel like propaganda.

Government Agency/
Public Relations

Problem: Assorted pieces of information—highlights of recent research, awards, and activities; sources for original documents or additional information; and media contacts—have to be presented as discrete units without looking choppy. The emphasis should be on the content, since the newsletter goes to the research community as well as the media.

Solution: *NIST Update* is short, simple, and unpretentious. No more than two or three announcements are printed on the first three pages; the back page is $\frac{1}{3}$ self-mailer, $\frac{1}{3}$ table of contents and return address, and $\frac{1}{3}$ mission statement, subscription information for print and electronic versions, and the editor's name and address. The media contact always appears at the far left on the scholar's margin. A note about more information is always at the end of the article in smaller type under a rule, like an informal footnote. A clue to the topic is run to the left of the headline, an on-the-line kicker. The two-column blurbs all begin with a large screened drop cap aligned under the headline. This economical format is no more and no less than what's called for to convey what are really short press releases.

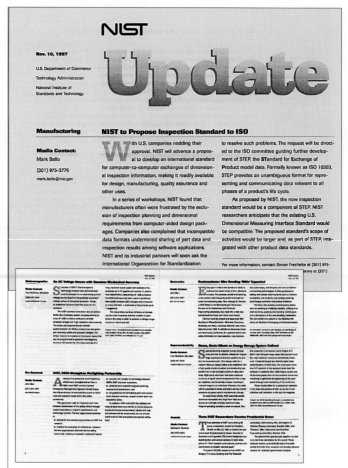

Subscription/
Nondenominational
Religious

Problem: With a small production budget and an emphasis on an ecumenical approach to the study of the Christian Bible, what kind of art will appeal to all readers?

Solution: The block initial capital in medieval style is well nested into copy and makes an attractive entry point. The candle isn't spectacular but doesn't need to be in order to balance two quotations about light in the scholar's margin. Just enough but not too much embellishment—and unlikely to offend anyone.

Nonpartisan, Quasi-Governmental Research Institute/External

Problem: Long analytical articles about international projects must be balanced with news of an institute's activities. How to set them off clearly so the 12-page newsletter has a predominantly "worldly" feel but doesn't neglect "internal" news?

Solution: Beginning with the lead article and the table of contents that lists only articles with an international focus, the first half or more of the content is devoted to one- and two-page reports about peace efforts overseas. The remaining half or less is a series of departments clearly flagged as "internal"—"Institute Events" and "Institute People." Here, half the self-mailer/back cover neatly advertises new books, a conference, and a grant deadline. This physical division of content into "front" and "back" content ratios is neither magazine-style nor random-sound-bite-style newsletter organization. The math works well for its editors—and readers—and that's all she wrote.

International Association/Training

Problem: This newsletter was redesigned from a large tabloid to an 8½- by 11-inch newsletter with four spot colors and full-bleed photos on glossy paper. You can't just send out a publication that's so obviously undergone plastic surgery without reassuring readers they can still depend on it.

Solution: On one crisply organized page were printed a short letter from the director of publications, a list of publications staff, and a masthead crediting the people responsible for the inaugural issue. The new look is presented as the product of a roster of attentive professionals who have retained "time-tested features" while adding such content as a readers' forum and pull-out order forms to make the newsletter more reader-friendly. If you redesign, explain why.

Association/Service, Free to the Visually Impaired

Problem: Making news about resources—talking books, large print publications, products with "low vision features"—available to people who have trouble seeing. The wish to distribute the newsletter free (with donations encouraged) makes the budget for production a negative number, so type is the only tool.

Solution: The obvious solution for the staff of the National Association for the Visually Handicapped seemed to be to print their newsletter in 18-point Helvetica Bold with a lot of leading. (This is a step in the right direction for any newsletter that wants to reach an older audience as well.) For people with macular degeneration and other vision handicaps, a serif typeface might be advisable for even greater ease in perceiving letter shapes. A heavy weight for body copy might seem logical, but it's a little like shouting in English at someone who speaks a foreign language—a lighter weight would actually reduce blurring or fuzzing around and inside words for many readers. But big is beautiful.

Nonprofit Bureau/ Education

Problem: Give readers information that's key but not directly on-topic without interrupting the flow of an article.

Solution: Create fact boxes (sidebars). A long *Population Today* article about the relationship of rising population and water supply begins with a strong statement: "The world's population lives at the mercy of the water cycle." There's little room in this analytical piece for facts about water itself—yet readers will gain perspective by knowing more about the nature of this resource. A box, lightly screened, sets off four "Myths About Water" without competing with copy. Statistics about per capita water supply in developing countries are easier to scan in another box than if they were buried in body copy. Fact boxes help the newsletter meet its stated mission of offering "News, the numbers, and analysis" without making long articles seem even longer.

You write the caption!

(Editor's note: After many hours of looking at this picture and trying to decide just what to say, we determined that anything we put on paper would be sophomoric. The old adage "A picture is worth a thousand words" is all too true. In reality the photographer was busy trying to get some "good shots" and failed to hear the conversation preceding the photo. For that he has been dealt with severely. Ken Hipp and Randy Babbitt will not divulge confidential information.)

Is this fellow in danger of losing his status as the state budget mascot?

Halloween festivities in Manufacturing Accounting in Winston-Salem included a Miss Sara Lee pageant. Winners of the event received enthusiastic support — and countless bad jokes — from all department employees. Cornell Brody, Mailroom, was voted Miss Sara Lee; runners up (left to right) were Dave Hampton, Charles Wiles and Bill Hauser, all of Manufacturing Accounting.

Desktop/Prepress • Commercial Printing • Envelope Printing

Direct Mail Package Design and Production Now Go Hand in Hand

The desktop publishing revolution has altered the designer's role in regard to the production process.

In the past, designers considered only a few production factors when creating a direct mail package. The creative process was basically separate from the production process.

The 1991 USPS rate case introduced new factors that affect cost, speed and deliverability of mail. These factors have many package design implications. Base postage rates increased substantially, but so did postage discounts available for easy-to-process mail.

Design must now be done with production in mind in order to take advantage of these discount opportunities. Where the major postal considerations in design need to be size, shape, thickness and weight, they now include a host of other items:

- Teaser and graphics placement
- Return address placement
- Folds
- Covering material
- Color of inks and stocks
- Clear space for sealing wafers (tabs)
- Stiffness and flexibility
- Loose contents
- Protrusions
- Labels and stickers
- Addressing method

- Processing category (size and shape)
- Window size
- Insert clearance

Each of these factors affects production and must be considered during the design phase in order to achieve the desired level of postal service and cost.

With postal penalties that can exceed any other production cost, it is imperative that new direct mail package designs be reviewed by production experts before you commit to the design.

Please call our Desktop Department if you have any questions about creating a direct mail package.

What's Up with Recycled Paper?

With the newly-elected Clinton-Gore administration the 1990's could very well be the decade of the environment. The new administration is promising to reward conservation and "green" business practices with the use of recycled materials.

Additionally, every poll shows that Americans' concern for the environment is here to stay. There is a genuine demand for recycled paper products.

Here's a brief update: In many cases recycled paper looks as good as its virgin counterpart...it is generally more expensive than virgin paper, but the cost differential is decreasing...it's significantly stronger than it was in the past...it has a much better "feel" than previously...it may still vary in performance and color a bit more than virgin paper....

EU customers are using a more than ever (recycled paper accounts for 50% of our paper usage)...most EU customers are asking for paper with 10% post consumer waste...we've added several new papers to our recycled paper portfolio. (See enclosed reply card.)

If you want to increase your use of recycled paper or to begin using it for the first time, it's important to work with a printer that is knowledgeable and experienced. Call us if we can be of help.

EU Still Prints Small Envelope & Letterhead Jobs

Over the past 24 years EU Services has grown from a small envelope printing company to a very large full service printing and mailing company. Yet today we will print small quantities of envelopes and letterheads — just like we did back in 1968 when we first opened our doors for business.

So if you think we've gotten too big for your small envelope and letterhead jobs — think again.

Give us a call. You'll find that in keeping with our commitment of providing the highest level of customer satisfaction, we'll give you the very best quality, superior service, and exceptional price/value.

Association & Corporate/Internal

Problem: In-group humor works only inside a cohesive group like an association or other affinity group (hobbyists, fans, sports/cooking/health, etc., enthusiasts) with a shared culture of references, problems, heroes, dreams, and experiences. If a newsletter that uses this kind of humor also distributes issues to readers outside the closed circle—lawmakers, allied professionals, vendors, clients, and potential clients, it's making a big mistake. It's for family only.

Solution: Be sure you're being very, very funny, as these examples are. And be sure you can weather hearing from someone who won't get the joke or think it's funny. A sense of what's humorous is even more subjective and open to disagreement than a sense of what's news.

Marketing

Problem: Find a way to stand out in current and potential customers' minds as a provider of competitive prepress and commercial printing services.

Solution: Market expertise first, specific services second. The printer of this newsletter, EU News & Insights, is a...printer. A tagline makes it clear that it's "A production newsletter for people involved in print buying, direct mail & production coordination." Readers get a ratio of useful content (news = service) to overt marketing (insight = how we can help you) of about 3 to 1. Of 14 articles in this issue, 5 were self-referential: a note about the newsletter itself, an invitation to a free seminar for clients, an announcement of a company award, advice for desktop file preparation, and the small low-key ad in the lower right corner of the illustration. The overall effect is of a newsletter full of help and a company full of pros waiting to help.

Association/membership

Problem: Getting members to volunteer for association projects.

Solution: A first-person testimonial touting the personal rewards of becoming active. A nice touch is the volunteer's reassurance that "volunteering doesn't have to mean 20 hours a week. It can be one hour a week. There are a lot of projects that come in bite-size chunks, and there is a lot of room to suggest your own project." The last paragraph mentions the networking that being a volunteer makes possible. Of our volunteer's three jobs following college, two came about as a direct result of association contacts.

Membership/User group

Problem: Getting members of a user group to participate in the work of the organization, let others know about independently developed applications, and write articles for the newsletter.

Solution: Instead of a note in the masthead generally inviting "contributions," a no-nonsense appeal outlines the specific ways in which readers/members can and should become active. The oversize, screened exhortation to "Volunteer!" makes it graphically clear what's coming and compels at least a moment of attention. Then a two-part message delivers the editorial payoff: (a) a series of rhetorical questions that show personal benefits to volunteering and (b) appeals for help with three areas where volunteerism is being encouraged.

The imperative voice makes the claim on readers' attention: "Share your perspective and ideas— and make an impact…," "Experience the reward of developing an exciting annual event," and "Develop and communicate valuable information to fellow…users—and help a publication come together." The boldfaced bottom line for each is a flat-out instruction to "join": the software advisory team, the annual conference planning committee, or the newsletter/publications committee.

3.2 Don't do that

Newsletters are built by hand from a finite set of conventions and standardized graphic elements that lend themselves to many simple variations in different hands. Creative ideas are great, but execution is everything. Simply looking at what your colleagues in newsletter publishing are up to makes you a better judge of your own work—especially when you can put into words what you don't want to emulate.

Remember the old skit? A guy goes to his doctor, pokes himself sharply in the ribs, and complains, "It hurts when I do that." The doctor considers, then drawls, "Well, don't do that." What follows is a rogue's gallery of samples, real enough although somewhat disguised, that don't work very well for anyone, under any conditions.

As consultants who evaluate publications and recommend ways to strengthen our clients' mission, EEI Press editors are always on the lookout for patterns of weakness, inconsistency, overdesign, poor organization, lack of hierarchy, inappropriate language, and lack of focus. Here are a few recurring problems that are difficult to illustrate here, but they're also "dont's" we see in print all too often:

- Articles that continue across spreads that have several other new and jumped pieces without a "continued from" line. Several jump heads that reiterate only a few cryptic words from their original articles are an even bigger headache.

- Continuations from several jumps that all end up on one page and turn it into a dumping-ground.

- A very short article or caption floating beside a large photo—it's better formatted as a photo-plus-caption "photo feature" in a box or vertical or horizontal solidly within the grid.

- Jumps to and from very short "legs" of text that make copy look insignificant coming and going.

- Inconsistent head-level styles—an attempt at "magazine style" variations usually comes off looking as if no care has been taken to reconcile style and content.

- Long pullquotes shoehorned onto a page with so little white space around them that they butt almost into copy or break up a short paragraph.

- Long, undigested blocks of direct quotation that ramble and repeat ideas.

- Leaving people out of photo captions or talking about people who aren't there—or aren't there in the order in which they're listed.

- Captions that repeat copy almost exactly from the headline or the story—use the caption to add something new to the story or lead back to it.

- Humor that goes beyond informality to flippancy and looks like the editor's showing off.

- Conclusions that seem tacked on—replace a vague or abstract paragraph that just repeats previous statements with a pertinent quote, a few words that end on a positive note, or a genuine summary.

- Redundant writing—places where the same things are really being said in slightly different ways that don't contribute new information or perspective.

This is a gallery of graphic shortcomings and basic editorial errors common to many newsletters. But having good company doesn't mean it's okay to ignore very real impediments to readers. *Don't* do what you see examples of here.

As you look at the don'ts, remember that you can't directly blame the editor, designer, or art director on whose watch they occurred. That's why we've tried to erase their provenance. Compromises get made for political reasons that can't be footnoted on the page (the executive director loves olive green ink; the president insists you use the goofy awards ceremony photo that's a sea of the backs of everybody's heads). And mistakes get made. Period. The trick is to learn from flubs so that next time, if you make a mistake, it won't be the same one. Hey, that's progress!

Site profile Successful sites and what makes them tick

Selling with specifics

Hilton's site breaks customers into small groups and gives each what they want

Hilton Hotels Corp. (www.hilton.com) makes clear the ultimate purpose of its Web site: to rent more hotel rooms. It employs many methods to do that, targeting some portions of the site to casual travelers and others to hard-core business travelers and members of its Honors frequent guest program.

"We want the business traveler to be able to get on the site, make reservations quickly and get off—because that's what they want to do," says Mike Wylie, senior account manager for Synapse Group (www.synapse-group.com), which designed the site for Hilton. "The leisure traveler wants to be able to go to the pages for individual hotels, see pictures of them, see where they're located and find out information about nearby attractions."

As a result, Hilton has created different content areas based on the preferences of these major customers. The emphasis on getting business customers into the site and out again quickly is evident on the home page, which is one of the graphically lightest home pages on the Web. The home page has two or three tiny GIFs of drawings or type, but otherwise completely consists of text that focuses on navigational choices.

"It's a little too stripped down," admits David Ayers, Synapse's senior technical consultant. But he says that it's important that the front page loads quickly given the firm's worldwide audience and the fact that many countries have slower Internet connections that the U.S.

Just as many airlines have devoted the resources of their Web sites to their frequent flyers, much of the Hilton site is aimed at customers in its Honors program. "It's a good audience to sell to," Wylie says, "they're already Hilton loyalists." Plus, Honors members tend to have high-speed Internet access, and they account for a large percentage of site traffic, he adds.

Honors members can access their full statement online, as well as see detailed information about their last three Hilton stays. The entire guidebook for that program is online, so customers can check on its rules, etc., whenever they want. This decreases the amount of costly telephone calls Hilton receives from people with questions about the program. And to save costs further, Hilton not only lets Honors customers make reservations online, it encourages them to do so by giving them an extra 1,000 Honors points each time they do so (normally members earn 10 points per dollar spent).

To provide content for the travel sections prized by the more casual travelers of the tourist market, Hilton has licensed tourism and travel material from the Worldview Corp. The individual hotels also send Hilton headquarters photographs, which Hilton puts on the Web site. In fact, some of the individual hotels have already set up their own sites—one of the reasons that Hilton is working on a site revision.

Consistency means reigning in franchisees

"It's very to important to Hilton to maintain consistency so it didn't want hotels creating their own sites," Wylie says. "The company follows a franchise model, and some of the sites hotels have already built don't necessarily reflect the corporate image."

Telling these hotels that they have to fold their sites into the main Hilton site and follow its guidelines for look and feel is a politically sensitive task. Hilton has made it less onerous by pointing out some of the benefits of being on the main site: Individual hotels won't have to pay hosting fees, they can integrate Hilton's content (such as its licensed travel material) into the pages for their hotel, and they won't have to pay for maintenance.

"A lot of the hotels went to little boutique Web shops," Wylie says. "They're finding that maintenance is costing much more than they thought it would; it's difficult every time they want to get something changed."

After the revision, every Hilton hotel will have the same look on the first page of its section. Hilton and Synapse Group have created several templates: one for this entry page and others for further down in the site—where design innovation will be encouraged more than on the entry page.

An example of a page on the Hilton Web site targeted toward a specific group—in this case the American Astronomical Association.

The revision will also present material in several languages. Not only will this make foreign business travelers feel more at home, it will save Hilton money. The company can put up brochures in Japanese or German, then send prospects a one-page mailer in their language directing them to the site. Printing entire four-color brochures in many different languages would be too expensive.

Finally, the revision will target the hotel chain's primary audiences even more carefully than they are currently. Group sales—blocks of rooms designated for conventions, for instance—account for 20 to 30 percent of Hilton's business. Special sites will be set up for large groups. They will include floor plans, and the ability to enter a booking code and get the reduced rate negotiated by the sponsoring group.

Finally, Hilton is setting up pages especially for its larger corporate accounts. For example, stock brokerage firm Charles Schwab already has six or so pages on which Schwab employees can access information such as Schwab's corporate rate with Hilton. Hilton is also setting up a forms-based system that will allow a Schwab employee to manage the content on its part of the Hilton site without knowing HTML.

"Companies like Schwab have preferred rate agreements with three or so hotel companies," Ayers points out, "and the individual traveler can make the choice about which hotel to stay at. We want to make it as easy as possible for them to choose Hilton—we even want to get a link to our site from their intranet."

Synapse Group: (214) 599-2929

Marketing

Problem: A copy-dense page with a single subhead and a graphic isolated at the top of the article.

Solution: There's always more than one place in long copy where subheads can be added as transitional devices—if only as run-in heads that take up less room. If not, don't use just one subhead. There's trapped white space all around the floating graphic and leftover space at the bottom of the far-right column; that just emphasizes how crowded the page is. Align the graphic deeper in one of the columns and distribute space evenly around it. Then the graphic can be visual relief and an editorial aid, rather than a parenthetical comment.

Cost and Quality Management

The January HFMA meeting which was held on Tuesday, January 20, 1994 presented members with various approaches to the concept of Cost and Quality Management. Continuous Quality Improvement, HMO Quality Score Cards, Operational Cost and Quality Management, Organizational Change Management and Patient Redesign were the topics discussed.

Shawn Haag, Vice President of Operations for Allegheny General Hospital, began the program with "Continuous Quality Improvement (CQI): Two Years Later". The basis for the CQI program that evolved at Allegheny General is "quality improvement being the integration of a strategy for controlling costs while achieving the vision of meeting customers expectations". Work groups, strategic aims, cultures to welcome change and strategic models were among the concepts implemented during the process.

"HMO Quality Report Cards" was presented by representatives from Kaiser Permanente: David Beal, Vice President and Regional Controller, and Dr. Allan Khoury, M.D., Ph.D., Vice President and Associate Regional Medical Director. The report card was developed to provide comparative information to the health care purchaser such as access to care, appropriateness, efficiency, outcomes of care and membership satisfaction with health care plans.

Robert Polahar, Administrator of Knox Community Hospital, and Marshall E. Winkle, President of the Knox Board of Trustees, presented their management tools for achieving an optimal balance between "Operational Cost and Quality Management". Investing in educational programs for management, concentrating on changing the culture at Knox and promoting the concept that ALL employees should be leaders lead Knox to develop their tailored strategic quality management program. The program focuses on four key areas: reducing mortality rates, improving the ease of data inputs, reducing variations in practice patterns and improving the use of resources. Some of their successes were shared with the group.

Jeff Jenkins, Manager at Plante & Moran, presented his thoughts on

Left to Right:

and included leadership commitment, obs

disciplinary involvement.

Nancy Schanz, R.N., Senior Manager at Erns

involves "defining optimal roles and system

produce excellent patient care, high quality

patient care. The phases of the process inclu

and evaluation. Nancy concluded her presen

Left to Right:

Association/Chapter

Problem: The line length is the entire width of the page. The photo isn't placed in any relationship to the grid—because there isn't a grid. The photo is badly in need of cropping, but we'll bet it's somebody's idea of symmetrical composition (too much of it is a dangerous thing—it makes all things equal). The hospital administrators, who should be prominent, are dwarfed by the wall behind them and separated by a blank podium they seem to admiring. So central they almost seem to need their own place in the caption are the podium, some light-blasted posters we can't read, and the light sconce on the wall. The caption is a painfully banal "left to right."

Solution: If you really have to print a photo like this, at least crop everything except the central third of it, size it up, and let us see what's on those posters. We don't need to see these fellows from the waist down—and the cropping would emphasize their hands pointing to evidence of their joint efforts. Better to run a smaller, more focused photo and a larger caption. In the story we learn that they presented some quality management tools at a chapter meeting. Tell us about that.

Association/Volunteer Editor

Problem: Trapped white space and an off-kilter feel that result from trying to place blocks of copy that are different sizes and shapes—and in different typefaces—without regard for a grid.

This is the surest sign of an amateurish effort and one of the most common problems when volunteer editors without graphic training are responsible for desktop publishing or worse, word processing the layout.

The page looks junky, so the content seems worthless by association. To compensate for the leftover space at the bottom, the association's logo has been stuck roughly at the center of it, but that merely calls more attention to the hodgepodge above—visually undercutting the care taken to produce a newsletter that's actually full of useful stuff.

Solution: Use consistent spacing, hanging indented bullets, and bigger margins around boxed text. And unbox at least one piece.

The "Employees Telephone Network"—a good feature—could easily be expanded to fill an entire column by using a type size people could bear to read. The masthead should repeat the entire official name of the newsletter and give contact names and numbers. The ad could easily be resized to fit within the right column. The margins within the text boxes should be the same. Fixing these omissions and style vagaries would solve the empty spaces like magic and let the copy breathe.

Educational/Alumni

Problem: The photo is misleading. There's no caption or callout in text, so it's impossible to know whether the photo is of the author of the article or the person whose appointment he's announcing.

Solution: Run a caption or build a reference into text after his name and title: "...Vice-Chancellor for Graduate Studies and Research (at left)."

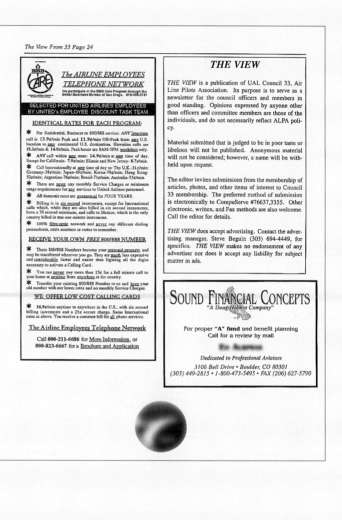

Graduate Studies Gets New Leader

It is with great personal pleasure that I inform you of the recent appointment of ██████ ██ ████ Kenan Professor of Chemistry, as Vice-Chancellor for Graduate Studies and Research.

RESOLUTION:	96.04.18	REQUEST FOR APPOINTMENT OF JOHN SCHLEDER TO THE POSITION OF CONTRACT ADMINISTRAT-OR FOR THE EGL-MEC
Motion to adopt by:		Passed: Unanimously
Seconded by:		

RESOLUTION:	96.04.21	THIRD REGULAR MEC MEETING
Motion to adopt by:	Peter Hoffley	Passed: Unanimously
Seconded by:	Bernie Neumann	

BE IT RESOLVED that the third regular EGL-MEC meeting be held in San Juan, PR, facilities permitting, with June 25-28 as target dates.

RESOLUTIONS NOT ADOPTED BY THE MEC

RESOLUTION:	95.12.15	STRAIGHT AND LEVEL NAME CHANGE BY CONTEST
Motion Reconsidered		NOT ADOPTED

TO change the name of the *Straight and Level* Newsletter and that the new name be decided by a contest announced in the *Straight and Level* Newsletter.

Association/Volunteer Editor

Problem: Trying too hard to use graphics to enhance a report on the results of the executive council's voting on resolutions or any other important but bread-and-butter association housekeeping.

Solution: Don't try to force simple text into an overly complicated graphic. Even a "simple" graphic is overkill if the content isn't suited to tabular format. Especially if a graphic has to do double duty as an ersatz subhead—each new table introduces a resolution—it must be instantly clear. The huge gray cells with all-caps titles take up a disproportionate amount of space, with separate cells for the word *resolution*, the resolution number, and, as a caption, the meaningful content: the subject of the resolution. The lower-right-hand cell is always blank, a clue that the graphic isn't the correct format. To add insult to injury, all these graphics are in a part of the report labeled "Resolutions Adopted." Only one, in fact, was not adopted, and it's listed last.

Reading stubs from left to right as for lines of text rather than using conventional table format goes against the grain. The reader keeps trying and failing to use the information like it's a real table. The result is an admirable attempt to be graphic that makes reading harder than it has to be. The only information that truly needs high-lighting is the nature of the resolution—we already know that almost all of them passed. All the rest of the details can be made subordinate.

Educational/Governmental

Problem: Old-fashioned, generic clip art and a windbag of a pullquote.

Solution: Allow room in the grid for a proper scholar's margin or do without; use a better-quality illustration or do without.

This stagy grouping of office workers adds nothing to support content or build interest—unless office meetings with people in suits is your idea of a treat. It's stuck atop the story and centered over the whole page but not over the text block, so the side of it above the right column looks cut off—it's almost an optical illusion of "now it's balanced, now it's not." And this isn't a useful scholar's margin that opens up a page with white space and lets an interesting quote draw readers into the text. It's a high-school-dropout's margin, with a quote too wordy to begin with and crowded into 20 lines so short that some have only one word on them. Remember that you can edit a long quote down to its essence so that it's a bright, short soundbite—or even paraphrase it into a nutshell.

Marketing/Value-Added Advice

Problem: Too much italic setting one category of information off from another.

Solution: Since a lot of light, steeply slanted italic makes readers squint (not all italic is this hard to read), use it to set off the least amount of text, not the most, on a page.

In this case, the reader letters are short and the expert's answers are long—and also more significant. The ratio of italic to roman should be reversed. The author bio at the beginning of the article shouldn't look like either a question or an answer. A different font, perhaps a sans serif, would indicate more clearly that it's an aside and could be used for other editorial notes. That would still be only two different fonts on the page; the italic counts as part of the body font family.

The NIDCD was proud to sponsor the NIH consensus development conference on the Early Identification of Hearing Impairment in Infants and Young Children, along with the NIH Office of Medical Applications of Research (See UPDATE, Issue 1). The conference was cosponsored by the National Institute of Child Health and Human Development and the National Institute of Neurological Disorders and Stroke. The consensus panel recommended, for the first time, that ALL INFANTS SHOULD BE SCREENED FOR HEARING IMPAIRMENT AT BIRTH because any degree of hearing impairment during infancy and early childhood can have devastating effects on speech and language development. The panel made this recommendation because advances in technology have led to improved screening methods that provide the capability to identify hearing impairments in infants soon after birth. A summary of the consensus panel's recommendations is given in this issue of UPDATE. • We are pleased to provide an article about activities from the National Center for Neurogenic Communication Disorders at the University of Arizona in Tucson, one of the multipurpose research and training centers (RTC) supported by the NIDCD. This is the first in a series of articles that will appear in UPDATE which provide information about RTCs supported by the NIDCD. Also in this issue is an article describing the newest publications available from the NIDCD. These publications include a monograph entitled DEVELOPMENT, GROWTH AND SENESCENCE IN THE CHEMICAL SENSES, new public information brochures, and the availability of some NIDCD publications in Spanish. • As this issue of UPDATE goes to press, we are planning a program for the NIDCD Fifth Anniversary, "A Celebration of Research in Human Communication," on Monday, October 25, 1993, from 3:00 to 5:30 p.m. The program will be held in Masur Auditorium of the Warren Grant Magnuson Clinical Center at the NIH and includes a keynote salute, festivities and performances. There will be three scientific presentations dealing with highlights of research and future directions: • "Recent Developments in Research on Hearing and Balance," by Dennis McFadden, Ph.D., Professor of Experimental Psychology, Department of Psychology, University of Texas at Austin • "Smell and Taste: Recent Advances and Future Directions," by Linda Buck, Ph.D., Assistant Professor, Department of Neurobiology, Harvard Medical School • "For Speech and Language, Time is of the Essence," by Paula Tallal, Ph.D., Professor and Co-Director, Center for Molecular and Behavioral Neuroscience, Rutgers University • A reception will follow the program and a dinner in honor of Geraldine Dietz Fox, the first chairperson of the National Deafness and Other Communication Disorders Advisory Board, will conclude the festivities.

UPDATE is published periodically by the National Institute on Deafness and Other Communication Disorders (NIDCD). Its purpose is to communicate NIDCD research findings and other activities of interest to those working in the field of human communication

Educational/Research Institute

Problems: Director's letter takes up an entire page of a four-page newsletter.

Solution: Don't ask the letter to carry so much weight: advertising upcoming programs and new publications, reporting the results of recent conferences, and recapping articles in the issue. Cut the letter to a column and let it cover one kind of content. Put news items in a clearly labeled roundup. In other words, let the letter be informal and cohesive; let the news stand alone.

Letters from top management to readers are notorious for being vacuous, or pompous, or a grab bag of miscellaneous information that trivializes potentially interesting content by mixing it with housekeeping like "also in this issue" promos. This example is the third case. Placing bullets between bits of news doesn't help much: A reader needs to see instantly what's table-of-contents stuff, what events to watch out for, and what's old news. Not one big spacey essay.

BITS & PIECES

■ The SEC approved new NASD rules governing the use of mediation proceedings to resolve securities industry disputes. Effective August 1, 1995, the new rules permit the NASD to launch a mediation program offering securities industry professionals and investors a less expensive and quicker alternative to arbitration or litigation. Mediation gives the parties involved a chance to talk through their dispute and try to resolve it with the help of an impartial mediator.

■ Altera Corporation (ALTR) of San Jose, California became a component of The Nasdaq-100 Index on July 19. Altera Corporation, with a market capitalization of about $2.2 billion, is a world-wide leader in high-performance, high-density programmable logic devices and associated computer-aided engineering logic development tools.

■ The NASD has named Dean Furbush as its new chief economist. Furbush previously worked at an economic consulting firm, where he specialized in the economic analysis of securities and derivatives. Earlier he served as a staff member on the Council of Economic Advisers and the Commodity Futures Trading Commission. One of Furbush's goals is to build further on Nasdaq's relationship with the academic community and focus on Nasdaq's and other's analyses in a way that will lead to the continual improvement of the Nasdaq market.

■ Manuel H. Johnson, a noted economist and former Vice-Chairman of the Federal Reserve's Board of Governors, recently become a member of the Board of Directors of The Nasdaq Stock Market, Inc. Johnson brings to the Board a broad range of experiences as a policy maker and economist and is currently co-chairman and senior partner in the consulting firm of Johnson Smick International, Inc.

■ The heads of the Shanghai Stock Exchange (SSE) and the NASD formalized agreements to provide American expertise to the emerging Chinese market at a joint signing ceremony in Washington, DC on July 24. The agreements enable the NASD to assist members of the Chinese exchange with regulatory and legal issues necessary to establish a self-regulatory organization. The SSE will encourage the listing of Chinese companies on The Nasdaq Stock Market, and Nasdaq will reciprocate for Shanghai. The agreement allows the two dealer markets to exchange price, trading, position, and other regulatory information about companies jointly listed on the Nasdaq and Shanghai markets.

■ Market capitalization of The Nasdaq Stock Market passed the $1 billion mark on July 5. The trading day ended with a market value of $1.004 trillion, up 27.7 percent for 1995 and more than double the $386.3 billion level in early 1990. Joseph Hardiman, President of The Nasdaq Stock Market, said passing the trillion-dollar milestone reflects the confidence investors and issuing companies continue to have in the Nasdaq market.

■ The Nasdaq Stock Market crossed the single-day, half-billion-share mark for the first time on July 7, with 512,201,000 shares traded.

Business to Business

Problem: Bulleted "bits and pieces" copy neatly crowded into two columns—the last bullet in the left column is even broken and continued at the top of the right column so text bottoms out. The problem is that there's a third of a page of wasted space and text is hard to read.

Solution: Throw some breathing space between the squibs. Bullets are a tool for setting off a series of related items, but these are unrelated. Having a short headline for each with space alone setting them off would be better, with or without the bullet on the first line of text (a common roundup style in newspapers). At the least, the bullets could be "hung" with each text block indented and extra space before each new block.

Advocacy/Political

Problem: Photos and captions shoehorned so close to the type in the rest of the article that they're almost touching it.

Solution: Don't do that. Claustrophobic graphics shoot themselves in the foot and ricochet into the innocent bystander, body copy, too.

Association/Member News

Problem: Lines are the length of the entire text block, and body text is neon chartreuse green, blunt sans serif justified right up against the edge of the box rules. (The headline is magenta.) No left and right margins for white space here! Instead, almost a solid block of text and only the empty lines at the ends of paragraphs and skimpy paragraph indents for relief.

Solution: Don't do that. Any of that. Black type on white paper is most legible. Use a grid with column widths comfortably proportional to the typeface and type size. Choose complementary colors; avoid using two of the least legible and least popular colors with readers: neon green, with Easter egg magenta. Use serif or a very clean, crisp sans serif for big text blocks.

Association/Member News

Problem: Photo collage of group shots with poor image quality and wildly different proportions. Half of the image of some of these photos is dark background.

Solution: Use fewer photos—only the best—and if several are of the same group posed almost identically in the same context, pick only one. Crop out dark backgrounds and size photos so that the images have approximately the same depth of field. Try putting an attractive group shot in the middle and circling it with smaller groupings, or let an enlargement of one of the groupings anchor the collage at a corner. Softening the edges of the shots instead of printing a rule around them would help the collage seem less stiffly assembled—and the human beings in it less like pinned butterflies.

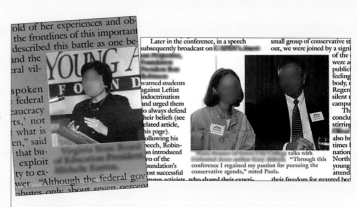

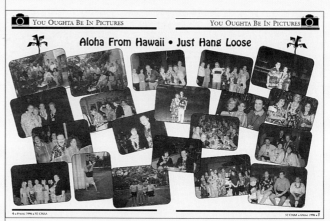

Association/House Ads Marketing Events to Members

Problem: Too many different type families (four) and type treatments—all caps, caps and small caps, sentence style, italic, black, red, serif, and sans serif.

Solution: Don't do that. Even for house ads, apply type styles consistently and use tinted type with restraint.

Association/Affinity

Problem: A great photo of four happy people, two of them shaking hands—but no caption.

Solution: Tell us who they are, where they are, and why they're so pleased. A photo caption can be a little story, and people love seeing their names in print. If the article immediately adjacent refers to the photo, a caption is optional but still desirable.

Association/Scholarly

Problem: A little leg of copy jumps from the inside cover (page 51) *backward* to page 50. Some designers think this is a neat trick for encouraging readers on their way out to step back into the issue. Many people, however, find it annoying or think it's a mistake—after all, nothing else in the issue jumps backward. In the case of a calendar, certainly, information should be kept together. Anyone who wanted to keep the calendar would have to tape the little square of runover to it.

Solution: There's no reason to waste all that trapped white space to the right of the calendar's headline. Get rid of the generic clip art graphic; put the range of dates the calendar covers in the headline; and make the head flush left. Then run copy in the far right two columns as high as the top of the headline, newspaper-style—perfectly okay for a tabloid format like this one. Copyfit to pull back about 12 short lines (like GUATE-MALA). Also reconsider all the bolding plus capitalization of organizations and countries. They compete and aren't easy to read.

Association

Problem: Even an article printed in heavy black type can't outweigh a big piece of clip art printed as a large watermark screened in too dark a percentage smack through the middle of it.

Solution: Watermarks have to be carefully screened back or else they compete with text. Lighten the screen so that the type will emerge the winner in the battle for the poor eyeballs pingponging between the two dominant elements of heavy type and big, pink image. Better yet, get rid of the art. It's purely literal; we know what a tennis racket looks like. What we don't know is the news we're trying to read around and through its interference.

Affinity/Volunteer

Problems: Using six exclamation points in a headline, and underlining the head when it's already boldface.

Solution: Don't do that. One exclamation point is acceptable occasionally, but be sure you need it: It's equated with amateur writing that's trying too hard to whip readers into feeling excited about something. Boldface alone is enough of a special treatment for heads; underlining as a genuine design element works only in the hands of a trained designer. The rest of us need to keep our heads simple.

Association

Problem: An entire page given to a calendar of events that lists the exact same pieces of information or events for each Sunday, Monday, Tuesday, Wednesday, Thursday, Friday, and Saturday. On only five days are variations on the daily theme announced.

Solution: List a simplified table-style rather than cell-style calendar, perhaps in a box, that's arranged by days of the week rather than dates. Announce the few special events at the top or bottom of it by date so they stand out.

Tennis Notes
The long wait is finally over... The Country Club of Bristol has signed a new tennis pro!

Todd Hall, originally from Elizabethton and a graduate of East Tennessee State University, will begin February 17 with full responsibility for our tennis facility and programs.

Todd has extensive experience and great success with his junior programs, including coaching Southern and Nationally ranked junior players. In addition, Todd has developed successful programs for players of all levels and ages, and has a demonstrated track record with increasing participation through special programs, tournaments and social events.

Todd and his wife, Patra (a Bristol native and graduate of Tennessee High), look forward to returning to the area with their two-and-a-half year old daughter, Emily. They are expecting their second child in June.

Before coming to Bristol, Todd served as Director of Tennis for the Lake Hickory Country Club in Hickory, North Carolina, as well as the Woodside Plantation Country Club in Aiken, South Carolina, and the Country Club of Orangeburg in Orangeburg, South Carolina. He also has been Assistant Tennis Professional at the Village Club at Martin Downs in Palm City, Florida, and the Johnson City Country Club (some people may remember Todd as Pete's assistant between 1986 and 1988).

We are excited about welcoming Todd and his family into the Country Club of Bristol family and look forward to an exciting tennis program.
Susie Williams & Kathy Robbins

Christmas is Coming!!! And I love it!!!

In my younger days I enjoyed going to the malls to watch the shoppers, some smiling joyfully, some wearing the worried looks which were easy enough to read: "I just don't know what to get for that special someone."

This is the season when we hear various attempts at "Messiah", Handel's masterpiece, good, bad and indifferent. There are also productions of "Hansel and Gretel", a story which has nothing to do with

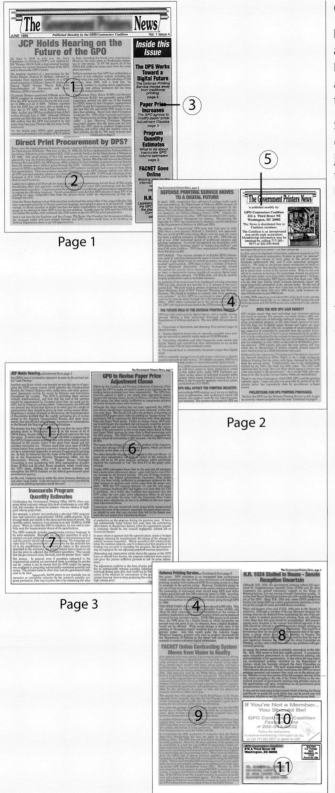

Page 1

Page 2

Page 3

Page 4

Government Agency

Problem: Needlessly distant jumps and awkward article shapes. The TOC is too large for four pages. News skulks beneath a too-prominent masthead at the prime spot of top right. This layout makes the news hard to find and follow.

Solution: Next-page jumps are easiest on readers. Plan—from page 1 forward—minimally jarring jumps, neat text blocks, and a pleasant flow of new and continued articles across pages. Here's a tour of advisable improvements.

Page 1: The TOC (3) needs to be reduced to a fourth of its size and placed at the bottom right corner. That will let you put more of article (1) on page 1. Then jump it to page 2, not page 3. Depending on where the masthead goes, the jump could be tucked into the lower left or right corner, or at the upper right corner, with article 4 flowing around it. Article (2) is fine as is.

Page 2: The masthead (5) at the top right probably should be moved to page 4. In a 4-pager, it belongs with the block of necessary-but-not-news content on the back page so that every other piece of real estate is dedicated to news. The long article (4) should continue at the top of page 2 as far as it can. The runover should flow onto page 3 in place of the article (1) runover.

Page 3: You now have the continuation of article (4) and new articles (6)and (7). The weird dog-leg in article (7) has to go. You might want to try switching (7) with a shorter article on page 4. Cut copy, including headlines, as much as necessary so that the shape of all articles is a rectangle (either a vertical one-column box or a two-column horizontal box).

Page 4: By now, page 4 should contain only 2 complete articles—no runover—and the mailing label (11), the ad (10), and the masthead (5). One block of rectangles in the far right column might work, but the leftover space at the top would allow only a small blurb. Or (5) could be placed in the left column, sized to align across from the other two blocks. You just have to play around with the text and the spacing until nothing looks too lonely or too crowded.

Corporate/Client Services

Problem: Too many screened boxes—in different styles—on a page and on a spread. The boxed items are all part of a feature called "Off-Site Highlights," but several factors work against recognizing that fact. There are as many different box formats as there are items, so there's no obvious visual relationship. And though the title is centered over the lot of them and does act as an umbrella, what we notice more is the box shapes, then the reversed-out type in three (which forms a pyramid across the spread), then the black type in two boxes diagonal across the spread. The eye hops all over the place to get some sense of direction about the content and some feeling for where to start reading first. All the clues are random. Nothing is more significant than anything else except that all the boxes are more dominant than the little introductory paragraph that explains what's going on but doesn't have much chance of being read first.

Solution: Calm down the graphics and use only one box style, since all the items are equal in importance and also need to be seen as part of a cohesive article. Anchor that floating box under the intro even if means writing a little more copy—you can always find some more to say—or reparagraph what you've said, or make a list of some bulleted items, or something! This intro could easily be made into three short paragraphs that would push the box down to earth.

Association/Member News

Problem: Where to put obituary announcements so as not to trivialize them or seem unwittingly humorous?

Solution: Not in a box on the back page next to the institution's "Hours of Operation." It's always hard to know where the best place is, but this isn't it. Many editors reserve a spot for obituaries in a section for general member news; others run the news as a department when the list of, say, former university alumni routinely runs to a page or more.

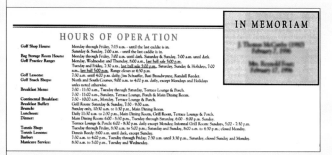

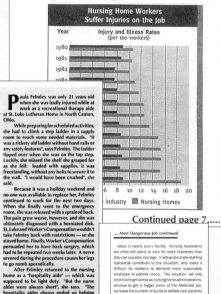

Dangerous Duty:

Nursing Home Work
Now One of the Most
"Dangerous Jobs in America"

What is the most dangerous job in America today? Ask any nursing home employee and they will tell you: working in a nursing home is bad for your health.

Over the past ten years, the rate of injury in nursing homes has doubled. In fact, nursing home workers are more likely to be injured than workers in industries typically considered dangerous such as manufacturing and construction. Nursing home workers are injured more often than miners. Nursing home work is fast becoming the most dangerous job in America.

Not only are nursing home workers more likely to be injured on the job, but they are more likely to be seriously injured. Lost time injuries affect 8.7% of nursing home workers, twice the rate for private industry overall. As anyone who has worked in a

**Nursing Home Workers
Suffer Injuries on the Job**

Year	Injury and Illness Rates (per 100 workers)
1980	
1981	
1982	
1983	

6   8   10   12   14   16   18   20

■ industry   ■ Nursing Homes

Continued page 7.....

.....Most Dangerous Job continued

nursing home knows, back injuries are the most common among nursing home workers. According to the Bureau of Labor Statistics, back injuries account for 43% of nursing home injuries, compared to 25% for private industry overall. Anyone who has suffered from a back injury knows the agony — as well as the limitations — such an affliction can cause.

One of the biggest factors contributing to the increase in nursing home injuries is the poor staffing

Continued page 8.....

In 1991, Wanda Proctor was putting in another shift at the Nicholas County Health Care Center in Richwood, West Virginia where she had worked for nearly 10 years as a restorative aide .

It seemed like just another day — until an injury put her out of work for 17 months. While working on the parallel bars with a stroke victim who was completely paralyzed on one side, Proctor bent to straighten the patient's knee when he lost his balance. "All of his weight fell on me", she said. As a result of holding up the patient, she suffered a strained neck and two protruding disks.

"I shouldn't have done this by myself", says Proctor. "It is normally done by more than one person but so many times we worked by ourselves, because we were shortstaffed most of the time, and there is a lack of training".

Proctor still endures a lot of pain and has to be cautious in how she moves. "I'm unable to do many things I took for granted", she says. "I can only get my arm up so far, and then I can't do it without pain".

Back at work now, Proctor is often still expected to carry a full lead because there is no light duty.

Paula Felmley was only 21 years old when she was badly injured while at work as a recreational therapy aide at St. Luke Lutheran Home in North Canton, Ohio.

While preparing for scheduled activities, she had to climb a step ladder in a supply room to reach some needed materials. "It was a rickety old ladder without hand rails or any safety features", says Felmley. The ladder tipped over when she was on the top step. Luckily, she missed the shelf she grasped for as she fell: loaded with supplies, it was freestanding, without any bolts to secure it to the wall. "I would have been crushed", she said.

Because it was a holiday weekend and no one was available to replace her, Felmley continued to work for the next two days. When she finally went to the emergency room, she was released with a sprained back. The pain grew worse, however, and she was ultimately diagnosed with a herniated disk. St. Luke and Worker's Compensation wouldn't take Felmley back with restrictions — so she stayed home. Finally, Worker's Compensation persuaded her to have back surgery, which had to be repeated two weeks later. A nerve severed during the procedure causes her legs to go numb sporadically.

After Felmley returned to the nursing home as a "hospitality aide" — which was supposed to be light duty. "But the nurse aides were always short", she says. "The hospitality aides always ended up helping them, What else are you going to do when a patient lies for hours in their own waste because no one has time to change them?" When she fell again when Vaseline and water went unnoticed on the floor, her career was ended. Felmley still takes pain medication constantly and doesn't know if she can ever work again.

.....Most Dangerous Job continued

ratios in nearly every facility. Nursing Assistants are often left alone to care for more residents than they can possibly manage. Inadequate state staffing standards contribute to the situation, and make it difficult for workers to demand more reasonable employee to patient ratios. The situation will only continue to get worse as nursing home administrators, anxious to get a bigger piece of the Medicaid pie, increase the number of acute or skilled care patients in the homes without increasing staffing levels.

Not only are nursing homes understaffed, but workers are also under trained. Most homes fail to provide proper training for employees, who then transfer and reposition patients without knowledge of proper lifting techniques. Management often prescribes back belts as a replacement for proper training, a National Institute for Occupational Safety and Health report issued in 1994 reveals that there is no scientific evidence that the belts prevent back problems. Evidence suggests that belts may actually increase a worker's chances of being injured by creating a false sense of security.

Combined with inadequate equipment and low staffing levels, lack of training spells disaster for workers who move thousands of pounds each day they work. But what is a nursing home worker to do? Torn between an obligation to the patients who rely on them and their personal safety, they often sacrifice their own health to get the job done.

In coming months, **Solidarity** will continue a series of articles on the crisis of nursing home injuries as part of the "Dignity" Nursing Home Campaign. Included will be data from a national report being compiled by S.E.I.U. as well as information you can use to prevent workplace injuries. Your input is valuable to us. To include your story in this series or to make suggestions, please phone the Columbus office of District 1199 at 1-800-227-1199 or write Attention Editor; District 1199/SEIU; 475 East Mound Street, Columbus OH 43215.

Advocacy

Problem: Double copy jump strains reader patience and strands two accompanying sidebars that seem unrelated to the article.

Solution: The first order of clarification here is the continued line: Where is it continued from? We need (a) a page number and (b) significant words from the original headline to help us return to the beginning of the article— "Dangerous Duty: Nursing Home Work Now One of the Most Dangerous Jobs in America." An acceptable jump line isn't "Most Dangerous Jobs Continued"—that's misleading. Something like "Dangerous Duty" is closer to home.

The article is cut in thirds by jumping to a squib on page 7 from a whole column on page 2 and jumping again to another whole column on page 8. Try to jump an article only once—newsletters are very different from magazines in this respect. Move other articles around and edit down until you find a way to keep copy together.

A complicating factor is the additional element of two sidebars that at first glance seem to be standalone but in fact are anecdotes about on-the-job injuries that are essential support for the article. But if we follow the text jump, we leave them behind; if we pay attention to them, we miss the text jump.

Side-by-side boxes not only predominate over the article itself, they compete with each other—while failing to provide graphic relief, one of the important functions of screened text boxes. This entire page is a waste of the time it took to lay it out because it does readers no good. An article this long with two sidebars big enough to need placement on different pages cries out for the simplest solution of all: Let it have an entire spread to itself. If that makes it look more important than it is substantively, there's another simple solution: Cut it back to a manageable size.

Association/Volunteer member editor

Problem: Classic case of a layout that screams lowest common denominator—justified type with too little leading, a two-column format with a too-long line length, rampant underlining that makes tightly packed text hard to read, and lots of hyphens and double dashes passing for real em dashes. Despite decent gutter space, there's no iota of relief within columns for the reading eye. Two small boldface subheads can't ventilate the smothering sense of grayness.

Solution: Pay a professional designer to create a template with a stylesheet for an appropriate format and typefaces—and let the volunteer editor take a course in using the publishing software. The basics of desktop typesetting beyond low-level word processing can and must be learned to produce a newsletter that looks as if it might contain credible information. And might not be punishing to read.

Advocacy

Problem: Spacing errors and carelessness. Display caps are three lines but are set into four lines of space; the spacing between columns is inconsistent; there's not enough space around the photo to set it apart from body copy, and it's placed asymmetrically across the gutter, making the text wrap awkwardly and unequally in the two affected columns. Perhaps most basic, paragraphs are indented, but there's also extra space between paragraphs—redundant paragraphing conventions.

Solution: Take care to set display type properly in alignment with the baseline, to use column guides consistently, to set a bigger frame for photos, and to size and place with more regard for the grid. Use either indentation or spacing between paragraphs, but not both.

Corporate/Marketing

Problem: Overuse of holiday clip art and failure to set it—or any of the copy—in any clear relationship to each other or to a grid.

Solution: Get rid of the clip art entirely, even if you have a symbol from every imaginable religious faction and "harmless" secular icons. And get a grid—you need it for your copy, if not for jingle bells, a menorah, and candy canes.

Association

Problem: Failure to see how a long article without any graphics works as a whole across the spread, as well as on each page.

Solution: Start over. Don't repeat the headline on the second page of the spread. Put the footnotes that run too deep on the left page at the end of the article where there's so much more space. Add subheads desperately needed to break up copy for the daunted eye and—more important—to serve as transitional devices to keep readers moving through the article. Lift out a quote to help brighten each page and fill out the space. Try a quote at the top of the right page to help it look less bleak, partly because there's no running head to anchor the page, just a blank bar.

No continued line is necessary across a spread. Redo the layout to achieve better balance between the huge empty column on the left page and the insufficient margin on the right—where type almost touches the edge of the page. Consider a more ragged text for copy-dense pages like these—the rag is so tight it looks justified. A generous rag is easier to read and adds a welcome sense of flow to copy; it's considered by many to be slightly less formal, so it's a nice counterpoint to lots of serious words.

Corporate/Marketing

Problems: Too many rules and too much spacing dividing the subsections of a reader letters feature. Especially since this is a long tabloid page, it's important to provide crystal-clear clues to where one thing stops and a new one starts. But here, it's not apparent even with a first careful look that all the material on the page except for the box is related—under three separate subheads and divided by rules into five columns are four reader "testimonials." Things look just lovely from a pure design standpoint, and it's always tempting to spread copy out to fill space, but an essential editorial clue—the physical proximity of closely related material—has been lost. Pullquotes, used for only two of the letters, could easily have been used as a knitting element but instead make the separate blocks of copy look unrelated—one pullquote is placed beside two of the letters, one letter is "illustrated" with a client's logo as if it were supportive clip art, and the fourth letter is formatted at the bottom of the page with a photo as well as a quote.

Solution: All the letters should be formatted alike to show that they're all client letters, not news stories. At the very least, remove or soften by screening the vertical lines that divide the parts of each letter internally and that also separate the letters from one another into skinny columns with a lot of space between them. Don't let tabloid format run away with the content.

Advocacy

Problem: Too many rules.

Solution: Delete as shown so that space and headlines serve as consistent cues to discrete blocks of copy. The only rule retained is the one that divides two columns that could be confused as belonging together.

Overruled

Not unruly—just benignly ruled

Corporate/Internal

Problem: Inaccurate photo caption. It states simply that these men are "recipients" of a prestigious award and then names them from left to right, inclusively. The clear implications are that all the men are recipients and that five awards were given. But of the five men shown, only four are holding an award. As a matter of fact, the fifth man seems to be holding his hands behind his back. Is he being shy? Is there something else we need to know about who he is?

Solution: You had to read the article to find out that only four employees were award-winners and that the empty-handed COO was the awards presenter. The writer of the caption took for granted that "everyone knows" who the COO is, but captions must be written to more exacting standards—people will read them first. Captions serve as teasers but shouldn't be cryptic; on the contrary, they should be meaningful apart from the article and include complete details about what's going on in the photo. You shouldn't have to read the story to get the point of the photo.

Membership

Problems: Copy organized with obvious care is nevertheless hard to read because basic layout rules have been ignored. The line length—the entire width of the box—is too long. The box itself is too complex, bounded as it is by 6 rules including top and bottom screened rules and a heavy vertical bar. Odd amounts of white space are trapped between the long blocks of copy followed by attributions. The graceful central oak tree and anniversary banner are meant to show pride and celebration. And they do. But at the expense of legibility—they're way too dark.

Solutions: Lose the rules—all of them. A whole page shouldn't be a set of Chinese boxes. Lighten, relocate, and maybe shrink the art. Shorten the lines of text. Perhaps divide the page into equal frames and run each note in its own lightly (less than 10 percent) screened color block (not a ruled box), presided over by the art used as part of the headline.

Business to business/ Subscription

Problem: Too much space above and below sub-heads. The extra space above makes it hard to know whether each subhead is really a new head for a separate section—especially since the preferable upper/lower case style has been used. The extra space below creates a literal and psychological gap between subheads and the copy they go with. Worse, the one-word subhead (one of three "empty heads") isn't flush left but floats at paragraph indent above the two estranged lines it introduces.

Solution: Tighten up spacing. Subheads should be only a line space or so away from the body copy they precede and no more than two spaces below the previous text. Indent subheads consistently, and actually write them: "Women" (what about them?) and "Content Preferences" (whose? women's, still, or somebody else's? what kind of content?) are too generic.

Professional association/ Membership

Problem: Too much space between each subhead and the text it introduces, between the end of a paragraph and the next subhead, between indented paragraphs, and around indented bullet lists.

Solution: Use less space between the heads and body text, and vice versa—instead of two line spaces between a subhead and the first line of text, use one; instead of three line spaces between text and the next subhead, use perhaps two. Either indent paragraphs and close up the space entirely, or make the paragraphs flush left and use a line space—not a double space—between them. A little extra space above and below blocks of bulleted items can be a good idea, but not when there's already as much leading as there is here.

Inc. (http://www.researchconnections.com), women who responded to a survey said they spent an average of $400 online in the past year and plan to spend $600 in the next year.

* According to the American Internet User Survey, FIND/SVP determined that news is the most popular content choice for adult Internet users, placing ahead of travel, entertainment/movies, sports and music content.

* New from **Chilton Research Services Express** poll determined that while significant numbers of Americans who access the Web do so to get product information, the vast majority of them do not yet use the Internet to place orders for those products.

Women

According to Research Connections, the best way to lure women to Web sites is to offer

information she needs.

Women shoppers online also ex sire for ease of payment and refund reliability, customer service and th cancel orders, the study determine

Content Preferences

With news the most popular con for adult Internet users, according SVP, such usage increases significa number of years a viewer has been researcher noted. Seventy-seven viewers in American Internet User S said they who used the Internet be access news content, compared to who started going online in the firs this year.

The survey also showed that medium is "redefining how people

Service/Educational for Potential Clients

Problem: At the bottom of a dense page of continued text, a wordy three-line head leaves space for only two lines of lead paragraph to draw readers in before requiring them to turn the page for the rest. References that—at a superficial glance, which is exactly how readers glance—might be connected to either the continued article or the new one float ambiguously above the headline. There's no extra space between articles to help set them off, and the long continuation overwhelms the new article. The head is ineffective either as a visual cue to something significant or as an editorial hook. The back page that follows has space to spare; the continuation doesn't look very interesting.

Solution: Cut the long continued article so the new article, which continues on the back page, begins no lower than two-thirds down the right-hand column. But since the shorter article already leaves the back page looking skimpy, better to trim all articles so that none starts at the bottom of a page or continues on the back. The shorter article could run there, complete, and the long continuation could be lightened with a pullquote or subheads.

Association/Member Education

Problem: A photo of an informal group of committee members "working hard to help meet member needs" is shot from an angle that makes several people look like toadstools.

Solution: Remember that a candid shot shouldn't mean an unflattering shot. Even informally posed association photos tell readers a little bit about the value of membership. A tight focus on the faces of the two people in the foreground interacting in a friendly, direct way would have made a nicer comment.

Committee Members working hard to help meet member needs.

Civic/Community News

Problem: This photo caption is trying to do too much and does none of it well—there's real news buried in a long list of names and the listing itself is suffocated by extraneous details. An oddly worded headline attempts to turn the caption into a photo essay, and the lead sentence introduces the list of 14 kids who graduated from a city-run baby-sitting course, but halfway into the paragraph, the caption shifts to naming the local volunteer fire and city recreation department personnel who ran the course. The names of the graduates are in no way keyed to the fewer than 14 kids (and one of the trainers—but who?) pictured. At the very end, a telephone number is given for 12-year-olds who want to take the course.

Solution: Make the headline do its work of highlighting the news hook (some hook, any hook: Youths Earn Baby-Sitting Certificates; Fire Dept. Prepares Kids for Baby-Sitting). Then write a coherent blurb with information about how long the course lasted, how many have graduated from it, and what the payoff is (a certificate, a ceremony, a speech). Or if there's not enough time to do more fact checking, write a clear caption that takes a few details from the middle and end of the story, ties them together into a summary statement, and lists everyone who is recognizably present in the photo.

Corporate Internal

Problem: Two full pages of employee anniversaries and birthdays in alphabetical order begin on page 16 and jump backward to continue on page 14. That's awkward enough, but maybe you could justify a couple of dreary pages if everyone listed knew each other and cared. They don't, though: It's a national company, and the names appear in sublists for 30 cities.

Solution: Abandon forever the condescending idea that a list of the names of strangers having birthdays in distant cities counts as content, is heart-warming, or matters to anyone. It's a goofy way to fill up space.

Baby Sitters Graduates

The following boys and girls recently completed the Baby Sitters Course sponsored by the Takoma Park Volunteer Fire Department and the city Recreation Department: Derek Apfel, Rachel Cox, Eva Daryabeygi, Evan Ernst, Lauren Grady, Lauren Hanson, Maggie Holobaugh, Joanne Lee, Claire McMahon, Maria Ortado, Cathy Rowe, Matt Schechter, Gaelan Varn, and Lisa Weir. Deputy Chief Jim Jarboe was again assisted by the following: Deanna Stewart EMT and Ingrid Scarpelli EMT, both of Takoma Park Volunteer Fire Department, and Officer Stevette Bryant of the Takoma Park Police Department.

Boys and girls at least 12 years old who are interested in taking a Baby Sitters course should contact the city Recreation Department at 270-4048. The next course will start in September.

Photo courtesy T.P.V.F.D.

National Council/ Membership & Networking

Problem: When almost every page jumps at least one article—even if they're relatively short pieces of about 500 words—continuations that have nowhere to go tend to clump up toward the middle and back of the issue. Even a tabloid runs out of fresh real estate under those conditions, and it becomes increasingly difficult to avoid whole pages of continuations—leftovers, in effect. That means some pages have nothing new to offer readers—bad news for browsers. In a single issue of this 16-page newsletter, editorial competes with as many as 14 vendor display ads and several quarter-page classified ads—not to mention a Job Bank department.

Solution: You may have to institute a policy of ganging up ads onto dedicated pages. Whatever you do, never make editorial fight ads for readability—especially text that's already at a disadvantage because it's continued. Ads will be less effective, too, in such a layout. The reader's eye is simply pulled too many ways by pieces of different messages to settle comfortably anywhere for long. In the spread illustrated, five continued articles are packed into a layout governed by four ads, taking up more than half of each page. Don't do that. The entire issue needs tighter editing and a layout that from page 1 makes sure ads don't take over.

Association/Networking

Problem: Old-fashioned, childish clip art has been used to balance out a page that contains only a brief Editor's Letter and the Newsletter Committee. Unfortunately, the clip art emphasizes not only the lack of design talent but the lack of content. Both detract from the image of a dynamic organization and make us wonder why they bothered to publish the newsletter at all.

Solution: If there really isn't enough to fill an eight-page newsletter, print a four-pager that looks fat and sassy and brimming with news instead.

Industry Association

Problem: Justifying of the right margin causes big gaps between sentences and between all the words on some lines—an overall effect known as rivers of white space meandering through copy. Although the typeface is obviously intended to evoke the homely newsiness of typewritten copy, only word processing software that hasn't had its defaults tweaked causes this effect.

Solution: Adjust the tracking, or try a ragged right margin. In fact, try either ragged right or more tightly tracked justified type with at least two full columns so lines aren't so long (especially since the scholar's margin isn't being effectively used anyway). The long line length exaggerates spacing problems.

Association/Membership & Lobbying

Problem: One way to meet the goal of being a forum that "presents a variety of viewpoints" is to invite four association leaders to speak to an issue. But with only eight pages, running their photos and about 150 words apiece means the forum has to be printed in a tiny type size in order to cram it all onto one page.

Solution: Cut copy ruthlessly so the point size can be brought up to a readable 10 points or so (depending on the x-height of the font). Any interview response can be cut by at least 25 percent to bring out one or two high points and get rid of rambling. Make sure that such valuable editorial isn't shrunk visually—tiny type makes for uncomfortable skimming. Another way to get room for sizing up the copy would be to get rid of the vertical rules and pull it closer to each photo.

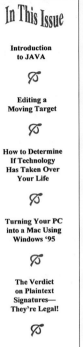

Marketing

Problem: A contents list but no page numbers telling readers where in 12 pages the articles can be found.

Solution: Don't do that. The TOC should raise interest in articles; don't make readers then hunt for what they're most interested in reading.

Association/News Roundups & Lobbying

Problem: Four completely different articles are stacked on a page without a crumb of differentiation as to content—though one is a resignation letter from an association officer (housekeeping), one is a summary of proposed legislation, one is an inspirational essay about teamwork, and one is a calendar of upcoming educational events.

Solution: Don't use the crutch of centered, all-cap heads as the only visual cue to where a new piece starts. Create blocks of information with space between them and make full use of the three-column grid to allow for more comfortable left-to-right reading in smaller sections than across the entire page. Don't use all-cap subheads and terms in body copy that's already crowded. And separate the news from the views from the alohas.

Association/Membership Education

Problem: Two crammed pages lack subheads to set off two main sections and cry out for bulleted list format or perhaps run-in boldface subheads for itemized groups. The crowdedness and grayness are made worse by the empty column at the far right. Sure, text ends neatly at the bottom, but what for? That kind of neatness doesn't count in newsletter copy flow.

Solution: Set up two real subheads (not all caps) with some space around them where major signposted copy points occur, and use bullets or run-in subheads to help browsers gain entry into the monolithic-looking spread. We'd like to see the rules go away—they're so heavy they're another barrier to the flow (more like a downpour) of copy. Run-in subheads are probably the best choice for so many items—more than five in each section. Spreads with great clots of bullets start to look measley.

Government/Armed Forces, Internal

Problem: A quotation is placed in a box and placed on a page to round out a layout—but it has nothing to do with the content. It's not attributed to anyone famous; it was "submitted" by someone listed as part of the newsletter staff. If someone famous said it, we need to know. If nobody famous said it, why quote a staff person saying something pious and irrelevant?

Solution: Unless you're editing a church newsletter, leave the homiletics to preachers—such filler quotes don't belong in professional newsletters. Leaving a small blank space would be preferable if there's nothing really newsworthy to be said. (But there's always, always more news than space for it—if the newsletter editor is doing the job.)

3.3 The redesign of a real, live newsletter

This is a case study of how one art director pulled all the pieces together for a community newsletter in need of an updated image. The case study includes an overview of the design challenge and a narrative about the specifics of a kickoff brainstorming session, the presentation of comps for the client to choose from, and the finessing of a finished prototype.

The "art director's choices" offer a glimpse into the many small decisions that must be made as a new image is refined. Tracking the process of the redesign shows how the creative synergy of editor, publisher, and designer relies on give and take, trips back to the drawing board, and at every stage, listening carefully and speaking honestly. This is the ultimate real-world exercise in the creative diplomacy that can, with talent and vision from a professional designer, produce a publication everyone's happy to see (and maybe even read).

3.3.1   Background and overview

For more than 50 years the Animal Welfare League of Alexandria (AWLA) in Virginia has published a service newsletter for the good of two distinct communities, each in turn composed of diverse members:

- Animals of all kinds—companionable family pets, exotic "designer" pets, indigenous wildlife, guard and guide animals, dangerous strays

- The human beings who live with them or near them—pet owners, nature lovers, the zoophobic, the philanthropic, those concerned about public health issues (the threat of rabies, "scooper" laws, stray animals)

Spotlight on Animals is distributed free four times a year to residents of this Washington, DC-area suburb and neighboring communities. It's mailed to about 22,000 readers, mostly individuals who have supported the League's activities and benefited from its programs. (If you adopt a pet, buy a coupon that gets you a discount on spaying fees, or call to report a lost animal, you'll be added to the mailing list.) A few thousand copies are also mailed to businesses and placed in local veterinarians' offices.

By fall 1997, League director Kate Pullen and *Spotlight's* editor Megan Brooks had become convinced that it was time for an updated look, partly to remain competitive with the publications of other animal welfare organizations in the community. (See old design on p. 192.) About five years is average between redesigns, and they'd been tinkering piecemeal for a couple of years already. They'd decided not to rely on volunteer efforts any longer and were planning to ask for professional design help.

The old *Spotlight* passed through the hands of volunteer editors who concentrated on telling the AWLA story. *Spotlight* grew in a topsy-turvy way. Naturally enough, different kinds of content and graphics were added over time without reconciling little design incompatibilities or discarding outworn treatments to make way for new kinds of material.

But grow it did and settled down to be the newsletter pictured here. Certainly, care was taken to neatly box in many pieces of copy and art and pack them into pages so solid they barely have space for outer margins.

Serious commitment is shown, but those pages didn't show signs of vitality or invite browsing. The smallish, dark photos and the clutter of different art styles (including the ads) didn't open up long columns of type but instead multiplied the sense of arbitrariness.

The nameplate with its Happy Days-era logo needed updating, the content needed reorganizing into departments with a tighter focus, and the redesign needed to add, in two words, more flavor.

The Newsletter of the Animal Welfare League of Alexandria   Summer 1997

Pet Ownership: A Family Affair

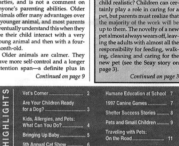

Many people grow up thinking that children and puppies or kittens are made for each other. While children and pets can be great companions, the age at which they are introduced to each other is critical to both the child's and the young animal's well-being.

Most national humane organizations and prominent animal trainers agree that very young children and young animals are not a good match for several reasons:

• Small children like to pick things up and carry them around; they are usually unaware of how tightly they may be holding a puppy or kitten, and the pet may react by biting or scratching the child in an attempt to escape.

• In time, young animals will often try to avoid small children by hiding under furniture, putting these fragile creatures at risk of being pulled out by their paws or tails.

• Puppies and kittens use their teeth and paws a great deal in play and while learning self-confidence, and may scratch or bite a child accidentally out of frustration.

• Children will often treat an animal as a doll or a stuffed toy, putting it in a stroller from which it can take a tumble, "putting it away" in a toy chest and causing suffocation, or trying to brush its hair too roughly and hurting the pet.

• Depending on the situation, parents may focus so much on supervising the child that the puppy or kitten is left to its own devices.

• Perhaps most important, young animals need a great deal of consistency in their lives in order to learn household rules and general good manners. As any parent knows, young children are absolutely not consistent.

The League's adoption policy matching children under the age of six years and puppies or kittens over the age of four months benefits all parties, and is not a comment on anyone's parenting abilities. Older animals offer many advantages over a younger animal, and most parents eventually understand this when they see their child interact with a very young animal and then with a four-month-old.

• Older animals are calmer. They have more self-control and a longer attention span—a definite plus in

Continued on page 9

Is Now the Time?

Pets can be a great addition to your family but there are many aspects to consider before you head to your nearest shelter to adopt a four-legged companion.

• Does your family need a pet? Many family members, especially children, *want* a pet, but does your family really *need* a pet? Animals should be viewed as a four-footed addition to your family; it's much like adding another child, especially if you get a younger pet who needs training and supervision.

• Are your expectations for your child realistic? Children can certainly play a role in caring for a pet, but parents must realize that the majority of the work will be up to them. The novelty of a new pet almost always wears off, leaving the adults with almost all the responsibility for feeding, walking, cleaning and caring for the new pet (see the Seay story on page 3).

Continued on page 3

Meanwhile, Davie Smith, EEI Communications' art director, and I had decided that we needed to do something rather obvious that no other newsletter guidebook had quite done: take a perfectly healthy but dated newsletter—non-negotiable warts and all—and describe the step-by-step process of redesigning it. *Spotlight* had many of the elements that editors in the newsletter classes I teach consistently say they want to improve in their own publications. We called AWLA and began the process of negotiating a redesign we'd all be proud of.

Brooks had started out planning to use Ventura software for page layout "because somebody on the board had gone out and bought it," but we talked her out of it. Smith recommended either QuarkXPress (for its ease of service bureau output) or PageMaker (for its ease of use). Either would give Brooks greater flexibility in placing graphics in columned text. Smith worked on the design with the final production process in mind. He wanted the template to be flexible enough to handle the real content that Brooks would be designing pages for. Meanwhile, she took a PageMaker class at EEI Communications to get up to speed, and the League set about acquiring the necessary software.

What we achieved was even more than we'd hoped for. We met two powerhouse animal lovers and advocates, not to mention witty, gracious people and perfect clients—who trusted in Smith's vision for the newsletter but spoke up clearly when we veered away from their vision. And there's the rub. If clients have a lot of ideas but no knowledge of design, all the words in the world can't help them cross the bridge to communicate with their design consultant. Art directors think in images, and they can see what we can't see even when they've roughed it out for us on paper. Good faith efforts to find the words for the images and the images for the ideas are the only ticket out of that situation.

We also got a model of the redesign decision-making process. As we made notes about the launch, the fits, the starts, and the final synthesis, we saw clearly the value of doing considerable research before investing time in preparing comps.

Pullen and Brooks were worried about one thing: They might find it necessary to change aspects of our design over time. But of course, we replied. A redesign is just a departure from the ordinary. A jumping-off point. A planned set of intelligent departures from the overly familiar to draw fresh attention to the original mission. But not just a new spotlight on old ground. Editorial has to shed flabby old habits so as to inhabit its new, tighter skin. That stretches the design and forces it to be resilient, to give where growth can't be stopped.

From the time the inaugural issue leaves the gate, a redesign is on its way to the place where old grids, overused fonts, stylish illustration styles, and trendy colors go—but if the groundwork has been done thoughtfully, a good design will have a healthy run at handling the vagaries from issue to issue.

3.3.2   Reconfirming the client's publishing mission

A newsletter like this has several goals, but they boil down to mainly public relations and education. All roads will, with luck, lead to more pet adoptions, universal protection for animals and safety for humans, and donor and community support for laws and voluntary intervention programs. Over the years, the design evolved into contained chaos: green-and-white, text-heavy format; small, dark, badly cropped photos; randomly placed, intrusive vendor and house ads; and generic styles—half a dozen—of clip art. The newsletter wasn't broken: It did its primary job of letting people know about community-based programs pretty well. But not as well as its creators knew it could.

A redesign also "fixes" perfectly acceptable publications that are showing signs of growing pains. Rethinking the visual package goes hand in hand with rethinking the scope of the content—and helps redefine or reposition a newsletter so it can gracefully admit a new goal or two that have been waiting for an opening. A thoughtful redesign can stave off the impression of entrenched editorial reflexes.

But a redesign can be an uncomfortable process unless both editor and publisher (sponsor) agree it's necessary. Instead of treating change as a threat, our clients courted it as a way to bring new supporters into the fold and strengthen the work of the League.

3.3.3   The brainstorming before the bargaining

We started by holding a kickoff meeting to find out what our client's dream newsletter would look and feel like. Jennifer Stewart, an EEI Communications staff designer, interviewed Pullen and Brooks to get a sense of what the boundaries for change were and what the production constraints would be. We asked leading questions about the kinds of stories—how long, how many, how linked—they planned in the future, and what former editors and illustrators had accomplished in past issues that they'd like to build on or keep intact. It emerged that the League wanted to

- add outreach stories for non-pet owners,
- streamline ads and fundraising efforts,
- organize issues around seasonal program themes,
- professionalize the quality of the artwork,
- boost the image of the League with readers, and
- encourage reader loyalty to League activities.

Other issues—politics, housekeeping, personal style—surfaced during our brainstorming. Here's how the notes from our genial but frank interview ran. The overlap of concepts evident in these notes is inevitable and desirable when conducting a brainstorming session to kick off a redesign; it's not a waste of time to keep coming back to the same items. Repeating ideas in different words is part of the process of distilling the essentials. At bottom is the need to fix points for the degree of novelty, and what sorts of novelty, a redesign should introduce.

- What we all wished the newsletter to keep

  A friendly, low-tech, approachable tone. First-person articles about successful pet adoptions, reports about League initiatives, advice from experts, and ads from pet supply vendors. Photos and illustrations to help brighten copy and add interest.

- What the client wished to add to the newsletter

  —A new nameplate that highlighted the League itself, not just "animals."

  —More articles for everyone in the community, not just pet owners.

  —A theme for each issue beginning with the lead article and continued in features on different aspects of that topic.

(Oh yeah, we said, how about a letter from the director to give a human face and voice to the League? With an ongoing rabies scare in Northern Virginia and exotic pet escapades, the media were always interviewing Pullen. Why not capitalize on her strong image as a calm, articulate, intelligent representative of the League?)

  —Hand-drawn illustrations by several League volunteers who are artists.

  —Pullquotes to humanize the often didactic content.

  —A regular round-up or two to gather up similar bits and pieces of news.

  —A more flexible layout for the editor to fill with copy but also more orderly patterns so pages don't look like a random mix of bits and pieces that nevertheless all seem the same. More white space but not empty space to lighten spreads. All that translates to a more reasonable grid to replace the present two-column (with variations and fudges) grid.

  —More readable type for text, headlines, captions, and sidebars.

  —Maybe a classified section, a minidirectory of vendors, with only four basic sizes to organize laying out the ads?

(Brooks' eyes brightened and she confessed that she'd wanted that for a long time. Laying out ads is a pain for anyone, and no matter how neatly done, they steal something from the full effect of carefully copyfitted news articles.)

—More consistently attractive graphics, starting with fewer but bigger and better-quality photos.

—Fewer cutesy illustrations. Develop a couple of recognizable characters—a dog and a cat—in different poses.

—Keep styles of clip art and illustration to one or two to avoid a perception of fickleness and add to the effect of a coherent editorial plan.

- What we all wished the client to lose

—Dark, dense pages of text.

—Clumsy organization of content so that ads, although clustered at the bottom and inside gutter margin, were dominant and messy-looking. Provided as camera-ready copy by advertisers, they all looked different and were many odd sizes.

—Cutesy, awkwardly placed stock clip art that didn't support stories.

—Too many articles that were too long.

—Too many similar articles placed wherever they fit instead of being grouped in categories.

(We were told that one of the board members always complained about "wasted white space" though there was little white space at all; "trapped" space that resulted from forcing copy and art into the boxy two-column grid was the actual culprit. We had it in for that, too.)

3.3.4   Mutually agreed-on redesign goals

Spotlight's sponsors wanted to expand the focus beyond the traditional image of a shelter promoting pet adoption by a nuclear family of one cat or one dog to include articles for a diverse community. A key to this newsletter is the demographic character of the community it serves: well-educated, multiethnic, with many singles, single-parent families, and same-sex households. As a suburb reflective of the metro Washington, DC area, Alexandria juggles extremes of income and political preferences. But the League also has to continue to appeal to a solid middle class still trying to preserve "normal family values" that include owning a shaggy dog even though mom and dad both work a 50-hour week and the kids are in daycare almost as long.

Spotlight, in short, needed to cover more territory and look more urbane. Many kinds of family arrangements and the attitudes of those indifferent to or antagonistic toward animals had to be taken into account. Pullen and Brooks wanted to add articles and regular departments to showcase new League programs, promote special fundraising efforts, encourage activism on behalf of pet welfare, educate the public about laws and safety, and offer practical information from a wide group of "experts," not just veterinarians.

Vendor ads, although awkward to place, were a must, but Brooks was interested in a new way to present them that gave her better control over the layout, for which she was also responsible. We all wanted pages to look less fragmented, but we also wanted to avoid rigidly boxing off a lot of competing copy.

3.3.5 The redesign process

Eventually, the head of the board of directors would have to approve the redesign, but he trusted Brooks and Pullen as knowledgeable delegates for the bargaining process. (Obviously, any redesign becomes more complicated when a committee must sign off on every concept and stage of production.)

Success is likelier to come more quickly—from the designer's standpoint—if the client agrees to wait for finished comps, rather than tinkering. But the truth is that the redesign process is always a little messier than that. Designers make a series of educated guesses and take a number of inspired risks as they attempt to translate the concepts in a client's head into the subtle language of nonverbal type and graphics. There are bound to be little slips in vision—and when what a client sees is what a client has asked for, many a client is dismayed. Interim signoffs on the direction a redesign is taking are essential.

Speaking clearly about what isn't verbal is difficult even for people of goodwill. Only after paying careful attention to stated wishes can a designer interpret what those wishes imply.

1 So first of all, to test our interpretation of where the redesign should be headed, art director Davie Smith roughed out by hand some individual elements that might work for a new nameplate. (See preliminary sketches, page 198.) He was interested in putting a literal spotlight on the League as a player and using it as a recurring element in the newsletter. He also wanted to experiment with using images of people with pets.

Our clients had said that they were open to other name suggestions if we were inspired, but we kept coming back to *Spotlight*. (We just wanted to be sure that the new treatment didn't evoke a deer-in-the-headlights image!)

2 With the spectrum of possibilities narrowed, Smith and Stewart independently came up with two very different cover pages with nameplates that built on those two different aspects of the client's mission. (See prototypes A and B, page 199.) Many clients prefer to see three design samples, but in this case, two allowed us to put on the table all the optional elements that we'd recommend. The final mix depended on our client's reaction.

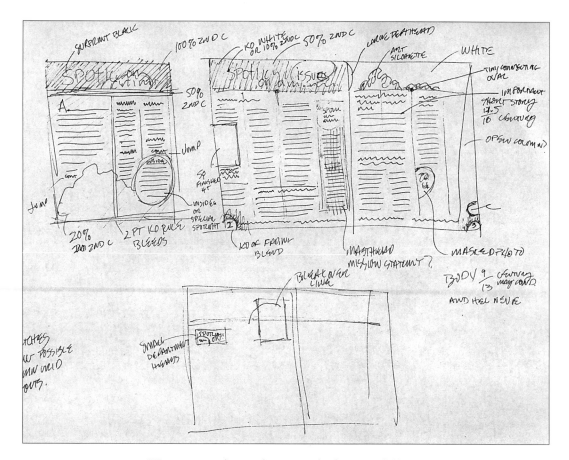

3 We presented our clients with the two different cover comps to see
how well we'd interpreted their priorities and how many of our
innovations their expectations could tolerate. Both comps used similar
type, illustration, photo, and clip art styles. Both used an eight-column
grid underpinning it all. Starting with the logo, the focus for both was
on the League as an agent of animal welfare rather than on animals in
general. But the paths Smith and Stewart took to that new emphasis
were quite different.

Cover A relied on a contemporary illustration style (freely drawn
rather than static clip art) and a scene of dog-walking by a group of
people—we thought they could be anybody and so evoked an active
yet definitely not Spot-Dick-and-Jane context.

Although our clients liked the illustration style, they were still concerned that the figures could be taken as members of a traditional
family, something they preferred not to seem to be endorsing at the
expense of single-person adoptions. The lack of rules and freer play
of text and graphics, though appealing to a sophisticated, active audience, also appeared to require more of a design background than
Brooks had to lay out effectively, rather than randomly. A bit more
defined structure was considered desirable.

Spotlight cover prototypes A and B. Although the clients liked A's loose illustration style and open layout, they preferred cover B, with its use of the spotlight element for emphasis and structured color-blocking.

They preferred—and thought their board would prefer—cover B overall, especially the strong nameplate with its oval spotlight into which subtly stepped the words "League of Alexandria." The reliance on a cover photo of a silhouetted dog-child scene and large, simple logotype were welcomed, and the more obvious separating of the nameplate with a bar of color from the articles on the page struck the right note. Likewise, they liked the big blocks of color and rules dividing stories from each other.

4 Time out for an even more definitive round to create a third cover that, we hoped, combined the significant elements preferred from both initial comps. But new relationships were of course created, making this less a compromise version than a third new design. Smith also "greeked" a sample spread and a unified classifieds page (that is, he used text in Latin to stand in for real copy).

He repeated actual headlines and department heads from past issues so Brooks and Pullen could envision future content in the new skin, but the text itself was greeked. Photos and new clip art, including ghosted spot art, were placed where we imagined they'd do the most good on the typical page. Screened color for boxes, tinted body type, and reversed type were used to show how easily a sense of vitality could be built into the copy, when and as warranted to show shifts between different articles and also the relationship between companion pieces. The use of an oval spotlight emerged as a useful continuing element.

5 We met with our clients for a second round of feedback and asked for their evaluation of the layout's utility and potential adaptability. (See the interim prototype, C, on page 200.)

Prototype C, which combined the free illustration style of cover A with the more structured layout of cover B, helped our clients specify what the cover should communicate.

But while we were working on a comprehensive final design, Brooks and Pullen were so excited about the prospect of it that they had been planning the issue that would launch it. The editorial changes they were making in response to the redesign in turn affected the layout we thought would cover all editorial changes! At this second presentation/bargaining session, we learned of some recent decisions our layout didn't yet offer a treatment for. The news roundup would now always be a whole page, the "Coming Up" table of planned events would be a whole page, and the masthead would be at least an entire column, listing more than simply the newsletter staff and League address and phone number.

Our clients, partly speaking for their board president, thought the stylized art on cover C too stereotypical to be a standard element, and they regretted the small size of the photo—after all, we had talked them into using larger ones! They were now committed to the idea of running a different large photo each time as part of the lead, and limiting illustrations to the inside pages. By now, they had a stronger sense of what they wanted the cover to say, and they outlined for us the effects they envisioned.

A subtle shift occurred at this meeting: Instead of merely agreeing to our ideas in the abstract, our clients were engaged with the redesign and actively making it one they could see themselves using. This meant a clearer definition of what "worked" in their minds—not that the interim design failed, but that it was out of focus. Smith, despite his own investment in the evolution of the design, agreed to rethink the role of the illustrations versus a large cover photo (which he had worried might be harder to come up with each time than attractive art).

6 Back to the drawing board. Finally, we presented revised comps and a template; we later helped troubleshoot file preparation difficulties when, naturally enough, graphics files too large for her computer to handle bit Brooks the first time around. We knew that the particulars of each issue would test both the resilience of the redesign and the editor's skill in working within it, as well as her ingenuity in breaking out of it whenever necessary to serve her readers.

When the first issue was distributed, readers were enthusiastic. All of us counted this exercise an artistic and a practical success. As Brooks said, "I think it's pretty simple to understand why we've been getting such positive feedback. The new look of the newsletter draws people in, and that gives our messages more power to be persuasive. That was our hope when we started the redesign process."

3.3.6 The art director's choices

Davie Smith wanted most of all to break the long-standing patterns of vertically stacked articles and tiny, sandwiched photos. He chose a three-column format with quasi-scholar's margin in an eight-column grid for its flexibility to accommodate a lot of copy as well as a variety of photos and illustrations. Every page will have a block of color.

The cover's lead article was intended to be printed in black text in a white block reversed out of a color background—for emphasis. The continuation of this article inside should echo this format for ease of identifying it and to save a reader who has followed the jump from having to readjust to a different line length and so forth. It's a small courtesy that will require a bit of extra care on the editor's part.

The spotlight-oval became a cheerful, simple way to set off standing material—the "Ask the Experts" column, the table of contents, the masthead—and make a simple, visually graceful connection to the nameplate and its mission of "caring." As the design evolves, overuse of the spotlight oval will have to be guarded against.

Smith chose what he called "kind of a peculiar typeface for body copy"—Century Schoolbook Condensed—because although it's condensed, it's highly readable and not fussy-looking or distorted. With its high x-height, gently rounded characters, and restrained serifs, he judged it a distinctive face that would work for what he calls "pretty copy-intense pages." (He considered and rejected Fenice as a little too formal and not quite as readable for this newsletter.)

Smith explained, "I wanted to open up the dark layout without too much editorial sacrifice of copy on a page. Because type is set a bit small at 10 points, leading is generous at 14 points to keep readers from straining. A smaller size of body type has an upscale feel that's more appropriate for an educated readership than a larger size."

As a compatible display type that offered good contrast, Smith chose the more informal-looking Adobe Helvetica. He liked the fact that it could also serve as a readable sans serif for sidebar body text and comes in a number of different weights to give some play when using display type for different kinds of articles while "keeping it all in the family."

The final cover design featured larger type in the nameplate and strong silhouetted photographs to illustrate the cover articles.

This spread demonstrates design treatments for standing items such as a masthead and departments, as well as ways to use clip art and photography to support editorial throughout the interior of the newsletter.

As for the choice of oversized, lowercased letters in the nameplate and in department heads, it's not the favorite technique of all editors, but as an unpretentious yet stylized element used sparingly (only for top-tier display, not for headlines), for *Spotlight*, it's just right.

Production details can make or break a new design. Century Schoolbook has both italic and bold faces should the need arise for them. They'll be used sparingly, but we've taken them into account.

Because of the art and photos throughout, Smith recommended Mohawk Options 80-pound bright white text stock. He said, "It has great ink hold-out that allows for fine reproduction of halftones, and it's also economical. Options is one of a new generation of offset papers with an ink hold-out that approaches that of coated paper. Ink isn't absorbed and dulled."

Heads, subheads, and runover heads have been set up in the style sheet as different sizes of the same typeface. Head styles get inconsistent very fast if too much "play" with display type is introduced—newsletters can tolerate only so much in their limited space. We recommended three or four consistent treatments to help Brooks avoid hit-or-miss formatting. We're skeptical about the magazine-like design that we see in the hands of amateur typesetters—it's too often a license for chaos. Newsletter design is intended to impose order on a little slice of the universe called "service news for an in-group." Since heads are the primary place readers glance before deciding to read an article, they shouldn't introduce distracting variations.

Smith's redesign uses Art Room's "Lifestyles" clip art package, but it's just a placeholder for what we hope will be hand-drawn and scanned-in art by League artist-members. The short list of software tools: PageMaker for text layout, Photoshop for image editing, and FreeHand for illustrations.

Smith said, "For silhouetted photos, I created simple clipping paths in Photoshop and exported scanned images as EPS files. But oval or rectangular masks are easy to do in PageMaker.

"I try to make sure that screens are appropriate for art or words that appear over them. Seldom is a 20 percent or greater screen suitable for surprinting type. I also don't usually reverse type out of less than a 50 percent screen."

Smith talked our clients out of printing a huge masthead each time and designed a new mailer that lists all their contact information. That's better for the layout and better for people looking for that information. He hopes they'll choose one clip art style and build up a core of 12 to 18 recognizable, stylish, all-purpose pieces, augmented by special art for each issue. We also hope they pick a second color and use it consistently, because "seasonal" variations come with problems of their own (not least of which are dismaying screens of certain colors, such as red, orange, and so on)—not to mention undercutting the recognition value of a consistent color.

The new advertising format gathers all display ads into an attractive "classifieds" section, eliminating the need to lay articles out around the ads.

But the very moment a design is handed over as a software template for an inaugural issue, that design will begin to change and evolve toward its next incarnation. A redesign is just a stage of growth in a process; as the message is transformed and the audience grows, shrinks, or plays assorted demographic tricks on an editor's assumptions, the design will, and should, be discarded in favor of a new one.

3.3.7 Putting the design into practice

Turning three or four pages of template design treatments into a 12-page newsletter with real articles and photos is a challenge for any editor, but not only was *Spotlight* Megan Brooks' very first layout project, the inaugural redesign issue was her first experience using desktop publishing software, preparing electronic files, and overseeing the printing process. To ease the transition from editor to layout artist, Jennifer Stewart helped Brooks test the boundaries of *Spotlight's* design template, practice software options, and get an overview of the steps of newsletter production.

After purchasing and loading the necessary software and fonts on the League's PC, Brooks began by looking carefully with Stewart at the design elements in the comps to see what new treatments they would need to create for the actual content. They identified stories that would be good candidates for art and searched the League's photo archives for simple, warm, good-quality images. After selecting and scanning photos for placement, they tackled laying out the text (the printer had agreed to scan and place high-resolution art).

Using the design comp as a constant reference, Brooks pulled text into the already designed pages. She used the electronic file of the comp to experiment with PageMaker's features and learn how the design elements were constructed before working with "live" content. Then thumbnails were roughed out for the rest of the newsletter, taking into account how new elements could build on the existing design treatments without overpowering the text or becoming monotonous.

As the layout progressed, Brooks discovered that creating a newsletter involved far more than just positioning text and graphics. She learned about graphic file formats, image resolution, spot-color separations, electronic file preparation, and a host of other production considerations. Like even experienced designers do, she had her share of frustrations, including system and software crashes that forced her to re-create part of the layout.

Printing *Spotlight* underscored the importance of good communication between printer and customer. As a beginner, Brooks relied heavily on the printer for production expertise. A text reflow problem revealed that the printer had cross-platformed her document to a Macintosh because the shop didn't own a PC, and *Spotlight* was designed as a PC file. New editors wouldn't think that scenario was possible, but making such assumptions is the first production error to correct. Never assume that your files are compatible with a printer's equipment: Ask. (The printer has since purchased a PC workstation.)

Brooks was a quick study. The following snapshots of *Spotlight's* first issue after the redesign show some of the decisions we made as we translated the template for the content. The sign that the redesign was a success is that in subsequent issues it has permitted the little tradeoffs that all editors have to make for the sake of their readers.

The cover layout will remain essentially the same for each issue. The primary task will be to identify a photo that's a good candidate for silhouetting. We decided that, although the other elements should remain static, the "highlights" box could move laterally as necessary from issue to issue to accommodate the photo. The back page will contain boilerplate such as the mailing panel and shelter hours.

The design for this spread translated beautifully into a real layout. "Directly speaking," "pawsing for the news," and "ask the expert" are all standing columns that appear in each issue. We created new text styles for captions, bylines, and subheads based on the typography. Because the League's logo no longer appeared in the banner, we placed it prominently above the director's column.

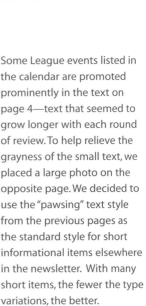

Some League events listed in the calendar are promoted prominently in the text on page 4—text that seemed to grow longer with each round of review. To help relieve the grayness of the small text, we placed a large photo on the opposite page. We decided to use the "pawsing" text style from the previous pages as the standard style for short informational items elsewhere in the newsletter. With many short items, the fewer the type variations, the better.

We wanted a central place to highlight League success stories with letters from adoptive families and other correspondence. The eight-column grid offered great flexibility in laying out the letters and snapshots sent in by readers. Centering the department head over each page allows this feature to be run as a single page if necessary. The spotlight theme was extended to a sidebar about a special animal ready for immediate adoption.

Like pages 2 and 3, this spread contains a combination of standing columns and feature articles. Strong color blocking helped separate the information, and clip art in the preferred illustration style is a consistent thread throughout. A few variations on existing text styles were developed to aid copyfitting, but keeping the template clean and uncluttered is important when an editor is tempted to add new styles instead of editing to match format options.

The ad spread was set on a six-column grid for a more flexible layout. For the first issue, the old ads had to be reduced to fit the new format until advertisers could supply new art. A few grumbled briefly about having their ads grouped with others, but all agreed that having a classified section will help readers find their services more easily. We think that it makes all the ads look more professional too, and that people are more likely to buy from league "supporters."

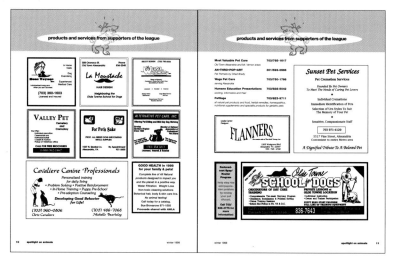

4 Writing and Revising Newsletter Content

Creating a Newsletter: Start to Finish

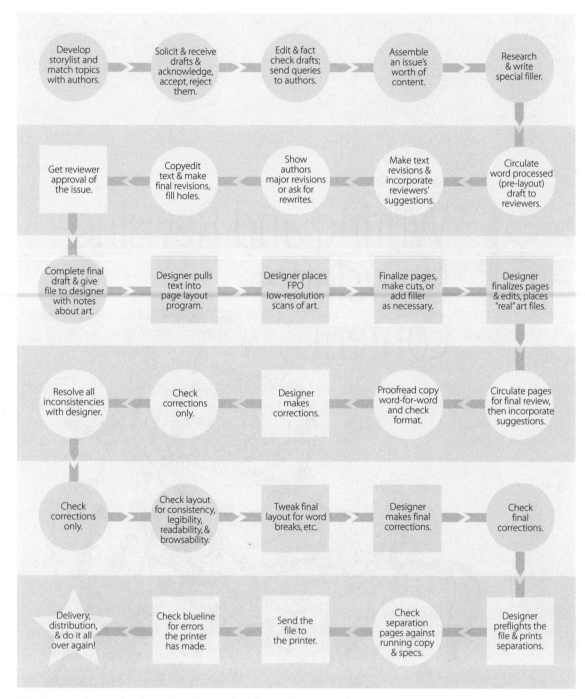

| Develop storylist and match topics with authors. | Solicit & receive drafts & acknowledge, accept, reject them. | Edit & fact check drafts; send queries to authors. | Assemble an issue's worth of content. | Research & write special filler. |

| Get reviewer approval of the issue. | Copyedit text & make final revisions, fill holes. | Show authors major revisions or ask for rewrites. | Make text revisions & incorporate reviewers' suggestions. | Circulate word processed (pre-layout) draft to reviewers. |

| Complete final draft & give file to designer with notes about art. | Designer pulls text into page layout program. | Designer places FPO low-resolution scans of art. | Finalize pages, make cuts, or add filler as necessary. | Designer finalizes pages & edits, places "real" art files. |

| Resolve all inconsistencies with designer. | Check corrections only. | Designer makes corrections. | Proofread copy word-for-word and check format. | Circulate pages for final review, then incorporate suggestions. |

| Check corrections only. | Check layout for consistency, legibility, readability, & browsability. | Tweak final layout for word breaks, etc. | Designer makes final corrections. | Check final corrections. |

| Delivery, distribution, & do it all over again! | Check blueline for errors the printer has made. | Send the file to the printer. | Check separation pages against running copy & specs. | Designer preflights the file & prints separations. |

Newsletter writers and writer-editors have to find the inside story readers will care about—not just a dry listing of facts with a few vague quotes thrown in. Reader-centric copy sounds like human beings talking to other human beings. In both print and online newsletters, content rules. Newsletter writing is journalism.

4 Writing and Revising Newsletter Content

How to help readers see and hear what you're saying

In case you haven't yet read or don't remember every syllable of the book so far, we said that newsletter editors, in their dreams, select and arrange a complementary group of newsworthy articles in a well-balanced issue, see it through a production process that results in a congenial layout, and get information into the hands of attentive readers. We spoke of the necessary project management skills and relationship-building that go with that territory.

We said that service newsletters have a strategic mission—a handful of specific actions or attitudes it would be nice to see readers do or show. Newsletter content is the jumping-off point for persuading people to support whatever the mission is, once they buy into it. So content (text) is both the point of publishing and the means to an end (subtext).

We also said that no matter what, editors must give readers real benefits, a sense of belonging, and a welcoming forum—the pretext for paying attention in the first place. Readers deserve and require all three, even if they're part of a captive organizational audience.

It's pretty basic: If a reader's attention to the text goes missing, so does reader action on the subtext. That is, if your target readers—the folks who *ought* to be interested—*don't* see the point of reading the newsletter, they won't cooperate by doing the things you were hoping they'd do (think, learn, vote, buy, be a better parent, have fewer on-the-job accidents, feel good).

4.1   Reader-centric copy gets read

Readers, more than writers or editors, are the ones who finally determine whether a news writer has hit the mark with information they want, formatted in a way they like, told in a variety of ways so that every story doesn't sound the same. What a given audience *thinks* is news and *expects* to see presented as news defines whether a particular story has value. How can editors produce consistently engaging copy? By avoiding writer-centric copy like this explanation of a new corporate program, found in an employee newsletter that we'll leave nameless:

> "Our relationship with retail technology suppliers, exposure to the technology in use and best practices across all channels of distribution provide us with the expertise to deliver solutions to our customers," says [the executive director]. "Our focus is on meeting the needs and objectives of our retail partners through the strategic use of retail technology."

When people read stuff like that, on some level they're thinking, "This is a recorded message." Its abstract language offers robotic precision but lacks the warmth and energy of a human being who's saying, "Listen, I've got to tell you about this, it's the neatest thing: We're using distribution technology to get the goods to our customers faster and it really works. Here's how."

Editors have to find ways to make even the driest piece of pro forma same-old column sound as if it's been written *by* a real human being *for* other human beings and *about* people and things that matter. Writing reader-centric copy, that's what this section is about: making sure that the life doesn't get leached out of the news in the editorial process. If a quick connection to reader curiosity and signs of benefits aren't there to begin with, it may be well written, but it's not good newsletter copy.

Don't let the life get leached out of the news.

Considering the stakes, it's amazing how few newsletter editors have any formal training in writing. Being articulate is a good start, but writing is much more than thinking out loud. Good writing involves making important decisions about how words will be deployed long before setting them down in a draft. Let's start by looking at how much original writing you're really doing and what kinds of articles you're creating.

4.1.1   Words: theirs, yours, 'ours'

Most newsletter editors are really writer-editors. Even peer-reviewed newsletters that rely on articles written by experts in the field always need bits of filler, an announcement of some kind, an invitation to participate in some event, perhaps a correction or an update, and a sidebar to round things out. Editors write to fit holes in a layout and

Make each
reader feel
you have him
or her in mind.

Writing to One Reader at a Time

Donald Murray said in *Writing for Your Readers*: "We should never forget that even in an age of mass communication, the act of reading is private, one writer speaking to one reader." Keep these observations (based on Murray's insights) in mind so all your readers will feel that an article is intended just for them:

___ Most good stories say one thing.

___ Avoid being overly formal or didactic; nobody likes to be lectured.

___ Avoid clichés that keep your writing from seeming fresh.

___ Readers like to know where a story has come from and where it's going.

___ Providing perspective isn't the same as imposing personal opinion.

___ An effective story has a shape that both contains and expresses the story.

___ Organize stories around events, ideas, or people—not just facts.

___ People like to read about other people—introduce news in a human context.

___ Everything should seem to be moving toward, and all loose ends should be tied up by, the conclusion.

to take care of the housekeeping details that come with nurturing an audience. This is the territory:

- The ability to knock out *blurbs*, *brites*, or *squibs* (short pieces) quickly is a skill editors acquire over time. Two ground rules for filler that's worth the space it takes up are (1) it's got to be true as far as it goes and (2) it's got to go far enough not to be just fluff. Editors may research and fact check their own copy or work with junior staff to develop both evergreen filler and on-the-spot copy relevant for a particular theme.

- Most editors also write critical reviews of resources such as books, products, or services. They may report on previously published professional material by paraphrasing, summarizing, and analyzing it for their readers. And they may do a roundup of news items taken from periodicals or internal departments or field offices. Even if others do the reviews, the editor has to constantly scan the horizon for likely-sounding products and resources, find out how to acquire review copies, and watch for reviews in other publications in order to compare viewpoints.

- It's also common for editors to write a column of their own or ghost-write a column for the CEO or the publisher. In either case, the "letter" or column that results can be a politically charged piece that requires a deft editing hand. See the section on page 234 on the art of "ghosting" copy for someone else's byline.

- Revising the original writing of others—members, volunteers, subject matter experts who are nonwriters, outside authors, a staff member who did interview notes—often ends up turning into rewriting when this material lacks a clear focus, a lead, a conclusion, and enough supporting details. Coaching writers is a rewarding way to educate them so that copy is in better shape earlier in the process and less subject to editorial intervention by fiat. "You write the draft and I'll fix it so I can use it" is a way of working that's hard on editors and writers alike.

- Last, but by no means least important, editors of consumer, employee, and organizational newsletters learn to act as moderators, inviting comments, questions, and criticism and then selecting letters and e-mail notes to print in a readers' forum. The trick is to referee disputes, research answers, and deflect naysayers so that nobody feels like a loser and your editorial credibility remains intact. Reader feedback can be used as a springboard for articles on larger issues—but only if people keep talking to you.

The biggest problem with most newsletter writing is that the editor, the arbiter for acquiring and developing content, can get so caught up in the process of dealing with authors and the demands of filling the issue that one person gets left out of the equation: every editor's silent partner, the reader.

Editors can get so busy they ignore readers.

As writer-editors, we tend to pay hardest and longest attention to the *look* of our words in a series of paragraphs divorced from how they will *sound* to someone else. We tend to forget what William Zinsser, in his classic book *On Writing Well*, told us about readers: They read with their eyes but "hear what they are reading—in their inner ear—far more than you realize." Of all publications, newsletters most invite the down-to-earth, friendly tone of a conversation between people on common ground: me and thee.

4.1.2   It's only words, but words are all we have....

Newsletter articles should appeal to readers the way some personalities charm dogs, children, and strangers—at first glance. Likewise, newsletter content has to please without visible strain, guile, or aggressive neediness. After browsing the headlines and layout, people should want to spend a little time with the collection of articles. If enough readers feel that way, the newsletter has succeeded in its most fundamental task: acquiring the voluntary commitment of attention. Without that, nothing else is possible.

Newsletter articles can make a little corner of work or personal life seem relatively orderly and comprehensible, and they can take many hours of research and preparation, but readers shouldn't be aware of all that. "A quick read" isn't necessarily a superficial read; it's just not uphill work. Like the best of friends, highly readable articles seem *unassuming*. What does that mean? "Exhibiting no pretensions, boastfulness, or ostentation; modest." Honesty. The real thing. And the beauty is that when newsletter articles seem straightforward and genuinely helpful, they acquire the ring of authority that comes only from authenticity.

That's the ideal. What pragmatic tools do editors have at their disposal to make it likely that readers will experience this happy sense that things are under control and they are in good hands? Words. Phrases. Sentences. Paragraphs. Syntax, grammar, and techniques that appeal to both logic and emotion. The imaginative language of ideas, images, analogies, comparisons, explanations, quotations, and descriptive details. Newsletter editors have to learn how language works and how to fix it when it goes kaput.

'Somebody out there is listening.'

Word by word and line by line, we editors build our own unique personalities and perspectives into the writing of routine news, special features, recurring topics, personality profiles, interviews, editorials, "think" pieces, photo essays, case histories, surveys, reviews of resources, standalone fact boxes, and every headline and caption.

Zinsser has told us to get over the sound of our own voices, though: "Words are the only tools you will be given. Learn to use them with originality and care. Value them for their strength and diversity. And also remember: somebody out there is listening."

4.1.3   The reader's shoes

What we have to remember, along with the fact that the sound of our words matters, is that we need ways to keep people reading from article to article. Each time an article stops, the reader is either motivated to go looking for more or discouraged enough to say, "That's enough of this."

Roy Peter Clark, of the Poynter Institute for Media Studies, has said that stories should be organized around "high points" that engage the reader in special ways: direct quotes that make us care about the speaker, memorable or humorous anecdotes, telling descriptions and unexpected phrasing, sharp point-counterpoint dialogue. He calls these bright spots of color and human interest "gold coins," and reminds us that we have to break our self-preoccupied habit of assuming that people will want to read what we've written without incentive:

> This way of writing goes against a bad habit many journalists have: packing all the good stuff into the first three paragraphs and making the rest of the story the dumping ground for the toxic waste in their notebooks.

Richard Weiner, a contributing editor for the *Editorial Eye*, has said that "newsletter readers expect brevity, but you can't just list a series of facts in bulleted lists and checklists."

Articles have to be reader-based, not writer-based, or writing becomes an exercise in brain-dumping: "I have all this to say about that and you should be interested." Explanatory journalism—service journalism—is all about offering readers information they can do something *about* besides admiring the writer (although that's always welcome, too). Weiner calls the addition of little reader rewards "putting raisins in the cake."

4.1.4   Looking for news angles

It can be difficult to find a way to make routine, even negative topics seem newsworthy to readers. You really have to be constantly on the alert for angles. It's a good idea to keep in mind that the "worth" in newsworthiness means "of value to readers." Copy that's worth the time it takes to research, write, and edit is copy that *readers* feel is worth the time to read and understand.

It's also a good idea not to take for granted where the "news" in news-worthy comes from. The first definition of *news* in *The American Heritage Dictionary* is "information about recent events or happenings, especially as reported by newspapers, periodicals, radio, or television." The last definition is "of sufficient interest or importance to the public to warrant reporting in the media." Together these are the characteristics that make people think an article is worth reading: The information seems (a) fresh, (b) interesting, and (c) important.

Those are simple criteria, but they can be hard to meet when you're writing on deadline. Why? Because being in a hurry tempts us to sort of dump everything we know about a topic into a word processing file and then start moving paragraphs around, hoping they'll click. Sometimes we can't find the right facts and quotes to support what we started out trying to say, so we fudge by slipping in what we've managed to glean, hoping nobody will notice that our direct quotes are off point or that the statistics aren't quite relevant.

And sometimes we writers just miss the point because we haven't done enough homework or enough planning *before* trying to write.

4.2   The process of writing an article

Here's one way to think about the process of writing an article. Writers all work differently, but at some point all these steps have to happen:

■ **Make a decision about the newsworthiness** of information for your readers. Deciding whether a topic is worth exploring at all is the first step on the way to creating a useful article. If *you* don't know why you're writing about something, your reader's in trouble.

- **Select a focus for reporting** on a topic. Writers call the "hook" or angle around which the story will be created different things: It's the *thesis statement*, *North Star*, *point statement*, *so-what statement*, *message strategy*, *meat*. Whatever you call it, you can't begin writing an article without it. You need to be able to state the point of the story in a few declarative sentences. What are the one or two things that you want your readers to understand and remember if (as they're likely to) they forget everything else? Note that I'm not saying to summarize "what you mean" or "what you've learned from your research." Selecting a focus is the first step away from a brain-dump mentality and toward reader-centric copy.

If you have trouble organizing your ideas, try using a 'formula.'

- **Outline all the details**—facts, statistics, quotes—that will support and make the thesis crystal clear. It really *is* necessary to outline the corollary points that will be necessary to round out your story or help you make a series of points that will cohere. An informal outline will work quite well to get all the pieces out on the table, and outlining isn't cheating, as some people seem to feel. You might want to use one of the freeform outlining techniques on pages 216–217.

- **Start organizing related pieces of information** and connecting them in light of your thesis. Every story has many individual threads; when you pick a pattern, some threads will become predominant, some will recede, and some won't appear at all because they're part of another pattern—one you're not making this time. The act of physically grouping related threads will ensure that they aren't scattered throughout. You want to save your readers the work of hunting for and trying to evaluate separate connections.

- **Watch out for disconnections** or shifts of topics and details in the paragraphs you're creating. You've 'woven' them from different threads, and they may not make a coherent pattern. You'll eventually anchor the story with a lead and a conclusion and a paragraph that crystallizes the gist of the news. Writers do these things very differently:

  — Some expand the thesis statement and use it as a lead.
  — Some write the key paragraph (*nut graf*) that crystallizes the news hook first, and then write a few paragraphs to precede and build up to it.
  — Some write the conclusion first, go back and write the lead, and then line up material in tiers between the two.

- **Bring the story to a conclusion** that reinforces the thesis or nut without repeating it in exactly the same words. Often a paragraph that doesn't work early in the story because it anticipates too much that hasn't been told yet will serve nicely as a conclusion. When we write leads we're often thinking of where we know the story is going, so discarded lead paragraphs may be concluding summaries in disguise. Save all discards when drafting leads!

Once you have a focused lead paragraph (or several), writing is essentially making a series of fairly arbitrary choices about what to emphasize. Making good choices at the word, sentence, and paragraph level increases the odds that the overall architecture of the narrative will be solid.

That's why it's important not to stint on the lead paragraph (or the sequence of the first few paragraphs). It's impossible to overemphasize the importance of the lead. For a reader, it's the linchpin of all the copy that follows and it determines the path a reader takes to get to the news hook. For the writer, though, it's not a starting point in the actual drafting process; writing the lead is the payoff for organizing notes and ideas until a focus emerges.

Issue Tree Outline

Construct an issue tree upside down with your topic at the apex and related issues branching downward from it. Represent your ideas on the issue tree with key words or phrases. You can encourage the flow of new ideas by asking questions as they occur to you. For example, an issue tree on the subject of public resistance to seat belts might look like this:

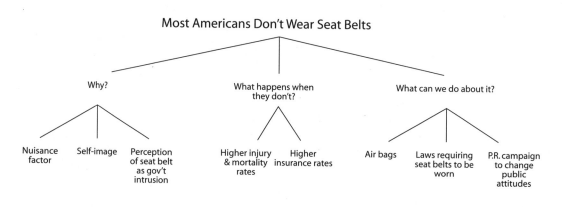

Cluster Outline

This is a largely intuitive mapping process, and making associative connections isn't linear. Writers think up or pull from their research questions, facts, resources, etc.—whatever seems to them to be meaningful chunks of information, circled and labeled with key phrases. Lines can then be drawn between chunks that seem closely connected. Overlapping topical clusters can be combined as logical relationships become apparent; dominant and subordinate chunks will emerge. For example, a cluster outline on conserving heirloom seeds in the garden might look like this (You'd write phrases in your ovals):

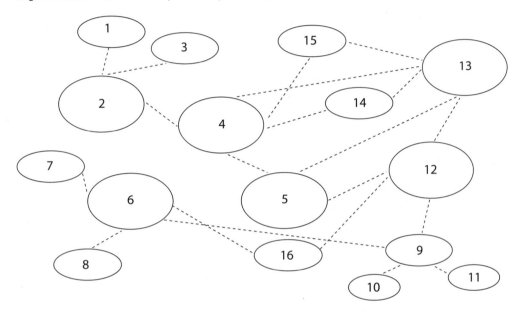

1 vessels of genetic diversity=nonhybrids
2 nasty crunchy flavorless tomatoes
3 shelf life and low price=hybrids
4 why gardening suppliers like hybrid seeds
5 100 companies sell 5,000 varieties
6 50% of all varieties available from only 1 source
7 seed suppliers bought by greedy conglomerates
8 tradeoffs=flavor, odor, disease-resistance

9   the Garden Seed Inventory
10 1,794 lost varieties recovered
11 collect and plant seeds=predictable offspring
12 Seed Savers Exchange International
13 Flower and Herb Exchange
14 Heirloom seeds
15 Southern Exposure Seed Exchange
16 Native Seeds/Search=offers 22 varieties

4.3   The lead's the linchpin

A linchpin literally holds together the elements of a complex arrangement. The lead paragraph holds the key to the success of any story because it can either make someone want to read or serve as an announcement to this effect: "Reading this article is not only going to be uphill work, it doesn't have anything to do with you in the first place, and anyway, does the world really need another article about this topic? Enough already."

Many people love to read. The recent report of the ASNE (American Society of Newspaper Editors) literacy research committee—based on one of the best and only surveys of reader preferences—suggests that the willful tuning out of print journalism isn't as inevitable as other surveys have suggested. Perhaps for newsletter editors, a bigger problem is the trend toward *aliteracy*: the tendency of people who *can* read to choose not to read, opting for other media.

Most of the time, we're stuffed to the gills with information from many media, all claiming they have what we want: "News you can use," "We get it first so you get it fast," "The exclusive story," "All the news you knows you need," "If it's not here, you don't need to know." If we're honest, at times we've all put out our personal version of "All the news I had time to dig up before deadline, and you're lucky to get it." Newsletters haven't always done such a good job of presenting content, and even now some publishers think that content is enough to carry the day, with no attention to the quality of the writing. That's a shame, because of all genres, newsletters can take advantage of what's known as "relationship marketing." In an increasingly technologically complex world, newsletter journalists can tell stories that ring true, seem personally rewarding, and inspire trust.

The lead is like the first move in a chess game.

A linchpin lead delivers an irresistible news hook, and that in turn sets the story on one of the many paths it could in theory take. Almost any of those paths will lead to the communication of some useful information, but remember the one technique that will draw more fellow travelers to any given story: cutting to the chase fairly quickly.

When drafting an article, writers tend to build up to the true news hook in a series of paragraphs. After you carefully construct three or four paragraphs, be sure to look for where the brightest quote or best analogy or most telling fact has ended up. Then consider moving it up and using it as the first paragraph. It can take a few paragraphs to work up to a confident stride; try deleting everything you've drafted and start right in with paragraph three or four. You can always restore copy if you decide you need more of a build-up. The goal is to head off writing that's going in the wrong direction before you stray too far.

Leading Them On

Newspaper and magazine editors often use jargon such as *graf* for paragraph or *lede* for lead, the first paragraph or so of a story. *Lead* (both spellings are used now) also is used to mean the most important article in a publication. It's fun to throw jargon around, and it also helps us remember different kinds of reporting techniques.

Types of leads. The most common type of lead in newspapers and newsletters is still the *direct lead*, which presents the main point right away. The workhorse of journalism, a direct lead can take various forms: a traditional who-what-when-where-why-how summary, an anecdote, a quotation, a question, or a single sentence, phrase, or word.

The other basic type of lead is the *delayed lead*, a more leisurely approach often used for soft news and features. Weekly newsmagazines have long used descriptive, narrative, or evocative details to set a scene or establish a mood, but delayed or soft leads are also widely used in major newspapers for hard news as well as feel-good and service articles (see below for more about those types of articles).

Types of articles. In a *broadsheet* (a full-size newspaper), the lead article is usually on the upper right side (above the fold) of page one. The *off-lead* or second-most important story is usually on the upper left side.

So far so good. But journalism jargon gets trickier still. Suppose you've been asked to write a *violin piece* with a *warm and wonder lede* as a *grabber*. What's a writer to do? Certainly not go off and draft a *thumbsucker*.

- A violin piece is a major article that sets the tone of the publication; a warm and wonder lede is a heartwarming and upbeat first paragraph. A grabber is humorous, startling, provocative, or human-interest material used in the beginning to get the reader's attention.

- Better a grabber than a thumbsucker, a superficial or ponderous article, which causes readers discomfort that can only be alleviated by thumbsucking. Thumbsucker can also be used to describe an article that's speculative or tries too hard to appeal to emotions—a little too "creative" for its own good.

- A feel-good article, often a firsthand report, is the opposite of a feel-bad article about tragic circumstances.

- A service article includes information that's useful to the reader—look in food, home, health, hobby, and finance publications.

Last and least. Let's not ignore the importance of a great ending. On a television or radio broadcast, an inconsequential, humorous, or even zany final item is called a *zipper*.

One of my favorite words is *weenie*, slang for a gimmick or trick device that's dangled in front of the viewer (or the reader) to tantalize them. Ah, the never-ending search by deadline-driven people for yet more efficient shorthand!

—Richard Weiner, from an article in *The Editorial Eye*

Paragraphs can often be shuffled in many combinations. There's an arbitrary aspect to writing the lead: It's the place where a writer exercises perhaps the greatest creative judgment. Like the first move in a game of chess, the lead is partly the calculated risk of editorial strategy, partly a psychological ploy, and partly a way to set interesting consequences into play for readers.

4.3.1 Finding the focus for the lead

The material assembled for a draft sometimes seems to have a mind of its own—or several minds, all taking off in different directions. You know you need to develop the story so it can go where it needs to go. But how? The biggest problem in most news writing isn't so much a lack of newsworthy material as a lack of focus—too much possibly important but diffuse stuff that's hard to put together.

A writer beginning a first draft is thinking about everything at the same time. No matter how interesting or, on the face of it (to a writer), significant all the tangents seem to be, a news story should have one dominant meaning for readers. Before you start writing, follow these steps to get unruly material—and the temptation to be all-inclusive rather than selective in the lead paragraph—under control:

You can't write until you choose one main point to make.

- Without looking at your notes, try to write down one sentence or phrase that summarizes the main thing your story must say. This is what writing coach Donald Murray calls his North Star. *It's your guiding thesis and every sentence from the first one on must support or advance it.*

- Find in your notes all possible perspectives you're toying with—first person, second person, 5 Ws, anecdote, direct quote, statistic, you-are-there, scenery, metaphor. You can number all the tangents to help you see related ones—and head off redundancy. Sometimes what look like many promising offshoots are the same ones over and over with different hairdos.

- Instead of rewriting the lead later to support what evolves as your main point, or writing the lead last as an afterthought, quickly draft several versions and then pick the one you feel goes with least diversion to the heart of where you want your story to go.

- Stand back and list a handful of questions any attentive reader might ask about your draft—whether you want to hear them or not. You'll have to decide whether you should build in some more information, clarify what's there, or delete material that raises questions you can't answer within the scope of *this* story. It may be best to acknowledge unresolved questions and state that a future article will deal with them. However, remember that this is a commitment to write another article!

- Finally, revise paragraphs so they're in a natural order that carries a reader along from point to point. Donald Murray says that if you let the story move forward from a logical starting point, "There is no need for transitions, a device meant to make it possible to wrench information out of the natural order and present it to the reader….Try to find an order that makes them unnecessary."

Sometimes a lead is really the conclusion.

You may discover that a paragraph tucked farther down would make a better lead and that what you started out with would really be better as the conclusion. These things happen. Writing isn't a science. Make decisions about what matters most and pick one good way (out of many possibilities) to show it to readers. Help them see what you see. Just remember not to trap yourself too early into thinking things can't be changed. It's hard to make yourself take a draft apart when new associations, relationships, and implications that you hadn't known were there when you started suddenly emerge—but you have to. Keep revising and rearranging sentences and paragraphs until what can be said has been said and what can't be said has been whistled.

4.3.2   Types of leads

The news writer has to find a way to make even mundane topics interesting. If you start with the attitude that all news is deserving of the most interesting treatment possible, you'll find that at least one of the following types of leads will almost always work for getting readers hooked:

- **Summary of the news.** To identify the five Ws: who, what, when, where, why and with any luck, also how and what's in it for the reader. Novelty, relevance, and immediate impact must be clear right away.

- **Setting the scene,** lighting the stage for the theme. "It was a dark and stormy committee meeting."

- **Quote plus context** to announce the theme. "We're on the verge of making our first million," the first-ever vitamin-fortified candy manufacturer announced at a trade show.

- **Anecdote** to illustrate the theme. "One day the newly named president of America Online placed a phone call to the Vienna, Va., home office to ask senior management a question. Enraged that he couldn't get through the voicemail system, he vowed that anyone who called in the future would be able to reach a human being. No detail is too small to be targeted for his planned professionalization of the company's operations, which are somewhat laid-back and erratic."

- **Analogy** to show how the theme is like something else familiar. "The little engine that could, did, after much strain and self-discipline, and so did the Natural-E Candy Co., which after first-quarter losses now enjoys a hard-won position as the industry leader in vitamin-E-fortified candy."

- **Metaphor** to explain the significance of a theme or idea by equating it with a vivid and often emotional, poetic, or literary image. "The vitamin candy company is the little engine that could" is saying one thing is something else to make the point. For metaphor to work, people have to understand the reference.

- **Simile** to explain the significance of a theme or idea by comparing it with a vivid and often emotional, poetic, or literary image. "The vitamin-candy company is like the little engine that could" says one thing is like another to make the point. For simile to work, people have to understand the reference.

4.4 Creating narrative perspectives

Perspective is a way of looking at things—a matter of emphasis. Organizing words within sentences and sentences within paragraphs is the way to show perspective. It's that literal and that subtle.

Unfortunately, news writers often work under such tight deadlines that they overlook simple ways to give readers clues as to what's most important. A lead metamorphoses into details and quotes (in what are called *follow paragraphs*) and the article starts to seem finished before it's been completely built. The problem is that, as Joseph M. Williams has said in *Style: Toward Clarity and Grace* (University of Chicago), "Structural flaws will show through if too much 'polish' goes on too early—unlike structure, polish rubs off easily."

The focus essential to constructing the strong lead, together with the effective emphasis of related ideas in the body of the article, is the one-two punch that develops a memorable piece. Faulty emphasis can create misleading elements, irrelevant details that eclipse the intended point, and unwittingly weird or comical juxtapositions. You could think of the opposite of emphasis as stress—as in stressing out your readers with prose that's off balance. Starting with the lead and continuing throughout the body of each article you're working on, try to watch for the way emphasis is more or less effectively achieved all along the way.

Be Careful When Addressing Readers as *You*

One of the simplest ways to invite newsletter readers into a story is by addressing them in second person—a nice "Hey, you!" It's conversational and places readers near the news—on the scene, in fact, at least in their imagination.

Addressing readers as *you* can take two forms: The subject can be what's called the *understood you* (often in the imperative mood) or the *rhetorical you* (meaning everyone). The problem with both is that they presume the reader will feel included in the *you*. But the very reasons that addressing readers as *you* is a good way to draw them in—it's direct and personal—are the reasons it's a risk. The scenario into which they're being invited won't apply—can't apply—personally to everyone. *You* isn't inclusive, so someone is being excluded. A stylistic problem comes up when copy shifts suddenly to you from a mixture of first and third persons. That's jarring. Watch out for these problems in your writing:

Just like hearing 'Hey, you,' addressing readers directly may get their attention—but annoy them.

- A newspaper story began, "Act up in Elizabeth Lodal's current affairs class and you won't have far to go to see the principal. Lodal is the principal." The problem is that the you of the article meant a high school student, not the adults who were the main readers of the newspaper. The subsequent shift to third person reporting in the rest of the article made the understood you an ineffectual, merely cosmetic technique. It would have been better to stick with third person from the start.

- In a service article about weight loss, a writer used the rhetorical you in the lead to make flat statements about the causes and effects of being overweight. At least some readers, whether they identified with having a weight problem or not, would surely have resented being addressed personally in statements like this: "You tend to open your mouth to eat too much and too often." Such statements pitched the article only to the overweight, when it could easily have been a piece recommending healthful eating habits for everyone who wants to keep fit. What the writer managed to do was come uncomfortably close to lecturing "you slobs."

- A magazine service feature on herbal teas uses first person early on: "About ten years ago, I turned to herbal teas when drinking even modest amounts of coffee made me twitch." Soon the voice shifts to rhetorical second person: "Growing your own tea herbs, you're in charge of quality control." The writer switches back and forth between "I like herbal teas that smell intriguing and taste as good as their fragrance" and "If you like licorice, you'll love anise hyssop's fresh, eye-opening flavor and fragrance." Several imperative yous were thrown in for good measure, like this direction: "Provide full sun and average soil." The mixture of persons makes for bumpy reading. Nothing personal.

4.4.1   Selective emphasis vs. stressful monotony and distraction

Selective emphasis in a piece of writing—for example, highlighting some words and statements, subordinating others; linking some closely, contrasting others—is a matter of

- clear construction and logical organization of ideas,

- telling detail and fresh images,

- concrete language, and

- concision (because no relationships are clear if all sentences are muffled with verbiage).

Stress (not as in creative tension—"bad" stress, like "bad" cholesterol) here means the opposite of emphasis. Boredom and distraction are not restful states; they're stressful states. Readers find language that's monotonous or full of illogical leaps and sticking places stressful going. Stressful writing is characterized by

- diffuse or illogical organization of ideas,

- redundant details, stereotypical images, clichés, and purple prose,

- abstract language, lots of numbers, and legalese, and

- prolixity (even "good writing" may contain wordy phrases when one word will do—all prepositional phrases are suspect).

4.4.2   Missing the point

Here are some examples of rote newsletter writing that obscures the point. In the most emphatic positions in these sentences—the ones readers will see first and remember best—are the least important words and concepts. The true news is placed in subordinate positions—a mistake that's graphically illustrated by informally "diagramming" two sentences into their component parts. Modifying prepositional phrases are in parentheses. Note the meaning being emphasized on the bare-bones subject-verb baselines:

> Our legal team is currently defending a meeting sponsor involved in a litigation suit pending in Federal Court over paying attrition fees for a no-go event at a hotel.

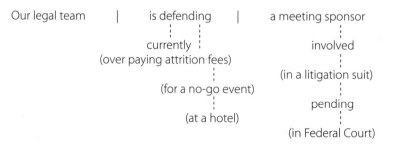

One of the issues is the payment of the tax on the damages owed the hotel.

```
       One      |    is    |      the payment
        ┊                            ┊
   (of the issues)               (of the tax)
                                    ┊
                               (on the damages)
                                    ┊
                                   owed
                                    ┊
                               ([to] the hotel)
```

The way to highlight key nouns and verbs is to develop an awareness of a logical *hierarchy of information*. Don't worry, it isn't as self-conscious and pedantic a process as it sounds. For a writer, it translates to remembering that the sum of every detail from using a semicolon to breaking material out as a list—and everything in between—should be an impression of meaningful order for the reader. Writers have to remember that placing two elements side by side creates a relationship; so does distancing them.

Here are some basic kinds of verbal relationships and simple ways to achieve them:

Relationship Established	Elements That Create Hierarchy
Equal importance	use semicolons, parallel phrasing/lists, equal amounts of copy
Dominance	use thesis statements, large sidebars, repetition of key terms/phrases, color; placement at the beginning or end of a sentence/paragraph/story and in the nut graph, headlines, pullquotes, captions
Subordination	use footnote/endnote/small sidebar; placement in the kicker/deckhead/subhead/middle of a sentence/paragraph/story; the ultimate way to show subordination is to leave something out
Set off/Contrast	use em dashes, parentheses, colons, periods, questions, transitional words, rules, different sentence patterns, italic/boldface type placement in boxes; vary font sizes; alternate long and short sentences and paragraphs
Orientation in time and space	use logical development and signpost terms to show "that was then, this is now"; "this is reality, that is theory"; "this is us, that is them"; "this is a problem, that is the solution"; "you are here, we're going there"

4.5   What's newsworthy?

Newsworthy simply means being of sufficient interest to readers to deserve coverage. Explaining the source and resolution of a problem and relating a surprising or edifying turn of events are the pivotal points of any news-based article. The degree to which the elements of breaking news should be an integral part of a newsletter's content reflects the editor, the publishing context, and the nature of a particular story.

Readers have an idea of what feels like 'news.'

The six generally accepted criteria for newsworthiness won't be met by every article, but if none of them ever show up in any articles, there's a problem. If a newsletter has no content that seems current or future-directed, it can only be read as a publication "of record." Keep these criteria in mind when you evaluate a topic to see whether it's worth developing and when you look over your storylist for balance. (For more about balanced content, see pages 30–32.)

Four elements of newsworthiness will vary by locale and readership:

1. **Impact.** Does your news directly affect readers' lives?

2. **Proximity.** How near geographically to readers is the location of the news event or its impact?

3. **Prominence.** Is someone in the story well known to the readers involved?

4. **Unusualness.** What's out-of-the-ordinary, one-of-a kind, the-first-ever, or never-before about your news?

Two elements of newsworthiness apply universally to stories people most enjoy reading:

1. **Timeliness.** "Breaking news" seems fresh and has discernible consequences for readers—the opposite of "old business" that's over and done with and just a matter of record. Making articles seem fresh when they're reports on past decisions, recurring events, and overly familiar oatmealy situations is one of the hardest tasks organizational editors face.

2. **Conflict.** "Hot news" is built from a core of creative tension: between old and new facts, received wisdom and discoveries, beliefs and debunked myths, the expected and discovered outcomes, a perennial problem and a future solution, traditional and innovative policies. A tug between any two antagonistic players or sets of circumstances allows the writer to set up a scenario that captures readers' imaginations and piques their curiosity. The exploration that leads to resolution is a natural story pattern that helps a writer put a fresh spin on any story.

Assigning Importance to Ideas

- Place the most important words at the beginning or the end of the sentence, paragraph, or article. *The least significant place for an idea is in the middle.*

- Build to a climax by arranging a series ranked from least to most important or most important to least. Illogical ranking makes copy seem disorganized, and readers can't retain the information without a framework.

- Use the active instead of the passive voice if you want to make the actor or doer important; using the passive deflects attention away from the actor and makes the recipient of the action or the "done deed" itself more important than the doing.

    Active: Gatekeepers control the ability of patients to get care from an HMO.

    Passive: The ability of patients to get care from an HMO is controlled by gatekeepers.

- Repeat key words or phrases as you move forward to new material; use the same vocabulary instead of introducing slightly different synonyms, a practice that diminishes reader recognition and remembering of key points.

- Make grammatical elements parallel to highlight differences or similarities: *To err is human, forgiving is divine* loses a bit of its impact when the infinitive form isn't repeated: *to forgive* completes the pattern memorably.

- Avoid monotonous sentence patterns; vary sentence length within rough units of two or three sentences, use other forms besides declarative sentences, and avoid long introductory modifiers and long end-of-sentence modifiers.

4.5.1 Classic news writing style

If you didn't go to journalism school, don't worry. The mysteries of the news formula are easily unmasked. It's a predictable sequence of paragraphs that introduce the story: *a specialized lead, follow paragraph(s), backfill paragraph(s),* and *the body,* which is a series of summary paragraphs and quotations. In theory, there's no formal conclusion. Journalists have effectively trained generations of readers that it probably isn't worth reading to the end of an article written in pyramid style, which places all that important detail in the beginning. But this formula is the workhorse of reporting in newsletters, newspapers, and news magazines.

Here's the traditional news formula:

- The lead contains all the 5 Ws. Includes a conflict angle whenever possible by setting up the news as a report on a problem that needs resolving, a question that needs answering, or a change in the status quo that needs explaining.

- The main players or organizations are identified in the first paragraph or immediately afterward in the follow paragraph. Proper names usually come soon after (not in) the lead sentence that sets up and defines in general the "who." By the third paragraph, readers need some names and human voices.

- The brightest quote (interesting, forceful, even controversial) appears by the third paragraph.

- Backfill—additional stage setting, context, or essential background should come right after the bright quote in the third paragraph, not after the lead.

- Story-moving quotes in action-reaction pairs are arranged from most to least interesting. These quotes appear after the backfill (fourth paragraph or later) to show point-counterpoint among sources.

- Paragraphs are short—perhaps even a single sentence. Paragraphs function differently in columned periodicals than they do in longer documents—keep them to two or at most three sentences.

- No formal concluding paragraph appears. Final sentences may be edited away, which is why they should be limited to inessential backfill; place all powerful, evocative, or significant information higher up (earlier) in the story.

4.5.2 Narrative style: a variation on the news pyramid

Using a feature-type lead, even if you revert to the pyramid for relaying facts and background, is just a way to freshen the reader's overburdened palate. Newsletters seem more lively when they include a mix of reporting styles. But most experienced writers mix and match story-telling styles without thinking too deeply about conscious techniques. They know that beyond a certain point they have to get out of the way and let readers see for themselves.

In this scenario, the writer gets out of the reader's way and presents news directly. Narrative style is a bridge.

In this scenario, the reader has to get past the writer's style to get to the news. Narrative style is a barrier.

New writers may feel self-conscious about using narrative patterns—selecting the "shapes" information takes as it's introduced, presented, and concluded. But the only way to be sure that a piece of writing will move readers from point A to point B without detours or U-turns is to make a map. You don't become a professional architect without learning about construction; you don't become an accomplished writer without learning about construction, either.

News articles that are built with the 5 Ws still need to include the human element.

And news articles with more of a narrative structure need to answer the 5 Ws sooner or later. The shapes of the stories will differ according to where facts, summaries, quotes, and background details are placed.

4.5.3   The news feature formula

Show the people in the news and affected by the news.

Both news and narrative news-features are more appealing to readers when the writer lets a person—even a made-up composite character—illustrate the main point of the story. The difference with the narrative structure is that the writer doesn't pack the answers to every one of the 5 Ws in the first paragraph. Instead, a narrative article formula introduces a specific person who is caught up in a specific event or experience, gets the reader involved, and zooms out to the bigger story.

A narrative article with a human-interest focal point will still use at least some of the 5 Ws to develop, analyze, or explain the kernel of news. The paragraph in a narrative article that puts the details into a larger context and offers that kernel is called *the nut graf* (or *graph*). This is likely to be a "how" paragraph since the "who" happens early and the "what, when, where, why" are usually offered in the paragraphs following the initial scene-setting.

Leisurely storytelling is something everyone enjoys, but it's a luxury most newsletters don't have space for and most newsletter readers don't have the time or patience for. So writers of short narrative reports generally follow a diamond pattern of development to make sure the news gets delivered. Lacking the no-nonsense off-the-bat punch of the news formula, human-interest-based narrative articles, also called "*Wall Street Journal* style," usually present information in a modified news pyramid:

- Begin with a three- to six-paragraph story about a person involved somehow in the news event.

- Step back from the personal and supply perspective and purpose with the nut paragraph, a summary of the newsworthiness of the story: the "so what" factor.

- Finish with an outline of the basic facts of the story and a few salient details or with an identifiable conclusion. Sometimes this part of the article is written in pyramid form, creating a hybrid structure that tapers off with less-than-essential details. That structure shouldn't stick out; try to move to a stop without an obvious grinding of gears.

4.5.4   Relative strengths of news vs. news-features

Poorly written straight news leads force a reader to chew through complex facts, trivial details, and long descriptive sentences to get to the meaning and relevance of the news. A poorly written narrative report (news-feature) lets readers down by being overly simplistic, because it can develop fewer topics in the same amount of space than the fact-packed pyramid can deliver. It takes more words to set a scene, place a person in it, let people speak for themselves, and link the protagonist to the larger story.

Perhaps worse, narrative structure, with its emphasis on storytelling, can tempt writers to editorialize and thus can impose a biased perspective on readers, unconsciously or deliberately (radical clarity). Many readers deeply dislike the feeling of manipulation such a story evokes.

For Every Reporting Trend, a Backlash

Writing in his *New York Times Magazine* column "Word & Image," Max Frankel makes the case against "colorful scene-setting" and "information coated, like distasteful medicine, with anecdotal capsules." In what he admits are the best articles being written by the current generation of reporters, he sees a struggle for attention between style and substance. He's of the old-fashioned school of editing that believes in cutting to the chase—and many readers agree with him—despite a "growing faction" of journalists who prefer to set up "establishing shots" before "zooming only slowly toward the heart of their reports."

Frankel cites reader complaints to the *Washington Post* about hard news being buried in what he calls "slice-of-life yarns" and "cinematic feature stories," but notes that only in the opening paragraphs are adjectives and "throat-clearing trivia" rife. He thinks that "reporters themselves have only a passing interest in the anecdotal style" and merely try for brief effect before moving to less discursive writing. Even so, that seems like a good idea, as long as the news appears within the first three paragraphs.

It's paradoxical: Storytelling style is meant to make hard news palatable. But in fact, a long delayed nut graf may be a nut graf denied. People who suspect the nut's going to take a lot of cracking tend to move on to content that demands less patience. Unless they just plain love nuts. And some people do. Rules about writing news should be taken with salt.

The three strengths of narrative style are also its risks:

- It focuses on specific people who are caught in a larger news story or are creating news. People are drawn in by the sight and sound of another human being, but an anecdotal lead is also a delay in getting to the news.

- It usually uses chronological order—telescoped or generalized—to tell the story of specific people and what they're doing or experiencing. Again, the human connection may be appealing, or it may leave out anyone who doesn't identify with the protagonist.

- It's written in very specific, human language, using everyday words and analogies and a minimum of numerical data. This is a good way to tell a story, but to some readers it may seem to dumb down or trivialize the news.

Why bother with a story form that's harder to write, harder to guarantee results for, and that takes up more space? Because research shows that, in the hands of a talented writer, that kind of story is likelier to be read all the way through than a dry, so-called objective news story.

4.6   Editorializing vs. objectivity

Is editorializing the antithesis of good reporting? Good editors have learned the fundamental tenet of keeping their credibility with readers: Don't try to feed people advocacy as if it were unvarnished reporting. Recent research sponsored by the Literacy Committee of the American Society of Newspaper Editors and the Poynter Institute of Media Studies (among others) suggests two corollaries editors need to balance:

- People will read a boringly presented article if they want the information.

- People will *not* read a brightly presented article if they're *not* interested in it.

In short, people read what they *want* to read. They resist being manipulated by extreme forms of reporting, but as much as they may dislike slanted news, they positively flee boring news *that doesn't seem to have anything to do with them*. That's why it's important to give readers a chance to figure out for themselves what they think about a piece of writing. All writing has perspective simply by reason of the countless small decisions to put word next to word, cause one sentence to follow another, and set paragraphs like building blocks in a meaningful pattern.

Good reporting of news isn't just about separating opinion pieces from fact. Good reporting means making people think twice about information, about the status quo. It means encouraging them to reassess what they think they know and want to learn more. And that means news writers must do some analysis, some correlation, and a lot of background research.

In the *Essays of E.B. White* (1977), White, the champion of writing that honors readers with clarity but also with perspective, summed up the need for both:

> I have yet to see a piece of writing, political or non-political, that doesn't have a slant. All writing slants the way a writer leans, and no man is born perpendicular, although many men are born upright. The beauty of the American free press is that the slants and the twists and the distortions come from so many directions, and the special interests are so numerous, the reader must sift and sort and check and counter-check in order to find out what that score is.

4.6.1   What is 'style'?

Style isn't something superficial you can successfully impose on language. It's not "attitude." It's the sum of the small choices a writer makes to say what he means to say, and most of those choices are words. Joseph M. Williams defines style as "the direct attainment of a foreseen end." What does that mean for practical newsletter writer-editors?

Direct attainment. Writers must translate central concepts into key words that resonate with readers. Resonant words are direct because they make a strong first impression, and they're powerful because readers retain them, "continuing to sound in the ears of memory," as the *American Heritage Dictionary*, third edition, says, with "a prolonged, subtle, or stimulating effect beyond the initial impact." Direct language bypasses the excessively descriptive, prefatory, and tangential in favor of the essential.

Style is the sum of countless small choices.

Attainment of a foreseen end. An effective writing style is one that takes a narrative and its readers where they were intended from the beginning to go. That means keeping the thesis, the editorial North Star, in sight every step of the way. Such stories read as if there's been no uncertainty about them, no patching together of stray bits and pieces into an uneasy pattern. The words and sentences and paragraphs must read as if they've put themselves together the only way they could have been written, developing naturally from start to finish like any good children's story—all loose ends tucked under, all trials and puzzles accounted for if not solved.

ComputerUser, a publication sized and formatted like a newspaper, is written in engaging newsletter *style*. Here is a stylish paragraph from a column by Michael Finley in which a wry list of truisms combine accuracy and humorous appeal for the universe of people so often waylaid by computers:

If a thing is not worth doing, it's not worth doing well. As H.L. Mencken accused Warren G. Harding of writing in the margins of his Bible: "How true." How many times have you dithered over a document, adding borders, fonts, indents and clip art when all you needed was to hand it to someone to read. Prioritize. Do what is important and move on.

A foreseen end. As writers we can't know ahead of time each word or image we'll use, the same as a sailor can't chart the course of each individual wave. But we can have a picture of what arrival—conclusion—will look like. We must keep in our mind's eye a compass tilted toward our chosen port. Some writers are of the "How can I know what I think until I see what I say?" school. Contrary to Aldous Huxley's pronouncement, the desired end of a piece of writing not only justifies the narrative means, that end recommends those means.

Voice is perspective plus diction.

4.6.2   What is 'voice'?

"All writing has a voice, although that voice might be described as objective, dispassionate, or neutral," wrote Joseph M. Williams. If content is the message, and style is the vehicle, the voice of the writer is the messenger with claims on the attention of other curious people. A piece of good writing creates the illusion that a single writer is talking to a single reader—the very opposite of speech from a committee issuing a dictum "for general distribution" or a talking head at a podium addressing an auditorium of strangers, the way so much newsletter copy sounds.

As Williams says, "The reader depends on writers to make sense of the world—to provide what Robert Frost has called 'a momentary stay against confusion.'"

Voice is partly the narrative perspective that a writer imposes on reality. That means *your* choices about what's going to appear side by side and create psychological associations, what's going to be placed in the position of expendable background or supporting detail, and what's going to stand out as most important. But creating a stay against confusion in newslettering is less like building a wall and more like putting up a tent. Unless you're doing advocacy writing, the perspective you confer will shift as you move from topic to topic, giving voice to the ideas of people who don't agree with you or with each other, and reporting new developments you have no opinion at all about.

And voice is partly diction, the selection and arrangement of words themselves. We always hope for sentence patterns that build toward effective

Sometimes No News *Is* the News

Sometimes the news is that there *is* no news, as in this lead paragraph from an article by Jim Hoagland in the *Washington Post*:

The most important fact in the current debate in America on defense spending is that there is no current debate in America on defense spending.

expression. Appropriate diction depends on the context, and that means a different vocabulary for medical, actuarial, sports, banking, religious, or political advocacy content—to mention just a few specialized newsletter subject areas. In no case, however, will abstract terms be preferred over plain and friendly mainstream English that means the same thing.

Newsletters reflect their times; newsletter writers offer perspective on a few slices of the reality at hand; as reality shifts, so do narrative perspectives. Your voice—the combination of perspective and preferred vocabulary that are your signature as a writer—will develop over time and become recognizable. Your intuitive way of organizing information and making observations is the result of all you've done and all you know. But watch out for the excesses of some "creative nonfiction" writers who inject themselves into the news. First-person reporting is still considered suspect by many readers, whose teeth are set on edge by having the news filtered through the writer's persona. You don't want to get pegged as a news writer with an in-your-face attitude unless that's part of your job description.

Here's an example of the wrong tone of voice—abstract speechifying—for a newsletter or anything else. Each declaration seems unrelated to every other (no governing perspective), and there's no sense of one human voice speaking to another in plain English (just between "me and thee"):

> The answers to these questions require more than forecasting; they require industry foresight. Forecasting simply starts with what exists today and attempts to project what might happen tomorrow. Foresight begins by identifying what could happen tomorrow and then determines what must happen in the interim to accomplish the desired result. Industry foresight requires deep insight into key trends in technology, demographics, lifestyle, and regulation in order to rewrite industry rules. Only then can you create competitive space.

4.7 'Ghosting' for someone else's byline

The "From the President" column in many corporate newsletters almost never is—written by the president, that is (that can be a good thing, too). It's very common for senior executives to rely on newsletter editors to draft articles for them. While that's a sort of compliment, implying as it does that the editor is plugged-in enough to speak for management about issues, communicating "authentically" in someone else's voice can be tricky. That goes for inventing "direct" quotes from management to reinforce articles, too.

"Ghostwriting" for an employer means not only figuring out what somebody else should be saying but also figuring out—and adapting to—someone else's personal style. It's a mistake to try to clean up the boss's act *too* much; that's as bad as trying for a phony casualness. Much as a good editor keeps in mind a writer's voice—tone, diction, mood—while revising copy, a ghostwriter "channels" the sound of the voice being assumed.

Trying to put natural-sounding words in someone else's mouth means taking inventory of that person's strengths, weaknesses, and preferences. Does the "author" tend to use anecdotes or facts, historical references or statistics to make a point? Are there certain topics or words that should *not* be used because the person "would never say that"?

No good writing is a waste of your skills.

Even if you've got the appropriate writing style down pat, you may dislike the nature of the message you're supposed to be handcrafting. Writers are selected for their skills, not their personal opinions, but if your heart really isn't in it, there's a risk of becoming cynical. Remember that a ghostwriter has to give voice to what someone else believes. This is a matter of pragmatism. If it starts making you get migraines, you need another job. A perfunctory attitude will leak through to readers like the fear of a polite hostess that an entrée won't go far enough: "You don't want another helping of that, do you now?"

As with any writing assignment, the more information you have, the better. It's best to discuss together in detail the scope of a ghosted article before you draft it for approval, rather than guessing now and mopping up later. But conflicting schedules can make it difficult to sit down and work closely with your employer, and the two of you may not have much direct daily contact. Slightly better than having nothing at all to rely on are comments from second- or third-hand sources that you can then rework as direct quotes or use as thesis statements. Your judgment always comes into play when choosing the turns of phrase and details that will ring true, so you're practicing your craft, more or less, aren't you? Things could be worse.

Journalists Agree: No Such Thing as a Perfect Story

Now that you've bought a handbook full of advice, here's the truth, as told by Roy Peter Clark and Don Fry in *Coaching Writers*:

> Unfortunately, no one has yet managed to get any group of journalists to agree on what constitutes a "good story." Confronted by a fine clip, journalists will tend to "tear it apart" by focusing on one detail after another. They tend to elevate their style preferences into universal rules. Some serious journalists (and teachers) seem to equate starting a sentence with the word *but* as a violation of the structure of the human mind.

Writers are critical, and even they forget that it's easier to criticize than create. If the content is going to make a difference to someone, if the dates and facts are all straight and all the names are spelled right, and if it has a beginning, a middle, and an end, it's a good story. Art is long, life is short. You'll be fine if you adopt novelist Elmore Leonard's standard: "I try to leave out the parts that people skip."

No good writing is a waste of your skills. When you can't take cranking out another word of propaganda, maybe you'll find a way to delegate the column or change it to a more interactive "Interview with the President." Then you can get out of the ventriloquism business altogether.

As for editing bigwigs who dare to tackle their own compositions: Do it. Find a way. Nobody doesn't need editing. This is your rationale: "I like it too much and it's too important to leave out the polishing step. If there's anything you miss when you see my revisions, we can always cut something else a bit and add it back in." Remember the ultimate out: "I hated to cut a word, but the layout made me do it. Once the subheads and pullquote and photo were in place, something simply had to go." Like maybe that third sports metaphor in a row about quality control—the one about the best offense being a proactive defense.

Actually, when you think about it, it's sometimes easier being a ghostwriter than a real, live editor.

4.8   Editing the writing of others

Much of a newsletter editor's time is spent editing the writing of others. That requires considerable tact and energy, as well as the ability to believe that there's a useful kernel in every draft. This kind of editing is actually substantive editing—that is, looking for all the inconsistencies, errors, and omissions that a copyeditor corrects, as well as rewriting and reorganizing copy to make it the clearest, plainest English that will do the job for your readers. Newsletter editors who work with authors have four main substantive editing tasks:

- **Finding the pulse.** Check for the vital sign of a thesis or news hook that could easily be restated by the average reader in the first paragraph or that's crystallized in a nut graph no later than the midpoint of the article.

- **Creating appropriate emphasis.** Rescue key ideas that have been subordinated (in sentences and paragraphs and across the entire story), complete or delete ideas suggested but left undeveloped, and test each sentence for some payoff that moves the story forward.

- **Cleaning out debris.** Delete redundancies, correct blatant grammatical or logical errors, and make sure elegant variations, passive and unparallel constructions, incomplete and vague comparisons, abstract and vague generalizations, and non sequiturs haven't crept into the copy.

- **Giving readers a sense of "Aha!"** Clarify and distill whatever call to action, benefit, or other resolution the story was intended as a vehicle for and make sure (a) that the story developed it and (b) that the conclusion distilled it.

> ## The Last Word on Getting Volunteer Writers to Cough Up Those Articles
>
> When the writers are mainly the members of the affinity group that reads the newsletter, it's hard to please and nag them at the same time. Their help in compiling news and announcements is essential but always late and sometimes never arrives. This note from one editor to her readers/contributors took the blunt approach, but has overtones of desperation that probably evoked pity as well as guilt. We recommend it to only those editors who have tried everything else:
>
> > PLEASE! If you want your newsletter out on time, you must submit your articles on time!

4.8.1   Editing to fit

All stories benefit from copyfitting edits.

Of course, besides being an advocate for plain English, smooth flow, and logical development, you're also editing copy because it has to fit the space you have for it. Citing the need for copyfitting edits can be a way for editors to tactfully encourage a writer to get rid of well-written padding: "I'll try to find room, but if you had to cut 150 words, what could you live without?" Copyfitting edits are a writer's best friend—if the editor making them keeps a good grip on the chief copy points, doesn't let important transitions get lost in the shuffle, and doesn't cut everything that's "color" (human interest, descriptive details, nuance). Too often, humorous or punchy asides are the first to go when space is tight, which is a shame because they can add warmth to copy.

But generally all copy benefits from a gimlet eyeing. When all but the essential statements and quotes are removed, subtle but jarring misalignments start showing up, as well as illogical leaps over undocumented, alienating shortcuts. If paragraphs don't seem to fit together smoothly and logically when you start to trim copy, maybe key points have been hiding behind verbiage.

The flow should just get better and keep moving in the same direction if you have a basically sound story and need only to clean out the normal stuff that gets in the way of all good news writing. (See the Writing Gallery on page 285.)

Copyfitting edits can reveal these flaws (or cause them if carelessly done):

- **Omissions.** Subjects or ideas hinted at in the lead may never be developed. Get rid of them and the ones that are left will look stronger.

- **Potholes.** Information may be missing or incomplete. Fill the holes or detour around them.

- **Transitional faults.** They can appear anywhere—in quotations, identity, place, time, ideas. If you build transitions, especially in a long, complex article, readers will stay with you. Without a little help shifting from conceptual point to conceptual point, even short pieces can leave readers nonplussed.

- **Elegant variations.** Readers grow restive when slightly different wording is used to refer to the same concepts or items each time they're repeated across paragraphs. Writers may think sprinkling copy with synonyms is a sign of creativity and verve, but readers lose the sense of continuity because each variation introduces different connotations that have to be tracked. It's annoying to try to follow what seem to be clues to different meanings only to find out that the writer meant the same thing all along.

- **Redundancy.** This means more than repeating the same words. It means starting over with the same thoughts in each paragraph without addressing a conflict or adding new information. The plodding of repetition masquerading as development renders a storyline inert. Readers look in vain for connections but it's just the same wheel being reinvented in each paragraph.

4.8.2   Revising until you get it right

Once you've got a respectable story put together—maybe you wrote it, maybe you edited someone else's draft—and it's almost ready to go, sometimes you have to hold on to it in order to work through a series of refining edits. The best wording doesn't always present itself on the first pass, and it's often tempting to keep copy moving through the pipeline—you'll fix it later, right? Well, later is usually too late. Today is the first day of your most recent "later," or something like that. If you become annoyed and bored reading copy like the Case 1 example below, what's the answer? Fix it. It matters. You owe it to yourself or that hard-working volunteer author or your publisher.

Editors are just writers who count all the bears and chairs and bowls and beds. Editors can see what's not there as well as through a glass darkly what is. They won't let a story say in one place that Goldilocks is a strawberry blonde and later on that the sun is glinting off her mahogany curls. In fact, they may ask if hair color is relevant to the story. It's always best to have someone else edit your own copy, and if you've developed someone else's article through several drafts, you've lost your ability to be a clear-eyed proofreader or copyeditor, then, too.

But the point stands: Copy that at first blush seems acceptable always benefits from a cold, hard second or third look. Here's a good example of how editing happens in layers of recognition as relationships become clear and the cracks widen. This list lead-in looks like just a case of faulty parallelism. But once you start unraveling it, the lack of focus is obvious. In fact, depending on what the real context was for it, this sentence might need to be completely rewritten by the writer, the editor, or by you-the-both-of-them. How do "real editors" do it? Here's the thinking, a step at a time, in two cases.

Case 1. Making inferences. The lack of a serial comma is only the most obvious of the reasons this deceptively simple statement doesn't mean much and invites a weak response of "Well, that's nice":

> The following services have been designed to provide revenue growth, cost-effective service solutions, and bolster the competitive position.

Editors can see what's not there—and what's wrong with what is.

The second verb is parallel with *provide*, but something's missing. A comma after the phrase *cost-effective service solutions* cuts it off from *provides*, the verb we assume it's meant to go with. But if *bolster the competitive position* introduces a third item in a series, that means the expectation that the writer set up a series of nouns completing *to provide* is wrong to begin with. So the faulty parallelism isn't a new verb in the third item but the lack of a verb in the second.

Edit 1

> The following services have been designed to encourage revenue growth, provide cost-effective service solutions, and bolster the competitive position.

The wording *to provide revenue growth* can be improved by saying what's really meant: *encourage revenue growth* or, better, simply *increase revenues*. Once that edit is made, *provide* can be moved to its more logical place in the series. But now it's clear that saying *services have been designed to provide service solutions* is circular. All the list items that follow are examples of services, so delete *service* as a modifier of *solutions*.

Edit 2

> The following services have been designed to increase revenues, provide cost-effective solutions, and bolster a subscriber's competitive business position.

Who are the services cost-effective for? Presumably both *subscribers* to the services and the provider of the services, though you can't always make such distinctions from the information given. Finally, the phrase *bolster the competitive position* is stilted. Whose position is it? Is it one of a kind? The answer can be inferred from the context: *a subscriber to the service that offers all these benefits*. So mention those it's directed at: the guys you're trying to persuade to sign up.

Edit 3

> We've designed the following services to boost revenues and bolster your competitive business position while providing cost-effective solutions for your subscribers' support problems.

If your newsletter style permits you to take an overt marketing approach, why not address the reader—your client—directly and bump up the wattage of the verbs with alliteration? You might want to shift the emphasis to profits in the first part of the sentence and finish off with what seems to be a consumer benefit that won't hurt the bottom line. It's been left a little too loose—ambiguous, really—what those *solutions* are for; but an edit this substantial would have to be reviewed with the writer to make sure that the facts haven't been misstated by filling in the blanks.

Case 2. A metaphor run amuck. Here's an entire lead paragraph from an expensive business-to-business newsletter. It's great information but the news is impeded by many disagreeable elements:

> Unlike earlier this decade, when the effects of the recession/downsizing gave the impression that media executives were reincarnations of Emperor Nero—they fiddled with hefty paychecks while the employees and shareholders were around them burning—the sector's mostly robust **financials gives** more **justification** to there being 37 "payroll" millionaires out of the 138 execs from 27 publicly held media companies charted on pages 4 and 5. But not totally....

A 36-word adverbial phrase contains (a) a 4-word adverb modifying the main verb that's 42 words away, (b) its own 18-word internal adverbial clause, and (c) an aside of a 14-word clause. All before the subject is reached, and then it disagrees with the verb. **Financials gives [sic] justification,** the main clause, is delayed—and immediately followed by a long, awkward (*to there being*) modifying phrase filled with prepositional phrases and verbals.

Elegant Variation in Attribution

Here are the attributive verbs used with the direct quotes sprinkled throughout a real newsletter article about new software. The names here are substitutes for the director of technology for the software publisher and the CEO of a satisfied client business who were alternately quoted in the article. *Said* would have been preferable in every case:

offered Paul Bunyan	John Henry *noted*
reported John Henry	he [John Henry] *added*
Paul Bunyan *stated*	

All these verbs have slight—but definite—connotations about *how* something was said that intrude into the reading of *what* was being said. As readers we look for those differences, but they're beside the point. Especially silly is ending the article with John Henry *adding* (as an afterthought?) to what he had just *noted* (deliberately?). Spokespersons don't *report*—writers report.

This copy is almost uneditable because there's no focal point—just a string of parenthetical comments wrapped around a cryptic subject and verb. The short phrase that follows, *But not totally*, pulls us up short after that long windup, but since there was no payoff, it's not clear what's being qualified. The financials don't give justification? But so what? Even if they did, we don't know where we're going with this article—and we're tempted not to follow it to the jump. An editor can only ask the writer to talk through what the main point is or systematically break the complex sentence into several shorter ones.

4.9 The most common news writing problems

Here's a crash course in the errors to watch out for when editing your own work or that of others. Increase your skill at catching and rewriting errors like these by examining the samples in the gallery that begins on page 285. As you compare problematic and edited sentences found in real published newsletters (slightly disguised to protect the malapropos), you'll see that we all come up against the same challenges. Probably the biggest sources of error for all periodicals editors fall into one of these categories. Master the art of seeking out these errors and the quality of your writing will improve perceptibly.

1. **Subject-verb disagreement**—caused by tricky collective nouns and pronouns, compound subjects with a single verb, prepositional-phrase red herrings, delayed placement of the true subject and verb, and sentences that are just too darned long and get away from us:

> There are a minimum of rules—books are supposed to be checked out at computerized stations near the entrances—and a maximum number of places to sit, alone or in groups.

> Perhaps one of the most striking elements of the Douglass house are the portraits that fill it.

2. **Listless verbs**—passive, linking, and smothered verb forms, verbs made unnecessarily subjunctive—make sentences sound like announcements or the minutes of a PTA meeting:

> From a sales perspective, the new line is both innovative and ingenious.

> The Founders Merit Awards were designed to reflect the appreciation of individual voluntary effort in the chapter environment and Individuals who held chapter offices and otherwise contributed at the chapter level would earn points toward personal recognition.

3. **Expletive constructions**—hidden subjects, delayed verbs, sound and fury making what's significant hard to find:

> What he has not yet established is the different roles of the different tools.

4. **Antecedent confusion**—where did that *it* come from or which of two preceding plural nouns does a *they* refer to?

> *They* [members of a crime ring] targeted mostly middle-aged or older foreign visitors, especially women, thinking that *they* would be easier prey....They also liked tourists who seemed unable to speak English, meaning that *they* would be more disoriented as victims....

5. **Modifier overload**—participial and prepositional phrases, compound adjectives, and infinitive phrases—make it hard to tell what goes with what and what the point is:

> Merchandising options for maximizing the striking visual impact of the new multi-part photo-sequence posters, when showcased side by side, are in development, with special captions identifying for customers the options for placing posters for various graphic "punchlines."

6. **Danglers and wandering modifiers**—unwittingly funny, misleading because the writer doesn't mean what the words say, or parked like an afterthought at the beginning or end of a sentence:

> A 1993 study found that 40 million U.S. adults, about one in five workers, can barely read or write, among other things.

> Educators say they are increasingly frustrated by families with one parent or two working parents who have little time to read to their children.

7. **Abstract nouns, unexplained jargon, and noun strings** (several adjectives and nouns in a series used to modify other nouns) that offer no contextual clues to meaning:

> On the other hand, the Internet and intranets that accept full information with interdigitalized current awareness and business research services may be better offerings for many things.

8. **Shifts in construction**—nonparellelism, time-warps, ambiguity:

> Company sales representatives were on hand when the doors opened on the first day of the expo, held in two buildings at the County Fairgrounds. "This is an opportunity for us to spearhead our products for small-business customers," said Dave. "We're here talking to people about their communication needs." "We've been able to hand out some literature," added Steve. In addition to our booth, the expo featured....

9. **Mixed metaphors and purple prose**—the opposite of boring, abstract wording but just as unwelcome, and often seen in personality profiles and first-person think pieces:

> As I sat with the rest of the audience, I was impressed with the barrage of entries flashing before us.

> Even on the hustings, with his arcane lawmakers' lingo, he can seem to be speaking from the engine room of the grimy, hissing, clanging, unretrofitted factory that is Washington in the public mind.

10. **Non sequiturs and false cause-effect relationships**—one thing doesn't follow from another that immediately precedes it and seems to set it up:

> The club's purpose is to heighten driver awareness of vehicle safety by placing a bumper sticker on company vehicles which asks "How Am I driving?" and offers an 800 number for comments.

> Despite the fashion industry's "thin is in" obsession, health professionals and nutrition educators are baffled by escalating rates of obesity in the U.S. and a pervasive ant-diet sentiment among today's overweight Americans.

Ten specific tricky usage problems and grammatical constructions news writers often have questions about are discussed in 4.9.1–4.9.10.

Keep Clichés at Arm's Length

Rene J. Cappon said in *The Associated Press Guide to News Writing*, "No writer can do entirely without the large stock of familiar expressions that includes hardworking idiom, phrases somewhere between idiom and cliché (off base, snowed under) and clichés unalloyed." There's nothing inherently evil about clichés; they can be apt and make a observation in a friendly way that everyone will get. When there's really no crisper way to make a point, by all means use a cliché—but be aware that the very reason everybody will get it is that everybody has heard it a hundred times. The trade-off is freshness of language.

If you use a cliché, at least use it exactly, don't mangle it. One editor swears that this line in a CEO's letter made it into print: "We have to head this problem off at the pass before it puts down roots."

Some clichés are just plain up to no good. Cappon advises news writers to pass on using tired phrases like these: *selling like hotcakes, like a breath of fresh air, last but not least, shun like the plague, leave no stone unturned, throw out the rule book, not take it lying down, out of the closet, spread like wildfire, a rose by any other name.*

Other corporate-speak clichés that could use a rest also come to mind: *keep a low profile, make a quantum leap, raise the performance bar, "Check out our Web site," "There's good news and bad news," at the end of the day, world-class, turn things around, launch an aggressive campaign, affect the bottom line.*

4.9.1   Mastering using verbs with collective nouns

As the classic reference *Words Into Type* says, "A collective noun takes a singular verb unless the individuals forming the group are to be emphasized":

The committee adheres to its decision.

The committee have signed their names to the report.

Most Americans would add *members of the* before *committee* to emphasize the individuals in action. The same goes for most similar collective nouns, such as *audience, chorus, jury, orchestra, public,* and *team. Staff,* however, is one collective noun that seems to sound natural with a plural verb.

Words Into Type advises using a plural verb with a singular noun if the "real" subject is individuals: "If the subject of a sentence is a group of words that conveys the idea of a number of individuals, the verb should be plural *even though the governing noun is singular.*"

A racial majority of the population are....

A wide range of bacterial phenomena are....

A subject modified by *the number of* always takes the singular, but *a number of* always takes the plural.

Sentences in which a number acts as the subject can also be troublesome, though the rule here seems relatively straightforward: Use a singular verb with a number that is thought of "as a whole," as opposed to "distributively." *Words Into Type* gives these examples:

Four years is too long a time to spend in college.

There was six feet of water in the hold.

If the rules don't help, simply rewrite around the weirdness.

How Do Good News Writers Do It?

To make news stories strong, here are the kinds of things Roy Peter Clark and Don Fry recommend in *Coaching Writers:*

___ The best writers invest time in organizing their materials.

___ Good writers see the world in story form.

___ Good reporters find the person behind the story, the story behind the person.

___ To the tuned-up journalist, even nothing can become something.

___ Good writers spend a lot of time on their leads.

___ Good writers go one step beyond what's expected of them.

___ Good writers rewrite their rewrites.

___ Good writers write too long, and they know it.

___ Good writers guide readers all the way to the bottom of the story.

Forty inches of air space filters out almost all the short waves.

Millions of dollars were lost by the citizens of America.

When all else fails, rephrase the sentence to avoid the weirdness if you hate the way the correct version sounds. Maybe that's a cop-out, but life's too short to worry about such things. There's always more than one way to say something.

4.9.2   Splitting infinitives

Adverbs should be near but are not bound by law to immediately precede the verbs they modify.

The governor plans drastically to revise the $30-billion crime bill so laboriously passed in legislative session.

The governor plans to revise drastically the $30-billion crime bill....

The governor plans to drastically revise....

To drastically revise sounds clearer and more natural than any other solution to the problem. A lot of editors—or their publishers—have some old conflicting rules rattling around in their heads. Those rules tell us on the one hand not to separate the parts of any verb, but on the other to place adverbs near the word they modify.

In practice, not splitting the infinitive can lead to awkward constructions. What sounds more natural? Editors have to trust their ear for the way most people speak. Today, only the most rigid grammarians forbid split infinitives across the board.

4.9.3   Bleeping expletive constructions

Try not to start a sentence with *it*, a demonstrative pronoun (*this, that, these, those*), or expletives such as *here* and *there*. When one of these is followed by the verb *to be* alone or with an auxiliary—*is, are, was, were, has/have been*—the sentence pattern that results is called an *expletive construction*. It sounds like this:

There are serious philosophical and monetary differences between them on health care issues and no assurance that the two sides can agree on a plan for a balanced budget.

Don't make readers struggle for a subject and a verb.

Writers often have to write sentences like this to get their ideas down on paper, but space-conscious newsletter editors will watch out for this construction. If you analyze this example, you find the first part of the compound subject, *differences*, is the fifth word after its verb, *are*. The second part of the subject, *assurance*, is trying to ride along elliptically as the fourteenth word after *are* but shouldn't because it's singular, not plural. The point of the sentence seems to be "Differences exist," but if edited, the real point (the consequences of the differences) would stand out better and the splayed subject-verb disagreement would be avoided:

> Serious philosophical and monetary differences on health care issues may prevent the two sides from agreeing on a plan for a balanced budget.

Postponing the true subject misdirects the proper emphasis, and a weak subject-verb connection makes copy vulnerable to disagreement. Such sentences tend to be wordy with modifying clauses and redundant with nouns trying to do the work of the deflected verb—as for example in this sentence:

> There are several causes for this employer reluctance to hire local residents. First,....

It would have been a stronger statement edited as

> Employers are reluctant to hire local residents for several reasons. First,....

The best reason to avoid expletive constructions isn't because their tortuosity annoys the author of this book. The reason they're best avoided is their potential for causing your readers to utter another kind of expletive (Bah!) when forced to hack through them.

4.9.4 Shedding light on a glaring dangler

This sentence needs help:

> One of the pioneers in the field, he was named by Science Watch magazine as the No. 1 light-emitting polymer researcher in the nation.

Don't let your modifiers get away from you.

He isn't giving off rays. A possible fix:

> A pioneer in the study of light-emitting polymers, he was named by Science Watch magazine as the No. 1 researcher in the field nationally.

4.9.5 Overloading with modifiers

This 64-word lead sentence was meant to be clever, constructed almost as an objective correlative to the amazing saga of the skater who believed she never got an even break. But the lead struggles for breath (just like Tonya did) under the weight of a seven-part predicate studded with ten prepositional phrases, three verbals, and numerous simple adjectives and adverbs. It's got everything going for it! Even a silly dangler boldfaced:

> Tonya Harding arrived late to the Winter Olympics, never completed a short or long program in practice, ended up a disappointing 10th after the technical program, had a shoe lace snap in tonight's warm up,

broke into tears on the ice, never tried her triple Axel and ended up struggling for breath while watching Nancy Kerrigan skate **from backstage after vomiting into a trashcan.** *—Washington Post*

Actually, there's a dangler and a half. Tonya was struggling for breath while watching Nancy skate. That much is clear. But starting with the phrase *from backstage*, things get funny. Had Nancy skated onto the ice after vomiting into a trashcan backstage? Or was Tonya gasping backstage after having upchucked? This sentence got away from its author.

Verbs can be powerful words—if you let them.

4.9.6   Setting verbs free

Verbs are the most powerful words in the language, the words that spin the tales we like to read and hear. What happens to those verbs when bureaucratese takes over? They become smothered. Such lifeless verbs are also called *camouflaged* or *buried*. But whatever you call them, editors have to unbury them so they can do their work. Unfortunately, all too often, perfectly good verbs are turned into nouns or adjectives, which are functionally weaker parts of speech—still informative, but weaker in the sense that they don't deliver action. Note the following snoozers; in each, the verbs-in-hiding have been boldfaced and the existing passive verbs have been italicized:

Authorization for the new vacation schedule *was given* by the project manager. (The project manager authorized the new vacation schedule.)

Consideration *is being given* to your proposal, and if **approval** *is given*, an **adjustment** to the present procedure will be made. (We're considering your proposal, and if we approve it, we'll adjust the present procedure.)

Thanks *are extended* to those who **made a contribution** of their time. (We thank those who contributed their time.)

The **preparation** of the new procedural manuals *will be accomplished* by an outside consultant. (An outside consultant will prepare the new procedural manuals.)

4.9.7   Shifts in construction

Careless shifts in tense, voice, mood, person, or number can distort meaning and confuse readers. Editors have to locate the shifts—sometimes called *mixed constructions*—and make inconsistent elements parallel, supply missing elements, or correct pronoun-antecedent ambiguity. In some cases it's better to rewrite the sentence. Here are two examples of common shift errors:

If a food poisoning **victim** has severe symptoms, **they** should notify a doctor.

(The sentence shifts from a singular antecedent in the first clause to a plural pronoun in the second. Use one or the other consistently in both clauses or rewrite the sentence: *If you are suffering from severe food poisoning symptoms, notify a doctor.*)

Anyone can learn CPR if **you** try.

(The sentence shifts from third person to second. Pick either one: *Anyone who tries can learn CPR* or *You can learn CPR if you try.*)

4.9.8   What's included in *including*?

Include and *comprise* are often used in newsletters to introduce summaries or lists. Traditionally, *include* meant that no claims are being made that all or even most of the components, examples, or elements that belong in a category are listed—only representatives; *comprise* meant that a list is comprehensive, inclusive—nothing has been left out. *Comprise* is really the equivalent of *composed of*, which is why *comprised of* is incorrect.

Many writers are skittish about using *comprise* at all and, to avoid the error of letting *comprised of* slip past, prefer to use *include* as a synonym. But through wide misuse *include* has become an ambiguous reader cue, and dictionaries don't help because they say *include* can mean either a partial list or an inclusive list. It's best to just say, "Here are some of the people who attended the workshop" or "Here's a list of all the workshop participants."

4.9.9   Should sentences begin with conjunctions?

Edward D. Johnson, in *The Handbook of Good English*, gets the last word:

> *And, but, or, for, so, yet,* and other so-called coordinating conjunctions are often used to begin sentences, despite an older rule, still sometimes heard, that a sentence should never begin with a conjunction because the conjunction makes the sentence a fragment. It is true that a sentence that begins with a conjunction can hardly be anything but a fragment of the complete thought, but that is no justification for such a rule. After all, in a well-written paragraph each sentence should add its thought to the thoughts of preceding sentences whether or not it begins with a conjunction. Sentences that begin with conjunctions are now accepted except in very formal writing.

4.9.10   Sentence fragments

Are sentence fragments ever acceptable in formal writing? Readers may think they've been used in ignorance rather than as a conscious style decision. Are they worth the calculated risk? Worth the risk of annoying people who dislike reading sentences without verbs?

There's nothing new about fragments; journalists have been using them for more than 30 years. The idea of sentence fragments in the first place is to avoid monotony and enliven copy by varying the rhythm. But a series of too many short fragments sounds contrived— the opposite of what's intended. Fragments intended to approximate informal speech patterns, when overused, simply seem self-conscious.

According to the great commentator W.H. Fowler, verbless sentences can serve six purposes. They can express

- transition (*So far so good.*)

- afterthought (*Well, almost.*)

- dramatic effect (*We will face difficulties as we always have. Together.*)

- critical commentary (*Brilliant!*)

- description (*It's an office designed to nurture whizkids. Complete with video games and other toys. An underground gym. And two snack bars. All free, all the time.*)

- aggression/advocacy (*The particular dynamics of the group spring, of course, from the unruly school of journalism that nurtured it. Defying the conventions.*)

Many verbless sentences, of course, can't be so neatly characterized. Longer verbless sentences can be mixed with short ones quite effectively. A good example of such writing can be found in the fiction of

---

Avoiding Tired Language: Journalese

Journalese is the style of writing people criticize newspapers and magazines for when reporters settle for clichés, sensationalism, and triteness of thought.

According to William Zinsse, in *On Writing Well*, journalese is so prevalent that it's easy to slip into without being aware of it. Novice writers are especially likely to be tempted to write news the way they've always seen it written:

> The only way to fight it is to care deeply about words. If you find yourself writing that someone recently enjoyed a spell of illness or that a business has been enjoying a slump, stop and think how much they enjoyed it. Notice the decisions that other writers make in their choice of words and be finicky about the ones you select from the vast supply. The race in writing is not to the swift but to the original.

Pulitzer Prize winner E. Annie Proulx. Here's an example from her book, *The Shipping News*:

> At last the end of the world, a wild place that seemed poised on the lip of the abyss. No human sign, nothing, no ship, no plane, no animal, no bird, no bobbing trap marker nor buoy. As though he stood alone on the planet.

Granted, this style is a bit poetic for most newsletters and probably for all strictly business writing, and it's infuriating when overdone. But it's worth a try now and then to add a sense of rhythm and freshness to a topic that might otherwise be a bit boring. As Fowler said, "Used sparingly and with discrimination, the device can no doubt be an effective medium of emphasis, intimacy, and rhetoric."

4.10 Basic story types you can build from the lead

The five basic contemporary forms most often employed for organizing information are

- **The chronology** ("a day in the life of"). In a chronological news article, time itself is the thread that links events: the story of how the public relations v.p. prepared for a hostile television interview hour-by-hour from morning to night or an account of crisis management from bad news step-by-step through to the happy ending— like the story of how communications personnel in a branch of the armed services worked with vendors to bring their equipment back online after a tornado.

- **The trip** ("been there, did that, lived to tell"). Copy corresponds to a kickoff, a journey to somewhere new, and a return safely home— literally, emotionally, intellectually, or all three. The trip can be a physical tour, a visit, an adventure, or a metaphorical voyage from the known to the unknown. The trip piece resembles the search in giving the effect of having traveled through information to reach a conclusion.

- **The search** ("looking for my roots"; "lost and found"). The search presents a series of events, facts, or relationships and ends with a sense of having gained insight or knowledge, or having moved from loss or lack to closure or reward. Such a piece may be the story of literally locating something or someone desired, needed, missed. The search can be a story framed as simply as a question that's answered by sifting systematically through information. Ideally, the search piece leads to an answer or outlines the options, but sometimes searchers turn up disappointed or empty-handed. That's news, too.

'Make Me See'

Newsletter writers steeped in the culture of their organization or expert in a subject may think they're being specific and using concrete details when actually they're relying on abstract language. "Make me see!" demanded a blind editor at the *Philadelphia Inquirer* when reporters failed to use revealing details. Abstract language is injurious to the health of news writing.

- **Use foreshadowing.** A writer can plant suggestive details early in the story that pique interest and take on full meaning later on in the narrative. This technique rewards readers for paying attention (if it doesn't frustrate them). Don't delay the payoff for too long.

- **Place key material at key points of emphasis.** Key words, facts, anecdotes, and quotes stand out at the beginning and end of sentences, paragraphs, and stories. When they are buried in the middle, weaker information surrounds and overshadows them.

- **Selection, not compression, gets ideas across.** Roy Peter Clark says in *Coaching Writers*, "Good writers use only a small percentage of the information they collect. In that sense, the story is like an iceberg, with the visible part supported by the weight of massive research and evidence. Too often, writers fall in love with their material and in an effort to squeeze it all in, make bad decisions about what should go into the story."

- **Show, don't tell.** Re-create evidence for the reader, but don't make pronouncements. People may resist being instructed, but they enjoy feeling they've discovered new things for themselves.

- **Problem and solution** ("if it's broken, diagnose it and then fix it"). Problem resolution is a systematic effort to define and clarify a source of stress or conflict and produce an answer or options. The problem-and-solution scenario takes a practical path, perhaps starting by describing some physical or psychological conflict and then telling what can be done about it. Generally the problem-solution piece is less theoretical than the trip and less emotional than the search.

- **Narrative** ("once upon a time in a deep wood"). In a narrative, key players—their actions, statements, and reactions—are the thread that links unfolding events and moves people meaningfully forward through them. Think of *Goldilocks and the Three Bears,* the template for any news story with its scene-setting vivid characters we learn about through detailed description and direct quotes, repetition of key actions/elements building to a climax, and a dramatic (or didactic) finish.

4.11 How to write under deadline pressure

Three kinds of deadline pressure are artificial—they're self-imposed and tied to human inefficiencies:

- **Dithering** until the last minute before starting to organize information instead of typing up notes and interviewing people, which would then help copy points emerge.

- **Mulling** until the last minute instead of outlining a story and starting a draft, which would then take on a momentum of its own.

- **Wrestling** until the last minute with an uncooperative story's complexities instead of using a formula to build it, which would ensure at the very least that one thesis—a news hook—is communicated in the lead and that everything included contributes to it.

Novelist Isak Dinesen advised a friend to sit down to write "without hope and without despair." She meant that we should do what we can for as long as we can and then stop. Being human, we shouldn't expect to produce deathless prose or perform miraculous editing every single moment of our working lives. There's a lot to be said for mere competence: Writing copy that does no harm, gets written on time, and adds to the sum of the newsletter's worth is nothing to sneeze at.

For some, underlying writer's block and procrastination may be the fear of being not so much bad as merely okay. All writers want their writing to be wonderful. Nobody sets out to do a mediocre job: "Hmm, I'm feeling tired today, think I'll subvert the true emphasis of my story by using a lot of expletive constructions. Nobody will notice."

But those blank pages of newsletters are a little like a nest of baby birds. They're always hungry for content. Take a cue from the patient mockingbird ferrying bits of nourishment a little at a time until every needy beak is filled and the babies are quiet. The payload might be a nice fat worm, part of a mealybug, a mulberry, or maybe something from a fast-food parking lot. There are many kinds of articles you can

---

How Two Prolific Writers Get Going (or Not)

Notwithstanding advice books that tell us to "prewrite" past our unproductive moments (if you're blocked, you're blocked), sometimes only a personal pep talk gets words rolling. And sometimes only a nap.

Planning to write is not writing. Outlining…is not writing. Researching is not writing. Talking to people about what you're doing, none of that is writing. Writing is writing.
—E.L. Doctorow

When action grows unprofitable, gather information; when information grows unprofitable, sleep.
—Ursula K. LeGuin

write; all of them will be useful in their way. The best way to beat deadline stress is never to back yourself into a corner by thinking you have to write *only this* article but you *can't* so therefore *you can't write anything.*

Instead of fighting the clock and your copy at the same time, try for steady creative output so that you always have a number of articles at an early or semifinal stage of development on your storylist. If writer's block ever really hits, or your sources don't come through, or the story you planned to run gets a thumbs-down from management for political reasons, you'll be able to pull out one of your sketched-out ideas, quickly pick a thesis, and dip into the background material you've gathered and stored in a futures file (keep one and add to it all the time, now and then weeding out old news or using it to track the progress of some current topic).

The goal is steady creative output.

In short, stop agonizing and put an article together strictly by formula if you have to. Every deadline met is a victory over inertia and self-doubt. It may sound like a platitude, but it does get easier to produce copy on deadline the more you just plain do it.

4.12 Targeted message strategies

Limitless kinds of articles are worth writing and constitute news, but most of them can be characterized as having one of six basic message strategies:

- **Education**—teach me the difference between freshwater and salt-water fish.

- **Information**—tell me where to go to get a fishing license.

- **Entertainment**—tell me the story of how you caught Moby Flounder.

- **Persuasion**—convince me to start eating more fish instead of red meat for my health.

- **Identification**—make me want to join the Flyfishing Association.

- **Emotion**—show me how watermen are hurt by the pollution of the Chesapeake Bay.

Regardless of what you may have read, being interested in something just for the sake of knowing about it is a legitimate bottom line for news. After all, people choose what to read and they seldom choose to be bored if there's an alternative. Boredom is a form of criticism, as the wit said.

Do remember, though, that ASNE research showed that people will read dense, straightforward, unenhanced text if they're interested in the information or see how it can help them. And they won't read what doesn't seem beneficial or relevant to their lives no matter how beautifully it's packaged.

The sections that follow cover some of the issues writers need to be aware of as they develop message strategies.

4.13 Why writing short is harder than writing long

It's hard for good writers to write less than they know. All good writers have trouble writing spot news or tight features. That's because they realize that "short" is only half of "short and sweet."

It's hard to know what constellation to aim for with the lens of tele-scoped prose—you select and emphasize one set of facts or ideas by shutting out or subordinating the alternatives. There's nothing intrinsi-cally magical about short words and short sentences if the real story and the important news don't spring from them.

As journalism professor Walter Fox said in *Writing the News*, "Today's readers, who are also viewers and listeners, have less time for print media. When they turn to print—as they must when seeking informa-tion and understanding not available elsewhere—they expect to find it in a concise, interesting form." He continues:

> Words such as "brief" and "concise" do not necessarily refer to an absolute measurement of length. When applied to news writing, they mean that the writer should present ideas and information as simply and effectively as possible. This notion of brevity, then, applies to long articles as well as to short ones.

> To write in a concise, interesting way, the journalist must begin at the level of words. Each word must justify its place in the sentence or be eliminated. Governing all word choices, however, is the fundamental rule of accuracy, which requires that words evoke in the reader the exact meaning intended by the writer. But writing can be accurate and dull, or accurate and verbose, or—as is often the case—all three.

World's Shortest Newsletter Story

Reprinted here by permission of editor Elvia Thompson from *Lubbers Line*, the newsletter of the Pentagon Sailing Club in Washington, DC, is possibly the short-est narrative report ever written. In its entirety:

World Famous Hydrilla
Cup Races Held
on September 13

Boys won. Girls lost. Next subject.

So for journalists, the choice comes down to this: Among several words, all of which may be accurate, which contributes most to brevity and to the reader's interest and understanding? The best writers will likely choose among four categories of words in making this decision.

These are the words brevity always has room for:

- Short words—the simplest word that says what needs saying

- Concrete words—the word that creates the strongest image

- Nontechnical words—the word that sounds most conversational

- Fresh words—the unexpected image, humor, the truth underneath the cliché

4.14 When the longer article works better

This is an excerpt from an article, "Going the Distance," which was written by Jon Franklin and published in the former *Washington Journalism Review*. A two-time Pulitzer Prize winner, Franklin is also the author of a wonderful book—really a memoir about his professional life—called *Writing for Story*.

To journalists accustomed to dealing with inverted pyramid and delayed-lead stories, the longer piece can be daunting. The biggest hurdle can be the idea that there is something unnatural about the long story. There isn't. In fact, the current fashion in sound-bite journalism notwithstanding, the natural length for stories is long.

…[D]espite the epic nature of life, most news stories can be short bursts of information encapsulating what happened yesterday, with perhaps a bit of background to jog the memory. The ongoing story already exists in the reader's mind. The new story simply moves it forward a notch or two.

The key point here is that the long piece is justified only when the reader either does not have the context for the story or when that context is wrong or superficial. When that's the case, nothing but a long story will do. And when it's done correctly and for the right reasons, almost nothing else in journalism packs quite the same wallop.

Franklin says that a long piece is preferable in two circumstances:

- When the story is so novel or significant that readers need the perspective only context brings. They have to be taught enough about the story to be able to understand its significance.

- When the story itself has the potential to take readers somewhere they wouldn't normally be able to go. They have to follow turns of events, the development of characters, and the interplay of variables to gain insight into the news.

Franklin warned, "Unfortunately, too many journalists delude themselves into thinking their stories meet the criteria for long-piece treatment when they clearly do not.... But length lends gravity only if there is a strong narrative line. Otherwise, it anesthetizes. Many profoundly important stories can be told briefly, and if they can be, they should be." In most newsletters, the lead article is about 2,000 words.

4.15 Giving the story a human voice: texture in writing

Texture in language is hard to define, but readers miss it when it isn't there. Have you ever found yourself reading and rereading a paragraph that just doesn't come together in your mind, even though it's technically impeccable? Actors say of a script that, though literate, doesn't come across vividly on the stage, "It doesn't play." Texture is part of what makes prose "play." As a writer, you have no exact equivalent for tone of voice, gestures, or movement. Writing that has texture is easier to absorb because it offers toeholds on the way to understanding. Here are four tools for giving readers copy that sounds human:

1. **Punctuation.** Punctuation and sentence structure add the extra element of texture that gives prose the charge it needs to leap the gap between writer and reader. For example, commas, em dashes, and parentheses can be used to dilute the force of nonessential material when it's enclosed away from the main statement. But a parenthetical statement can also drive the point home when it's set off as a "significant aside." Parenthetical walls can act as a sounding board against which a phrase resonates.

2. **Sentence patterns.** Varying the length and structure of sentences further creates a pattern or texture that's appealing to readers. Why? Anything unvarying—including sentence length—is monotonous (not to mention ugly on the page), and long chains of ideas, facts, and logic are better digested in small bites. Literacy essays are fine, but no contemporary news writer would turn out an unbroken series of long, complicated sentences crammed with details.

But a steady diet of short sentences is just as hard to digest. This style has enjoyed a certain vogue, but it can become ludicrous. Even the respected short-story writer Raymond Carver sometimes lapsed into Dick-and-Jane style like this:

> He had a necessary trade. He was a baker. He was glad he wasn't a florist. It was better to be feeding people.

Deliver the occasional punch of a long summary sentence or a short, explosive sentence as variations. A paragraph as short as a single line can read like the voice of revelation—so don't waste it on "A good time was had by all."

How to Avoid Verbiage

Verbiage doesn't mean "words"; it means too many words, repetitive words, redundant words—an excess of words for the purpose. Here's how to streamline news writing:

1. Don't say the same thing in two ways: "About one-third (34 percent)...."

2. Don't say the same thing in several places. Look throughout a paragraph or manuscript for whole sentences that repeat what's already been said.

3. Don't use "about" or "approximately" with "estimated": "The police estimated the crowd at about 400,000." And, of course, don't use "about" or "approximately" with a number that is exact: "about 11,483."

4. Avoid vague, trendy words and terms. Here are some that spring to mind:

Don't say	Say instead
a problem area	a problem
a program involving employees	a program six employees participated in/helped with/volunteered for
the American history field	American history
additionally	also, too, and
as such, in turn, existing	delete!
assure an outcome	ensure an outcome
concerning, regarding	on, about
dilemma	problem
firstly, secondly, lastly	first, second, last
etiology	cause
for a period of years	for years
impact the economy	affect the economy
in the area of education	in education
including but not limited to	some of
individuals	persons
is knowledgeable about	knows
local-level government	local government
methodology	methods
my sense is	I think
on behalf of	for
on the other hand	but, however, conversely
on the part of	by
prior to	before
share experiences	discuss/compare experiences
to the extent that	if
utilize	use

If people developed the habit of making every word count, they'd avoid saying things like this about a county supervisor's repeated absences from board meetings: "His attendance pattern is such that he's often not there."

—Priscilla S. Taylor, from an article in *The Editorial Eye*

Make every word count, and stop when you've said something clearly once.

3. **Conversational rhythms.** When we talk about the voice of an article, we're talking about more than stylistic conventions and first versus third person. We're talking about the rhythms of human speech. If your writing has a recognizable voice—pitch, volume, inflections, accent—other people will perk up and pay attention.

4. **Metaphor and analogy.** They do windows. We've taken it as a writer's mandate to remember how language sounds and use natural cadences so people will want to listen, as they would politely listen to anyone trying to tell them something. What readers will hear is important, but helping people "see" something more clearly is also the writer's job.

Figurative comparisons give readers a way to visualize abstract ideas

Describing something by comparing it to something else sounds at first like a hard way to get the dust washed off the windows, but figures of speech—metaphor and analogy—open readers' eyes to the meaning behind abstract terms and concepts. Imaginative language isn't beside the point in journalistic writing. It's a way to make the point of a news story more vivid in an almost nonverbal way—by reflecting a concept or a description off the surface of another image.

Think of figurative language as analogous to the perception of colors that seem to be what they are—blue, green, yellow—but in fact are reflections of light off surfaces. Pretty arty, huh? Not necessarily. The best news writers never use figurative language in a self-indulgent way that would call attention to the words instead of to the meaning. They use it the way a good children's story does, to make us feel and hear the dark forest, see the breadcrumbs on the damp trail, see the plume of smoke rising from the witch's gingerbread house.

Even if the topic is a dry summary of new cost-cutting measures to be implemented immediately by the Task Force on Right-Size Strategies in order to facilitate the just-in-time staffing plan so integral to meeting our goal of maximizing the capabilities of each and every employee to do the job of several others who have been deaccessed (ugh), it shouldn't be expressed baldly, without regard for the human wish for color and warmth.

A *New York Times* feature on an interactive exhibit, "Liquid Vision: Lasers, Holograms and Virtual Reality," at the opening of the Liberty Science Center in Jersey City goes far beyond announcing an event and becomes an eventful, exciting vicarious experience:

> The idea, says the tour manager, Sean Kozack, is to give a sense of the fluid possibilities that emerging electronic technologies offer: hence the name, "Liquid Vision."

> This point is underlined by the lack of a fixed path through the exhibition....You can dive in anywhere.

A gleaming, silver, 124-foot sphere and a 170-foot tower preside over harbor and grassland, rising like some futuristic apparition. "Oz in a can," the writer John McPhee called it. Inside, the spirit of things is established by the first thing you see: a spectacular hanging aluminum ball.

The 700-pound sphere…unfolds on 1,700 hinges from a little ball of 4½ feet in diameter to a giant globe of 18 feet, then folds back up again. A motorized high-tech blossom.

Indeed, the everyday attractions at Liberty are hardly everyday. There are hotdog-size millipedes (sorry, just 250 legs a bug) you can hold in your hand…. There is a real ambulance to crawl through…an electron-microscope to peek at the bristles on a flea's belly and some awesomely interesting written comments: Did you know, for instance, that there are female cockroaches who mate just once and stay pregnant for life? That tarantulas taste like shrimp?

The charm and newness of the place have obviously captivated the author. He's been moved to a state of almost child-like curiosity and eagerness to learn what new wonders are around each corner and makes no apologies for having written a piece that's close to being apologetic. But the writing doesn't gush; it makes us smile as readers, maybe even say "yuk" or "wow" as we see the exhibits through his eyes. We— at least, those of us who haven't become grouches—wish we could go see the museum for ourselves. Soon. With or without children.

4.16 Writing display elements: a case study

One of the best ways to make sure that a story's focus is clear is to see whether you can pull display elements to highlight the thesis and the main transitional points. The point of writing display is pretty clear-cut: to offer readers a taste of what's there for them, like a series of little open doors. If you can't find the high spots—what we've called the gold coins that reward reading—and highlight them, they may be missing to begin with. (See Section 5, the Real-World Newsletter Writing Gallery, for more advice on writing heads and captions.)

Done properly, writing display elements to accompany the layout of a story is like the art of fishing. Belief in the act of fishing (for attention) is as important as having good equipment and good weather. The reader hook? Great display elements. The line? Great storytelling. The sinker? Also great storytelling. The best weather? Your own interest in the story.

Arranging entry points into a story—places that invite readers to browse—is partly a design decision but editors should never delegate writing these vital elements to designers, who simply can't be as familiar with the content. The complementary writing and layout of

This Is a Sample Headline

Caption 1

Pull quote

Caption 2

a feature by Keith Bradsher in the *New York Times* (April 14, 1996) created intriguing, organic entry points. They don't seem contrived or pasted on just before deadline, but instead seem to be natural outgrowths of the story.

Most of us go straight for attention-grabbing bits of display copy, photos, or graphics before we've even decided whether to read a story. We all hunt for clues about the worth of a story. Here's the anatomy of the Bradsher piece, which any casual reader—even one who isn't a hockey fan—can see is not run-of-the-mill. A reader might begin skimming this story at any one of the entry points and backtrack to read more about the fairly horrifying tendency of some fans to indulge in octopus-throwing.

(Headline)

Extends over all four columns of the story and makes the reader wonder how the statement finishes. In fact, the answer—Playoff Time—is the whole story.)

When Octopuses Are Flying in Detroit It's…

(Photo and caption #1)
A guy in a seafood warehouse has his arm lifted as if he's about to toss a strange blob toward the foreground.

> "You've got to be esthetically perfect to be an octopus thrower," says John Messina, a Detroit fish wholesaler and Red Wings fan, who demonstrated the technique on Friday. He admits to throwing a few onto the ice.

(Photo and caption #2)
A different guy is carrying a similar strange blob off what appears to be an ice rink.

> Albert Sobotka, the building manager for the Red Wings who is known as "Octopus Al," carried a fallen octopus off the ice Friday.

(Pull quote)

A ritual peculiar to hockey fans in Detroit is about to resume.

Readers can sample any or all of these information snacks. Together they get the point across: This is a story about Detroit Red Wing hockey fans who throw octopuses onto the ice at games. That message isn't in any one place; it's telegraphed in bits and pieces, but it quickly adds up.

All the clues lead to a more or less unconscious decision to give body copy a chance. Will the hook and line hold? We bite. And in this case, we're landed, no matter how we tack through the copy. The lead and conclusion are equally hilarious. Check all the entry points.

A reader who starts at the first paragraph will see this and want to keep reading if only out of morbid curiosity or indignant revulsion.

> The secret to throwing a large octopus onto an ice hockey rink is to boil it first for 20 minutes on high heat with a little lemon juice and white wine to mask the odor.
>
> A well-boiled octopus can be hurled close to 100 feet, its rubbery purple tentacles waving, and will bounce and roll satisfactorily across the ice when it lands. A raw dead octopus is a smelly ball that will stick to the ice on impact and often leave an inky stain.
>
> "They just splat" when not boiled properly, said Alphonse C. Arnone, a fish monger at the open-air Eastern Market here.
>
> For more than 40 years, Detroit hockey fans have had the peculiar tradition of lobbing dead octopuses onto the rink whenever their beloved Red Wings reach the National Hockey League playoffs....

A reader who starts at the end will see this teaser and be challenged to read backwards into the story or even start at the beginning:

> When the Red Wings are in the playoffs, the management throws hundreds of pounds of octopuses into dumpsters, often tossing in a little ice to lessen the smell before the garbage collectors arrive.
>
> Yet the Red Wings have no plans to try to put the octopuses to profitable use, such as by selling them to restaurants. "I wouldn't even think about it," Mr. Sobotka said. "You don't know where they've been."

Readers who skim randomly across the columns of text will encounter gems like these:

> Strictly speaking, it is against the law...for a fan to throw anything onto the ice during a game.... As a result, fans resort to a wide variety of stratagems to smuggle the octopuses into the Red Wings' arena. Mr. Messina usually stuffs an octopus into a zip-lock plastic bag and slides it down the front of his black pullover with the red octopus insignia. "It looks like you've just got a pot belly, like a typical beer belly," he said. "If I didn't have the plastic bag, I would have had a stinky belly all night."
>
> "You could hurt someone if you didn't know what you were doing," Mr. Messina said. "You've got to be esthetically perfect to be an octopus thrower."

The sheer popularity of the octopus here has even provoked a debate over the correct plural for the sea creature. While most fish mongers use "octopi," language experts say the fish mongers' version is etymologically unsound…. While "octopi" and "octopuses" are both sufficiently common to be acceptable, octopuses is three times more common. The purists' favorite, "octopodes," is virtually never used. "Other things being equal, I would probably always use 'octopuses,'" said Dr. Mish.

Whatever the correct term, animal rights advocates are not amused…. "People wanting to have fun is one thing, but when it's at an animal's expense, it's not funny," said Michael V. McGraw, a spokesman for People for the Ethical Treatment of Animals. "What's next, dead kittens or dead puppies?"

There's no way most readers can escape this article, despite the fact that the octopus isn't a widely beloved creature. It's *got* to be read! Entertaining copy appears in almost every paragraph: gold coins galore. Perhaps only an audience of environmentalists or People for the Ethical Treatment of Animals would dislike the article. But even they could learn from looking at how such articles are constructed—even ones far more exotic than the ones most of us get to write about. It gets easier to pick the brightest copy *you've* got and bait *your* version of the hook. It's not an all-or-nothing proposition.

Developing an eye for the way details can be used in steady, strong concert is partly a matter of having a good hook, line, and sinker at hand and part sheer love of the sport. Just remember that as the distinctive tone of your copy increases, the potential for it to explode in your face increases, too. Never underestimate the propensity of some readers to be hair-splittingly unhappy about anything that risks humor or "attitude." Decide whether it's worth it to you to crack wise. Are you showing off or breathing life into an otherwise tame story?

4.17 Displayed lists can help organize complex copy

A short series of items can often be run smoothly into text, but lists longer than eight lines or so tend to stray in the reader's mind from the starting point. Displayed (also called vertical) list format makes the information more approachable and has been shown to help readers absorb—and retain—three or more relatively complex items more easily than if they had been run into the body of a paragraph.

Displayed lists are also welcome visual relief in newsletters, but they aren't foolproof. Considerable care in writing and editing is necessary to make lists meaningful to readers. Lists establish either sequential or coordinate relationships among ideas or facts. The two flaws in writing lists are (1) camouflaging coordinate information with inconsistent writing or punctuation and (2) formatting sequential items erratically so that readers are distracted or left in the lurch.

4.17.1 Choose the right style for visual order

Use numbers and letters for list items only when sequence or hierarchy matters; numbers imply priority. If "the following four steps must be followed" to open the emergency exit when the plane crashes, please use numbers. (Numerals with periods are preferable to numerals with parentheses.)

Displayed lists aren't foolproof and may obscure the true relationships among facts.

But if there's no reason to emphasize the number of items or their order, and if you won't be referring to the items by number later in the text, use bullets instead.

Numbered and bulleted items alike look best when set with hanging indention—a uniformly indented block of text or a block with additional indention of runover lines.

Paragraph style is also acceptable when most items are about one-third of a manuscript page long or longer and when copy is typeset in two or more columns.

Use the same bullets for the same levels of text throughout the document. For example, if a square bullet flags the main elements in the list, use a round bullet for subsections. If you have run-in paragraph bullets, they should look different from display list bullets. But don't use too many bullet styles within a single document or on any two-page spread.

4.17.2 Make items parallel in form and grammar

Editing elements in a list to be parallel can be difficult and annoying, but it's worth the trouble for readers. Parallelism is the principle that says the parts of a sentence or list that are parallel in meaning should be parallel in form. Why? To emphasize coordinate relationships.

Here's an example of structural and grammatical parallelism doing its work well in a newsletter:

To achieve its mission, the National Breast Cancer Coalition focuses on three goals:

- research—increasing appropriations for high quality, peer reviewed research and working within the scientific community to focus research on prevention and cure;

- access—increasing access for all women to high quality treatment and care and to breast cancer clinical trials; and

> ■ influence—increasing the influence of women living with breast cancer and other breast cancer activists in the decision making that impacts all issues surrounding breast cancer.

4.17.3   Punctuate and capitalize lists consistently

Phrase- and sentence-style lists can be mixed in a document, but the choice of lead-in sentence or phrase always determines (a) the punctuation that precedes the list and (b) the options for punctuation and capitalization within the list. The one rule without an exception is that a sentence fragment introducing a list should not be followed by a colon. Here are the basic guidelines.

- Use a colon after a complete statement that leads into a list and ends with the words *as follows* or *the following*. Use either a colon or a period after other complete statements introducing lists.

- When the introduction is not a complete sentence and one or more of the items on the list are needed to complete it, don't use a colon or dash.

  Wrong: Among the most common phobias are—

  Wrong: Among the most common phobias are:

  Correct: Among the most common phobias are

  > __ arachnophobia,

  > __ claustrophobia, and

  > __ zoophobia.

- Within the lists of items, a comma, colon, or dash may be used between a term and its description or definition. Use a comma when the definition is a simple appositive, a colon or dash for a more involved description or definition.

  Three conventions that define displayed lists are, in order of importance:

  1. List style: dingbats and indention

  2. Parallel construction: form and grammar

  3. Consistent formatting: capitalization and punctuation

- Within lists of items that are not complete sentences, the items may begin with either uppercase or lowercase letters and end with either periods or no punctuation. Whatever style is chosen should be followed throughout the publication for the same type of list.

- Within lists of items that are complete sentences or that combine a phrase and a complete sentence, each item should begin with an uppercase letter and end with a period. It's also acceptable to capitalize the first word of each item and drop all punctuation—but semicolons are incorrect.

Like too much of anything good, displayed lists can become monotonous, and writers who use them as a shortcut to telegraph difficult material or mask inadequate research give lists a bad name. But well-constructed displays earn their keep in copy by

- helping readers understand and remember multiple items, factors, and ideas;

- breaking up copy visually so that even complex information seems approachable; and

- encouraging writers and editors who are breaking copy out as a list to think carefully about the relationships the list is really creating.

4.18 Quoting from published works: 'Who said that?'

Accurately quoting or paraphrasing someone else's words is like truth-in-lending. The fine points are important because a writer who uses quotation marks promises readers that the words are being reported exactly as printed—or if paraphrases, as intended to be understood. If we don't use quotation marks, we aren't making that promise. In both cases, however, there is an implicit promise that we are reporting the meaning accurately. (See the editing section, page 72, for guidelines on requesting permission to reprint previously published material.)

Indicating material that is being quoted. In nonfiction, indentation (that is, block quotation) usually replaces quotation marks for quotations of more than a few lines. A block quotation makes the same promise of strict accuracy that quotation marks do.

Quoting unfairly means giving a false impression of the source speaker. Adding ellipsis points to a quote is a signal that we've left out words or sentences, but it's not an excuse for skewing the meaning so the quote fits the borrower's present purposes.

Punctuation within a quoted passage shouldn't be changed or omitted, but punctuation at the end can usually be dropped or changed to suit the enclosing sentence. Note also that if words are omitted not at the beginning of a quotation but in the middle, ellipsis points aren't optional—they must be used.

Just as ellipsis points are mandatory to indicate the omission of words in the middle of a quotation, brackets are mandatory to mark any additions or changes to a direct quotation beyond capitalizing or lowercasing an initial letter.

When to Paraphrase Someone You're Quoting

The main advantage of paraphrasing someone's words is the same as the main disadvantage: The writer summarizes what's been said instead of presenting it to stand on its own.

Paraphrasing—putting someone else's thoughts into your own words and attributing them back to the speaker—has to be responsibly done to preserve the speaker's meaning. Paraphrases lack the force of a direct statement; worse, the writer, acting as interpreter, can get in the way or seem to be editorializing.

But sparing readers all the speaker's actual words is better for all concerned—and just plain necessary—when (a) the quotes can't be used as is and (b) they'd require a lot of editing to sound good or make sense.

One commentator, Michael Schumacher, says in *The Writer's Complete Guide to Conducting Interviews*, "The best support quotes are unique, corroborative, well- or cleverly stated, informative, clear, and useful to your narrative. They will make your text better with them than without them." Not all interviewees measure up to those criteria, and crisp partial quotes threaded through a report can be more effective than long undigested ones.

Here are six categories of quotes you're better off paraphrasing:

1. **Fixer-uppers**—rambling, inarticulate musings or reluctant hedges that don't produce any strong quotes at all, only a few memorable phrases.

2. **Disquisitions**—long histories or anecdotes whose main points are puzzling or would require too much work for readers to extract.

3. **Stiff-upper-lippers**—cryptic statements that wouldn't be meaningful to readers without benefit of bridging details: scene-setting, context, definitions.

4. **Reinvented wheels**—rehashes of what's certain to be common knowledge, which disappoints readers once they realize there's nothing worth hearing.

5. **Lectures**—stilted statistical or technical information that sounds like so much boggling trivia.

6. **Party-line parrots**—platitudes so dusty they're patently propaganda.

Incorporating quoted material. If we want to report only a specific comment, a short quotation and straightforward attribution may be best. Often, though, rather than rely on bland paraphrases or simple attributed quotations, we want to work quoted material into our own sentences, enlivening our text and giving our readers direct contact with our source. That's fair—but it should be done properly.

What about compiling one great direct quotation from several scattered sentences? Minor edits can lead to trivial lies, but they're still lies. Misreporting the sentence structure of the source is as irresponsible as misreporting the words. The conventions of quotation have their limitations, but we at least can make sure we don't tell lies. That's why, if we have to change person, and tense, and put a lot of contextual information in brackets to make a direct quotation suit our new enclosing sentence, we should just use *indirect quotations*—and they should not be put in quotation marks.

A direct quotation often has a punch that an indirect quotation lacks, but it may take some effort to fit the borrowed words into good sentences of our own. Paraphrase is weaker than a succinct indirect quote but better than a long indirect quote. Paraphrase may not communicate everything the speaker had to say, but we can be fair without quoting the whole thing. If all we want is the gist of the original, freely paraphrasing would be better.

(This material is adapted from an article by Edward Johnson in *The Editorial Eye*.)

4.19 Lies, damned lies, and statistics

Even the best of us goof when it comes to using numerical analysis to make inferences. But if the math doesn't add up, it makes everything else that's being said suspect.

Disraeli said, "There are three kinds of lies: lies, damned lies, and statistics." Even writers who have no intention of misleading readers can be guilty of spreading "damned lies" when they venture into statistical territory. Why? Because 90 percent of all writers and 98 percent of all readers approach statistics with a combination of bafflement and awe. Where did these statistics come from? Nowhere—they're made up to sound more convincing than the phrase "most writers and nearly all readers." See? Statistics convey an air of authority, but readers are at the mercy of how they're reported.

The Statistical Assessment Service (STATS) tries to prevent bad data from entering the media stream by reviewing news items for errors in statistical reporting. The STATS Dubious Data Awards for the Top Ten Silly Science Stories in the News points out where writers have gone astray. Here's one of the 1997 winners:

> The Associated Press (Sept. 11, 1997) reported on a new study that linked low levels of radioactivity to cancer deaths among nuclear workers. This was the report's headline: Study Links Cancer Death to Site

Researchers had indeed found that 29 percent of all deaths among former employees of the Rocketdyne Santa Susana Field Laboratory were attributable to cancer. But the reporters failed to note that among the general population between the ages of 44 and 65, 35 percent of all deaths are attributable to cancer. A single statistic can be alarming, reassuring, or simply meaningless unless the writer asks, "Compared to what?"

This checklist is for alert newsletter writers and editors who want to avoid earning a Dubious Data Award:

___ **Ask the next question.** It's a mistake to think that numbers mean anything by themselves. As the bumper sticker says, "Question Authority."

___ **Do the math.** "Half of all those who…" is a percentage of a sub-sample, not of the whole, and exponentially less significant. Rounded off percentages can give a false picture of whole numbers.

___ **Verify sample size.** The smaller the sample, the less credible the finding. What's reported as a trend in a small sample may, under scrutiny, turn out to be merely a statistical anomaly.

Indirect Discourse, Yes; Oblique, No

Why paraphrase a direct quote? For several good reasons: to knit background or key information more smoothly into a narrative or to telescope a sequence of events that would take too much space or be less than clear if revealed with direct quotes. But sometimes so many speakers are loosely folded into copy that it becomes hard to tell who has said what to whom or who's doing the quoting. Take a look at these examples from a *New York Times* squib. Indirect quotes make for oddly discordant and very confusing discourse—at times the person speaking seems to be muffled from backstage:

> When the White House first started planning the event, an official there called Police Commissioner William J. Bratton, who said he would be delighted to attend, said a top city official familiar with the exchanges.
> *(Speakers: New York City Police Commissioner Bratton responds to an off-stage White House official as reported by a New York City official being indirectly quoted by the reporter)*

> Then the White House official called Deputy Mayor Peter J. Powers, told him how much the White House hoped the Mayor would join the President, and mentioned in passing that of course, Mr. Bratton was a national leader in crime-fighting.
> *(Speakers: White House official speaks to the deputy mayor to relay the president's invitation to the mayor as reported by a New York City official being quoted)*

> To which Mr. Powers coolly replied, the city official said, that the only national leader in crime-fighting was Mr. Giuliani [the Mayor] himself.
> *(Speakers: Deputy mayor responds to the White House officials' relaying of the president's invitation to the mayor as reported by a New York City official being indirectly quoted)*

What could have been an amusing anecdote (the headline was "City's Only Big Enough for One Top Crime-Fighter") lacks the authenticity and immediacy of first-person and also the clarity of third-person reporting.

___ **Don't confuse correlation with cause.** Given enough time and technology, almost any pattern can be "detected" in a large data set. A fund manager who analyzed some United Nations data found that historically the single best predictor of the Standard & Poor 500 stock index was butter production in Bangladesh.

___ **It's not the things we don't know that hurt us...** it's the things we know that ain't so. Once faulty information hits the headlines, it has a ripple effect; people all over the country parrot flukish stats to friends and family as confirmed truth. The STATS Web site (www.stats.org) features other examples of some things we all "know" that, in fact, aren't facts. Here are two:

- Suicide rates rise around the holidays. (In fact, suicide rates decline in December.)

- Children are at risk from poisoned treats at Halloween. (Of the few actual incidents reported, most have turned out to be mistaken or fraudulent.)

As veteran writing trainer Rudolph Flesch advised, we should "get used to the idea that this is a world of multiple causes, imperfect correlations, and sheer, unpredictable chance." It's tempting to take shortcuts and make facile generalizations, but readers, who get the news after it passes through our editorial filter, deserve better.

(This material is adapted from an article by Lee Mickle in *The Editorial Eye.*)

4.19.1   Making over-qualified statements

To qualify something is "to describe by enumerating the characteristics or qualities of; characterize" (*Merriam-Webster's Collegiate Dictionary*, 10th edition).

To qualify news is to introduce emphasis and priority—when key points are clearly and logically presented, significance emerges. When key points conflict, are underdeveloped, or lack signposting, the news is diffused into unrelated bits of information. Both readability and credibility suffer.

This has to be the ultimate in hedging, fudging, homogenizing—the evil triplets of qualification. We'll withhold the publication's name.

> Many association offices up and down the eastern seaboard were paralyzed by Mother Nature last week as back-to-back storms dumped more than 30 inches of snow. New York City schools were closed for the first time since 1978 and the federal government closed all Washington-area offices despite a break in the three-week budget shutdown. Association offices in eastern cities had little or no staff manning the phones and events were canceled or postponed because of dangerous travel conditions. Nearly all airports were closed, some for several days,

and many flights from other parts of the country were canceled or delayed. Association staffers were unable to return to work throughout the week because of the arrival of the second storm. Many from the East Coast who were attending the Professional Convention Management Association conventions in California were forced by flight delays to enjoy the sunshine an extra day or two.

4.19.2   Generally speaking, try not to

Try to pin down vague or all-encompassing terms of measurement. When an author's statements contain subjective measurement or proportions open to misinterpretations, editors must isolate the ambiguity and identify the missing information needed to make the point clearer.

Here are excerpts from a survey of communicators. It attempts to make generalizations on the basis of statistics but leaves the reader feeling engulfed by a cloud of gnats:

> Everyone writes and edits, the survey found, but only 21% spend more than half of their time on either. The great majority (83%) work on design/layout, but half of those people spend less than 10% of their time on it. A big majority (79%) have management responsibilities.

> Writers and editors work hard, with half reporting an average 50-hour work week. Most (85%) work in an employer's office, but only 45% prefer to work there. Many take work home. Two-thirds think telecommuting is a great idea, and a fourth see it as desirable but not feasible.

> Half the respondents consider their salaries good or very good, and a third call them average. Only 15% make more than $50,000, but 31% expect to by next year. Almost two-thirds (63%) now make between $25,000 and $45,000.

There's just no way to evaluate the larger patterns because the data are not presented in a way that allows the reader to answer the question "compared to what?" In some cases, the measurement may not need to be more specific because a great deal of detail isn't essential to the meaning of the sentence. But since newsletters have a duty to be concrete and practical, modifiers and some sample terms to avoid are *virtually all, almost none, as soon as possible, a relatively short time, many, often, a time or two, seldom, a substantial amount, a slight majority, a great majority, a modest number, a few, more than a few, a minimal amount.*

4.20 Coming to strong conclusions

Why are conclusions hard for writers to come to? Why don't we just say "in conclusion" and stop? Why do we have a sense that a feature article ought to have a recognizable ending, that it's unfinished without one no matter how much information has been presented? The inverted pyramid report just stops; nobody expects much of a conclusion and nobody wants one.

But as Walter Fox says in *Writing the News*:

> In a feature, the role of the ending is twofold: to restate the angle in a way that will leave a lasting impression on the reader and provide a clear, graceful finish to the story. While these may appear formidable

Percentages, Data, and Statistics

Try to explain statistical patterns in terms of common physical analogues or metaphors—that is, translate numerical verities into practical terms. The goal of condensing news into a set of vivid "objective correlatives" just compounds the already difficult task of making mathematical findings graspable by the math-impaired among us. Here's an example of the two imperatives working at cross purposes:

> The longer unemployment continues to be chronically high, the more corrosive the effects on self-confidence. In France, one recent survey of 500 people between 18 and 25 years old, taken by the Sofres organization, showed that more than half expected to be living less well in 20 years than they did now, compared to only about one in four Germans surveyed last summer by the Emnid organization.... Little wonder that French youth today are more worried about jobs than any generation since the 1930's.

Rudolph Flesch, in *How to Write, Speak and Think More Effectively,* recommends 12 ways to make statistics painless for readers:

1. Help your reader spot trends.

2. Pick the right average: mean (socialistic average), median (middle-of-the-road average), or mode (fashionable average).

3. Point out the range.

4. Point out the exceptions.

5. Don't bury figures in text.

6. Beware of tables—readers like them least of all.

7. Use spot tables [short, illustrative rather than encyclopedic].

8. Make your figures round.

9. Make your figures small.

10. Keep pictorial statistics simple.

11. Explain your symbols.

12. Don't try to use pictorial statistics for two things at once.

criteria, they are not that difficult to satisfy because of the range of options available. As in constructing a lead, writers may use a direct quote, a segment of dialogue, an anecdote, a descriptive paragraph or—less often—a summary of the story angle.

Most news reporting trails to an end and just stops. But some stories require a more deliberately constructed final paragraph or sentence. This shouldn't be an editorial comment by the writer (that's beside the point), or a strained or coy punchline ("bird-brained crows"), or a repetition of the points in the lead paragraph. Coming full circle should not feel like reading in circles or a dead end.

An article can give readers a striking direct quote that sums up the essence of the story, a summary statement of fact that provides perspective on the news, a prediction that suggests a trend, a forecast of future developments, or—my personal favorite—a coming full circle, wiser now, back to the thesis sketched early. And sensible of having traveled and come back home.

If you think of the contemporary news feature as a diamond, it makes sense that some of the techniques that work in the lead will be effective in the conclusion. With an important difference: Instead of preparing a reader for the trip ahead, the ending paragraphs are a glance back at scenery that's already receding.

As Jack Botts says in *The Language of News*, "Every paragraph in a story should maintain its own unity of subject for proper cohesion." That goes for the conclusion, too: "An ending that concludes smoothly will leave readers more satisfied than one that stops abruptly." But unless the writer qualifies as an experienced news analyst, no conclusion should be built around the writer's editorializing on the news.

> [Good] writers will resist the urge to put something of themselves in the last few lines. Nothing can cancel hard work more effectively. Readers don't care what a news writer thinks.

Here are four techniques recommended by Botts, a professor emeritus at the University of Nebraska-Lincoln School of Journalism and a reporter and editor for 17 years:

- Summarize the story's point.

- Use a poignant or revealing quotation to "give the reader something to chew on."

- Bring the story full circle to the starting point (but don't repeat the lead).

- Paint a scene of continuing action.

And a final thought: The very things that work against a summary "packed" lead may be used to advantage in wrapping things up. Remember, too, that some people start reading at the end of a story

Computer-Assisted Reporting

Many beleaguered writers have slipped into the habit of using online information and press releases as the basis for their articles in place of original research. That's how the dreadful stuff in so many volunteer-edited newsletters gets published.

One reason to be skeptical of secondhand facts: They come with secondhand analysis and interpretation because, as we've seen, news writing flows from early premises. If the premises are unsound, no amount of writing talent can save the reporting. As media critic James Fallows has said, "The temptation of the Nexis age is for journalists to write stories they didn't report. That, it turn, reduces the chances that reporters will ever discover things that they didn't know they were looking for."

In the *Columbia Journalism Review,* Andrew Schneider examined what he called "The Downside of Wonderland"—online resources and data.

> When asked whether computers improved the overall quality and readability of stories, 28 percent of the editors [surveyed] said they saw improvement, and 16 percent noted no change, but 56 percent said the impact, the relevance of the topic, and the overall quality had diminished.

What can be the reason for such a negative attitude toward computer-assisted reporting? Perhaps the ease with which stories can be *compiled* tempts writers to cut corners when it comes to personal interviews, storytelling, and making old-fashioned revisions for copy flow. The article quoted a *Washington Post* metro projects editor's best guess: "A well-structured computer database can generate enough statistics to kill the best written story....Reporters must fight to keep the human factor in their copy. Editors must keep all but the most relevant statistics in a box or out of the story. Numbers, even those never before reported, should be used only when examples of real people can't be gotten." Schneider added:

> Inaccurate information is another concern. Most of us who have done many stories based on databases have learned that it's only too easy for bad data to get into stories.

See the appendix that starts on page 321 for a discussion of computer-assisted journalism.

It's easier than ever to find and compile information— but readers are still readers.

and backtrack. All the more reason to use a summary or full-circle conclusion.

Here's the gist of the sweet three-paragraph conclusion to that excerpt from the *New York Times* feature on the Liberty Science Center on pages 258 and 259. The writer broke the rule about injecting himself, but in this case, that's part of why it works.

> But you know what's even more fun...? Electronic finger-painting.... You dip your fingers in whatever [onscreen] color you want to use and go crazy. Needless to say, the next time I visit, I'm bringing my two boys.

Though I must admit to a worry. If science and learning is this much fun, maybe it's possible they'll never open an old-fashioned book. Could it be that all this wham-bang entertainment eventually takes the learning out of learning?

But then I have to admit I never had remotely this much fun with computers. "Our goal is to teach people slyly," Mr. Vanderer said, smiling mysteriously.

4.21 How to write news that's not fun to read

Roy Peter Clark, a senior scholar at the Poynter Institute for Media Studies, is widely considered the most influential writing teacher in American journalism. With Don Fry, he's the author of *Coaching Writers*. Clark wrote two articles for *The Editorial Eye* that are reprinted below to reinforce all the advice in section 4. These articles summarize the essentials of editing and writing copy that will make the news easy to read and clear enough to understand. The practice of explanatory journalism can make the most difficult copy with nothing but hard facts to recommend it come to life for readers.

4.21.1   Making hard facts easy reading

I hear it all the time from staff writers. "Sure, I could write a great story. But I don't cover wars or volcanoes. I write about utilities! I write about bond issues, municipal finance proposals, rate hikes! Tell me how I'm supposed to make that readable and interesting!"

Explanatory journalists take responsibility for clarity.

No circuses or oyster-eating contests for these scribes. They have the toughest assignment: the essential stuff of countless newsletters, magazines, newspapers, white papers, press releases, and sundry other reports.

These stories aren't going to go away. They're killers to write—but they're also killers to read. Editors who routinely assign these kinds of stories can help writers turn their frustration into a concern for the needs of readers.

Professor John Robinson of the University of Maryland draws an important distinction between *making information available to the public* and truly *informing the public*. Under time and space pressures, he says, writers subconsciously say, "If I can understand it, if I get it into the paper without any inaccuracies, then readers can muddle through it and make whatever sense they can out of the story."

But writers who take some responsibility for what readers get from their stories practice what *St. Petersburg Times* editor Gene Patterson has described as *explanatory journalism*. Some of the heroes of this school are the *New Yorker*'s John McPhee (for writing about Alaska and energy and oranges), Tracy Kidder (for writing about computers in

The Soul of a New Machine), the *Atlantic's* William Greider (for analyzing the American budget), and Chris Welles of the *Los Angeles Times* (for explaining the secrets of Wall Street).

Explanatory journalists try to make technical stories simple, clear, and relevant to the reader's needs. Here are some of the techniques they use—techniques that any writer can adopt (provided he or she is willing to take responsibility for what readers know) and that nurturing editors can teach.

Too much news writing is densely packed.

Envision a general, rather than a specialized, audience. A sense of the audience controls a writer's voice. If you imagine an audience of specialists such as lawyers, you may be tempted to use convoluted language like this:

> To avert the all too common enactment of requirements without regard for their local cost and tax impact, however, the commission recommends that statewide interest should be clearly identified on any proposed mandates, and that states should partially reimburse local governments for some state-imposed mandates and fully for those involving employee compensation, working conditions and pensions.

In contrast, although Sharman Stein, a business writer for the *Orlando Sentinel,* was writing about the technical topic of venture capital, she wrote a lead that invited *all* readers into the story with vivid, appealing imagery:

> It's too bad dollar bills don't grow inside Florida oranges. The state's entrepreneurs could just pick capital off the trees.

Even specialists who *can* read material with a Fog Index of 20 don't want to work that hard to get the news.

Tell it to a friend; read it out loud. When I'm struggling to make something clear, even to a general audience, I imagine a conversation with someone I know well. If a friend asked me, "What happened at the council meeting today?" I wouldn't respond, "The council agreed by a one-vote margin Friday to apply for federal matching funds to permit them to support a project to aid small businesses in the black community by giving them low-interest loans." I'd be more inclined to say, "Well, black businesspeople are struggling, and the city council thinks it's found a way to help them out." Sometimes, when you imagine telling your story to a single human being or actually read it out loud, your voice changes and your language becomes more direct.

Slow down the pace. Introduce new characters or difficult concepts one at a time. I've read news stories that introduced 19 characters to readers in a dozen paragraphs. The frustrated reader turns back again and again to keep things straight or just gives up. In a long, difficult story that aspires to explain techniques or events, introduce them one by one, in a way that allows the reader to relax, to think, to understand.

A good teacher doesn't assume that pupils know everything about a subject. Nor should they be expected to learn everything at once. Yet too much writing on difficult subjects is of the densely packed variety: information stuffed into tight, dense paragraphs and conveyed at a rate that takes the reader's breath away:

> The billing structure and data-gathering procedures are geared toward providing cost-based reimbursement to satisfy federal regulations under Medicare, he said, which insures about 40 percent of Arizona's hospital patients.

I wouldn't want to have to pass a comprehension test after reading a story that packed with information. Jim Ludwick of the *Decatur Herald and Review* shows concern for readers by easing them into what's going to be a complicated subject. Consider the beneficial effects to the reader of this lead, with which Ludwick sets up the story at a slower pace:

> When the price of sugar was plummeting last year, the federal government tried to help. Things didn't work out as hoped.
>
> What emerged is a complex struggle involving an interplay of governments, sugar producers, Third World economies, corn farmers and two grain milling giants based in Denver.
>
> At stake are the price of sugar, the marketability of corn and the future of high-fructose corn syrup.

Use simple sentences. Difficult ideas can be expressed in short sentences with one clause and one main idea. A series of short sentences also slows the pace for the reader. Each period gives the reader time to assimilate information. Donald Murray of the University of New Hampshire has pointed out what can happen when brevity is lost in an example like this:

> A 3.6 billion-dollar compromise budget was agreed to by House and Senate Ways and Means Subcommittees yesterday that pares one billion dollars from the previous compromise budget of 4.6 billion dollars, of which 993 million dollars may be restored when it returns to the floor of the Senate next week.

"The more complicated the subject," says Murray, "the more important it is to break the subject down into digestible bites, writing in short paragraphs, short sentences, and short words at the points of greatest complexity when the meaning is too often lost."

Remember that numbers can be numbing. Numbers turn off most readers, especially when a paragraph is full of them or when they bump and collide in a relentless series of abstract paragraphs. Only the most important numbers should be used, and they should be explained in context. Good writers help readers understand the significance of large numbers. Jim Ludwick did that in this lead on the farm debt:

'Rejecting Anonymity'

Geneva Overholser, *Washington Post* ombudsman, wrote about the necessity of making sources clear in a column headlined "Rejecting Anonymity." Her advice, excerpted here, can be extrapolated to all kinds of news writing. Careful attribution honors the intelligence of the reader as well as the source.

"The practice of publishing unattributed news…goes on unchecked—needlessly in many cases—because it suits our convenience and interest; it makes the job easier. But there is real reason to question whether it always suits the public convenience and interest and whether it is not time for a change."

That's from a *Post* ombudsman's column—25 years ago. There has been a change: The use of anonymous sources has become even more acceptable. Readers have less ability now to judge the source of information. And the people quoted—most commonly officials—have greater leeway to speak irresponsibly.

A column I wrote recently on anonymity roused passionate hurrahs, mostly from veteran news professionals and from readers. It also roused passionate criticism mostly from practicing journalists….There are defensible and vital uses of anonymous sources. But they are rare indeed. And, having decided that they are, sometimes, essential, we in newspapering have brought the barriers against their use far too low.

What should be the limits on the use of unnamed sources? Here are some thoughts:

- Never allow a pejorative comment from an anonymous source.

- Use them only in the most critical instances—the quotation must be important enough, the source valuable enough, the story weighty enough.

- Word all anonymous citations so as to tell the reader as much as possible about the source. Be sure any critical piece of perspective [bias] is included.

- Always give the source's reason for requesting anonymity.

- Too often we quote anonymously someone easily identified by everyone [else]…; only the reader is left in the dark. In the circle of insiders, it's easy to forget that the goal of the press must be to give readers more information—and more tools for weighing the information we give them.

Numbers aren't beloved by readers.

Last year, the nation's 500 largest industrial companies had total profits of more than $84 billion. That's a lot of money, but not half what it would take to pay the debts of U.S. farmers.

Farmers now owe around $200 billion, and are paying so much interest that a half-point drop in their rates would save enough to cover all U.S. foreign aid in the Western Hemisphere.

Think graphics. Informational graphics are reaching new levels of excellence. Our ability to explain complex issues in words and then illustrate them provides the reader with valuable reinforcement. A good writer doesn't leave the graphics to the editor. Writers should be on the lookout for important information that might be communicated more effectively in a chart, graph, or picture.

Use analogies to translate jargon. A term like *infrastructure* can put readers off until a writer compares the decay of the national infrastructure to a family "whose income has been cut, is behind on the mortgage payments, and is unable to buy shoes for the children, only to learn that tree roots have plugged the drainage pipes, the furnace must be replaced, and termites have weakened the foundation of the house."

Analogies are fun and interesting because they can help readers visualize a thorny process or a cloudy abstraction. Tracy Kidder attempts to explain the system of "rings" that protects information in a computer:

> Picture an Army encampment in which all the tents are arranged in concentric rings. The general's tent lies at the center, and he can move freely from one ring to another. In the next ring out from the center live the colonels, say, and they can move from their ring into any outer ring as they please, but they can't intrude on the general's ring without his dispensation.

Help readers see relevance in abstract information.

Find the human element. Good writers understand that readers are attracted to the presence of human beings in the news. And readers want to know the human significance of the news. Budgets aren't human documents, but graphs that look like pizza. Stories filled with the clichés of economic writing—bottom lines, tightened belts, economic spirals, chopping blocks—seem not to be about people at all. No wonder people look away. John Gouch of the *Anderson Independent-Mail* explains the plight of poor South Carolina farmers by focusing on the life and words of a single farmer:

> Furman Porter was 4 years old when he first walked behind a mule plowing up Anderson County's red clay.

When used wisely, these techniques help the writer toward a cleaner, clearer style. Clarity is the explanatory journalist's grail. The quest to achieve it is more than an occupational disposition. It's a form of vision, a way of looking at complex events and issues that's analogous to a great mountain climber scaling a mighty cliff. When writers face and master the challenge of meeting the reader's needs, they practice one of the truest and purest forms of journalism.

(This material is from an article by Roy Peter Clark in *The Editorial Eye.*)

4.21.2   Making hard facts clear

In the 1960s and 1970s, a wave of reform encouraged reporters to make stories interesting and lively, to write about trends and personalities, to experiment with techniques of fiction, and to test newspaper conventions. Today's journalists have somewhat different goals. As I explained in "Making Hard Facts Easy Reading," *explanatory journalism* tackles important, complex topics and tries to help readers see their relevance. Here are the basics of making abstract information clear enough to let readers decide what to think about it, what to do about it.

Don't clutter leads. Writers must pay special attention to the lead when a story is difficult or complex. A lead with confusing statistics, technical information, or bureaucratic names demonstrates merely that the subject is beyond a reader's casual interest and may cause that reader to turn elsewhere:

> Efforts to improve housing for Buffalo neighborhoods will receive $5.6 million of the city's 1995-96 federal community development block grant money according to the application to be submitted to the Common Council tomorrow.

The combination of numbers, bureaucratese, and needless attribution dooms that lead.

Recognize the Value of Repetition

Teachers know that repeating ideas is necessary to communicate them effectively. They adhere to the old strategy "Tell them what you're going to say, say it, and tell them what you've said."

Repetition has a bad reputation with editors. It takes up space, and it adds nothing new. But why not repeat key information to demonstrate its importance to the reader? The heart of a story can be repeated in a headline, lead, and caption. Repetition increases the odds that the news will get through to browsers.

"I always try to teach reporters that if they have an important point they want to make, make it repetitiously but in different ways," said William Blundell, formerly of the *Wall Street Journal*. "Make it with a figure, make it with an anecdote, and then maybe wrap it up with a quote."

"You cannot be explicit enough in communication," says Professor John Robinson of the University of Maryland. "Leaving something between the lines and thinking the reader is going to get it is a very dangerous practice."

—Roy Peter Clark

The alternative is to escort the reader into what may be a complicated story. That's what Neil Skene of the *St. Petersburg Times* did in a column criticizing IBM for opposing Florida's unitary business tax—not a lightweight topic:

> The state is going to spend $1,250,000—yep, one and a quarter million dollars—to widen a road for IBM.

The repetition helps the reader absorb the number, the "yep" establishes an informal relationship with the reader, and the lead is uncluttered so the reader can enter the story with ease.

Translate jargon. It may take a new writer a month to learn the acronymic alphabet soup of government- or finance-based news or the shorthand of a specialized context, but suddenly he or she will feel comfortable sneaking terms like *UDAG* into stories.

A journalist's language can become contaminated by singleminded contact with specialists. Unless terms like capitalization, amortization, and indexing are translated, many readers will be left in the dark. Bob Whereatt of the *Minneapolis Star and Tribune* did his readers a favor by taking a paragraph to explain the meaning of indexing in his story about Minnesota income taxes:

> Indexing prevents a taxpayer from being pushed into higher tax brackets merely because his income goes up with inflation. Before indexing, a taxpayer whose income rose at the pace of inflation had a constant purchasing power but could find himself in a higher tax bracket. Indexing was designed to offset that negative impact by expanding the brackets with inflation.

According to former page one editor Glynn Mapes, the *Wall Street Journal* defines the GNP (gross national product) each time it's introduced in a story as "the total market value of the output of goods and services in the nation." The *Journal*'s zeal for translating jargon once extended to defining "batting average" in a story about Ted Williams.

Find the microcosm. The key to writing stories about abstract topics clearly and well is to find a single, concrete example that anchors the larger reality. William Greider, formerly with the *Washington Post* and *Rolling Stone,* focused on two tennis courts, "a minor anomaly in the idyllic rural landscape" beside David Stockman's family farm, to profile a controversial fiscal philosophy. The tennis courts represent what Stockman thought was wrong with the way the federal government had been spending money:

> "It's all right, I suppose," Stockman said amiably, "but these people would never have taxed themselves to build that. Not these tight-fisted taxpayers! As long as someone else is giving them the money, sure, they are willing to spend it. But they never would have used their own money."

Find examples that anchor the larger story.

Develop a chronology. When writers write in chronological order, they explicitly invite readers to enter a story and stick with it. Readers understand the demands of chronology—it's the oldest narrative bargain—and they know that when the time line ends, they'll have reached a heightened level of understanding.

"I always try to find a chronology," said Chris Welles, who has written some of the most complex business stories in American journalism. Welles may have been writing about a marketing war between razor manufacturers, or the collapse of a major government securities firm, or the criminal indictment of a famous woman entrepreneur, but in each case he found a chronological rope for his readers to hang on to.

'They held a meeting Tuesday.'

Compile lists. Use a laundry list to spell out the most important information in meaningful order, and list major findings early in the story. Lists create order, or at least a sense of order, and they demand that the writer convey information tightly. Lists also create white space and typographical structures (bullets, indented lines) that invite the reader's eyes to move down the page.

Reward the reader. Stories contain at least two kinds of information: what reporter Joel Brinkley of the *New York Times* has called BBI (Boring But Important) and what might be called IBLI (Interesting But Less Important). Sometimes a writer will use an interesting morsel of information as a lure into a difficult story, hoping readers will stay for the meat and potatoes. The ingenious writer learns how to alternate Important and Interesting to reward the reader.

I once attended a lecture on macroeconomics. At various points the professor would explain why he bought Persian rugs or hoarded spaghetti or decided to buy a sailboat. The rugs, spaghetti, and sailboat were included to illustrate theories, but they were also there to reward us for listening to him talk about monetarism all day. In the same way, a good writer will link a paragraph of numbers with an interesting quote that explains them. Too many Boring But Important paragraphs in a row and the reader checks out.

Consider the impact. My first editor, Mike Foley of the *St. Petersburg Times*, taught me to avoid writing leads that said, "They held a meeting Tuesday." The meeting itself isn't important; what people did or failed to do is important. The writer must show the impact of a story and, if necessary, educate the reader to be able to appreciate the impact. Too many stories fail to answer the reader's most challenging question: "So what?"

Announce difficult concepts. Some medicines go down hard, and some concepts, issues, or procedures are so hard to grasp that even careful, thoughtful writers can't make them palatable. That's as it should be. It's dishonest to give readers a false sense of simplicity, so good writers tell them that certain information will be rough going. For example, Chris Welles let his readers know what they were in for if they wanted to understand "risk arbitrage":

> Until recently…risk arbitrage has been largely unknown beyond Wall Street. One reason was arbitrage's image as a highly intricate, arcane, even mysterious art well beyond the ken of ordinary investors.

Such announcements give readers greater tolerance for harder information—or at least give them a quick out—by signaling the need for a change in concentration level. When a writer plays it straight with them, some readers will stick with a story out of reflexive courtesy.

Eliminate information that's just too difficult. The best way to deal with some material is to leave it out. Our readers may understand more of the implications if we give them a less encyclopedic story to digest. The key to leaving out information responsibly is to make tough value judgments on the material we've collected. The result of being selective is a more precise, more readable story. If it does turn out to be boring and difficult to read anyway, at least it will be brief, boring, and difficult. Our readers will forgive us if we waste less of their time to tell them what they need to know but wouldn't enjoy reading under any circumstances.

(This material is from an article by Roy Peter Clark in *The Editorial Eye*.)

5 Real-World Newsletter Writing Gallery

5 Real-World Newsletter Writing Gallery

The cautionary, the sadly ordinary, and the exemplary

This section, like the design gallery, offers a tutorial based on published samples. Excerpts taken from news-based periodicals, nearly all of them newsletters, fall into the categories of the cautionary, the sadly ordinary, and the exemplary. Brief analyses of each sample's problems will help news writers look for similar problems in their own copy. Some samples would be uneditable without slowing down to gather more information; some samples would be uneditable at any speed. Alternatives have been suggested wherever possible.

Here's how this gallery is set up:

- First, 19 kinds of problematic prose—body text analyzed at the word, sentence, and paragraph level, including lists. Also in this section are sidebars with guidelines for writing captions (page 292) and pullquotes (pages 296–297), which tie narratives together into an attractive package when they're written with care.

- Second, 10 kinds of problematic headlines—too short, too long, too weird. Also in this section are sidebars with guidelines for writing heads (page 302), deckheads (page 304), and subheads (page 310).

- Third, 24 examples of a range of exemplary leads—both direct and delayed. Also in this section are a description and samples of the two most common mistakes in writing leads (5.3.1 and 5.3.2, page 311).

5.1 Parsing prose with a high 'huh?' quotient

Get ready (it would be trite to say, "Put on your seatbelt," right?) for an analysis of all-too-real-world writing that's bound more or less to confuse, mislead, intimidate, or bore the average reader—sometimes all at the same time.

The first sample that follows is a little bit of an exception. It's long, but it illustrates the problems that creep into news writing done quick and dirty—the way lots of newsletters get written. These problems aren't covered by other newsletter handbooks precisely because they're miserably hard to discuss without referring to a specific block of narrative, and they don't mean much without slogging through a critical analysis cringe by cringe. So that's what we're going to do.

Here's the narrative sample to which the discussion in subsections 5.1.1 through 5.1.4 refer:

Are Former Mental Patients More Violent?
If They Don't Abuse Drugs or Alcohol, the Answer Is Generally No, Study Finds

People discharged from psychiatric hospitals who do not abuse alcohol or drugs are no more likely than their neighbors to be violent, one of the largest and most detailed studies of mental illness and violence has concluded. At the same time, newly discharged patients who have a substance abuse problem tend to be more dangerous than the general population.

Patients with drug or alcohol problems were five times more likely than the general population to be violent, and three times more likely to commit a violent act, researchers found. Ex-patients who don't abuse drugs or alcohol, however, are no more dangerous to other people than their neighbors.

[A team researching ex-patients and other residents from the same neighborhoods] found that the prevalence rate for violent acts was 31 percent among patients with a major mental illness [schizophrenia and manic depression] and substance abuse, and 43 percent among the group with "other" mental illnesses [personality and adjustment disorders] and a substance abuse problem. Among the group with a major mental illness and no alcohol or drug problem, the prevalence was about 18 percent, which, the researchers noted, was "statistically indistinguishable from the prevalence of violence among others in their neighborhoods without symptoms of substance abuse."

5.1.1   Poor definition of key terms

In the "Former Mental Patient" excerpt, intended for a general interest audience, we're asked to pick up on three categories of people; the potential of each for committing violent acts has been researched and is going to be reported in this article. The players in this drama are

- patients with major mental illness,

- patients with "other" mental illness, and

- their neighbors who aren't patients.

All of those people have two possible statuses with regard to having a history of substance abuse—yes or no—and the documented commission of violent acts—higher or lower tendencies.

Add to that the slightly but significantly different terms that are used to describe the patients, and things are already confusing. It's unclear what the researchers counted as behaviors of violence and drug abuse. The reporting of the essential terms that map the scope of the research is fast, loose, and annoyingly inexact. No objective criteria are given so the reader can know whether to be alarmed by the potential for violence or just interested. Are we talking about murder, popping tires, or slamming the garbage can lid down too loudly? We're not given a clear context within which to evaluate the findings.

5.1.2   Elegant variations

Elegant variations—several slightly different ways of referring to the same thing—make copy seem more complex than it is. And this is pretty complex copy to begin with. The reader who is sent looking for trivial differences that aren't there may miss out on significant points.

In the "Former Mental Patients" story, all these slightly different terms are used for people who have been hospitalized as mental patients:

- people discharged from psychiatric hospitals who do not abuse alcohol or drugs

- newly discharged patients who have a substance abuse problem

- patients with drug or alcohol problems

- ex-patients who don't abuse drugs or alcohol

- patients with a major mental illness and substance abuse

- the group with "other" mental illnesses and a substance abuse problem

- the group with a major mental illness and no alcohol or drug problem

All these terms are used for people who have not been mental patients, with whom ex-patients are being compared. The ballpark just keeps getting bigger and vaguer:

- their neighbors
- others in their neighborhoods without symptoms of substance abuse
- the general population
- substance abusers who are not ex-patients

5.1.3 Too many apples and oranges and grapefruit, too

Using a statistical term that has a specific meaning in a loose, quasi-scientific way bothers everyone—the experts who know the jargon and resent the misuse and the rest of us, who just don't know what's going on. In this excerpt, *prevalence rate for violent acts* misuses *prevalence*, which has a specific meaning in tracking the number of people with a disease. It's an unnecessarily convoluted way to describe the relative frequency of violent events by people in the three subpopulations. The writer uses *prevalent* when merely *widespread* or *the percentage of a group that commits violent acts* is meant.

All these percentages and quasi-statistical ratios are used to compare the occurrence of acts of violence by all the subgroups described:

- no more likely than their neighbors to be violent
- tend to be more dangerous than the general population
- five times more likely than the general population to be violent
- three times more likely to commit a violent act
- no more dangerous to other people than their neighbors
- prevalence rate for violent acts was 31 percent…and 43 percent…
- the prevalence was about 18 percent
- statistically indistinguishable from the prevalence of violence…

5.1.4 Meaningless generalizations

The headline and deckhead for the "Former Mental Patient" excerpt superficially express a clearly focused thesis, but in fact they generalize on the basis of only part of the findings. Are Former Mental Patients [which ones? those with major or "other" illness?] More Violent [than whom? than each other or the general population?]? If They [which ones?] Don't Abuse Drugs or Alcohol, the Answer Is Generally [ah, but the exceptions are significant!] No, Study Finds [we aren't sure exactly what was found because we can't track it].

Perhaps the most startling "findings" aren't findings as such, but the implications of comparing the statistics. To whom do the most significant comparisons of rates of violence really apply? In other words, which groups are actually being compared?

- The 31 percent of the violent patients who have been (and probably still are being) treated for major mental illness and substance abuse and the 18 percent of the general population without symptoms of substance abuse who are violent? (Of course, having no overt symptoms doesn't mean having no problems, either mentally or with regard to substance abuse. That's an important story that could be told, but it's not told here.)

- The 43 percent of violent patients with other mental illnesses who are substance abusers and the 18 percent of violent patients with major mental illness who aren't? (The other mental illness patients are probably succeeding at least superficially, are marginally better, and are getting less outpatient treatment and medication than the ones with major illness. That's another important story worth telling, but it's not even acknowledged here.)

- The 18 percent of the people who haven't been treated for mental illness and don't show symptoms of substance abuse but who commit violent acts, and the 18 percent of seriously ill patients who stay sober but still commit violent acts? (Statistically indistinguishable: How can the rates be the same given so many variables? And what does it mean that they're reported as the same?)

The real news is so much more interesting than the garbled version reported here. And what's put forth as the news is so little of the truth. The article states that substance abusers who are not ex-patients are three times more likely to commit violent acts than the general population; it also states that patients with drug or alcohol problems were five times more likely than the general population to be violent. We want to know what to think about that, but this article doesn't help us.

Let's leave these beleaguered mental patients and their neighbors in (here's hoping) relative peace and move on to more categories of news writing problems illustrated by a wider range of examples. Keep in mind that the examples are all taken from publications edited by people who have a lot in common with you: They have the best of intentions but, being human, make a mess of it now and then. It takes one to know one, so a little charity is in order before we begin our dissection of these frogs. But first, a moment of silence to ponder the ponderous wisdom of Nathaniel Hawthorne, who said, "Easy reading is damned hard writing." Okay, that's enough understanding, back to the work of being critical.

5.1.5   Saying what's really meant

In the sample below, the USDA offers reassurance that its findings won't harm the public health. While carelessly written announcements may be annoying, they're not disease agents. Obviously, what should have been said is...the USDA's findings show no threat to public health.

> No cases of the disease have been reported in the United States, and the USDA said that at this point its findings do not pose any public health threat.

If you think about it for a moment, this is a very long way of saying, He told people he had picked them out and if they agreed, he knew he had a mentor, which is stating the obvious. It's not clear what this newsletter writer had in mind—maybe, Mentoring is a two-way street; you have to pick each other.

> By notifying the people he had identified as mentors and asking them if they were comfortable with that, he had confirmation that those mentoring relationships were established.

5.1.6   Verbs of attribution

Attributive verbs—the verbs preceding or following a direct quote that hook it to its speaker—have body language. Better most of the time just to say *said* or *says*. In news writing, that's preferable because other verbs of attribution—*agreed, added, noted, offered, observed, explained,* and the sometimes clunky *according to, stated,* and *remarked*—have distinctive connotations that color a comment. You want readers to be paying attention to the direct quote, not busily distracting themselves with mental pictures of how someone looked when he or she chuckled, or barked or—perhaps most interesting of all—intimated some remarks for the record.

Read these examples out loud, listening for the self-consciously varied attributives. Doesn't this guy ever just talk or does he always posture?

> "We're in another transition in how we relate to an ever-changing market," Doughty explains. "This is a major breakthrough," Doughty states.

5.1.7   Attribution to experts

Watch out for loose attributions; they don't carry as much weight as a specific name and affiliation.

Loosely attributed

No medical specialty has made more progress in improving patient safety and reducing errors than anesthesiology, **medical experts say.**

Specifically attributed

Much of the credit for these improvements is attributed to the Anesthesia Patient Safety Foundation, a 10-year effort that has sharply reduced injuries and deaths, **according to Harvard researcher Lucian L. Leape.**

What Not to Let Your CEO Say in That Letter

The alarming mixture of Dilbertesque corporatespeak, biblical analogies, and mythical overtones in the following paragraphs, excerpted from the front page of an employee newsletter, is rare only in its degree. All too many of these letters sound as if they've been handed down from the Mount and carved in stone. That's a shame, because obviously they're meant to make people take heart and feel good about working for the company. Then why not talk to them in the voice of a normal human being, instead of someone in a forensics competition?

> What you have accomplished has been epic and the world has not witnessed anything like it since that certain stroll across the Sea of Galilee. I am proud to be on your team.

> Our Strategic Planning seminar, courageously scheduled, adroitly planned and masterfully executed, resulted in superb results that will serve as the alchemy for us to achieve our Olympic strategic objectives....Our Strategic Plan will be made available to you soonest. It will serve as your pharos, so I solicit your buy-in and request your support.

> Our future is as bright as that bolt from the heavens that Saul observed on the road to Damascus.

If you're the lucky editor whose CEO insists on writing gems like these, you've got to find a way to tone them down. If you're the writer and you're asked to add such smarmy stuff, resist as charmingly as you can. Your reason is the best: Language that's too highly charged (you can call it electric, if that'll help you pull the plug on it) calls attention to itself instead of the message—and many people just plain won't get the fancy references. You don't want the wonderful message to get zapped in all those extension cords.

Use Captions as Links to Get Stories Read

Captions can do more than define who's pictured left to right or state the obvious about what's pictured. If you tend to write captions quickly at the last minute because you think they're not as important as body copy, and if you always keep them very short and perfunctory because you think they're not as important as the image, think again. The first thing readers look at when they skim a page is photos. And the second thing they look at is the captions.

So if captions merely describe what's pictured, their potential to pull readers into the story is lost. Effective captions do identify the people or actions that photos depict—that's their first job—but they can and should also make a connection to the article. The best captions highlight a snapshot of the news story and make readers want to know more; in fact, captions can explicitly refer readers to the article for the rest of the story.

The four main types of photos—mugshot, action, event, and group—all merit a caption that ties back to the story. And so do most illustrations like an artist's rendering, floor plan, or flow chart. But a caption should be more than perfunctory.

The hardest photos to caption may be the group shot and the static "award" shot with two people facing the camera. You can be sure of 100 percent readership by all the people—and their relatives—who are pictured (left to right) in a group photo. But to attract other readers, you'll need more than just names. You'll need to tell what the players have in common, why they're there, and what they have to do with the topic of the article. Try to write in present tense to make the scene come alive to you instead of recalling it as a done deal: *Teamsters march for justice for strawberry workers.*

Here are some examples of captions to try not to write:

> *Person A (right) received the Division of the Year Award from manager, Person B.*

> *L to R: Employee association negotiators Person A, B, and C are congratulated by those assembled.*

> *Person A, Person B, and Person C.*

There's nothing wrong with having a little fun in a caption for an employee publication. Many photos aren't of stellar quality, and if everyone knows everyone, why not crack a little wise instead of defaulting to formalities? Here's the caption for a candid group shot of association representatives just before the official photo of a contract signing:

> *Not a bad picture of everyone.*

Here's the caption for the actual posed signing photo:

> *Once the official photograph is taken, we're ready to sign.*

(For more about effective photo caption packaging, see the Design section, page 85, and the Design Gallery, page 143.)

5.1.8   Embedded partial quotes

It's okay to use only a short phrase from a direct quote; in fact, it's a great way to get rid of the boring part of a quote and highlight the crux. But not when the patched-in results sound more awkward than a seamless paraphrase and weaker than a direct quote.

- Don't put quotes around illogical groups of words in an effort to fit them into a sentence that needs the original verb in a different tense. Instead, start the quotation at a logical, significant word and just paraphrase smoothly up to that point.

- Don't put quotation marks around common terms that anybody might have said. If you're only quoting one significant word, and it's not one-of-a kind, you aren't honor-bound to use quotation marks just because it rested in someone's mouth for a moment.

- Finally, remember that in newsletter publishing, "knitting edits" to make direct quotes more cogent are considered acceptable. A slight refocus doesn't have to undermine the meaning; in fact, rethinking what the important words are makes it more accessible.

Original

Hunter said it was "clear that we need to bridge the gap as quickly as possible."

Revised

Hunter said, "It's clear that we need to bridge the gap as quickly as possible."

or

Hunter made it clear that he thinks we need to bridge the gap as quickly as possible.

Original

He said that the new model is "almost twice as expensive" as the old model and it will be "extremely difficult" to fund it.

Revised

He said that the new model will be extremely difficult to fund because it's almost twice as expensive as the old one.

Original

The senator whose district is near the plant that manufactures the new model said the proposed denial of funding "makes no sense whatsoever" and represents a "gigantic shift in policy."

Revised

The senator whose district is near the plant that manufactures the new model said he thinks "it makes no sense whatsoever" to deny funding and would be a "gigantic shift in policy."

Original

One official said that if the debate holds up funding the new model "they might as well kill the entire program."

Revised

One official said, "They might as well kill the entire program" if the debate holds up funding the new model.

Original

The panel says the two models are too different to offer "meaningful" comparison.

Revised

The panel says that the two models are too different to offer meaningful comparison.

Original

Pike noted that in a time when the Russian spy program is "falling apart," the launch of a Russian satellite is important because it is "in the ballpark" with the most advanced U.S. technology.

Revised

Pike noted that in a time when the Russian spy program is "falling apart," the launch of a Russian satellite is important because it's competitive with the most advanced U.S. technology.

5.1.9 Windy speechifying

This quote is just too darned long and pompous to belong in a newsletter story—but that's where it was:

> "We are the nexus of these three groups—participating in a very team- and partner-like way—not as the leader, but as a team player," he notes. "Our goal," he says, "is for the group to be considered at the forefront of partnership and activity along the program paradigm, to stress the importance of trust and values-based leadership, to truly live by those rules, and be honest and open in our communication. Only on that basis can we operate effectively as a team."

5.1.10 Too many players, no score

The point—the action—is completely lost in the cast of characters here. This is the hardest kind of newsletter story to write interestingly, a report on a report:

> **Original**
>
> Had the board determined that reporting entities had not made enough progress, it could have required them to take additional actions or pay a fine.
>
> According to the report, the resin industry has invested in 120 programs.... The report also identified 102 programs for using post-consumer resin by resin manufacturers and their customers....

The progress report has already been submitted, but it doesn't have to be reported as old news, which the subjunctive *had...determined...had not made...could have required* construction emphasizes rather than counteracts. Use simple present tense whenever possible for the sound of fresh news.

And why not emphasize the positive outcome instead of the power of the board to punish the negative report, which didn't actually happen?

But it's easy to understand why the writer resorted to lumping together as cryptic reporting entities the previously identified cast of players with these cumbersome names:

- the board = California Integrated Waste Management Board (CIWMB)

- the law = to reduce and recycle rigid plastic packaging containers (RPPCs)

- the reporting entities = those required by law to report on efforts to reduce the use and increase the recycling of rigid plastic packaging:

  (a) the American Plastics Council (APC)

  (b) a consortium of six food and cosmetics trade associations, two cosmetics-only trade associations, and 60 manufacturers

> **Revised**
>
> If the APC and industry consortium fail to report enough progress in reducing the use of RPPCs, the CIWMB can require additional efforts or levy a fine. But the report shows that the resin industry has....

Exercising Quotes: Pull, Lift, and Call Them Out

How do you pick quotes to highlight editorial and add graphic interest to a text-dense layout? Look for the shortest, most emphatic direct quotes from someone in the story, or paraphrase a key point, or lift out an especially crisp or spicy statement in the narrative itself. Edit very slightly if necessary to make the quote clear. Attribute it when it's a direct quote to distinguish it from an authorial observation or plain fact. Format is a consideration when writing, especially if the line length is short and will force hyphenation:

Original	Revised
Experts agree that clinical trials are needed to determine whether higher dietary intake of folate and vitamin B will reduce cardio-vascular disease and whether the evidence supports increasing the recommended daily amounts of these vitamins.	Increase B and folate in diet? Clinical trials will tell, experts agree.

Here's an example of a wordy paraphrased pullquote that needed to be a tightly edited direct quote:

Original	Revised
Ott complained that she could not understand why she could sell condoms to minors, but not magazines.	Ott can sell condoms to minors— but not magazines.

5.1.11   Mixed metaphors

Metaphors are already tricky. Don't trowel them on too thick or the point will be submersed in murky waters—like that mixed metaphor. Walls are not usually thought of as the source of roadblocks.

A "green wall" between the environmental and business staffs of many companies has created a major roadblock to successfully managing corporate environmental issues, according to a recent survey....

Pullquotes That Pull Their Weight

Here are some better real-world examples:

This was really our first opportunity to put our vision into print for the world to see. We've talked about it a great deal, but now it's revealed in our annual report.
—*corporate executive*

"I don't take things for granted anymore. Something like this really makes you appreciate the little things."
—*critically injured employee*

Let your printer know right away if you're unhappy.
—*(no attribution, lifted from narrative)*

"I lived the American dream. Then the airport took my job, my way of life and stability. I'm 47, a carpenter's apprentice, trying to do a 25-year-old's job."
—*a father of five in Louisville who lost his job after 22 years*

"The movement toward diversity will be driven by training and career development for all employees."
—*senior vice president*

5.1.12   Too much crammed into bulleted lists

Rigid plastic packaging containers (RPPCs) must meet one of four criteria. Here's how the criteria were listed:

Original

They must—

- be recycled either at the rate of 25 percent for all RPPCs; 55 percent for RPPCs made primarily from PET; 45 percent for product-assisted RPPCs, such as Tide detergent containers; or 45 percent for all RPPCs in one generic category, such as milk containers;

- be made from at least 25 percent post-consumer material;

- be reusable or refillable; or

- be source-reduced.

The first bullet contains too much complex information. Packing a bulleted list cancels out the effectiveness of bullets at highlighting key points. Recycling rates needed to be broken out and presented separately, and it would be helpful to rank them in order of percentage.

No need to repeat a word like *be* four times—pulling it back into the lead-in highlights the verbs in the bullet items. Commas for a simple list are preferable to semicolons since all four criteria are listed as equal options (that is, one is required, and it can be any one). Here are a better list lead-in and bullets followed by recycling rates written as a separate little table:

Revised

RPPCs must be

- recycled,

- made from at least 25 percent post-consumer material,

- reusable or refillable, or

- source-reduced.

A table is preferable to trying to tell so much tangled-up information in text—people need help with trying to picture data across categories:

Acceptable recycling rates vary by category:

Container category	% that must be recycled
All RPPCs (minimum legal criterion)	25
Product-associated RPPCs (e.g., for Tide detergent)	45
All RPPCs in a generic category (e.g., milk containers)	45
RPPCs made from PET	65

5.1.13   Better a split infinitive than cracked syntax

But better, no infinitive in a headline. Watch out for "found to" constructions—they sound like a hedge, perhaps because they so often are. And they tend to come with adverbs—l-o-o-ong adverbs like *dramatically*. Don't try to qualify everything in the headline—tell us enough to hook us, then qualify it in the story with who did the research and "found" the finding, what stage of cancer was most responsive to the treatment, and those dramatic statistics. (Patients aren't *early*.)

> **Original**
> Taxol Found to Dramatically Increase Survival in Early Breast Cancer Patients
>
> **Revised**
> Taxol Boosted Patient Survival in Early Breast Cancer

5.1.14   Expletive construction

The sentences below are weighed down by several linking or passive verbs, boring redundancy (…policy has been in effect. It was established…), and a wordy deflection of the true subject in the second sentence. The expletive construction (…there were valuable experiences career employees could have…that they couldn't acquire) clouds what's supposed to be the benefit of the policy.

> **Original**
> The five-year policy has been in effect since the late 1960s. It was established because the Department of Defense recognized that there were valuable experiences career employees could have overseas that they couldn't acquire anywhere else.
>
> **Revised**
> The five-year policy was established in the late 1960s because the Department of Defense recognized that career employees could have valuable experiences overseas that they couldn't have anywhere else.

5.1.15   Shooting a benefit in the foot

Here, a benefit of receiving the association newsletter is couched in tepid terms and a chance to remind readers what you're doing for them is wasted. A future passive verb makes the statement sound conditional instead of confident, comma faults trick the quick reader into losing track of syntax, and a circular statement masquerades as a benefit. News about the association will be reported in the association newsletter—oh, really?

> **Original**
> News about the Alumni Association, its chapters and societies and the various programs offered to alumni, will be reported to you in the newsletter.
>
> **Revised**
> The [name of newsletter] will bring you reports on the activities of the Alumni Association, its chapters, and its societies, as well as news of programs offered to alumni.

5.1.16   The unnecessary subjunctive

If you'd like to thank people, do it, don't just wish you could acknowledge their work. This appreciation is oddly worded. Participation already means time and effort, and you don't participate in a committee but in the activities of a committee or on it. Unfortunately, the thanks feels canned.

> **Original**
>
> I would like to acknowledge the time and effort put forth by our members and the industry executives who participated in our joint committee.
>
> **Revised**
>
> To our members and the industry executives who joined them on the joint committee: Thanks for your time and hard work.

5.1.17   An invitation you could refuse

Expletive construction makes a weak appeal (what we will need are...), and verb tenses are all over the place: the plans are expressed in passive future tense (will be held), the appeal for reader action in present and subjunctive tenses. Glaring typos reflect poorly on the organizational skills of the party planners (and *cookout* is one word). No contact information is offered or deadline specified for replying in case someone is willing to forgive such sloppy copy and wants to volunteer. If you want to encourage people to participate in an activity, who-what-when-where-why-how plus "what's in it for you" have to be crystal clear and...inviting!

> **Original**
>
> What we will need are members to volunteer. The first "Work Party and Cook Out" will be held on Monday, July 15th starting at 6pm. We plan on working for one hour and then enjoyng a free dinner cook out for all of the participating members. Should you be interested in participating in this program, please call.
>
> **Revised**
>
> We need all the volunteers we can get for our first "Work Party and Cookout" on Monday, July 15th. Build an appetite by working for an hour—from 6 p.m. to 7 p.m.—and then relax and enjoy a free [whatever's on the menu—steak? hot dogs and hamburgers? be specific] dinner grilled especially for volunteers. Please call [telephone number] by [deadline] if you can help out so we know how many of you we can count on for work and fun.

5.1.18 Lost in the obvious, the whole point

This sample is wordy and diffuse, and the reader can't tell what the point is. What's the action that's been taken? Why are you telling us? All that can be gleaned from these words is that the associations' need for succession planning…was obvious. The information in the two sentences needs to be combined and condensed into a statement of the very real two-part problem: (a) the association's need to develop a succession plan (because there hasn't ever been one) that began when the director announced his retirement (because he was the first and only director the association has ever had). The data on the history of the group has taken over the news—it should be used as background for the need to continue progress instead of the rather negative way it suggests a panicky need to protect against high-stakes loss.

Original
Attention to succession planning began as the retirement of the only executive director in our association's 10-year history approached. With more than 1,600 member firms, 38 staff, a broad and vibrant membership program, and an annual budget in excess of $7 million, the association's need for succession planning to ensure continuous competent staff leadership was obvious.

Revised
When the only executive director our association has had in its 10-year history announced his plans to retire, we realized the need for succession planning. Continuous staff leadership is essential to a smooth transition of leadership for more than 1,600 member firms, 38 staff, and a broad and vibrant membership program—and oversight of an annual budget of more than $7 million.

5.1.19 Motivating members to advocacy

When trying to make a group or association sound proactive and dynamic and all those good adjectives for "your membership dues at work," use vivid language instead of static bureaucratese. Compare Churchill's "We will fight on the beaches, we will fight on the…" with this ringing statement, which translates to the pallid "We've been making efforts to tell people who we are and what we're trying to do"—the bare minimum members could reasonably expect. The *call to action*, the kind of support that's being asked of members, should be pitched more closely to rabble-rousing than to a polite invitation to participate. In the sample on page 302, energy and an emotional appeal are missing.

Original

Our Society has been increasing educational and advocacy efforts within the profession and with state agencies that have jurisdiction over our field.

Revised

We need some friends in the legislature. We're in the middle of many hot issues, and members need to be an active part of the legislative lobbying process. We must stay competitive because our adversaries and competitors are lobbying the legislators very actively against our platform.

How to Write Heads That Lead Readers to Body Copy

1. Take a phrase or part of a spicy quote from text and elevate it to the main head instead of settling for a pallid statement or summary. The headline **More Open Season Instructions to Agencies** doesn't cause a salivating drive to read about yet more regulatory details.

2. It's not against the law to be amusing—try word play as long as it's tied back somehow to the subject. The headline **Summer Heats Up Along with Membership Drive** is contrived—and makes the season seem more important than the drive.

3. Too many imperative main heads (especially negatives, like *don't*) can make the entire newsletter seem overly dogged. Good advice is welcome, but nobody wants to be bossed around. Soften with gerunds: Not **Take stock of the options** but **Taking stock of the options.**

4. Try to find unusual or blunt—but not weird—verbs to give heft to the news hook: **Creative Approaches Combat High Staff Turnover** works. **Individual Touch Transforms Conn. Child Care Center** works. **Governors Nudged to Examine Child Care** works. But **Science Group Ponders Pre-K Learning Standards** doesn't work—too stiff. Rodin's statue "The Thinker" ponders; people *consider*, *evaluate*, or *review* standards. In fact, the lead states, "A national science group is eyeing the feasibility of setting national math, science and technology standards for preschoolers." **Eyes** belongs in the head.

5. Verbs are not required but they sure are nice to have. Heads shouldn't be composed of only nouns and adjectives unless you're really stumped or there's no real action going on, only steps in a process or an overview. In that case, try verbals—participles and gerunds that at least have the cheekbones of a verb in them—to give readers a clue to the kind of article they're buying into: **Mapping, Defining, Approving, Agreeing, Disputing, Threatening, Debunking, Rating, Predicting, Performing, Starting, Checking, Building, Changing, Cleaning, Polluting, Looking, Finding, Proving.** Just be sure to use the shortest, simplest verbals for the job, or you might slip into pompous spacehogs like Reassessing, Supplementing, or Individualizing.

6. Alliteration is allowed: **A bitter backdrop for bargaining** says it all, with bite.

5.2 Deconstructing display copy

Here are succinct guidelines for writing display copy, with an emphasis on headlines; the principles are illustrated with more and less effective samples.

- Real-world headlines don't have to be boring to be true. But they do have to be truly reflective of the article's content.

- Real-world headlines don't have to be encyclopedic to help readers decide whether an article is relevant to them. But headlines do have to touch on some significant aspect of the news.

- Real-world headlines should be sharply focused. But that doesn't mean joining highly specific declarative statements with semicolons in a quasi head-cum-deck-style reminiscent of newspapers.

- Real-world headlines don't have to be filled with facts and statistics to be descriptive. But they shouldn't be so cryptic or telegraphic that readers can't tell what's going on in the article.

5.2.1 The boring summary statement

Original
Members Active on Many Fronts

Pick one verb that crystallizes the efforts members are making—surely there's either a thread of similarity or one astonishing achievement to highlight—and the article will seem less like fluff and more like real news from the frontlines.

Revised
Do You Know What Your Colleagues Are Up To These Days?

5.2.2 The cryptic umbrella headline

Original
Dos and Don'ts of Medical Records

This headline is too cryptic to be a good sound bite, and doesn't reflect the valuable content of the article at all. "Of" doing what about or with records? It turns out to be about "medicolegal" dos and don'ts. And there are three key precepts:

- Maintaining good records is a part of providing competent service.

- If it's not written down, it didn't happen.

To Deck or Not to Deck the Heads

Some newsletter writer-editors just love deckheads. And there's a place for them in a newsy publication, especially if it's tabloid-style with longer articles.

But sometimes decks aren't formatted on a separate line; they're doubled up with the headline, placed like a subhead would be after a semicolon, but they're functioning as decks:

> ### FDA Approves Over-the-Counter Medication for Migraine Headaches; Available Early This Year

> ### EAPs Changing to Meet Growing Needs of Today's Workforce; Internet New Treatment Tool

That semicolon just isn't enough to link two disparate statements. If you're writing these kinds of heads, it's probably because somebody told you that they look and sound more "journalistic." It's true, they're a take on newspaper style heads. But in a newsletter, they're overkill. The articles they go with are almost never long enough to merit such exhaustive headlining. Trivia tends to creep into too many tiers of information.

But the real problem is that heads like this look and read too much like body copy. They're not a taste, they're a gulp. And yet they're more often than not too telegraphic to be informative. Use decks judiciously and only when a topic is so complex you need two cracks at headlining it. In this example, the "deck" is ambiguous (a role in the plan or in lobbying for legislation?) and actually detracts from the news hook because it's the last thought readers take with them into the story:

> ### President Proposes $21 Billion Child Care Plan; Business Plays Role

- The psychiatrist owns the records, the patient owns the information.

And it turns out to be about keeping "good records"—they have to meet a lot of criteria:

- Dated, timed, signed, and legible entries and later emendations

- Crisp, clear, detailed, and objective observations

- Written diagnosis and risk-benefit appraisals of interventions

- Documentation for major management and treatment decisions

One reason the generic headline was chosen might be that there really isn't one good headline that easily encompasses two such different kinds of content. The article probably should have been broken into a main article and a box detailing record-keeping material, with its own headline:

Rewrite of box headline
Legal Criteria for Good Records

Then the main article—about the legal aspects of storing patient information—could have a more focused head like this:

Rewrite of main headline
If It Happened, Write It Down

5.2.3 Headlines that ask unanswerable questions

Original
Managed Care and Psychiatry: What Does the Future Hold?

In a trends or predictions piece, if there's an answer for uncertainty, foreshadow it in the headline; if not, don't ask a question that you're not going to be able to answer in the text. Say the future is uncertain, lift out a point of controversy, or characterize the drift of the conclusions.

Any of these points could be the fulcrum: "Practicing medicine will be very different; clinical decisions will be more data-driven. The level of physician quality is going to be higher because of more good information. It will be exciting and rewarding, but the days of people making a million dollars as physicians are going away."

Revised
The Future Will Be Rewarding (But Not in Dollars)

5.2.4 Headlines that introduce us to people in a picture

Original
SAY HELLO TO OUR STAFF

Hello. Well, okay, then. Good-bye. This kind of head leads nowhere and is infantilizing. Even if it's "just" a last-minute head slapped on a brief photo essay, don't waste the opportunity to show that your group is actively doing…something besides facing the camera.

Revised
Our Staff Is Getting Ready for the Convention

5.2.5 Wordy, repetitive headlines

Original

Workplace Flexibility Works Better with Management Flexibility

Flexibility is too long a word to be in a headline once, much less twice. It's boring, and worse, meaningless; it bears no relationship to the article. The first half told the short, sweet story of how a "total flex" program helped a money-losing regional office become productive and turned it into one of the locations where people wanted most to work. Better headlines were everywhere in the copy, including this quote by an employee relations consultant: "The ability to set your own schedule is a powerful motivator." But it turns out that the last half of the piece was a laundry list of obvious mistakes managers make (not listening, not being open to change, not anticipating problems and making new rules) in launching innovative programs like flexible work hours. "'We can't afford not to...alleviate today's increased worker stress,' said the consultant."

Why not a headline that ties together the case scenario and the list of management mistakes?

Revised

Workers Thrive with Innovative Management

5.2.6 Headlines that foster unhealthy relationships

Original

Job-Related Stress May Be Cause of Some Sick Building Syndrome Cases

This headline makes it sound as if stressed-out people are making buildings sick. It's also confusing to mix sick people and stressed people with "sick building cases"—that's asking readers to think of several kinds of relationships at once...and relate them! Edit to support one point.

Revised

Job Stress, Not 'Sick' Buildings, May Cause Illness

A Roster of Empty Heads

Main headlines must say something about the story. They must say or suggest something meaningful, period. They can be short and sweet: **Minimum Wage, Maximum Debate**. But these samples—and they're what 75 percent of newsletter headlines look like—are devoid of interest or meaning. There's nothing real there, maybe because the writer or editor has taken a shortcut in hopes of making do with a quasi-kicker-style phrase. But that effectively screens out whatever initial burst of curiosity a reader might bring to a story. These heads lack the ability to whip readers into even a polite stupor of attention:

PRESIDENT'S MESSAGE

Workers Queries

Installation of Officers & Directors

A Return to Work Success Story

Relocation Completed

Deaths from Improper Use Rising

Lessons Learned

5.2.7   Perpetual headlines

This head is too long and too complex, and it's ambiguous.

Original

Chamber, OSHA Butt Heads Over CCP, Organization Asks to Withhold Funding

Main heads shouldn't try to be encyclopedic—that's why they invented kickers and deckheads. Also, to what is the word organization referring? The point of a headline should be clear without having to read the story first. Since we haven't, we don't necessarily know whether CCP is a technology, an organization, or a regulation. (The in-group does, you say—or does everybody in an in-group know the whole scoop? New members as yet unfamiliar with the jazzy acronyms and shorthand don't.) And the more information you try to telescope into a head, the more you're forced to rely on potentially ambiguous wording that doesn't resemble human syntax. Uneditable except by the writer-editor who knows the inside story. And only then by taking the time—even if it's after the fact—to identify the thesis and let the headline be a headlight for it. If it can't be edited, the reader can't get it at a glance—which defines a head that's no more than a waste of space in big type.

5.2.8 Headlines that make deadly declarations

The tired this-is-that formula is only a few moments away from "And? I would care because…?" Clue: *Portends* isn't a word anyone says.

Publications Services Branch Has News

Workgroup Reports to HHS on Computerized Patient Records

Publications offer vehicles to spell out ethics code

Editors' key assignment is educating employees

Bridging of Wireless Networks Portends Further Integration

Administrative Simplification Key to Healthcare Reform

5.2.9 Headlines that ask rhetorical questions no one cares to answer or that may be answered negatively

Don't ask a question your readers can answer with "Nope, and what of it?"

Original

Do You Follow These Safety Reminders?

Revised

Five Tips to Keep You Out of Traction

Is There an Echo in Your Head?

Sentence-style headlines that echo the exact phrasing in the first sentence of the lead waste readers' time and patience—not to mention the chance to slip in emphasis for a key point instead of making it seem redundant. The headline should be a jumping-off point to new information. Here's an example of what not to do; the head is too long to begin with, and then gets substantially repeated:

Survivors Prepare To Vie for Customers at Paris Air Show as End of Jetstream 41 Production Highlights Overcapacity

As regional aircraft manufacturers prepare to vie with each other in promoting their competing designs next week at the Paris Air Show, the death of British Aerospace's Jetstream 41 marks another step toward bringing the industry's global capacity into line with demand for its products.

> ### One of the Most Unfortunate Headlines Imaginable
>
> Watch out for wording that readers might misinterpret in your headlines—after all, they haven't read the article yet and the words you use may have other associations for them. In this example, the writer has inadvertently undercut the serious message for non-clinicians about new breast imaging technology. The average reader could be forgiven for taking the headline the wrong way:
>
> **New Ways to Look at the Breast**

5.2.10   Headlines that repeat your group's name over and over

All these heads appeared in a 24-page issue with the company's name, an acronym, represented here by ACME to protect the tedious.

ACME Announces New Software Release

ACME Acquires Management Corporation

ACME Interview with the Executive Vice President

Product Launches Continue ACME Market Leadership

ACME System Improves Deliveries

ACME-Supported Program Wins Leadership Award

ACME Tracking False Alarms

Reuse Solution Offers New ACME Capability in Data Warehousing

ACME at Legal Tech Conference

ACME's Key Contacts

ACME Regional Office Wins Recognition as a Preferred Supplier

Sure, it's a combined employee-marketing newsletter, and people may photocopy selected articles so they can pass them around, and you want them to know who you are. But that's what running headers and footers can do for you—enforce awareness of your identity. Try not to trumpet the obvious too loudly. That gets tiresome, and so does the unrelieved pattern of "We Did This" and "We Did That."

Subheads Don't Have to Scintillate

There's a little less pressure to be scintillating when it comes to subheads (also called *crossheads*). In fact, it's a mistake to get too awfully cute with them. The virtues of subheads are modest but true. They

- act as logical transitions whenever a narrative shifts topic;

- hoist a truce flag that says, "You can dip in anywhere you want; there's lots going on here worth a look"; and

- visually break up unrelieved gray blocks of copy.

Placement. Subheads should seem neither to be squashed into place nor floatily detached from body copy. They come in pairs, so if you need one, you'll have to find a way to write two. If you don't have a lot of extra space, format them as boldfaced run-in subheads.

Length. Keep them short. They do good advance work but they're not the star performer: The information in body copy is. But don't write them cryptic: They should be minimally but concretely informative, not just a single flat noun like the series below. (We all fall down on this, though—we think we'll go back and write better ones, but we never get around to it.) In an article about scan-to-Web technology for getting images and documents from paper onto the Internet, subheads work mostly as visual placeholders. Not tremendously exciting, but a perfectly acceptable thing for subheads to do, if that's all the time you've got:

> A Significant Advancement/Possible Applications/
> Web Made Easy/Is There a Need?/Blurring the Line

Phrasing. Like heads, subheads shouldn't repeat the exact phrasing of the first sentence that follows, or body copy will seem redundant. Or it will seem that you just picked up a phrase from the first sentence of the paragraph and tacked it up as a subhead. That's the way a lot of subheads do get written, but they should really signpost something about copy, not just echo it.

Parallelism. Parallelism is a goal. It can be hard to make all the verbs in a long article parallel, but sometimes it's worth the extra effort. Take this series of subheads in an article about the sub-prime mortgage business:

> Understanding the Market/Targeting Sub-Prime Offers/
> Maintaining High Standards/Banks Track Loan Portfolio Performance

That last subhead could have easily been edited to **Tracking Loan Portfolio Performance.** When it comes to subheads, gerunds and participles are your friends—they still have the faint odor of verbs about them but none of the aggressiveness.

Summary value. Sometimes subheads are more helpful to readers than headlines because, although they generalize, too, they're closely tied to a specific text block. For example, in one newsletter (about health for women), these were the subheads:

> What You Need/What Happens to Protein/Too Much of a Good Thing

Much more useful than the empty main headline—merely, **Proteins.**

5.3   Crafty leads for the rudderless

The examples of direct and delayed lead paragraphs in this section can be used paradigms for your own articles. But first, let's nail down what we don't want to do. The two biggest problems with most newsletter leads are that, in effect, they

- in so many words announce that the story that follows will be dull and unpleasant and

- set up the story without regard to what's relevant and of immediate concern to readers.

5.3.1   What you're about to read salutes you

It's not a good idea to make a not-too-thrilling article sound even more boring than it is. That's why this is not a good lead:

> Following is the text of outgoing Board President Vince Lambers' address to the members at the Annual Meeting December 9....

Let me outta here! Why do you think I skipped that meeting in the first place? You can hear readers voting with their feet.

5.3.2   Keep reading and you'll get there eventually

Here's a lead that "explains" the benefits of a new teeing-off system for golfers without taking into account readers' resistance to the system. In fact, reading between the lines, we discover that some golfers resent the system, and an explanation of how it works isn't going to make them feel better about not getting the starting times they prefer. The lead misses a chance to be pure service journalism. The writer concentrates on the mechanics of describing a system "we" set up instead of acknowledging that "we've heard some grumbling about the drawbacks." (Readers are country club members.) A "Helpful Hints" section comes last, at the very end of the story, but it should have been first—it explains what readers can do about their frustration.

> The pro shop staff has been using a computerized tee times system called First Tee to assign members' starting times for over two years now. We implemented this system in order to be equitable to all members. This will become increasingly important as we get into our peak months. Hopefully, this article will shed some light on this sophisticated and effective system.

5.3.3   Far, far better leads

Bad leads don't—lead anywhere anyone wants to go, that is. The examples that follow do. Borrow from them. The subject matter almost doesn't matter. Most of these samples could be adapted for most any sort of topic in any sort of newsletter. Leads are the part of an article than can—and should be—the most systematically built.

The primary focus of any intelligent company, says any intelligent CEO, is shareholder value. We'll drink to that—as soon as we know what shareholder value means. Well, shareholder value means...well, dammit, what does it mean? What would it mean if we decided the primary value of a company was "employee value"? Or even "customer value." Or "public value." Or "CEO's bankroll value...."

&

When lawyers at Microsoft Corp. and the Justice Department agreed Thursday to sit down and talk—rather than brawl—they demonstrated one of the enduring truths about the art of negotiation: There's nothing like the threat of war to focus the search for peace.

&

Many of you may be wondering why the sign that has traditionally advertised Sugar Mill at the SR 44 corner of Sugar Mill Drive has been painted over by Ocean Properties and what will be happening to it now.

The Club and the Association have been in discussion with Ocean Properties....

&

When the Ladies Golf Union of England tried to organize a major tournament in 1893, Horace Hutchinson, a true golfing legend, wrote the women: "Constitutionally and physically women are unfitted for golf. The first women's championship will be the last....They are bound to fall out and quarrel on the slightest, or no, provocation." Ironically, Hutchinson later became vice president of the Ladies Golf Union. If he could see us now!

We are still feeling good about the success of our two big tournaments....

Huntley Meadows is making landscaping plans for the community's common areas, but the landscaping we do on our own property can make a big difference, too. Colorful gardens and attractive plantings increase resale potential, create privacy, and add to the day-to-day-enjoyment of our homes.

Now's the time to start planning so small, inexpensive plants have plenty of time to mature during the growing season. Remember to coordinate your tree and shrub plantings with the ACC; allow a few weeks for approval. Your homeowner guidelines will help you determine if you need to get approval for your landscaping project.

ﻰ

The gray-haired little grandmother behind the big desk would stand 5 feet tall, if she was standing uphill. Pictures of grinning grandchildren decorate her warm and tidy office. Her ashtray holds a single, half-smoked cigarette. The filter is ringed with pink lipstick.

It is only when she speaks that you know that Marion Hammer, the first female president in the 125-year history of the National Rifle Association, is tough as a day-old biscuit. Her voice is startlingly deep, and her words pile up to form a rigid barrier against what she sees as an emotionally hysteric anti-gun movement.

"It truly is not guns that kill people," she said, repeating the gun owner's mantra. "Individuals do."

ﻰ

Alternative delivery of a print product and increasing Website traffic are the two primary reasons for publishing e-mail newsletters. Alternative delivery is an end in itself, but if you launch a newsletter to build Web traffic, there are many more profit upsides. Almost all Web-traffic-building e-mail newsletters sell ads or sponsors into the newsletter. But you will be surprised at additional, unexpected profit boosters uncovered in this article.

ﻰ

Join us for four days in our nation's capital at the 1996 Advocacy Training Conference. A special tribute to...scientific research and policy updates, and an opportunity to network with breast cancer advocates from across the country are among the highlights of the conference. All conference registrants are invited to a Monday evening reception a....We will mark the 5th year of NBCC and acknowledge our long-time friends, supporters, and activists.

The conference has a new and extended format....

For a company so associated with quality, goodness, and all that is cheerful in the world, the Walt Disney Co. has certainly suffered its share of sour public relations predicaments.

From Southern Baptists boycotting Disney theme parks because of their gay-friendly policies…to Catholics protesting Disney-owned ABC's "Nothing Sacred" sitcom…to feminists excoriating the Disney film, "The Little Mermaid," for its scantily clad heroine…to Civil War buffs objecting to Disney's plans to build a theme park on the historic Manassas, Virginia, battleground…to the company's own stockholders screaming about the outrageous sweetheart deal doled out to super-agent-turned-management-disaster Michael Ovitz—Disney's fire-fighting public relations department has been busy.

ε∂

Intranet developers are linking data warehouses to intranets as corporate demand for access to information reaches new heights.

Linking databases to enterprise networks is not new, but intranets offer users more choices in how data is offered.

The growth in data warehousing is leading to….

ε∂

Welcome to the first issue of our expanded monthly newsletter. We plan to use this format to better inform you about your club and promote the Stones River Country Club in the most professional manner possible. I would especially like to thank all of the sponsors who made this possible. Without them, we would not have been able to make this exciting change….Hopefully, each issue will be better than the one before. And as always, we welcome your comments and suggestions.

ε∂

Like their human counterparts, some dogs occasionally forget their manners and lash out. Rather than using words, they may bite—a most undesirable canine behavior from our viewpoint but a natural response from a dog's. "Most dog bites occur for a reason," says Dr. Linda Aronson, a veterinary behavioral consultant in Lexington, Ma. "Any dog is capable of biting given the right circumstances."

A recent study published in the Journal of the American Medical Association reports there are 4.5 million dog bites each year….

Final Congressional compromises on proposed tax law changes are expected by mid-August. There will be much maneuvering, politicking, and shouting between now and then, but we expect to see higher rates for individuals in upper income brackets and some restructuring of which taxpayers pay what share. Many publications are giving advice in what to do to protect yourself against the proposed changes. Equally important is what not to do!

1. Don't....

è❦

Methyl tertiary-butyl ether (MTBE) is a sore subject in California. Mandated by Congress as an oxygenate additive to gasoline to reduce hydrocarbon smog pollutants in 1990, MTBE has become a contaminant of surface water and groundwater in California. It may be a carcinogen and also cause respiratory problems. Tosco Corp. (Stamford, CT), a big independent gasoline refiner and retailer, has begun a six-month pilot program to market gasoline blended with ethanol rather than MTBE at 50 service stations in Northern California....

This could be the forerunner of an enlarged market for....

è❦

Being able to see into the future should help you plan how to squeeze the most profit out of your business during the next 12 months.

In this issue and the next, I'll give you 32 of my top predictions for 1998. Use them to your best advantage!

Forecast #1....

è❦

Why did I ever build a color darkroom in my observatory? It still has its advantages, but they are fading fast as digital imaging moves into the mass market. My purchase of the Hewlett Packard PhotoSmart system last year, specifically for processing astrophotographs, has made me a believer in this new technology.

The PhotoSmart system is attractive for several reasons....

Despite a nationwide upturn in the economy, SEIU public-sector [union] locals are facing tough bargaining.

The hostile, anti-worker political climate, coupled with slow growth in some state economies, is the backdrop for SEIU bargaining talks underway this year....

❧

Sexual harassment laws have always been notoriously confusing, so there was much cheering when the Supreme Court clarified things by issuing new harassment guidelines last month.

The Court made it clear that employers are always legally responsible for the harassing behavior of supervisors. But it made the world a bit safer for employers by offering them a defense: an effective anti-harassment policy and complaint procedures that employees disregard at their own risk. The Court helped both sides understand what harassment is by explaining in a case involving men that it is the conduct that is at issue—not the sex or the sexual desires of the people involved.

❧

The Sierra Club finds itself embroiled in a bitter and controversial debate, but the issue isn't necessarily about the environment per se. Members are fighting about immigration.

The topic of immigration has split Sierra Club membership, and already as many as 1,000 people have quit over the issue. Club officials expect more resignations no matter which side wins the argument.

The initial campaign over the argument started....

❧

A major thermoplastic material manufacturer just launched a new optical media development center, in a move that reflects a trend toward increasing use of advanced optical materials. GE Plastics has built the state-of-the-art facility to work with manufacturers and equipment makers in developing and testing innovative processing technologies and next-generation materials for optical media.

More importantly, this development....

Mental health associations have often been accused of being marketing dinosaurs especially where the World Wide Web is concerned. Not so anymore.

For an industry burdened with showing absolute cost justifications for marketing programs, the Web is being quickly being exploited as not only an exciting communications medium but a cost-efficient one as well.

੨

Drug addiction has always created concerns that go beyond the need to understand its causes and develop treatments. As individuals and as a society, we have been unable to decide whether it is a disease, a vice, or a behavioral problem—something that people do to themselves or something that happens to them. Now, with the help of scientific innovations that include images of the living brain and detailed molecular analysis of neurons, researchers are beginning to learn about addiction as a biological process. Their discoveries may not only aid in the search for treatments but throw indirect light on these moral, social, and philosophical issues, and even on the nature of desire and habit in general.

੨

Imagine two companies in the same business. The sales of Company A are one-nineteenth those of Company B. Company A has never shown a profit and is expected to report on Wednesday even bigger losses than had been forecast, while Company B is enjoying a strong quarter and figures to be solidly profitable for the third consecutive year.

Company B's market capitalization ought to dwarf Company A's, yes?

And investors ought to be piling into Company B and watching Company A nervously, right?

Wrong. The market value of A (amazon.com, the online bookseller) has rocketed past that of B (Barnes & Noble, king of brick-and-mortar bookstores) over the last six weeks....

੨

A Russian revolution in theater is taking place, not in Moscow or St. Petersburg, but in the heart of Arlington at Ballston, with Classika Theater for Youth's founders, Inna Shapiro and Alyone Ushe, as the protagonists.

317

Afterword

Editors are only human; we make mistakes and fail to catch others' mistakes. When we do, we need to set the record straight. We've all seen correction notices that told us both more and less than we ever wanted to know, like this one:

> A story in last week's *Fairfax Weekly* incorrectly identified the military title of the Rev. John Plummer. He was an assistant to the commander of the U.S. Army's Third Regional Assistance Command in June 1972 when he ordered the napalm bombing of a Vietnamese village.

Huh? The notice just raises new questions. Granted, a correction like this is probably meant to answer someone's objection rather than to enlighten readers. But it's a good reminder that just because something is phrased as a declarative sentence doesn't mean it's worded clearly or neutrally.

Fortunately, we don't have the same mandate that newspaper editors do to print corrections for the record, sometimes for quite small errors and omissions. But to be viewed as holding to standards of accurate reporting, we do need to acknowledge all substantial errors—and as soon as possible after they come to light.

Correct any misinformation that might

- offend, confuse, annoy, or harm your readers;

- offend, reflect badly on, or harm your authors or third parties;

- make you or your publisher look irresponsible.

Corrections call attention to the very fact that you've messed up, so try to write them in a way that doesn't make matters worse. An overly detailed and defensive "mistakes were made" notice doesn't help matters: "Due to a production error...." "The fact checker didn't...." "Because of a printing mistake...." "We deeply regret the fact that the recycled paper streak in the photo on page 3 of the fall issue made the southeastern regional sales manager seem to be wearing a mustache."

Just set the record straight briefly, in a helpful way. Because *The Editorial Eye* newsletter is a resource for exacting people, all errors are egregious, but we try to make corrections with a light touch:

> The title of a book we recommended in a recent article should have been *Medical English Usage and Abusage* by Edith Schwager (Oryx Press). Leaving the word *English* out made it sound like a book on malpractice—yikes! This little error serves as a reminder of an important principle of medical editing: The surer you are of something, the more important it is to look it up. (We *hate* it when we're not perfect.)

When You Feel Like a Witless Wonder...

...take a break from your routine, light into a big fat Cobb salad or tuna sub (if it's a really bad day, you'll require chocolate and quite possibly barbecue potato chips, as well), and spend an hour reading, not editing. Here are four print newsletters and a research report that will help you clear the cobwebs out and learn something new about copyright, direct marketing, the newslettering business, public relations, and literacy. You should be subscribing to at least one of the newsletters.

copyRights: The Newsletter on Rights and Permissions. Published by The Permissions Group, 1247 Milwaukee Ave., Suite 303, Glenview, IL 60025-2425. Call 800-653-7163 for a free sample. Visit http://www.permissionsgroup.com.

Fred Goss' What's Working in Direct Marketing. How to market your subscription newsletter. No-nonsense advice, analysis of direct mail packages, design and type tips, and reporting of focus groups, surveys, and other consumer research results. United Communications Group, 11300 Rockville Pike, Suite 1100, Rockville, MD 20852-3030.

Newsletter on Newsletters. The oldest trade publication that covers what's happening in the world of consumer and business-to-business newsletters. Covers acquisitions, start-ups, design, and marketing and offers snippets of editorial wisdom and insider gossip. Newsletter Clearinghouse, 44 West Market Street, P.O. Box 311, Rhinebeck, NY 12572.

The Ragan Report. Irreverent, often hilarious weekly reporting of the world of corporate communications, newslettering in particular. One of the few editors to take on the ludicrous hype involved in "strategic communications programs"—and the important principles that tend to get lost in the shuffle. Expensive, but worth it. Visit http://www.ragan.com or write Lawrence Ragan Communications Inc., 212 W. Superior St., Ste. 200, Chicago, IL 60610.

Ways With Words: A Research Report of the Literacy Committee. Prepared by the American Society of Newspaper Editors in cooperation with the Poynter Institute for Media Studies, the *St. Petersburg Times*, and the University of Wisconsin-Madison. Summarizes results of a readership survey after an experiment that tested reactions to four reporting modes: AP pyramid, narrative, radical clarity, and point of view. ASNE Foundation, PO Box 4090, Reston, VA 22090.

If a correction is clear and makes sense, readers will absorb it and move on—if they notice it at all. But it can be very hard to explain a serious error without a lot of contextual explanation, and readers often don't remember the original context. Even a correction for a wrong phone number should tell people enough so they know what to do with the new information. Pointing out any problems that were encountered by readers will go a long way toward mollifying the people who were inconvenienced (and probably told you about it):

To order *Wired Style: Principles of English Usage in the Digital Age* by the editors of *Wired* magazine, call HardWired at 800-401-6515. If you call the number we ran in February, someone will try to sell you lightbulbs and electrical wiring. That number was for a hardware store.

Why am I ending with a discussion about correction notices? This whole book has been a cheerleader for fine-tuning your newsletter's message and presenting it with graphic intelligence. But real-world newsletter editing has its ups and downs; even running a correction note can be tricky. Newsletters can only do so much; you can only edit them so far; you can't let the message get lost in the molecules.

I encourage you to make a little deal with yourself. For every time you feel like you're running on empty, spend an hour just for yourself. Step out of the traces and let yourself graze freely in other fields for a while.

Browse the newsstand in a good bookstore and buy a couple of newpapers you never normally read—say, the Sunday *Charlotte Observer*, the *Chicago Tribune*, the *Baltimore Sun*—and look at how differently editors and graphic artists interpret special sections. "Lifestyles" sections are especially fun to compare.

Look for interesting e-mail discussion groups and listen to people in a different community converse about what they value or worry about. Join in or lurk; doesn't matter. Just see the world through someone else's eyes.

Browse Web sites that you turn up from a spontaneous keyword search; follow links until you find a topic you've never heard of before or always wondered about, and pick up everything you can. Use feedback forms to talk to people. Tell them honestly what you think and ask them questions.

Read magazines that have nothing to do with your work or your background—*The Economist, Discover, Harper's, Astronomy, Rolling Stone, Brill's Content*. What are they doing to make you a happy reader? Did you become interested despite yourself? Anything you can borrow and adapt for your own readers? How long has it been since you read purely for fun?

An even keel: It's a goal. But you've got to develop sea legs. Here's the last of the cheerleading, a bit of silly verse from Richard Armour's *Going to Extremes*:

Shake and shake
The catsup bottle.
None will come,
And then a lot'll.

Appendix

The future: drive-by views of computer-assisted research and online newsletters

Does using the Internet in preparing print newsletters change the way editors compile and write content? Yes and no.

Every editor I know says, "Thank God for e-mail," which has drastically cut the time it takes to correspond with authors, send and receive documents, and forward information to staff (with an optional back-up paper trail). But every editor I know also says, "I'm sick of receiving unsolicited e-mail ads and endless messages from tail-chasing e-mail discussion groups. I never talk to people in person any more—I just sit at the computer."

E-mail is only the most widely used part of the Internet; the World Wide Web (Web) gives editors access—usually free—to many thousands of online documents and publications that in turn offer many thousands of links to other sites. Managing time and targeting priority topics can become a problem: You can look up and realize you've spent two hours moving through online resources without finding the answer to the question you began with, led far afield by intriguing but irrelevant sites.

It also takes time to perform searches with the instructions that tell search engines (portal sites) how to find what you're looking for, time for Web pages to load, and time for browsers to call up each link you're trying to follow. And then, there's printing waiting for pages to print out so you'll have back-up documentation....Computer-assisted reporting isn't magical and it isn't much of a shortcut. It's thoughtful work that requires making the same kinds of discretionary calls and critical evaluations as print resources—everything on the Web isn't an impeccable source. But ignoring online information is something editors do at their own professional peril—if only because employers expect online skills as part of even entry-level job descriptions.

Does the way online newsletters present and distribute newsletter content change the way editors do their jobs? Yes and no.

You may have to learn HTML coding and hypertext editing programs; you may have to learn about Web design and readability; you may have learn how to write text links into your copy, keeping a site map in your head instead of your usual John Dos Passos-like muse. Books on Web publishing, interactive forms, and "dummies" guides to integrating PDF and Acrobat files with Postscript files may join your desk dictionary and the almanacs on the shelf. But style guides and other essential editorial references are on the Web, too, as well as glossaries for hard-to-define technical terms, maps, and most major national newspapers.

Print newsletters will never be obsolete, but learn what the Web can do for you.

In one of my merrier newsletter editing classes, the participants and I were speculating that if the world ends with a bang, three creatures will survive: the rat, the cockroach, and the newsletter publisher. Someone will start up a two-color broadside called the Apocalypse Daily Advocate, and it will need an editor. You'll be there with the ability to gather the pieces and make news of your part of the world seem worth reading.

Or maybe there'll be a critical natural resources shortage that drives a backlash against technology long before the end of the world, and we'll all be using Royal portables again to save electricity. You'll be there with your organizational and language skills to help paste up the New Dark Ages Bulletin.

But until then, editors will do well to learn how to use whatever parts of the online library/cafeteria/laundromat/studio/conference they can discover that enable them to bring good information to their readership, with or without hypertext links.

Electronic media are becoming mainstays

As reported in *The Ragan Report*, the 1998 "Media in Cyberspace" study conducted by a New York public relations agency, Middleberg + Associates, and Steve Ross, an associate professor in Columbia University's graduate school of journalism, makes one thing very clear: Working online is the trend, the future is now, and neither is just for geeks.

Will online research and publishing destroy careful editorial practices and replace print publications? Nah, say most industry observers. But reporters who responded to the survey ranked the Web as a significant avenue for researching a story—in fact, they ranked it second only to live interviews.

On tight deadlines and when sources are hard to reach, editors and reporters increasingly turn to Web sites for background and facts. But reporters also use online sources to generate ideas for stories—in effect, discussion lists, e-mail, and Web sites are primary sources.

Half of all print journalists in the survey go online at least once daily, and a third use the Internet at least once a week. These journalists are using the Internet primarily to research articles and as a source of reference material, especially financial information, press releases, and photos.

Drive-by view of CARR

You could spend your life online trolling for useful sites—and you'd find them, along with time-wasters and dubious sources. Learning how to evaluate material from individuals and organizations you find online is half the learning curve in using the Internet to assist you in reporting stories. But once you develop some shortcuts, you'll find yourself turning to the Internet for a variety of resources. It's relatively quick and cheap, it never sleeps or takes time off, and it's full of information and people you'd never come across any other way.

Any editor working in any niche who's willing to invest some stumbling-around time can learn to use the Internet for computer-assisted reporting & research (CARR): fact checking, background information, and trolling for prospective article topics, expert advice, and potential

Newsletters: A Primary Web Marketing Tool

In *Web Marketing Today*, an online newsletter, Ralph F. Wilson wrote, "If you're serious about Web marketing, you ought to look long and hard at beginning a [Web] newsletter for your own business." He said that an online newsletter gets visitors to your site interested in your business, builds trust, and helps cement "branding"—the identification in a client's mind of you as the source for a certain product or service.

Do people resent being sold to this way? "So long as you're offering them information of value in your newsletter, they'll take a look at what you have to sell. When you have a special sale or promotion, the newsletter gives you a ready vehicle to let your very best prospects know about it."

Many Web users would take a cheerfully in-your-face marketing ploy over advertorial with a sneakier agenda any day. That's not so different from the reaction of readers to printed propaganda: Nobody likes the news mixed up with it, but as long as it keeps its distance, people will just ignore ads they don't find relevant or interesting—and read around them to get to the good stuff.

To subscribe to *Web Marketing Today*, send an e-mail to web-marketing-request@sparklist.com.

authors. The statistical reports, surveys, resources, and publications available through many U.S. government Web sites alone are resources enough to mandate that newsletter editors get online as soon as possible and make it using a habit as reflexive as using a dictionary.

It's also tremendous fun leaving your own set of assumptions and conventions to see what else is going on in the world. Just remember to take it all with a grain of salt:

- A caveat. As Christopher Callahan, assistant dean of the University of Maryland's College of Journalism, said in an *Editorial Eye* article about online mailing lists: "Treat all the information that comes your way with caution.…There's no guarantee that people are who they claim to be. The need for accuracy will never change, no matter the source of information." There's no replacement for solid fact-checking and verifying sources.

- Another caveat. Online articles are almost always copyrighted; treat them as you would any original printed material and attribute them properly to their authors. Even e-mail discussions are not public domain; postings should be considered the property of their owners. Intellectual property is still a valuable commodity, even in the ether.

The four r's of computer-assisted journalism

The Poynter Institute for Media Studies Web site offers a concise introduction to the enterprise of using the Internet for gathering information and finding experts to consult and quote. Briefly, the many related aspects of computer-assisted journalism (CAJ) can be broken into four main areas, two of which make up the CARR that's most applicable to newsletter editors rather than newspaper reporters:

- **Computer-assisted reporting.** Using databases, statistical analysis programs, and spreadsheets to spot trends and verify data.

- **Computer-assisted research.** Using online information as secondary sources such as reports, articles, surveys, and studies.

- **Computer-assisted reference.** Using dictionaries, encyclopedias, periodicals, glossaries, thesauruses, and the like to check definitions and facts.

- **Computer-assisted rendezvous.** Using mailing lists, news groups, and e-mail lists to tap into the advice and knowledge of a virtual community of colleagues and experts.

Successful CAJ calls for a combination of having the right software, acquiring navigational skills, and being willing to tolerate a lot of drek to get to the good stuff. Visit the Poynter site for more details of CAJ (http://www.poynter.org/car/cg_carfourr.htm) and a tutorial for the types of Web sites and navigational tools you need to know about: http://www.poynter.org/car/cg_carwww.htm.

To learn about online resources, go online!

Here's a range of Web sites that are helpful on their own or offer valuable links to other Web sites or articles. The list also includes a few electronic mailing lists and online periodicals (e-zines and newsletters) to help you get your feet wet.

AJR News Link. This *American Journalism Review* site gives you several ways to search hundreds of online news sources—just AJR articles, just newspapers, just magazines, or the entire site—by keyword, state, city, country, or topic. Visit http://www.newslink.org.

CARR-L. Largest e-mail discussion group for working journalists and educators to discuss doing research in cyberspace. To subscribe, send e-mail to listserv@ulkyvm.louisville.edu, leaving the subject line blank and writing "subscribe [your name] listserv@ulkyvm.louisville.edu" in the body of the message.

How Much Is Too Much? More Models of Web Newsletters

Some publishers think the (theoretical) lack of space limitations on the Internet means online newsletters can be as long as they wanna be, but people's brains don't have infinite reserves of attention and life is short. As for print newsletters, good content and a clear, appealing layout matter more than either brevity or many pages when it comes to whether readers like an online newsletter.

Digests (like the Edupage news briefs—send a request for information to educause@educause.unc.edu) abound; they may be more in keeping with the peripatetic spirit of the Internet, but try to take a look at some of these if a short format doesn't make sense for your content. All are models of well-edited, content-rich newsletters that succeed despite being quite long:

Iconocast—sub@list.iconocast.com

E-pulse—epulse@sna.com

Spectrum: Interactive Media & Online Developer News—
duberman@dnai.com

Science Week—prismx@scienceweek.com

@NY—newsletter@atnewyork.com

The Monday Review—specpress@earthlink.net

In an online discussion, the publisher who recommended these publications summed up a problem that nags at many online readers: He thinks that "click-throughs" are unpopular and most people would rather get a single long e-mail than have to follow links to stories—which themselves may have more links. If you find your newsletter getting longer and longer, maybe you should consider increasing its frequency. "Tough call, though, because more frequent editions means more work even if the number of words doesn't increase," the publisher adds.

Visit this commentator's site at http://www.veniceinteractive.com, which calls itself the newsletter of the Los Angeles interactive community.

Communicator's Library. Many links to articles about corporate communications management, copyediting, intranet design and development, media relations, associations, writing, and other libraries. Visit http://www.bccc.com/Schlee/library.html.

Contentious. An e-zine for online writers and editors. http://www.contentious.com.

Copyright Clearance Center Online. Acts as an agent and a clearinghouse by collecting equitable reprint fees and helping faculty, authors, businesses, copyright holders, publishers, and editors exchange information about ownership. Also offers guidelines for creating a policy for copyright compliance. Visit http://www.copyright.com/.

Direct Source. A store of links to government, humanities, and reference documents and materials put together by a George Washington University librarian. Bookmark this site to avoid repeated searches for others. http://gwis2.circ.gwu.edu/~gprice/direct.htm.

Editing for the Web. How to adapt and expand editing skills to the online context. http://www.towson.edu/~lieb/updates/chapter12/toc.html.

Finding Things on the Internet. And other articles about Web standards and practices, originally published in *The Editorial Eye* newsletter. Visit http://www.eeicom.com/eye/utw.

Fred Showker's Design & Publishing Center. Tricks for copyfitting printed newsletters are value-added information for people who come to this site looking for help with Web site production. Visit http://www.graphic-design.com.

Garbl's Writing Resources On Line. Many other sites have a link to this site, which is itself a bundle of well-chosen links to excellent resources that are grouped into categories. In some ways, the Web is like a small Southern town where everybody knows everybody and who you are related to is everything. http://pw1.netcom.com/~garbl1/writing.html.

Web Design Sites for Editorial People

These excellent sites offer suggestions for creating more readable and more professional-looking Web publications:

http://ppewww.ph.gla.ac.uk/~flavell/alt/. Alan J. Flavell of Glasgow University offers guidelines for providing text-based information as an alternative to image maps (for readers whose computers can't support downloading large, complex, multicolor images).

http://www.med.yale.edu.caim/stylemanual/Manual-3.html. This is an article on optimizing performance in Web pages, part of Patrick J. Lynch's Web Style Manual (from the Yale Center for Advanced Instructional Media).

http://www.sun.com/styleguide/tables/Graphics.html. Graphics guidance from the "Guide to Web Style" by Rick Levine of Sun Microsystems.

The Idea Station. Publishes the Online Publishers Moderated Discussion List Digest and Marketing with Online Newsletters; owned and moderated by Shannon Kinnard. Many articles are archived and can be easily retrieved by e-mail. Visit http://www.ideastation.com or send an inquiry to shannon@ideastation.com.

Inkspot. Many valuable links to references and publications. Visit http://www.vquill.com/inkspot.

Internet Writing Workshop. Serious, professional online critique group; minimum monthly contributions required (critiques or submissions). Categories for nonfiction and nature writing. For subscription information, contact writing-request@psuvm.psu.edu.

Journalist's Notepad. Links to journalism and public relations organizations and publications, reviews of Web sites and resources, and links to articles on media/communications/computer topics. Visit http://www.tech.prsa.org/journal.html.

Paradigm Online Writing Assistant. A rich, one-of-a kind site with information on how Web information should be organized with the best hierarchy and links. Topics include the relationship of the whole to its parts, mapping content to determine scope, creating logical categories, and paragraphing. Visit http://www.idbsu.edu/english/cguilfo…igm/organize.htm#Create Expectations.

The Poynter Institute. Results of media studies and resources offer journalists an overview by some of the best in the journalism business. http://www.poynter.org/car/cg_carwww.htm.

SPJ-L. One of the best and largest general journalism discussion groups, sponsored by the Society of Professional Journalists. To subscribe, send e-mail to listserv@lists.psu.edu, leaving the subject line blank and writing "subscribe [your name] listserv@lists.psu.edu" in the body of the message.

For a FAQ on how to publish an online newsletter, visit http://www.inkspot.com/~oki/ink/newsletterinfo/html/.

Drive-by view of online newsletters

If you're very lucky, you may get to work with a genius Webmaster who lets you hand over document files and pops them online for you. But you still need to be able to talk a little of the talk, and you should know what's involved in "repurposing" a print newsletter or spinning off a sister title for your organization's Web site. If you're a freelancer, odds are good that there's an online publication in your future, too.

What do online newsletters look like?

Many companies and associations have *intranet* newsletters (accessible only locally) to provide their employees and members with up-to-the-minute news. Typical contents are publications, a calendar of events, media clips, press releases, and new-hire orientation materials.

Direct marketing newsletters are a value-added feature of many Web sites meant to attract customers for products or services. Online newsletters may also be sister versions that offer information there's not room for in the print newsletter, or a way to send time-sensitive information. Newsletters online can be updated as often as necessary or desired, which means content may change overnight. (Many readers print out pages they want to keep.)

Newsletters can be delivered free by e-mail subscription or for a fee, with readers accessing a private site using a secret codeword or key. Some of the best free newsletters are supported by ads, a departure from most print newsletters and a big drawback or a minor annoyance depending on your point of view.

The Internet is packed full of all sorts of *e-zines*—newsletter-like publications that many be plain-vanilla text-only documents or formatted with graphics so screens look like printed pages, except studded with ads, icons, and text links to other pages. The traditional genre- and layout-specific definitions of what a newsletter, bulletin, digest, and magazine "is" pretty much break down online. See page 332 for a quick look at three online examples.

Some of the basics are the same graphically, in print and online:

- Use consistent typography.

- White space is good.

- Visually organize the "page."

- Keep pages short, and keep paragraphs short.

- Include elements of contrast.

- Use graphic elements in moderation, and for good reasons.

(For more on Web layout, visit http://sunsite.berkeley.edu/~morgan/waves/readability.html.) Online as well as on paper: Content rules. The quality of the research and writing, the integrity of the data, the relevance and veracity of original information—they're everything. Sophisticated Web site design can't hide superficial or error-riddled content that's just an excuse for advertising. And convenient e-mail delivery can't make up for half-baked writing or short-sighted thinking.

Readers of print vs. online newsletters

We have to give up some of our cherished expectations about readers; they can subscribe and unsubscribe online much more quickly and with less chance for intervention by us to retain them. People click through quickly if they don't find something worth pausing for. The term "browsing" doesn't quite describe how fast online readers skim for relevant information. Newsletter content online has to work harder at newsworthiness; it becomes a habit to just keep moving when you're reading online, and someone who follows a link may not come back.

Interactivity isn't an entirely new concept when it comes to what readers do with writing. We define the interactions that readers have with online documents differently, but paying attention, remembering, learning, and even now and then enjoying the content of a publication have long been devoutly desired reader responses, regardless of medium. Remember to:

- Anticipate how readers will use the information.

- Make the benefits to be gained from reading a piece of copy unmistakably clear—within a few seconds of browsing.

- Remember that most readers are intelligent but uninterested.

- Treat readers with respect by providing accurate information.

- Avoid writing for the lowest common denominator.

- Make sure any element that has its own real estate deserves it.

- Make sure any element that deserves its own real estate has it.

- Break big blocks of information into more accessible pieces.

- Make every word count.

- Remember that a piece of writing can't be engaging for readers unless the writer was personally engaged with the material.

But of course it's not quite as easy as checking off a few trusty criteria. Successful writers adapt their message to take best advantage of the medium in which it will appear, and the Internet has altered the traditional path from writer to page to reader. Some common assumptions about how readers process content written for the page don't apply to online content. The chart below shows some assumptions that writers can (and shouldn't) make. Newsletters are already organized into smaller units—articles—so you might think the translation to "screenfuls" would be one-to-one. It's not.

Writing for a printed newsletter

You come to readers and hope they will welcome you. Copy has to interest them or at least pique their curiosity within a few seconds of reading a lead paragraph or browsing a page. Articles that earn attention allow you to establish the credibility of your message.

Articles are written with well-defined copy points to appeal to the audience you have in mind.

Writing for an online newsletter

You hope readers will come to you; then you welcome them as best you can. You probably have their interest or at least curiosity to begin with, but to earn their continued attention you have to establish credibility within a few seconds.

Copy has to prove its value to readers who have found a document entirely by accident, too.

continued on page 330

Writing for a printed newsletter, cont'd.

Writing for a online newsletter, cont'd.

Information is presented as a package—an issue. If you don't get it all, you could miss something essential. Content covers a range of topics and is usually organized into recurring departments.

Even if the newsletter's front page is presented with the conventions of a nameplate, volume and issue, and table of contents, the content itself is made available as standalone bits with possible links.

Reading pages is essentially passive. Only brain synapses know for sure whether someone's formed new pathways!

Reading online can be interactive: People can do searches, move around, leave e-mail notes, or fill out forms.

Writers try to push readers through all the points in a closed system. The message is developed as a coherent whole to which each part contributes.

Writers pull readers through as many self-selected points of an open system as possible. There may be no ideal number of points.

The structure has a beginning, a middle, and an end.

The structure of the content has many points of entry.

Names and addresses on mailing lists, responses to direct mail efforts, and lists of employees and clients are finite. An issue of a printed newsletter has a finite print run. It has a pass-along readership but it's going to be among ilk.

A single file of a free newsletter for ostrich breeders can be downloaded, printed out, and read by anyone in the world, with or without an ostrich ranch. It can also be browsed online.

Targeted readers have a lot in common. Content is aimed at known demographics and the newsletter serves stated needs as revealed in reader surveys, focus groups, correspondence, etc.

There's no certainty about who's going to be reading. You can't anticipate who will be browsing or who will return (unless the newsletter is a subscription).

Texture and tone might—should—change from article to article to create variety and confer the idea of broad perspective. A sense of multiple authorship, joined by a unifying, coherent editorial vision, is desirable.

A site-specific tone and voice that carry across publication segments must be maintained. There's so much physical variety that a sense of unified authorship is essential to a coherent editorial vision.

Readers normally "taste" and then may read from A to Z or backward from Z to A.

There's no "normal" reading. Readers may skip from C to Z to B to M to L to K with points in between left out.

Some elements deserve more attention than others. Attention grabbers are expressly intended to keep people reading forward and following jumps.

All segments deserve equal attention. Links and navigational tools encourage random traveling around—one link's as good as another and none is subordinate.

Your message (your publishing mission, the benefits of reading your content) can be carried by the narrative of individual articles. Once you've printed a mission statement in your nameplate or masthead, no overt statement is necessary—even in a marketing newsletter.

You need to include your message in every segment because you don't have the luxury of context. All the "pages" of a Web site have to stand on their own merits, and no assumptions can be made about what someone has read.

Writing for a printed newsletter, cont'd.

Writers should scatter "gold nuggets" randomly throughout an issue to reward people for reading.

Writers have to "qualify" their readers before they can count on capturing their attention.

Readers can develop a sense of belonging to a group represented by a publication. Service content encourages them to take action in their world.

Over time a publication that meets reader expectations builds loyalty. People recognize and look forward to it, renewing that loyalty at regular intervals.

Errors and omissions in printed content live in infamy until someone lines a birdcage with the flawed issue. But at least the number of people who see them isn't infinite, and you can print a correction next time. In fact, acknowledging errors demonstrates editorial honesty.

Writing for a online newsletter, cont'd.

Writers should make sure each segment contains a "gold nugget." Each one may be your only chance to reward readers.

Readers tend to "qualify" themselves before going too far with material.

Readers can join a virtual community or sign a guestbook. They may just lurk. But there's no there there—it's a reflection.

A sense of "I'm glad I visited" is about the best you can hope for. Readers may find you by accident and forget how to return.

Errors and omissions in online content can be corrected in moments—as long as you find them. But millions of people may have seen them before you do, and anyone who bookmarks or prints out the problematic version will miss out on the correction.

Organizing content online

If a newsletter publishes numerous long articles, research shows that people prefer short descriptions of articles that they can use as a preview. Then readers can choose which links to follow in a Web site newsletter or which articles to retrieve, in an e-mail newsletter, directly from a special e-mail address. It should be clear that few of the graphic conventions for organizing information that we discussed in section 3 apply to most online newsletters. (In the examples that follow, we'll see that headlines are still important, though.)

To show the range of possibilities, let's take a look at three examples with very different formats and graphic standards for organizing and delivering their newsletter content to the public. Captions in the margin summarize what the newsletter or e-zine can do that a print version could not, and pinpoint some of the tradeoffs involved.

- Ostriches On Line, a free text-only e-mail newsletter that's sometimes very long, is delivered automatically each month to subscribers—http://www.ostrichesonline.com.

- The Feed Daily, an e-zine combined with an online discussion forum, delivers an e-mail "alert" promoting specific articles and lets readers link directly to the Web site to read them. The Web site looks like a magazine with its graphic complexity and advertising, but it feels more like a newsletter in its appeal to the concerns of a community—http://www.feedmag.com/html/feeddaily.

- Healthy, Wealthy, and Wise, a free electronic newsletter, is an "e-freemium"—a little something extra offered to respondents as part of an online direct marketing pitch. The newsletter is a sweetener for the main deal: sale of an inexpensive personal financial planning spreadsheet, Retire Right. The promise to help people reach their retirement goals is reinforced by the newsletter's focus on pragmatic lifestyle advice. This Web site illustrates the fluid nature of online publishing: The layout and major links changed three times after we selected it as a sample of an online marketing newsletter—http://www.reallygreat.lantz.com.

Sample 1: 'Another compelling newsletter'

Here's one of the most content-rich e-mail newsletters I've ever come across. This "issue" from shows very clearly which conventions can and should be retained from print newsletters and which simpy don't apply.

```
Date sent:      Mon, 20 Apr 1998 14:00:04 -0500 (CDT)
To:             ljorgen@eeicom.com
From:           Ostriches On Line
<ostrich@ostrichesonline.com>
Subject:        Another compelling newsletter
Send reply to:  ostrich@ostrichesonline.com


Ostriches On Line - The World's Largest International Ostrich
Company
================================================================

Newsletter - 19th April 1998
Publishers of the "World's Largest Ostrich Newsletter"
This newsletter goes out to 13,329 people in 131 countries


In this packed issue

1) Ostrich Industry gets 6 MILLION + readership boost - update
2) Using Probiotics for newly hatched chicks and livestock
3) Ratite Feeding - The Dilution Factor - Part 2
4) Sales, Marketing and getting the product to the consumer.
   Part 3 of a long running series
5) Ratite Egg Incubation - Part 5 of a series from Texas A & M
6) In future issues
7) Unsubscribing
```

TOC

```
================================================================
```
Ostrich Industry gets 6 MILLION + readership boost - update

As we mentioned in our previous newsletter, we have spent a
considerable amount of time recently on the International promotion of the Ostrich industry culminating in a number of
"featured" articles in prominent publications.

One of the widest read global newspapers, USA Today, have confirmed that their article will appear on Monday 20th April
1998 within the Money section. The article will be on page 1
or page 3.

Subsequent to our last newsletter, we have also completed many
other interviews with magazines around the world and are
delighted to advise that the Ostrich industry has received much
favourable press within a number of farming magazines, via a
syndicated column in various agricultural magazines and also a
long interview in the renowned Chicago magazine Cranes Chicago
Business.

All this publicity is a major boost for the global Ostrich
industry and I would like to thank the many people who have
sent emails, faxes and called us with their support. We very
much appreciate the ongoing efforts of the many professionals,
dedicated farmers, breeders and everyone else involved in the
"International Ostrich Chain" to bring our wonderful products
to the consumer.

Although it is indeed pleasurable to receive such accolades,
the focus must remain on the constant and never ending work we
all must do to continue to educate the population on the wonderful benefits of:-

1. Eating low cholesterol, low fat and low calorie Ostrich
meat.
2. Using Ostrich leather as a durable and fashionable alternative.
3. Purchasing natural household dusters made from Ostrich
feathers.
4. Utilising natural Ostrich oil in skin care and other derma-
tology products.
5. Farming a free range, unendangered, easy to manage and
resourceful animal culminating in a much cleaner environment.

Our focus and goals still remain the same and we should all be
striving for a similar achievement, namely

"To put Ostrich meat onto all the food tables of the world"
To contact Ostriches On Line and Steve Warrington send an
email to

steve@ostrichesonline.com Tel +1 708 452 7596 Fax |1 708 452
7510 Our address appears below

==

Service

article

Using Probiotics for newly hatched chicks and livestock

Probiotics - what are Probiotics?

The word probiotic means "For Life" as opposed to the word
"Anti Biotic" which means against life. In one of it's easiest
explanations, there is both good and bad in all forms of
organisms, and this is no exception when when we examine bacteria.

Bad bacteria includes Salmonella, E-Coli, Staph, etc. which are
usually found in the gut and intestine and can lead to severe
gastric problems and food poisoning.

On the other hand, good bacteria and naturally occurring beneficial organisms in the gut and intestine can aid in the
digestion and inhibit disease causing bacteria.

Newly hatched chicks need all the help and assistance they can
get and continual trials and field tests consistently show that
the addition of Probiotics to One Day Old chicks substantially
helps in their development.

Probiotics are available as direct-fed microbials and aid in
the balance between beneficial and harmful bacteria in the
digestive tract of all Ostriches, Emus and Rheas.

A healthy digestive tract is necessary for proper growth and
continued good health in young all ages of livestock - and
especially young chicks.

Many ratite breeders have reported that direct-fed microbial
products aid in improving the survivability of young birds as
well as producing a more thrifty and stress reduced older animal.

We have included many technical papers on this subject as well
as an easy to complete order form on our web site and you are
encouraged to see the benefits you can enjoy when you introduce Probiotics to all of your livestock.

Additional Web

resource

http://www.ostrichesonline.com/animalhealth/probiotics.html

For more information please send an email to
probiotics@ostrichesonline.com

```
================================================================
```
The Dilution Factor - Part 2

Protein, Fat, Fibre, Energy

Service article

In Part 1, I promised you we would get right to the nuts and bolts of "The Dilution Factor" beginning with Part 2, so here we go.

It is slightly complicated so you may have to give full attention but then, nutritional subjects usually are that way.

In order to fairly explain what happens to ratite feed when The Dilution Factor is involved, we need to start off with a point of reference that would be considered an adequate diet for ratites.

This subject, by itself, can be as controversial as anything you ever run across. But, I am writing this article so I will pick the parameters that I know would be a good example of a breeder bird ration that will result in reasonable production performance.

Chart

ITEM———————AMOUNT———PROTEIN————FAT———FIBER————ENERGY

Breeder Ration—100%——————21.0%—————4.0%——11.0%————67%

Allow me to explain the above chart. The AMOUNT column is the percentage portion of the birds total daily intake - in this case it is 100%.

The protein content of the example breeder ration is 21% crude protein.

The fat content of this ration is 4.0% crude fat and 11.0% crude fibre.

If you disagree with any of these numbers, that is fine, just keep in mind that this is an example and I am trying to demonstrate The Dilution Factor and not debate the who is wrong and who is right on nutrient levels.

In-group humor

For the nutritionists out there reading this information, when you are done laughing about the ENERGY column, allow me to put some reason to this category.

The average ratite rancher does not understand ALL the energy systems and cannot relate to them. There are probably more different ways to calculate energy than I have fingers and toes.

And, all livestock rations do not use the same one to calculate diets. This is very confusing to the average person. But, most everyone can understand the word ENERGY.

What method was used to calculate this energy number does NOT matter. What is important is the assigned number I have put in the ENERGY category and to see if it changes when The Dilution Factor in implemented.

Let's take a look at...

If you would like further information about how we can help you with all your sales and marketing requirements, please review our Internet site at

Additional Web resource

http://www.ostrichesonline.com/consultancy/consultancyindex.html

```
================================================================
```
Ratite Egg Incubation - Part 5 of a series

Coming attraction

Due to a lack of space, we were unable to bring you part 5 of this article - it will appear in our next newsletter.

```
================================================================
```
In future issues

Our next newsletter will be published within 10 days and will feature more information on sales, marketing and other benefits of utilising direct fed microbials.

```
================================================================
```
Unsubscribing

We cannot manually unsubscribe anyone.

How to stop subscribing

To unsubscribe, please review the full instructions on the Internet site at

http://www.ostrichesonline.com/general/unsubscribe.html

```
================================================================
```
Don't just do something, sit there

Appeal for reader contributions

We can't be everywhere - although we would like to be, and it would be great to hear some news and views from your part of the world. It doesn't take much, and you don't have to send something every week - just an article or item that is topical and informative, a chance to get your name and company printed (for free) and a view from your part
of the world. This newsletter now goes out to 130 countries on every continent and there is no deadline - just send us an

email with your contribution that you want to include and we will take care of the rest.

```
=================================================================
```

Copyright notice

Editorial note

All views and opinions in this newsletter are ours unless it was a contributed article.

Ostriches On Line are responsible for all material contained herein.

Print version available

You can receive this newsletter by First Class Airmail. To subscribe to the printed version please visit our Internet site at

http://www.ostrichesonline.com/general/newsletter.html

Thank you for choosing and visiting Ostriches On Line

Steve Warrington

```
=================================================================
```

Contact information

Ostriches On Line - The World's Largest International Ostrich Company
2218 N 75th Ave Elmwood Park IL USA 60707 E&OE
Tel +1 (708) 452-7596 Fax +1 (708) 452-7510 Member: BDOA, AOA, BBB of Greater Chicago Elmwood Park C of C The Ostriches On Line newsletter has over 13,000 subscribers - join now
http://www.ostrichesonline.com
ostrich@ostrichesonline.com

Sample 2:   Interactivity galore

An e-mail (below) arrives to highlight articles and encourage participation in an online reader discussion group. Readers can follow links
to the e-zine (shown on pages 340–341).

```
From:      Alert@lists.feedmag.com
To:        Alert@lists.feedmag.com
Subject:   FEED Alert 11.04.98
Date:      Wed, 04 Nov 1998 14:33:20 -0600
```

[Editor's note: We're very pleased to report that POV Magazine
named FEED the sixth best site on the web, in its annual survey of the top 100 web sites. POV's comments singled out the
"smarts and savvy" of our Loop conversations, and so the award
really belongs as much to all of you — Loopies and lurkers
alike — as it does to us here behind the curtain. So kudos to
you all — and let's make it to number one next year!]

Q U O T E   O F   T H E   W E E K

"Most people surveyed say they want the presidential scandal to
be over, even as network news coverage of the saga boosts ratings and the Starr Report becomes a best-seller. Does this
mean people are disingenuous when they respond to polls, or
are they just voyeuristic, on the one hand, and legitimately
disgusted on the other? Contrary to their reputation, the polls
don't simplify the things they survey. If you know how to read
them, they add layers of ambiguity and unresolved tension. In
the end, perhaps, that's the real reason the polls infuriate
so many people."

—Peter Dizikes, "The Sixty-Percent Solution"
R E C E N T   A R T I C L E S

ESSAY | 11.04.98
Pixels at an Exhibition: Tom Standage explores the past and
present of the Virtual Museum.
http://www.feedmag.com/essay/es124_master.html?alert

ESSAY | 11.03.98
The Sixty-Percent Solution: Peter Dizikes defends the fine art
of political polling.
http://www.feedmag.com/essay/es123_master.html?alert

MATERIALIST | 11.03.98
Junk TV
Stefanie Syman on artist John Wells' television reconstruc-
tions.
http://www.feedmag.com/column/materialist/cm122_master.html?ale
rt

RE: | 10.30.98
Re: Christine Vachon FEED talks to the "godmother" of independent films about the difficult art of production
http://www.feedmag.com/re/re121_master.html?alert

ESSAY | 10.29.98
Filling the Void in Berlin: Daniel Pinchbeck on art and politics in Europe's most schizophrenic city.
http://www.feedmag.com/essay/es120_master.html?alert

ESSAY | 10.28.98
Picket and Roll: Josh Ozersky on why the NBA lockout is about
more than money.
http://www.feedmag.com/essay/es119_master.html?alert

THE   LOOP

*This little promo
reminds sub-
scribers they
have a reader's
forum.*

Readers continue to joust over Steven Johnson's article "The
Brain's Missing Link" on the the new generation in organizational software.
http://www.feedmag.com/cgi-bin/loop/loop.cgi?function=areav-
iew&document=ci118.s html

Sick of the Gates monopoly? Confounded by America's anti-trust
laws? You will be in good company in FEED's Loop discussion of
the DOJ/Microsoft case.
http://www.feedmag.com/cgi-bin/loop/loop.cgi?function=under-
view&document=dy107.s html&stringhead=107.11

Once readers follow links embedded in the 'Alert' e-mail, they're transported to a bright, dynamic "front door" to the e-zine Web site.

Pages are graphically complex but carefully organized. Links are available to other FEED articles and other resources on the Web.

Graphics are amusing but never compromise text blocks.

SUBSCRIBE TO FEED

Subscribing to FEED is simple and free. Give us your email address, and every week we'll send you an update, listing the latest articles and events on the site, and pointing you to the most active discussions in the Loop. And until November 22nd, becoming a FEED subscriber entitles you to 20% off the list price of all BigStar.com products. FEED subscribers will also have first dibs on any special events. And of course we won't sell or give away your address to anyone, under any circumstance.

Before you subscribe to FEED, we'd love to hear a few words about how you found our site, and your impressions of it. What are we doing well? What would you like to see more of? Who are you, anyway? Your responses will be sent directly to FEED's editors, so please don't hesitate to let us know how we're doing.

If you simply want to sign up for the list, just put your e-mail in the subscribe form below.

[Click here to send us your feedback.]

Subscribe to FEED's weekly email Alert.
[Join]
Enter your email address, then click JOIN.

To **unsubscribe** Alert with email,
[Unjoin]
enter your email address, then click UNJOIN

Thanks for subscribing! After you submit your address, you will be automatically subscribed to the FEED mailing list. (We won't sell or give away your email address to anyone. We promise.)

As a thanks for subscribing to FEED's weekly email alert, we have arranged for you to get 20% off the list price of all BigStar.com products until November 22nd. Just click on or copy any of the links below to get your 20% discount on BigStar.com.

You can chose from over 100,000 videos, DVD and Laserdiscs at BigStar.com, your online movie superstore. And, remember videos make great gifts! Here are few ideas:

Subscribing is easy.

Special discount on merchandise for subscribers.

A table of contents has embedded links to take readers directly to an article. The closer we get to real content, the simpler the layout becomes.

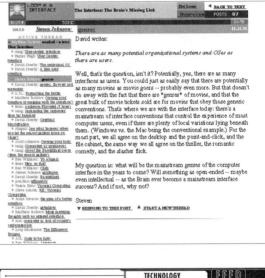

Articles are easy to read because text takes over and graphics finally recede.

Sample 3:   Not quite shameless promotion

The no-purchase-necessary newsletter offered by this Web entrepreneur isn't essential to the purpose of the site, but it underlines the bottom line effectively. Advice about health and wealth is a draw for potential clients, even if they're not yet in the retirement market. The newsletter is a relationship-building tool and a showcase for the trustworthy expertise that's presumably behind the software being flacked.

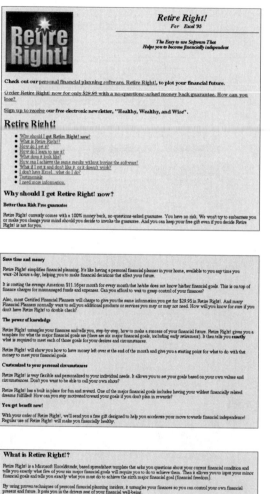

Table of site contents and offer of a free newsletter, 'Healthy, Wealthy, and Wise,' no purchase necessary.

Explanation of the reason for the site. The publishers make no bones about it: they're here to sell financial planning software.

This plain-text home page is set up like a FAQ (frequently asked questions) list.

What does it look like?

Look at these screen shots [58 K].

[Top]

How can I achieve the same results without buying the software?

Here's what I had to do to research and build Retire Right!:

- I attended a financial seminar to get started. Cost $459.00.
- Bought a financial calculator. Cost $49.95.
- Then I attended an advanced financial seminar. Cost $2249.00.
- Nine months of training in accounting. Cost $777.00.
- Six months of training in economics. Cost $518.00.
- Consultation with certified financial planners for 3 years. Cost $879.00.
- Training in advanced programming with Excel for 3 months. Cost $259.00.
- Anthony Robbins Wealth Mastery seminar. Cost $11,695.28 (including airfare and accommodations).
- Purchase personal financial planning software from my current competitors (They don't do the same things Retire Right! does—more useless and dated bells and whistles, less pure helpful content). Cost $876.23.

This does not include the four plus years of college for business and programming. Don't you agree that $29.95 is a much better value than the $17,762.46 I had to spend (mis-spend) to use Retire Right! the first time for myself?

Save Time and Money

Why would you want to go through all of that time and expense when you can get Retire Right! now and benefit from someone else's experience and trouble? It's smart to benefit from someone else's experience. After purchasing Retire Right!, the only thing you won't be able to do that I can is write personal financial planning software. Remember, I originally wrote Retire Right! for myself!

Benefit from economies of scale by spending $29.95 and a couple of hours instead of the $17,762.46 and 4 1/2 years that someone has already gone through for you. Instead, invest the $17,732.51 that you'll save for 4 1/2 years at 8% and you'll have a tidy sum of $25,396.18. That's in addition to the extra savings you will have from using Retire Right!

[Top]

What if I get it and don't like it, or it doesn't work?

Retire Right! comes with a no-questions-asked 100% money back guarantee. If you don't want it for any reason, we will refund your entire payment amount with no hassle. And you get to keep our free gift.

How can we do this? We are confident that Retire Right! will help you to earn more money for your retirement and other financial goals and easily pay for itself many times over! With this guarantee, how can you lose?

I don't have Excel...what do I do?

Please e-mail us and tell us what format you would like. If we get enough requests, we will re-write Retire Right! as a stand-alone program for Windows 95/NT and/or Macintosh. You are the boss.

[Top]

Testimonials

"What you've got here is golden! Everyone must use it." Chris

"I was amazed at the things it told me I should do. I need extra copies for my friends." Judy

"I thought being financially independent meant I had to be a millionaire. *Retire Right!* defined financial independence as a much more achievable goal for me! Now I feel like I can actually achieve financial independence, not having to rely on a job for my security!" Cathy

"Platinum [highest] rating for usefulness." Really Great Software Works, Inc.

I need more information

Click here for the story of Retire Right!

Order Retire Right! now for only $29.95 with a no-questions-asked money back guarantee. How can you lose?

Sign up to receive our free electronic newsletter, "Healthy, Wealthy, and Wise".

Home | Products & Services

Newsletter

Get our free newsletter-Healthy, Wealthy, and Wise by answering this survey question:

One of our marketing advisors said this site is too commercial. Another says that its to the point and doesn't waste your time. Should we change the site to make it less commercial?

In a rare burst of honesty and humility, the publishers try to survey reader reaction to the Web site.

I need more information

Click here for the story of Retire Right!

Order Retire Right! now for only $29.95 with a no-questions-asked money back guarantee. How can you lose?

Sign up to receive our free electronic newsletter, "Healthy, Wealthy, and Wise".

Home | Products & Services

Newsletter

Get our free newsletter-Healthy, Wealthy, and Wise by answering this survey question:

One of our marketing advisors said this site is too commercial. Another says that its to the point and doesn't waste your time. Should we change the site to make it less commercial?

[Change It] [Leave it the Same] [No comment, Please send the newsletter]

Feel free to leave a comment. Find out what other people like you think about this. We may follow-up with another question. Answers will be posted to your e-mail when the results are tabulated. You may remove yourself from our mailing list at any time.

Disclaimer

Copyright © 1997 Net Media, Inc.
If you have comments or questions, please feel free to contact us at info@realbuyeat.iunix.com.
We can also be reached by phone at (813) 296-9129,
by fax at (813) 296-7129,
or by mail at P.O. Box 260263
Tampa, FL 33685.
Last modified: March 25, 1998

As a value-added service, the software publishers offer a free subscription to a newsletter. Names and addresses become part of a marketing database as well, of course.

Selected Bibliography
for Newsletter Editors

When you work mostly alone and always on deadline, sometimes the creative well just plain runs dry. We newsletter editors need to see what other journalists are up to, stay open to new ideas for keeping our own publications up to speed, and listen to the advice of those who've produced excellent work.

When you work in a quite specialized niche, sometimes you also lose perspective. We newsletter editors need to remember that we're real news reporters—not just hacks for hire. We need to feel connected to the world of professional journalism and learn from the experience of the best practitioners we can find—whether by way of building a library of reference books or taking a workshop, joining an association, or bookmarking online resources.

This bibliography serves two purposes. It's a list of references that all come highly recommended for their clear instruction, friendly presentation, and practical approach. It's also a way to spotlight titles that were especially helpful in the research for the workshops out of which this book grew—they're flagged with an icon, and they'd be valuable additions to any editor's anti-ineptitude arsenal.

Most of these books are readily available in bookstores, but some are older, and even a new book may go out of print or into a new edition at any time. The publisher listed can be contacted directly (addresses are given, and many have Web sites), but online search services may be your best bet for books that are hard to find anywhere. Here are some services that will do the legwork for you:

- The Advanced Books Exchange (http://www.abebooks.com/). This site claims to be "the Internet's most popular service for buying and selling out-of-print, used, rare, and antiquarian books." Searches are free. Highly recommended for some of the older softcover books that aren't likely to be in libraries.

- Amazon.com (http://www.amazon.com). The backlist is deep and older titles are offered at a good discount. Service is usually quick, but sometimes the information about in-print status isn't totally accurate. Worth a try.

- Bibliofind (http://www.bibliofind.com). Search for out-of-print titles by keyword.

Editing / Editorial References

Coaching Writers: Editors and Reporters Working Together, by Roy Peter Clark and Don Fry. St. Martin's Press, Inc., 175 Fifth Ave., New York, NY 10010.

The Concise Columbia Encyclopedia (third edition), edited by Paul G. Lagassè. Columbia University Press/Houghton Mifflin Company, 136 S. Broadway, Irvington, NY 10533.

Copyright Basics. The Permissions Group, 1247 Milwaukee Ave., Ste. 303, Glenview, IL 60025.

The Copyright Permission and Libel Handbook: A Step-by-Step Guide for Writers, Editors, and Publishers, by Lloyd J. Jassin and Steven C. Schechter. John Wiley & Sons, Inc., 605 Third Ave., New York, NY 10158.

Editing Your Newsletter: How to Produce an Effective Publication Using Traditional Tools and Computers (fourth edition), by Mark Beach. Writer's Digest Books, 1507 Dana Ave., Cincinnati, OH 45207.

The Elements of Editing, by Arthur Plotnik. Macmillan Publishing Company, 866 Third Ave., New York, NY 10022.

The Elements of Nonsexist Usage: A Guide to Inclusive Spoken and Written English, by Val Dumond. Prentice Hall Press/Simon & Schuster, Inc., 15 Columbus Circle, New York, NY 10023.

The Elements of Style, by William Strunk Jr. and E.B. White. Macmillan Publishing Co., Inc., 866 Third Ave., New York, NY 10022.

The Essential Handbook for Writers (also published in hardcover as *The Little, Brown Essential Handbook for Writers*), by Jane E. Aaron. HarperCollins Publishers, 10 E. 53rd St., New York, NY 10022.

Find It Fast: How to Uncover Expert Information on Any Subject (third edition), by Robert I. Berkman. HarperCollins Publishers, P.O. Box 588, Dunkore, PA 18512.

❧ *Fundamentals of Successful Newsletters*, by Thomas H. Bivens. NTC Business Books, 4225 W. Touhy Ave., Lincolnwood, IL 60646.

Guidelines for Bias-Free Writing, by Marilyn Schwartz and the Task Force on Bias-Free Language of the Association of American Publishers. Indiana University Press, 601 Morton St., Bloomington, IN 47404.

The Handbook of Good English, by Edward D. Johnson. Facts On File, Inc., 460 Park Ave. S., New York, NY 10016.

Harbrace College Handbook (13th edition), by John C. Hodges, Winifred B. Horner, Suzanne S. Webb, and Robert K. Miller. Harcourt Brace College Publishers, 6277 Sea Harbor Dr., Orlando, FL 32887.

How to Conduct a Readership Survey, by W. Charles Redding. Lawrence Ragan Communications, Inc., 212 W. Superior St., Ste. 200, Chicago, IL 60610.

The Internet Handbook for Writers, Researchers, and Journalists, by Mary McGuire, Linda Stilborne, Melinda McAdama, and Laurel Hyatt. Trifolium Books Inc./GDS Inc., 85 River Rock Rd., Ste. 202, Buffalo, NY 14207.

LetterPerfect: A Guide to Practical Proofreading, by Peggy Smith. EEI Press, 66 Canal Center Plaza, Ste. 200, Alexandria, VA 22314.

❧ *Line by Line: How to Improve Your Own Writing*, by Claire Kehrwald Cook. Houghton Mifflin Company, 2 Park St., Boston, MA 02108.

❧ *Marketing With Newsletters: How to Boost Sales, Add Members and Raise Funds with a Printed, Faxed or Web-Site Newsletter* (second edition), by Elaine Floyd. EF Communications, 5721 Magazine St., Ste. 170, New Orleans, LA 70115.

❧ *My Big Sourcebook: For People Who Work with Words or Pictures*, edited by Linda B. Jorgensen. EEI Press, 66 Canal Center Plaza, Ste. 200, Alexandria, VA 22314.

❧ *New York Public Library Writer's Guide to Style and Usage*, edited by Andrea Sutcliffe, by the staff of EEI Communications. HarperCollins Publishers, 10 E. 53rd St., New York, NY 10022.

The Nonsexist Word Finder: A Dictionary of Gender-Free Usage, by Rosalie Maggio. Oryx Press, 2214 N. Central at Encanto, Phoenix, AZ 85004.

Publishing Newsletters (third edition), by Howard Penn Hudson. H&M Publishers, 44 W. Market St., Rhinebeck, NY 12572.

❧ *Starting & Running a Successful Newsletter or Magazine*, by Cheryl Woodard. Nolo Press, 950 Parker St., Berkeley, CA 94710.

❧ *Stet Again! More Tricks of the Trade for Publications People*, edited by Linda B. Jorgensen. EEI Press, 66 Canal Center Plaza, Ste. 200, Alexandria, VA 22314.

Success in Newsletter Publishing: A Practical Guide, by Frederick D. Goss. Newsletter Publishers Association, 1401 Wilson Blvd., Ste. 207, Arlington, VA 22209.

Usage and Abusage: A Guide to Good English, by Eric Partridge. W.W. Norton & Company, Inc., 500 Fifth Ave., New York, NY 10110.

❧ *Webster's Dictionary of English Usage*. Merriam-Webster Inc., 47 Federal St., Springfield, MA 01102.

Webster's New World Dictionary of Media and Communications (revised and updated), Richard Weiner, Macmillan General Reference/Simon & Schuster Macmillan, 1633 Broadway, New York, NY 10019.

Design and Production

Adobe Photoshop Creative Techniques, by Denise Salles, Garey Poyssick, and Ellenn Behoriam. Hayden Books, 201 W. 103rd St., Indianapolis, IN 46290.

❧ *Clip Art Crazy* (with CD-ROM), by Chuck Green. Peachpit Press, 2414 Sixth St., Berkeley, CA 94710.

Color for Impact, by Jan V. White. BookSmiths Inc., P.O. Box 23556, Lexington, KY 40523.

Color on Color: How Overprinting Two Colors Creates a New Third Color, by Richard S. Emery. Rockport Publishers/North Light Books, 1507 Dana Ave., Cincinnati, OH 45207.

The Copyright Permission and Libel Handbook, by Lloyd J. Jassin and Steven C. Schecter. John Wiley & Sons, Inc., Professional, Reference and Trade Group, 605 Third Ave., New York, NY 10158.

Designer's Guide to Print Production, edited by Nancy Aldrich-Ruenzel. Step-By-Step Publishing/Watson-Guptill Publications, 1515 Broadway, New York, NY 10036.

The Desktop Style Guide, by James Felici. Bantam Books/Bantam, Doubleday Dell Publishing Company, 666 Fifth Ave., New York, NY 10103.

Everyone's Guide to Successful Publications: How to Produce Powerful Brochures, Newsletters, Flyers, and Business Communications, Start to Finish, by Elizabeth Adler. Peachpit Press, 2414 Sixth St., Berkeley, CA 94710.

47 Printing Headaches (and How to Avoid Them), by Linda Sanders. North Light Books, 1507 Dana Ave., Cincinnati, OH 45207.

Getting It Printed (revised edition), by Mark Beach. North Light Books, 1507 Dana Ave., Cincinnati, OH 45207.

❧ *Graphic Idea Notebook*, by Jan V. White. Rockport Publishers/North Light Books, 1507 Dana Ave., Cincinnati, OH 45207.

Graphics, Design, & Printing Terms: An International Dictionary, by Ken Garland. Design Press/Tab Books, 10 East 21st St., New York, NY 10010.

The Gray Book: Designing in Black & White on Your Computer, by Michael Gosney, John Odam, and Jim Schmal. Ventana Press, P.O. Box 13964, Research Triangle Park, NC 27709.

Halftone Effects: A Complete Visual Guide to Enhancing and Transforming Halftone Images by Peter Bridgewater and Gerald Woods. Quarto Publishing plc/Chronicle Books, 275 Fifth St., San Francisco, CA 94103

HTML Visual Quick Reference (second edition), by Dean Scharf. Que Corporation, 201 W. 103rd St., Indianapolis, IN 46290.

Looking Good in Print: A Guide to Basic Design for Desktop Publishing, by Roger C. Parker. Ventana Press, P.O. Box 13964, Research Triangle Park, NC 27709.

Make Your Scanner a Great Design & Production Tool, by Michael Sullivan. North Light Books, 1507 Dana Ave., Cincinnati, OH 45207.

Making a Good Layout, by Lori Siebert and Lisa Ballard. North Light Books, 1507 Dana Ave., Cincinnati, OH 45207.

Newsletter Sourcebook (second edition), by Mark Beach and Elaine Floyd. North Light Books, 1507 Dana Ave., Cincinnati, OH 45207.

❧ *Newsletters from the Desktop: The Desktop Publisher's Guide to Designing Newsletters That Work*, by Joe Grossman and David Doty. Ventana Press, Inc., P.O. Box 2468, Chapel Hill, NC 27515.

❧ *The Newspaper Designer's Handbook*, by Tim Harrower. Oregonian Publishing Company, 1320 S.W. Broadway, Portland, OR 97201.

❧ *The Non-Designer's Design Book: Design and Typographic Principles for the Visual Novice*, by Robin Williams. Peachpit Press, Inc., 2414 Sixth St., Berkeley, CA 94710.

The Non-Designer's Web Design Book, by Robin Williams. Peachpit Press, Inc., 2414 Sixth St., Berkeley, CA 94710.

One-Minute Designer, by Roger C. Parker. Que Corporation, 201 W. 103rd St., Indianapolis, IN 46290.

The PC Is Not a Typewriter, by Robin Williams. Peachpit Press, Inc., 2414 Sixth St., Berkeley, CA 94710.

Photography for Graphic Designers, by Joseph Meehan. Watson-Guptill Publications, P.O. Box 2014, Lakewood, NJ 08701.

Pocket Pal: A Graphic Arts Production Handbook (16th edition). International Paper Co./Print Resource Group, P.O. Box 770067, Memphis, TN 38177.

Real World Scanning and Halftones, by David Blatner and Stephen Roth. Peachpit Press, Inc., 2414 Sixth St., Berkeley, CA 94710.

❧ *Type & Layout: How Typography and Design Can Get Your Message Across—Or Get in the Way*, by Colin Wheildon. Strathmoor Press, 2550 Ninth St., Berkeley, CA 94710.

❧ *Type in Use: Effective Typography for Electronic Publishing*, by Alex White. Design Press, 11 W. 19th St., New York, NY 10011.

Using Type Right: 121 Basic No-Nonsense Rules for Working with Type, by Philip Brady. NTC Business Books/Contemporary Publishing Group, 4255 Touhy Ave., Lincolnwood, IL 60646.

Writing

The Art of Styling Sentences: 20 Patterns for Success (third edition), by Marie L. Waddell, Robert M. Esch, and Roberta R. Walker. Barron's Educational Series, Inc., 250 Wireless Blvd., Hauppauge, NY 11788.

❧ *The Associated Press Guide to News Writing*, by Rene J. Cappon. ARCO/Simon & Schuster Macmillan, 1633 Broadway, New York, NY 10019.

Basic Media Writing (fifth edition), by Melvin Mencher. Times Mirror Higher Education Group, 2460 Kerper Blvd., Dubuque, IA 52001.

❧ *The Complete Guide to Magazine Article Writing: A Guide to Clear, Powerful, Salable Writing*, by John M. Wilson. Writer's Digest Books, 1507 Dana Ave., Cincinnati, OH 45207.

❧ *Error-Free Writing: A Lifetime Guide to Flawless Business Writing*, by Robin A. Cormier. Prentice-Hall, Englewood Cliffs, NJ 07632.

How to Write Fast (While Writing Well), by David Fryxell. Writer's Digest Books, 1507 Dana Ave., Cincinnati, OH 45207.

❧ *How to Write, Speak and Think More Effectively*, by Rudolph Flesch. Signet, published by Penguin Group, 375 Hudson St., New York, NY 10014.

The Language of News: A Journalist's Pocket Reference, by Jack Botts. Iowa State University Press, Ames, IA 50014.

ᵫ *The News Formula: A Concise Guide to News Writing and Reporting*, by Catherine C. Mitchell and Mark D. West, St. Martin's Press Inc., 175 5th Ave., New York, NY 10010.

ᵫ *News Reporting and Writing* (fifth edition), by Brian S. Brooks, George Kennedy, Daryl R. Moen, and Don Ranly. St. Martin's Press, Inc., 175 Fifth Ave., New York, NY 10010.

ᵫ *On Writing Well* (revised edition), by William Zinsser. Harper & Row, 1000 Keystone Industrial Park, Scranton, PA 18512.

ᵫ *Ways With Words: A Research Report of the Literacy Committee*, by the American Society of Newspaper Editors, ASNE Foundation, P.O. Box 4090, Reston, VA 22090-1700.

The Write Way: The SPELL Guide to Real-Life Writing, by Richard Lederer and Richard Downs. Pocket Books/Simon & Schuster, Inc., 1230 Avenue of the Americas, New York, NY 10020.

ᵫ *The Writer's Complete Guide to Conducting Interviews*, by Michael Schumacher, Writer's Digest Books, 1507 Dana Ave., Cincinnati, OH 45207.

ᵫ *Writing for Story*, by Jon Franklin. Plume/Penguin, 375 Hudson St., New York, NY 10014.

ᵫ *Writing for Your Readers: Notes on the Writer's Craft from The Boston Globe* (second edition), by Donald Murray. The Globe Pequot Press, 6 Business Park Rd., Old Saybrook, CT 06475.

Writing the News: A Guide for Print Journalists, by Walter Fox. Iowa State University Press, Ames, IA 50010.

Credits

This is one of the realities of newsletter publishing: It's ephemeral. By the time this book is in print, some of the design samples that show what good ideas and careful execution look like will no longer be around. Others may now be unrecognizable, having been redesigned, folded into a sister publication, or transformed into a magazine since we last saw them. Some will have skinnier or fatter alternative online versions. Editors and designers are likely to have moved on, too, and some publishers will have gone under, merged with competitors, or, sadly, abandoned their print communications programs altogether. The usefulness of the samples as paradigms nevertheless stands. The following newsletters were selected for signs of intelligent and even inspired decisionmaking:

The Affable Curmudgeon, Arvinmay Consulting Co., Inc., Carmel, California

Artes Liberales Today, College of Letters and Science at the University of Wisconsin-Madison, Madison, Wisconsin

Avon Outlook, Avon Products, Inc., New York, New York

Bedford News & Views, Bedford Court: A Marriott Retirement Community, Silver Spring, Maryland

Blue Ridge Ostrich Review, Blue Ridge Ostrich Ranch, Inc., Blue Ridge, Texas

The Choice, The Wings of Light, Mount Laurel, New Jersey

ComputerLetter, Technologic Partners, New York, New York

Connect News & Views, The User Group for Texas Instruments Software, Chicago, Illinois

CopyRights, The Permissions Group, Glenview, Illinois

DictaTalk, Dictaphone Corporation, Stratford, Connecticut

EU News & Insights, EU Services, Rockville, Maryland

Expressions, American Greetings Corporation, Cleveland, Ohio

Family Therapy News, American Association for Marriage and Family Therapy, Washington, D.C.

Farm Bureau News, American Farm Bureau Federation, Washington, D.C.

The Forge, Foundry United Methodist Church, Washington, D.C.

Fred Goss' What's Working in Direct Marketing, United Communications Group, Rockville, Maryland

GPPA Update, Georgia Psychiatric Physicians Association, Atlanta, Georgia

IABC Washington Update, International Association of Business Communicatiors/Washington, Rockville, Maryland

Insight Matters, Ohio Psychiatric Association, Columbus, Ohio

The Key Reporter, Phi Beta Kappa, Washington, D.C.

NAVH Update, National Association for the Visually Handicapped, New York, New York

NEWSlink, Sara Lee Hosiery, Winston-Salem, North Carolina

NIST Update, U.S. Department of Commerce, Technology Administration, National Institute of Standards and Technology, Gaithersburg, Maryland

NOVA Now, Calgary, Alberta

Office Worker Update, Service Employees International Union, Washington, D.C.

PeaceWatch, United States Institute of Peace, Washington, D.C.

PEPCO Seniorlines, Potomac Electric Power Company, Washington, D.C.

Planning for Health, Kaiser Permanente Mid-Atlantic States Region, Rockville, Maryland

The Polling Report: An Independent Survey of Trends Affecting Elections, Government, and Business, The Polling Report, Inc., Washington, D.C.

Population Today, Population Reference Bureau, Inc., Washington, D.C.

Prince Michel de Virginia, Prince Michel Vineyards, Leon, Virginia

Probable Cause: A Literary Revue, Improbable Publications, Miami Beach, Florida

The Prudential Leader, Prudential Communications Group, Newark, New Jersey

Publishing Forum, Canadian Centre for Studies in Publishing, Simon Fraser University at Harbour Centre, Vancouver, British Columbia

Quantum Traveler, Quantum Travel, Alexandria, Virginia

The Roar from 44, Air Line Pilots Association, College Park, Georgia

Speaking of Fire..., Oklahoma State University Fire Protection Publications, Stillwater, Oklahoma

21st C: The World of Research at Columbia University, Columbia University Health Sciences, New York, New York

UMS News, University of Maryland System, Adelphi, Maryland

The Vance International Report, Vance International, Oakton, Virginia

Water Environment Regulation Watch, Water Environment Federation, Alexandria, Virginia

Index

Linda B. Jorgensen is the editor of *The Editorial Eye*, a monthly subscription newsletter for writers, journalists, editors, and publications managers.

Photograph by Diana Adams

She developed the "Real-World Newsletters" and "Writing News" courses for EEI Communications and teaches them in Alexandria, Virginia, and at client locations across the country. She manages EEI Press and its Eye Exam publications critique service.

Jorgensen, who has worked in publishing for more than 15 years, was one of the associate editors who helped write the *New York Public Library Writer's Guide to Style and Usage* (HarperCollins). She holds a B.A. from the University of North Carolina-Chapel Hill and an M.A. from the University of Wisconsin-Madison. She thinks newsletters rock.

Colophon

This book was crafted by the design and production divisions of EEI Communications in Alexandria, Virginia, and printed by Carter Printing Company of Richmond, Virginia.

Lynn Whiteley created the final pages and cover. Davie Smith, who was the art director, collaborated on page design.

Jennifer Stewart contributed to the "Redesign of a Real, Live Newsletter" section. Loel Barr was the illustrator. Janis Hubbard indexed the book. Merideth Menken was the production editor.

The cover was produced using Macromedia FreeHand 8.0, Adobe Photoshop 5.0, and QuarkXPress 4.04 with Myriad MM fonts and Cornwall 10 pt. C1S stock. The text was produced using QuarkXPress 4.04 with Goudy and Myriad MM fonts and 60 lb. Touchglow opaque and Patina matte stock.